EXCHANGE AND MARKETS IN EARLY ECONOMIC DEVELOPMENT

The Human Economy

Series editors:

Keith Hart, Goldsmiths, University of London
Theodoros Rakopoulos, University of Oslo

Those social sciences and humanities concerned with the economy have lost the confidence to challenge the sophistication and public dominance of the field of economics. We need to give a new emphasis and direction to the economic arrangements that people already share, while recognizing that humanity urgently needs new ways of organizing life on the planet. This series examines how human interests are expressed in our unequal world through concrete economic activities and aspirations.

Volume 10
Exchange and Markets in Early Economic Development: Informal Economy in the Three New Guineas
John D. Conroy

Volume 9
Land and the Mortgage: History, Culture, Belonging
Edited by Daivi Rodima-Taylor and Parker Shipton

Volume 8
Commerce as Politics: The Two Centuries of Struggle for Basotho Economic Independence
Sean M. Maliehe

Volume 7
Credit and Debt in an Unequal Society: Establishing a Consumer Credit Market in South Africa
Jürgen Schraten

Volume 6
Money at the Margins: Global Perspectives on Technology, Financial Inclusion and Design
Edited by Bill Maurer, Smoki Musaraj and Ivan V. Small

Volume 5
Money in a Human Economy
Edited by Keith Hart

Volume 4
From Clans to Co-ops: Confiscated Mafia Land in Sicily
Theodoros Rakopoulos

Volume 3
Gypsy Economy: Romani Livelihoods and Notions of Worth in the 21st Century
Edited by Micol Brazzabeni, Manuela Ivone Cunha and Martin Fotta

Volume 2
Economy for and against Democracy
Edited by Keith Hart

Volume 1
People, Money and Power in the Economic Crisis: Perspectives from the Global South
Edited by Keith Hart and John Sharp

EXCHANGE AND MARKETS IN EARLY ECONOMIC DEVELOPMENT

Informal Economy in the Three New Guineas

John D. Conroy

berghahn
NEW YORK • OXFORD
www.berghahnbooks.com

First published in 2023 by
Berghahn Books
www.berghahnbooks.com

Library of Congress Cataloging-in-Publication Data

Names: Conroy, John D. (John David), 1938- author.
Title: Exchange and markets in early economic development : informal economy in the three New Guineas / John D. Conroy.
Description: New York : Berghahn Books, 2023. | Series: The human economy; 10. | Includes bibliographical references and index.
Identifiers: LCCN 2022054607 (print) | LCCN 2022054608 (ebook) | ISBN 9781800739680 (hardback) | ISBN 9781800739697 (ebook)
Subjects: LCSH: Informal sector (Economics)—Papua New Guinea. | Economic development—Papua New Guinea. | Papua New Guinea—Economic conditions.
Classification: LCC HD2346.P26 C66 2023 (print) | LCC HD2346.P26 (ebook) | DDC 338.9953—dc23/eng/20221116
LC record available at https://lccn.loc.gov/2022054607
LC ebook record available at https://lccn.loc.gov/2022054608

British Library Cataloguing in Publication Data

A catalogue record for this book is available from the British Library

ISBN 978-1-80073-968-0 hardback
ISBN 978-1-80073-969-7 ebook

https://doi.org/10.3167/9781800739680

To Janet for her continuing patience, and love

Contents

Maps

Preface

My early curiosity about Papua New Guinea[1] was sparked by an interest in 'human capital'. Demand for formal education surged in PNG through the 1950s, and in 1961 a plan to achieve universal primary education was announced. This was the last gasp of Australia's 'uniform development' policy – soon to be overturned on World Bank advice, and replaced by 'accelerated development'. I was interested in the behaviour of school leavers, on the hypothesis that surging popular demand for education reflected utilitarian attitudes to schooling. These could be seen (in the jargon of 'Chicago School' economists) as motivating 'private investment' in education. Personal payoffs from schooling came from formal employment. The search for jobs would impel educated young rural people to migrate to towns, to find 'white-collar' work. School leaver unemployment promised to become a national problem – as indeed it did.

After fieldwork in PNG in 1968–69, I was recruited to the Economics Department at the University of Papua New Guinea (UPNG) in 1970. In the early 1970s most students and staff were committed to an ideology of 'economic development', requiring a decisive break from the old colonial order. Discontent with race-based inequality had been growing, but no coherent dissenting narrative emerged until a report by the 'Faber Mission' in 1972 provided the necessary catalyst. Michael Faber, and colleagues including the anthropologist Keith Hart, proposed a new programme to curtail 'accelerated development', blamed by many for worsening inequality. For reasons of timing, and because of its redistributionist tone, the Faber Report proved very appealing to nationalists and their expatriate sympathizers.

Only a year or two earlier, Hart had introduced the concept of economic informality into the development literature. The Faber Report placed the informal economy at the heart of its strategies for development, urging the facilitation of a host of micro-scale, labour-intensive, *informal* economic activities largely absent from PNG. This proposal appeared to offer the prospect of a 'people's economy'. The Faber/Hart 'line' was adopted enthusiastically, if only briefly, by the new government. Its influence was sustained just long enough to inspire a national set of 'Eight Aims' suffused with the idea of informality, and for elements of the aims to be incorporated into the new state constitution.

Meeting Keith Hart in 1972, I found the idea of urban economic informality compelling, as was the puzzle of its comparative absence from PNG's few small towns. But by 1974 I had become aware of the paradox of attempting the *formalization of the informal*. The failure of official efforts to institute an informal economy was due to the misconceptions of its supporters, but also because entrenched business interests and bureaucratic prejudice combined to stigmatize informality as an impediment to 'modernization'.

Faber emboldened the Somare government to bring accelerated development to an abrupt halt and to adopt new approaches to development planning. The report fed into intellectual ferment in Port Moresby; at the university, Marxists in Law, Politics and Economics achieved marked changes in the orientation of their departments. In Economics, an assault

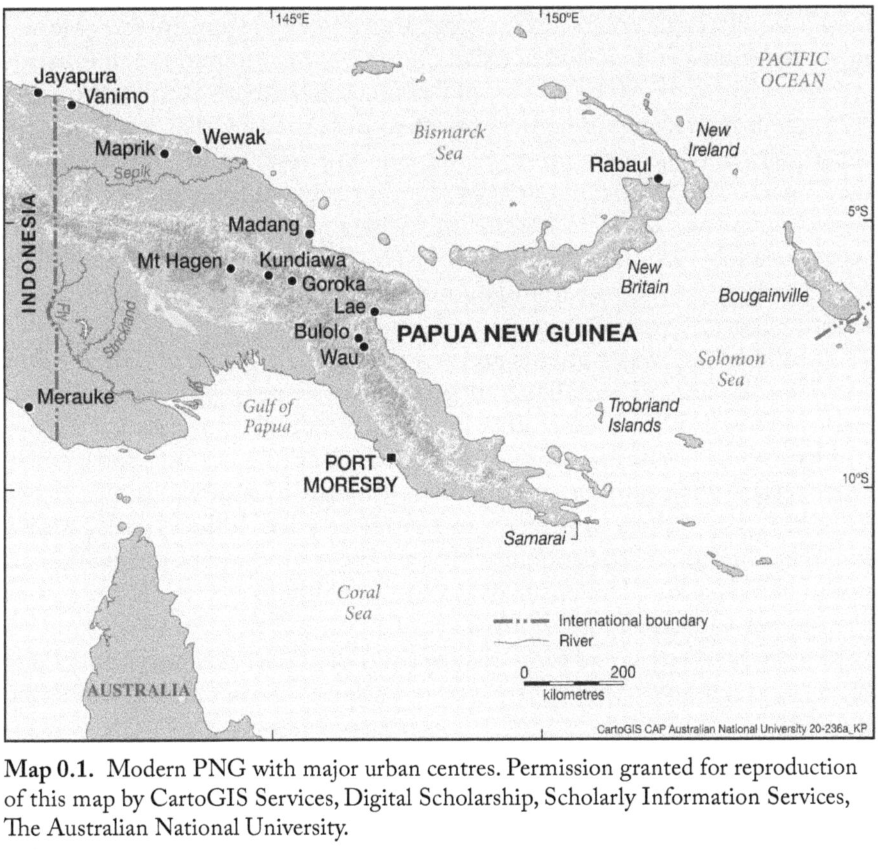

Map 0.1. Modern PNG with major urban centres. Permission granted for reproduction of this map by CartoGIS Services, Digital Scholarship, Scholarly Information Services, The Australian National University.

was mounted on 'neoclassicism' as the handmaid of neocolonialism, with the orthodox economists ill-prepared to meet the intellectual challenge. By 1976, my last year at UPNG, their numbers were finely balanced against the radicals. Curriculum innovation had proliferated, with many public policy skills neglected. Some students were rendered indifferent, even hostile, by the denunciations, while others were confused by the dissonance. Ross Garnaut observed later that, rather than inspiring political radicalism, this situation had encouraged cynicism among students about politics in PNG. It had diverted some of 'the best young people' away from 'concern for egalitarian and rationalist political objectives' and it had denied those politicians genuinely pursuing such objectives 'the political support they might otherwise have received' (Garnaut 1980).

Because they will recur later, I should mention some of the currents of thought swirling in and beyond UPNG, as self-government and independence approached. Members of a loose group (styled by one radical as 'colonial apologists') included academics whom the Australian administration had called upon for advice. They had tended to support the World Bank's 'accelerated' policy framework, and its elaboration in the colonial administration's first comprehensive Development Programme, published in 1968. Criticism came from several sources. Members of the nationalist and pro-independence Pangu Party were disturbed by the distributional consequences of accelerated development, and resented the highly managed character of policymaking by the Australian Department of Territories. Pangu was critical of forms of social and economic discrimination experienced by its (largely) indigenous membership; wage differentials applying to expatriate and indigenous public servants were a particularly sensitive issue.

Another group was students and academics attracted by the ideology of Nyerere's 'Tanzanian Socialism', an enthusiasm shared by at least one Faber team member. John Momis and Bernard Narakobi, associated with the Constitutional Planning Committee (Ch. 25), provided self-consciously 'Melanesian' perspectives, and found resonance in aspects of the Faber Report. Other radical critiques came from scholars influenced by 1970s Marxian thought – 'dependency' theory and/or a contemporary French strand of Marxism. These diverse influences should not be dismissed as ivory tower theorization; the universe of PNG politics was small enough to permit the ready circulation of ideas and of academics (as political advisers and technical consultants) between the governmental and academic cultures.

Ideas of the Australian economist, E.K. (Fred) Fisk, whose concept of *subsistence affluence* was influential in Australian policy and planning during the 1960s and early 1970s, were seen in radical quarters as the embodiment of neoclassical economic dogma. When members of the Faber team were introduced to 'Fiskian' orthodoxy they were not persuaded. Other critics, influenced by contemporary French structuralist Marxism and its anthropological correlates, saw Fiskian economics as colonial apologetics serving to justify the preservation of a 'traditional mode of production' and thereby to sustain the exploitation of rural labour by international capital.

Another ideological battle provoked by structural Marxism concerned whether an indigenous class structure could be discerned within traditional PNG 'social formations'. Presumed forms of traditional, hereditary leadership were asserted as providing the base for an indigenous capitalism. A new capitalist class whose status rested on principles of ascription, rather than achievement, would have implications for new forms of social stratification and wealth distribution. Countering such elitist tendencies would require mass mobilization and political education. Radicals had some cause for optimism as student strikes had shown a potential for mobilization, as had the emergence of widespread and spontaneous organization for local-level 'development' during the 1970s.

I left UPNG at the end of 1976 and spent four years as director of the PNG Institute of Applied Social and Economic Research before taking up an ANU appointment in Indonesia. After eleven years in Port Moresby, the Indonesian experience enabled me to view PNG from a new, comparative perspective, including the opportunity to observe the operations of a sprawling bureaucracy and a huge and complex informal economy. This experience is still the benchmark for many of my judgements about informality in PNG.

In Australia from 1991, I became interested in the relatively new fields of microfinance and financial inclusion. I now realize my attraction to financial inclusion stemmed from an abiding interest in economic informality. Among many things, poor people need access to an appropriate suite of financial services to support their economic activities – which are invariably informal – and to 'smooth' their consumption in the face of fluctuating incomes. But after 2009 I walked away from microfinance, disillusioned by the trend towards its 'financialization' as simply another asset class for Wall Street investors.

The puzzle of PNG's missing 'urban informal sector' had continued to intrigue me. I wanted to write an account of the *idea of informality* in relation to the ideology of 'development', which had taken hold after the Second World War, and to set this in the context of colonial economic history. This study is my attempt to view the economic history of the colonies – German, British and Australian – which came together to form the modern state, and to interpret their history through an informal economy lens.

Note

1. More correctly, the 'Territory of Papua and New Guinea' from after the Second World War until 1972, and thereafter 'Papua New Guinea' (abbreviated in the text as PNG).

Acknowledgements

Books have their reasons. Mine flow from events in late colonial Papua New Guinea between 1972 and 1975. Ideas have their seasons, but some are durable enough to shape a body of knowledge, changing how we view the world. Economic informality – to which I was introduced by Keith Hart in Port Moresby in 1972 – is such an idea. In this new century Keith encouraged my efforts to reconsider the processes of 'development' in PNG in terms of informal economy. Reflecting the separate lenses through which anthropologists and economists view the world, Keith retains reservations about my disciplinary and ideological approach. But whatever our differences, for more than a decade he has been the most helpful and patient of correspondents, during times when he has experienced personal difficulties that would absolve any reasonable person from such effort. I am profoundly grateful to him.

I am also indebted to Professor Ronald Duncan of the Crawford School of Public Policy, Australian National University, for seeing possibilities in the research proposal I put to him in 2010, and for his patience in waiting for this book. Access to colleagues and the university library, made possible by Crawford, has been invaluable. I have been heartened by guidance from Professor Stephen Howes of Crawford School's Development Policy Centre, to which I am now attached as a Visitor, and his role in bringing this book to fruition. In order to permit its publication in print form, and its wider distribution, Stephen has very generously agreed to waive, in favour of Berghahn Books, the copyright asserted by the Centre in regard to its previous publication. Richard Curtain, who has his own recollections of PNG's late colonial period, provided a most helpful review of the manuscript. I have been buoyed in recent years by the encouragement of Professor Ross Garnaut, although the connection is of longer standing. As an early-career researcher, Ross prepared studies of PNG rural–urban dynamics – empirical work (produced with Richard Curtain and others) that undergirds my account of the capital's population growth and labour market in the 1970s.

During the 1970s in Port Moresby, I learnt much from contact with senior Australian scholars including Anthony Clunies Ross, E.K. (Fred) Fisk, Nigel Oram and Charles Rowley, and have drawn on them for this study. Other contemporaries included John Langmore, the late Bill Standish and Christine Inglis, each of whom informed my understanding of the period – as did the former UPNG administrator David Sloper. Among Australian-based scholars of that period I should also mention W.R. (Bill) Stent, friend and recovering econometrician, whose work on *hybridity* in PNG 'transitional' agriculture has greatly influenced my argument. Later I had the good fortune to meet Ian Hughes, whose insights on traditional trade and exchange have been enormously helpful. I am grateful to him for his permission to quote freely from his landmark study *New Guinea Stone Age Trade*. In the new century I have been fortunate to encounter a new generation of young Papua New Guinean scholar/activists engaged in grassroots research, including Dr Nayahamui Rooney at ANU, Dr Elizabeth Kopel and Dr Fiona Hukula at the PNG National Research Institute, and Mr Busa Jeremiah Wenogo at the Institute of National Affairs/CIMC – for all of them, the informal economy is a matter of pressing social, political and economic concern. Finally, I am grateful for the assistance of my dear friend Alison Sloper, who prepared the index for this volume.

Acronyms

ANU	Australian National University
ASOPA	Australian School of Pacific Administration
BNG	British New Guinea
CMB	Coffee Marketing Board
CPC	Constitutional Planning Committee
DC	District Commissioner
DORCA	Directorate of Research and Civil Affairs
GDP	Gross Domestic Product
GNG	German New Guinea
HCE	Highlands Commodity Exchange
HFSA	Highland Farmers' and Settlers' Association
IASER	Institute of Applied Social and Economic Research
IBRD	International Bank for Reconstruction and Development (the 'World Bank')
ICA	International Coffee Agreement
ILO	International Labour Organization
LMS	London Missionary Society
MWB	Minimum Wages Board
NHC	National Housing Commission
NSO	National Statistical Office
ODG	Overseas Development Group
OPC	Office of Programming and Coordination
PCB	Production Control Board
PMV	Passenger Motor Vehicle
PNG	Papua New Guinea
PRS	Plantation Redistribution Scheme

TCP	Tolai Cocoa Project
TPNG	Territory of Papua and New Guinea
UN	United Nations
UNDP	United Nations Development Programme
UPNG	University of Papua New Guinea

Introduction

An 'Informal' Economic History

This narrative stands apart from more conventional economic histories because it is framed through a very particular lens provided by the idea of an *informal economy*. So far as possible, it is presented from the perspective of *popular* economic activity rather than the more common colonial vantage point – the commanding heights of an alien economic system. The study is organized around the notion of a *transition* by Melanesians from subsistence economy to market exchange, impelled by their introduction by Western colonialism to the monetized market economy. The island of New Guinea was divided between three European powers in the last quarter of the nineteenth century, with German New Guinea in the north-east quadrant, British New Guinea (later Australian Papua) in the south-east quadrant, and Dutch New Guinea occupying the western half of the 'big island' (Map 0.2).

During the colonial period, Melanesians were relatively quick to enter into monetized exchanges similar to traditional utilitarian barter, and later also into formal indentured employment. However, restricted by what W.E.H. (Bill) Stanner called 'a simple division of labour, little specialisation, and an undeveloped system of trade' (Stanner 1953), Melanesians proved generally unable either to initiate or to engage in more complex market processes. This incapacity constrained their productive engagement with the market economy, and retarded the transition from subsistence.

Colonial actors in what is now PNG included imperial administrators, together with traders, colonists and missionaries, and foreign minorities

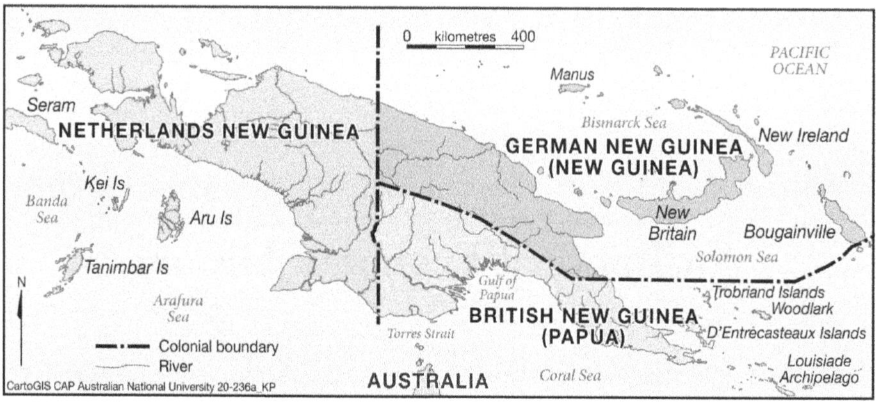

Map 0.2. The German, British and Dutch New Guineas. Permission granted for reproduction of this map by CartoGIS Services, Digital Scholarship, Scholarly Information Services, The Australian National University.

introduced as functionaries and intermediaries. Important as these actors were, their influence is less central to this account than what Keith Hart (speaking of West Africa) called 'the massive impediments to growth that originate in local material and social conditions' (Hart 1982). The lens of informal economy derives from Hart's observations of the livelihoods of African rural–urban migrants in Nima, a suburb of Ghana's capital Accra, during the latter part of the 1960s. The reification of their activities as occurring in an urban informal sector was a coinage of the International Labour Organization (ILO), applied in a subsequent study of employment issues in Kenya. Events soon gave Hart opportunity to compare his Ghanaian experience with the circumstances of late colonial PNG, as a member of the 'Faber Mission' – a consulting team contracted to recommend economic policies for the soon-to-be-independent state. Hart and his colleagues visited PNG in 1972 at a crucial moment in its history and he would later describe the experience as 'decisive' in his thinking.

This study considers the introduction of colonial-era Melanesians to a completely unaccustomed experiential environment – *the market*. I employ this construct while accepting the conclusion of a scholar of Melanesian economy, Karl Benediktsson, that 'no social group has ever taken commoditisation to its logical extreme, fully excluding non-economic aspects from economic relations'. My discussion moves between various historical periods and places to convey an understanding of how the market manifested in the prevailing German, British and Australian colonial systems. This requires some discussion of contemporary economic orthodoxies in each of the three New Guineas, governing the conduct of introduced economic activities and relationships. The reactions of indigenous Melanesians to colonial bureaucratic pressures flowing from these orthodoxies are represented here by a metaphor of *pushback*. This provides a dynamic element in the study, whose novelty lies in framing the account in terms of formality and informality in economic affairs. Consisting, for the most part, of the examination and reinterpretation of standard texts, the work is presented with little pretension to historical originality beyond that framework.

Certain writers of the late colonial period deserve reconsideration because of their continuing value for our understanding of the era. These include the historians Rowley and Oram, and anthropologists Salisbury, Hughes, Finney, Stanner and the two Epsteins, all of whom informed contemporary debates about PNG's preparedness for independence. Certain economists, also now relatively neglected, helped to frame post-war debate about economic development policy. In PNG these included the Australian economist E.K. Fisk and his school; beyond Melanesia, economic theorists in the classical mould including Peter Bauer, Hla Myint and W. Arthur Lewis were also influential.

Discussion of the interface between economics and anthropology impels us to examine the confrontation between two defining logics, supporting radically different understandings of economic processes. These logics are, first, a Smithian worldview (embodied in colonial ideology) which saw in humanity a universal propensity to 'truck and barter'. Second, there is a Maussian logic of *The Gift*. The allusions here are to *The Wealth of Nations* (Adam Smith 1776) and *The Gift* (Marcel Mauss 1925). Described by Chris Gregory (1982) as the exchange of inalienable things between non-aliens, *The Gift* influences Melanesian behaviour profoundly. Adam Smith's economizing instincts are at odds with such exchange, conducted (as Mauss put it) 'in ways and for reasons other than those with which we are familiar from our own societies'.

Of particular importance to the narrative is a conundrum that suggests a certain singularity in Melanesian economic behaviour. Evidence of this appeared during the Faber Mission's visit to PNG, when Hart observed that informal economic activity such as he had documented in Ghana was very largely absent from PNG's towns. This absence caused the Faber team to recommend measures to encourage the growth of an urban informal economy. But the dearth of informality in PNG was symptomatic of that deeper incapacity described in 1953 by Stanner (above). This constrained popular engagement with the market economy throughout the colonial period, and was still evident at independence. It is argued here that it was significant among what Hart called the 'impediments to growth' originating in 'local material and social conditions'. Melanesians would be slow to overcome this handicap, whether in formal or informal modes of market economic activity.

Hart's construct of informality cannot be applied to traditional (or pre-market) forms of exchange such as occurred in pre-colonial PNG, for it had no salience there. It became salient only with the commencement of market exchange, with the introduction of bureaucratic regulation, and with efforts by traditional subsistence agriculturalists to accommodate themselves to the modalities of markets. In many countries, such attempts at accommodation have thrown up economic informality, as indigenous people grapple with unfamiliar market norms and bureaucratic strictures. It is also common for the experience to induce *hybrid* behaviour among them. Hybridity occurs in situations where introduced market dealings sit uncomfortably alongside traditional norms, with one apt to compromise the other. The anthropological literature provides many instances of such hybridity in colonial-era PNG, some of which are examined in later chapters.

Instances of economic hybridity in Melanesia may be seen as arising from clashes between the Smithian and Maussian logics. An earlier analogue of this was seen in interactions on the western fringe of historical Melanesia, in the present-day territory of Indonesian Papua. There, Asian pre-colonial commercial norms – demonstrated in the behaviour of travelling Malay and Chinese peddlers – rubbed up against the ceremonial exchange of Melanesian 'Papuans'. The Dutch historian J.C. van Leur described a pre-colonial system of mercantile capitalism with its own conventions of bureaucratic regulation and market exchange. In this system, travelling peddlers – cast here as historical forerunners of modern informal 'micro-entrepreneurs' – were a dynamic element. They failed, however, to inspire significant emulation among indigenous Papuans. Van Leur should be seen as one of a number of 'precursors' of the idea of informality, each of whom anticipated Hart's observations and analysis to some degree.

Confrontation between market economy and traditional exchange also occurred later, and more emphatically, in the experience of colonial PNG. Its territory was located in the eastern half of the island of New Guinea, contiguous to modern Indonesian Papua. Encounters between colonial market economy and traditional exchange in the regions that became PNG are recounted here in an analytical framework of formality, informality and hybridity. This is applied to three case studies set in the major colonial centres of Port Moresby, Rabaul and Goroka. These document the transition from subsistence economy to market exchange that occurred in and around the towns. While it is more a sketch than a case study, a complementary account (Ch. 3) of events in former Dutch (now Indonesian) West New Guinea will support these three narratives.

Rabaul and Goroka were 'lucky' places, whereas Port Moresby was located in an economically unpromising zone and struggled to make its own luck. Rabaul had the additional advantage of an immigrant Chinese population. Recruited as artisans and intermediaries by colonial capital, many Chinese quickly became independently employed and demonstrated the entrepreneurial energy of monsoon Asia to Rabaul's Melanesian population. The case studies offer comparisons between German and 'Anglo' (British/Australian) colonial ideologies, and their consequences. As colonial regulatory and normative frameworks were derived from ideologies imposed by the European powers, there is also some discussion of imperial understandings of 'primitive' economic systems, and of how these influenced colonial economic policy.

In the late colonial period, after the Pacific War, an ideological transformation occurred in the newly unified Australian 'Territory of Papua and New Guinea'. The economic sub-discipline of 'development', whose origins are traceable to the eighteenth century and the classical economist Adam Smith, re-emerged in a decolonizing world after having been eclipsed by a 'neoclassical' economics more concerned with allocative efficiency than economic growth. While before the war the dominant ideology had been one of extractive, *commercial* development, in the post-war era of Bretton Woods and anti-colonialism the Government of Australia adopted an ideology for PNG based on notions of *economic* development. My account examines the implications of Hart's idea of informality for economic development, and considers how the new development orthodoxy both shaped informal economic behaviour and was itself reshaped by a dawning understanding of informality's significance in the development process.

Economic development in PNG was to be implemented under a rubric of *trusteeship* – the 'guardianship' of indigenous peoples by the colonial power. Among the obstacles to development was a lingering colonial legacy of social and economic obsolescence. This was sustained by entrenched attitudes, effectively hostile to the emergence of a committed indigenous urban workforce and the very notion of a Melanesian urbanism. The bureaucratic application of the new, post-war ideology in the regions of Rabaul, Goroka and Port Moresby, and the interactions between official policy initiatives and the *pushback* of indigenous peoples, are recounted here.

As the inevitability of PNG's independence impressed itself on the bureaucratic mind, governmental processes became more self-consciously 'preparatory', and efforts were made to quicken the pace of development. An account is given of this preparatory period, and of economic policy-making during the term of the first (pre-independence) Somare government, influenced by (among others) the Faber Mission and Keith Hart. Political change and redistributive (or economic nationalist) policies created opportunity for some indigenous entrepreneurs to flourish in the *formal* economy, although their rise displayed relatively little resemblance to Joseph Schumpeter's model of creative entrepreneurship. The Faber-inspired attempt to encourage economic *informality* failed, in part due to the 'entrenched attitudes' mentioned above. To understand the rise of formal indigenous enterprise this study looks to Baumol's conception of negative forms of entrepreneurship and to North's institutionalist account of 'stumbling blocks' on a path requiring actors to transition from 'personal' (i.e. Maussian) to 'impersonal' (Smithian) modes of exchange. As to *informal* economic activity, understanding the reasons for its failure to flourish is among the purposes of this book.

The experience of this last period, in which the idea of economic informality was briefly at the centre of political rhetoric, offers insights into an economic malaise which subsequently overtook the young independent state. During a late twentieth-century period of stagnation there seemed little reason to expect that the impediment to economic development, represented by the incapacity of Melanesians to engage with processes of specialization and exchange, would be overcome.

A Note on the Structure of This Narrative

The study is organized around three historical periods, seen through the experiences of three towns. The chosen periods are the early colonial (up to the outbreak of the Second World War), the late colonial (1939 to self-government in 1972) and an 'Independence' period (1972 to 1975, but with some necessary treatment of subsequent events). These are the subjects of parts II, III and IV of this book, respectively. For each period, accounts of events in the three regions are presented in parallel. Readers requiring a continuous narrative for any one region will find it by skipping through the chapters, although this will diminish their opportunity to see correspondences and contrasts between the regions in each historical period.

Part I

Economic Informality

An Idea and Its Relevance to Melanesia

Chapter 1

Keith Hart and the Idea of Informality

The idea of informality relates to economic activity, described in terms of *formality* and *informality*, and conducted in the context of market exchange. Although informality in economic life may be observed in a wide range of economic and social formations, this study focuses on the circumstances of emerging or 'developing' states, with particular reference to PNG. Keith Hart has described the genesis of the construct, and its widening frame of reference. The term 'informal sector' (later, largely superseded by 'informal *economy*') emerged during the1970s as a 'label for economic activities that escape state regulation'. It responded to the 'proliferation of self-employment and casual labour in Third World cities', and later also found applications in industrial societies where it 'competed with similar epithets – the "hidden", "underground", "black" economy', and so on (Hart 2010, 142).

In terms of this broader application, Hart identified a study by Pahl (1984) as among early efforts to apply economic informality to advanced industrial economies. Having begun simply as a label for the 'unregulated activities of the marginal poor' in cities of the Third World, informality became generalized as a 'universal feature' of modern economies. Activities as varied as 'home improvement, street trade, squatter settlements, open source software, the illegal drugs traffic, political corruption and offshore banking' could be seen as united under this single banner (Hart 2004, 6). This expansive formulation encompasses both the urban poor in their slums and wealthy international clients of Panama City legal firms.

But such broader applications are beyond the scope of this study, which remains focused on Hart's early concern for emerging polities and on the relationships between economic development and informality – 'the unregulated activities of the marginal poor'.

Consistent with Hart's original, 'Third World' context, PNG was among the first countries to which he applied a formal/informal framework. This occurred in a report on economic policy, prepared for the soon-to-be-independent Government of Papua New Guinea (ODG 1973). It drew on his initial description of the phenomenon in newly independent Ghana (Hart 1971, 1973) where he had encountered what the International Labour Organization (ILO 1972) subsequently styled an 'urban informal sector', or what Hart himself later termed an 'early-modern street economy' (Hart 2004, 7). As Hart recalls, 'for me formal and informal income opportunities were always joined at the hip, not a separate sphere called the informal sector or economy'. Whatever the labels, his intention had been (and remains) 'to make informal activities visible' and – employing an anthropological lens – to insist on the formal and informal as 'a dialectical pair defining each other reciprocally' (Hart, personal communication with the author, 18 May 2020). It will be necessary to consider Hart's initial account of informal economic activity, as observed in 1960s Ghana, before examining his later attempt to apply it to late colonial PNG. But first some further explanation of the nature of economic informality is needed.

The growth of market exchange in an 'underdeveloped' region has typically been associated with the imposition of bureaucracy, which creates rules to give *form* to its own activities and to those of the regulated. In this way, market activity becomes enumerated, and the status of being enumerated is a crucial marker of formality. The nature of bureaucratic frameworks and activity (as informed by a dominant economic orthodoxy) substantially determines the character and designation of economic activities as being either formal or informal. In many of the instances of informality discussed here, a metaphor of *pushback* is employed to describe how informal economic actors react against bureaucratic regulation. Informality challenges bureaucracy by failing to con*form* with bureaucratic prescriptions. If that were all, informality in economic life could be defined simply in terms of opposition to the processes of formal economy.

Conformity is not simply a matter of obeying regulations, however, as it also involves broad acceptance (or the 'institutionalization') of the particular set of norms and ideas underpinning a bureaucratic culture. What was referred to above as a 'dominant economic orthodoxy' is likely to be present and identifiable – whether explicit or not – in any given set of circumstances. The account here of economic informality in PNG will pay attention to the relationships between distinctive colonial economic orthodoxies, the action of bureaucracies informed by those orthodoxies, and the reaction of individual economic agents to such circumstances. In this framework of analysis informal economic activity is seen as occurring outside the strictures of bureaucracy, as possibly transgressing its requirements, and perhaps also signalling authorities' failure to secure popular acceptance ('institutionalization') of the necessary bureaucratic and cultural norms. But while informal actors may be able to avoid certain obligations, they must also forgo some of the advantages of conformity, such as the security that flows from operating in a predictable bureaucratic and normative framework. Such nonconformist actors are unable to access the protection of the state (Hann and Hart 2011, 113), an insight Hart attributes to Clifford Geertz (1963b).

If this explanation seems to set up a dialectic, a formal/informal antagonism, this is not inevitable. Hart has said that this dialectical opposition could be conceived as a bureaucratic war against ordinary people, in which informal economic life might be seen as a form of popular resistance. While this depiction may have some romantic appeal, he argues that bureaucracy is necessary to manage the 'large-scale coordination' of certain public functions, and that its origins lie in 'aspirations for political equality'. Bureaucracy and informality could be made to complement one another, and the task is to harness this potential (Hart 2008, 4)

Little evidence of this 'complementary potential' was apparent in Hart's original account of an informal economy in Ghana, where the formal/informal duality was reinforced by bureaucratic action impacting actors differentially. Between 1965 and 1968, Hart conducted fieldwork in Nima, a slum neighbourhood of the capital, Accra (Hart 1971, 1973). This was at the end of the Nkrumah period and during its immediate aftermath. In terms of *dominant orthodoxy*, a 'national bureaucracy' held sway, imbued with notions of economic development driven by state corporations. Living in the slums of Nima, and denied the *institutional protection* of this system, residents 'were excluded from (and victimized by) the state's monopolies [and] were busy making lives for themselves in the cracks between' (Hart 1994). This description serves to remind us that the idea of an informal economy emerged from, and is a critique of, the idea of 'economic development'.

Hart's discussion of bureaucracy began with Hegel's contention that society should be managed by 'an educated bureaucratic elite in the national interest', and he noted that Max Weber saw the alliance between Rhineland industrialists and Prussian bureaucrats as representing such a synthesis (Hann and Hart 2011, 30). The imperial bureaucracy offered institutional protection to corporations in an ideological framework described by Hart as 'national capitalism'. To repeat an assertion made above, he sees bureaucracy as an essentially positive construct, a democratically inspired attempt to allow people access to their rights – although he comments that it too often operates as 'the negation of democracy' (Hart 2004, 1). In nineteenth-century European colonies, Weberian bureaucracy was associated with the growth and elaboration of market exchange and the construction of institutions for its conduct and regulation, but without any necessary democratic engagement of the colonized. Most often it involved the state's extending bureaucratic protection to metropolitan capital, to the detriment of emerging indigenous enterprise. This proposition will be examined later, in the historical circumstances of PNG. There the predecessor colonies – German, British and Australian – were all bureaucratized entities. Indeed, as subsequent chapters will suggest, German New Guinea was the very model of a Weberian bureaucracy, directed from Berlin, and its Australian successor regime retained the Teutonic regulatory system to a remarkable degree.

Returning to Hart's experience in Ghana, he found that in Nima 40 per cent of active males and virtually all females were untouched by formal employment (Hart 1973, 63). Among the Frafra, an ethnic group of rural–urban migrants with little Western education and limited formal skills, most men got by on wages from unskilled jobs, earnings from self-employment and what he called private transfers – money or other support received from familiars. Hart observed high levels of 'unemployment' among the Frafra (in the then conventional sense of non-participation in regular 'waged' jobs). Those with such jobs were inadequately paid, so that multiple job-holding, or moonlighting, occurred routinely among waged (that is, formal) Frafra workers. These men resorted frequently to additional, non-wage, sources of income.

Frafra without access to 'formal' employment subsisted on earnings from casual employment, and by self-employment in the production of a wide variety of goods and services. Many benefited from private transfers received by virtue of their ethnicity and/or membership of social networks (as well as incurring their own obligations to make such transfers from time to time). In addition, resort to credit was pervasive and frequent. This served to smooth their consumption expenditures and allowed them to meet contingencies. Hart's account stressed the unreliability of non-wage incomes rather than their inadequacy. Returns to non-wage employment varied widely from period to period, around mean levels often higher (occasionally much higher) than unskilled wages. But because of this unreliability, Frafra were often reluctant to surrender low-paying wage employment, opting instead to juggle the demands of such work with the opportunistic, though sporadic, activities of the informal economy. As Hart observed it, everyday life followed a 'hand-to-mouth' pattern – an existence marked by 'unevenness of expenditures' over the payroll cycle, 'flexibility of consumption units' and the 'proliferation of credit' in all expenditures. He remarked wryly that '*haushalten*' (budgeting) – described by Max Weber as one of the 'two types of rational economic activity' – was rather uncommon in Nima (Hart 1973, 65).

Hart made an important distinction between legitimate and illegitimate informality, with the notion of legitimacy being that found in Ghanaian law, and broadly consistent with the morality of those Ghanaians who considered themselves respectable. Such judgements did not correspond readily with the *mores* of most people in Nima. It was a neighbourhood notoriously lacking in respectability, dominated by criminals, and supplying everything available in the 'red-light' district of a major city (Hart 1973, 74). He contended that any discussion of opportunities for income *beyond* formal jobs must consider certain criminal activities. In Nima, what Hart called 'illegitimate' activity seemed to him to be everywhere (ibid., 68).

The classification of criminal income opportunities commenced with service transactions, many of which might in principle (moral considerations aside) be valued in national accounting terms and regarded as productive. Hustlers, receivers, usurers and pawners at illegal interest rates, drug dealers, prostitutes, procurers, smugglers, bribe-takers, influence pedlars and protection men were accounted as productively, albeit illegitimately, employed in the informal economy (ibid., 69). Hustlers and spivs, 'Runyonesque' and often shady characters who jumped at every opportunity, were the largest single group. Many other Nima residents also engaged in making (and benefiting from) 'illegitimate transfers' involving thieves, larcenists, peculators and embezzlers, confidence tricksters and gamblers. Urban crime was an agent of income redistribution.

Among legitimate informal activities, Hart distinguished numerous categories of primary (urban agriculture), secondary (petty manufactures, artisanship) and tertiary activities, conducted by an urban proletariat (Hart 1971) or sub-proletariat (Hart 1973). This categorization suggests why the early ILO usage of the term informal 'sector' has been largely supplanted by the empirically more accurate term, informal *economy*. Informality is not itself a 'sector'; it occurs in all sectors – as categorized by statisticians – primary, secondary and tertiary.

At the apex of Nima's legitimate informal economy were tertiary activities conducted by the owners and operators of transport assets and cornmills, and speculators in commodity markets, all requiring relatively large capital. Beneath them was a profusion of small-scale distributors – some itinerants from 'upcountry', others resident in the city. They were distinguished by how and where they traded (whether from market stalls or roadside tables, or as mobile hawkers), or by the commodities they traded, or by their positions in distribution chains. Traders were flexible in response to opportunity, differing widely in terms of time devoted and scale of operation. But, reflecting the flexibility of trade and the relative ease of entry into it, the roles of 'petty traders, brokers, wholesale merchants, commission agents, and occasional dealers' were played to a greater or less extent by many members of what he called the 'urban sub-proletariat' (Hart 1973, 72).

The formal and informal economies were closely interrelated. While the informal economy provided a very large proportion of the daily needs of residents of Nima and other sub-proletarian suburbs, it also made substantial 'exports' of goods and services to middle-class neighbourhoods. In regard to illegitimate goods and services, he distinguished between the bustling local economy within Nima and its dealings with the 'bourgeois' population of greater Accra. The latter were avid recipients of many illegitimate services, but also unwilling donors of certain 'illegitimate transfers' (owing to theft and burglary, for example). Hart made a nice distinction between the private transfers circulating within his 'sub-proletariat' and the illegitimate transfers whose costs are borne 'predominantly by the urban middle classes' (Hart 1973, 86). The metaphor of symbiosis applied; both positively, in the sense of mutually beneficial transactions, and negatively, in the sense of exactions by one side from the other.

Hart's research in Ghana had a considerable impact on the thinking of some international agencies and on the governments of some newly emerging states, concerned by alarming projections of growing urban unemployment (see, for example, Jolly et al. 1973). In retrospect these may seem ill-conceived, but they generated considerable unease at the time. Briefly, Hart's Ghanaian insights suggested that urban poverty should be analysed in terms of the lack of sufficiently remunerative 'income opportunities', as distinct from any notion of open unemployment due to the absence of 'jobs'. When Hart arrived there as a member of the Faber Mission, his newly acquired celebrity prepared the way for a positive reception to the idea of informality in PNG. That experience also caused him to consider the idea of a *rural* informality. Further consideration will be given to this later in the volume (Ch. 25), dealing with the impact of the Faber Report (ODG 1973) on the political economy of PNG on the eve of its independence.

Later, Hart came to see informality as arising from anomalies between the conceptions of orthodox economic theories, as conceived for application in particular economic systems, and the messy reality of those systems. In any formal economic system, such anomalies between a dominant orthodoxy and the objective circumstances of livelihoods can only be accommodated by introducing the idea of informal economy. It applies wherever formal economic analysis – whether intended for application to, for example, a socialist or a capitalist economic system – is confronted by the merely '*partial* institutionalisation of economies around the globe' to one or another economic system. In such circumstances 'there will be a need for some such remedial concept as the informal economy. Its application to concrete conditions is likely to be stimulated by palpable discrepancies between prevalent intellectual models and observed realities' (Hart 2007a, 846, italics in original).

Hart's notion of 'form as rule' suggests how ideologies determine the forms that *ought* to be observed in economic life. Orthodoxy typically informs the policies to be implemented and guides bureaucratic measures applied for their implementation. Informality occurs when populations are only partially institutionalized to, and push back against, the prevailing economic dogma and its supporting bureaucratic measures. In that sense, the notion is as applicable to remaining socialist regimes (such as Cuba, North Korea and the People's Republic of China) as to the market economies of the industrialized world and the 'national capitalist', 'transitional' or 'emerging market' systems of the developing world. Conduct of market economy and the operation of bureaucracy appear as twin pillars supporting an economic system in which formal and informal economic activities coexist. As an extension of this principle, prescribed modes of organization for production and exchange in a socialist economic system may also induce the phenomenon of pushback among its population – hence behaviour that is informal in terms of socialist principles.

This prompts the question of whether economic informality could occur in quite different contexts, as in social formations occurring prior to mercantile or industrial capitalism. Any society with some semblance of administration had its own version of *form*. These derived from the principles on which societies were administered, so that economic activity occurring outside, or deviating from, prescribed forms might be considered informal. But such speculation is unfruitful. It amounts to the *reductio ad absurdum*[1] of Hart's understanding of informality, which cannot be applied to pre-market forms of exchange because it had no salience there. Informality becomes salient only with the adoption of market exchange, with the emergence of bureaucracy to regulate it, and with the efforts of economic actors to accommodate themselves to the emerging modalities of markets. This formulation could also allow for informality to appear in some liminal form, under circumstances where those preconditions are emergent rather than established. Such a situation may have occurred in West New Guinea (Ch. 3).

Even in a market economy subject to bureaucratic regulation, it is likely that some activities and societal attitudes from earlier socio-economic formations will persist. Hart dealt with these as *residue*, describing them as parallel to what he called the 'formal order'. Such activities are simply *separate* from the bureaucracy. Any attempt to label phenomena such as 'peasant economy' or 'traditional institutions' as informal puts excessive strain on the category. Yet they are significant, because the 'social forms' characteristic of such phenomena 'often shape informal economic practices' (Hart 2008, 14; Hart 2012b).

Our discussion will return to this subject later, when the idea of *hybridity* in economic activity (interposed between the states of formality and informality) is introduced. Just as the 'modalities' of markets were absent from other early economic formations, they were also foreign to traditional Melanesia. Later, in the colonial period, this absence had implications for the manner and degree of Melanesian acculturation to the colonial economic system. The persistence of Hart's 'residue', triggering what is called here 'hybridity', will be shown as crucial to understanding much Melanesian economic behaviour in the colonial period.

Note

1. *Reductio ad absurdum* is the disproof of an argument by reducing it to absurdity: in this case, by showing its inapplicability, because it attempts to take the argument beyond the boundaries within which the duality of formality and informality may be applied.

Chapter 2

Precursors of the Informal Economy

A number of earlier observers should be considered Hart's intellectual forerunners in that they described, and in varying degrees explained, what later became known as the informal economy. Among those acknowledged by Hart was the nineteenth-century English journalist Henry Mayhew, whose *London Labour and the London Poor* (1861–62) is unmistakably an account of the informality phenomenon. Appearing originally as newspaper columns, his reports remind modern readers that mid-Victorian Britain experienced phenomena – urbanization and population movement, technological change and social dislocation – found in contemporary developing countries. Mayhew's London is shown as supporting a historically unprecedented concentration of unemployed and casual workers, with a significant and complex informal economy.

Hart has also acknowledged the direct influence on his thinking of Clifford Geertz (1963b) and Oscar Lewis (1966), but other candidates – not nominated by him – are named here as precursors. Chosen for their relevance to themes of this narrative, they are the liberal economist P.T. Bauer, the formalist anthropologist R.F. Salisbury and the colonial historian J.C. van Leur. The discussion of van Leur (Ch. 3) introduces an even deeper time dimension to economic informality than Mayhew provided. It suggests the possibility that a kind of *liminal* informality appeared in the mercantile capitalism of the Malay Archipelago, at its furthest extent on the shores of West New Guinea. Van Leur's account of that period also supports the notion of a Melanesian 'singularity' in economic affairs.

The account here of Péter Tamás Bauer, a pre-war Hungarian émigré to Britain, provides a link with the origins of 'economic development' in classical political economy and acknowledges his role as the pioneer *economic* analyst of informality. As much of his early fieldwork was conducted in British West Africa, this also provides points of comparison with conclusions Keith Hart drew from his own work in Ghana. Richard Salisbury is nominated to bring this narrative closer to its geographic focus on PNG. It will show how closely he anticipated a generalized view of urban informality. Salisbury's formalist accounts of Melanesian societies in transition from subsistence echoed Bauer – both in their common adherence to the construct of 'transition' and in their emphasis on the role of the service sector in development. Both Bauer and Salisbury provided evidence to support the idea of a *rural* economic informality, an idea not emphasized in Hart's account of Nima, and it cannot be claimed he was influenced by them. In fact, Hart is extremely critical of the idea of transition from subsistence economy. These correspondences and discordances will become clearer as the narrative proceeds.

Peter Bauer, West Africa, and the Economic Analysis of Informality

Bauer introduced the idea of informality to the economic literature – in the sense of fine-grained description – in his studies of late colonial British territories. Because of his interest in the 'grassroots' economic behaviour of indigenous peoples, Bauer was an isolated figure among economists of his period. A comfortable, even arrogant, assumption – that orthodox economic analysis could be applied reflexively to the broad range of human societies – appeared to render unnecessary any close scrutiny of the specifics of particular cultures or economic systems. Bauer was also isolated in setting himself against the post-war vogue for interventionist planning, parodied by him as 'price-less' economics. Embraced by the victorious Western powers and the newly created Bretton Woods institutions, economic planning was the instrument of choice for achieving the new goal of economic development. But while Bauer was also a 'development' economist, his inspiration lay elsewhere: in Adam Smith's *Wealth of Nations* and the classical political economy that followed upon it.

Bauer's credentials as precursor include studies of internal trade and entrepreneurship in late colonial West Africa and Malaya (Bauer 1948, 1954). Colonial administrations created formal employment, while European capital controlled large-scale economic activity. An intermediary class of alien traders (Chinese, Indians, 'Levantines') often maintained the most direct economic interaction with indigenous populations, catalysing economic activity. Emphasizing the enterprise of these peoples, Bauer pointed to the spontaneous and substantial expansion of smallholder export crops in British West Africa and Malaya (just as occurred later in parts of colonial PNG). His paradigm of agricultural development was one of Smithian 'transition'. Smallholder agricultural investment, complemented by the intensive trading and service activities of African cultivators, had the potential to increase their levels of economic activity and income from 'subsistence' to an 'exchange' economy (Bauer and Yamey 1951, 743).[1] The indigenous economy was his primary focus, and in hindsight we may choose to characterize it as 'informal' (whether or not Bauer himself had such a distinction in mind).

Another reason for naming Bauer as a precursor of informality stems from a controversy he initiated, challenging conventional wisdom on the changing occupational distribution of labour during the course of development. Derived from William Petty's *Political Arithmetick* (Petty 1690) and buttressed by Colin Clark's empirical research (Clark 1940, *The Conditions of Economic Progress*), the accepted principle was that economic growth is 'generally associated' with 'distinct, necessary and predictable' changes in the distribution of occupations. Most particularly, there occurs a 'relative increase' in the proportion of those in tertiary (service) jobs (Bauer and Yamey 1951, 741). Bauer dismissed this generalization as deterministic, describing it as empirically incorrect due to a combination of flawed data and inadequate observation. He claimed that the Petty/Clark hypothesis was falsified by two characteristics of developing country labour markets – the 'imperfect specialization' of individual workers, and their 'occupational fluidity' (Bauer and Yamey 1957). These characteristics resulted in a greater allocation of labour to tertiary or 'service' occupations during the *early* stages of development than Clark had anticipated.

Imperfect specialization of labour (first identified by Adam Smith) was masked by unreliable colonial census data, though simple observation showed that many of those described as 'farmers' also spent much of their time in 'small-scale transport, porterage and trade', where, apart from selling what they produced personally, they also engaged in purchasing and retrading commodities (Bauer and Yamey 1957, 34). Specialization was 'imperfect' because such people operated in both the agricultural and service sectors, while in urban areas even many formally employed people also had sidelines (the moonlighting described by Hart). The second characteristic, fluidity of occupations, was also difficult to detect in census data. Bauer's explanation was couched in terms of farmers and their options (hence a case applicable to *rural* informality). But it was equally relevant to urban street traders in Nima (or in Mayhew's London) who gave time, opportunistically, to such activities – characterized by ease of entry – as mentioned above. Doing so was not difficult, so long as they had the small amount of capital required to conduct such relatively unskilled activities (ibid., 37).

Because of these two characteristics, the economic activity of such people is better understood as a varied series of tasks rather than the conduct of a defined occupation (Bauer and Yamey 1951, 742). Yet this diverse set of sideline activities was generally ignored in census data. When multitasking Africans were enumerated simply as 'farmers', the size and significance of the service sector was seriously underestimated. Bauer took such flourishing tertiary-sector employment in West Africa as an instance of a familiar theme, articulated originally in the eighteenth century by Adam Smith – the 'crucial role of trade and transport' in growing and extending the monetized economy (Bauer and Yamey 1957, 42).

Bauer and Yamey (1951, 1957) provided multiple instances of the microeconomic logic underlying the behaviour of West Africans at early stages of the transition from subsistence, describing the incremental processes by which Smithian specialization and exchange are elaborated. These were the processes Bill Stanner had found so lacking among the indigenous people of PNG immediately after the Pacific War (Introduction, above). As development proceeds, individuals become more clearly specialized in their occupations, and the degree of occupational fluidity diminishes. Rising personal incomes and improved transport systems lead to the extension of markets, so that specialization yields increasing profits. At this higher level of economic progress, the need for greater capital and more complex technological requirements act to reduce the freedom of individuals to shift between economic activities (Bauer and Yamey 1957, 34).

In retrospect, the importance of Bauer's polemic does not lie in its attempt to challenge the Petty/Clark generalization. Although he pointed to unsuspected levels of service activity at low levels of development, this amounted to no more than an intriguing qualification to the Petty/Clark hypothesis, which retains broad acceptance. Modern research is more concerned with the causal mechanisms underlying the 'shift to services', rather than the *direction* of that shift. In recent decades the shift has been observed, particularly in Latin America and sub-Saharan Africa, as taking the rather troubling form of 'premature deindustrialization' (Rodrik 2016). The share of manufacturing in GDP and in employment has been peaking at lower levels, and at lower levels of per capita income, than was observed historically in the Western world, or (more recently) in East Asia.

Bauer is judged significant here for his pioneering account of indigenous trading and service activities, which we now recognize as informal. A later critique of Bauer by Michael Lipton (1984) was concerned not so much with his account of the service sector, and still less with his 'discovery' of the informal economy, but rather with his generalized application of classical economic theory to modern issues of economic development. Lipton charged that Bauer's 'classical' prescription, that 'enterprise, trade, enlargement of markets' would act as 'engines of development', was persuasive only because he drew his policy prescriptions from the experience of 'lucky places' such as British West Africa and colonial Malaya. Lipton's assessment of Bauer (and, by implication, of the classical prescription) will recur frequently in this narrative because of its particular resonance for PNG.

Richard Salisbury: Services as Leading Sector

Given the centrality of Melanesia to this narrative, nominating an anthropologist of PNG as a precursor may appear opportunistic. However, Salisbury embraced the 'underdevelopment' economics of Bauer and Yamey (Salisbury 1962, 213) and was influenced by Clifford Geertz (whom Hart regarded as a precursor of informality). Bauer and Yamey informed Salisbury's view of the importance of services in development, leading him to undeniable premonitions of informality. Keith Hart respected his 'rich and nuanced ethnographic arguments' (Hann and Hart 2011, 68), but had little time for his anthropological formalism, and none at all for his adherence to the 'transition'. Nonetheless, that concept – integral to the dynamics of agricultural development as understood by Bauer, Myint, Fisk and Stent (among economists) and Salisbury, Scarlett Epstein and Finney (among anthropologists cited here) – underlies this study. Some Marxists may dismiss the informal economy as 'petty commodity production', and accuse its champions of 'mystify[ing] the essentially regressive and exploitative nature of this economic zone' (Hart 2008, 7). But the enthusiasm for informality crosses ideological boundaries, with the idea engaging commentators as widely separated as the eclectic Marxian Hart and Lord Bauer, that darling of modern economic libertarians.[2]

Salisbury's informality was derived from two PNG studies. One, the particular object of Hart's praise, concerned the Siane people from the region of Goroka, while the other dealt with the Tolai of the Gazelle Peninsula around Rabaul. Salisbury knew the Siane at an early stage of their transition, soon after steel tools revolutionized their agriculture and social relations (Salisbury 1962). The Tolai of Vunamami (Map 7.1) were already much further along that path (Salisbury 1970). Replacing stone axes with steel ones had released some of their labour time, to be used for political competition, gift exchange, land disputes and warfare. These activities induced processes of 'political consolidation' in both groups. Larger entities coalesced around emergent leaders exercising greater political control, leading to new forms of organization and the acquisition of new consumption habits (ibid., 10–11).

In an obscure paper[3] titled 'Development through the Service Industries', Salisbury (1971) synthesized his Siane and Tolai findings. He rejected the assertion by Colin Clark (also disputed by Bauer and Yamey) that economic growth is generally associated with distinct, necessary and predictable changes in the distribution of occupations, and that only with growth does there occur a relative increase in the proportion of those in tertiary (service) jobs. Salisbury followed Bauer in asserting that under certain circumstances the tertiary sector would become dynamic in the *early* stages of growth. Thus, among the Siane and Tolai, services had been the leading sector (Salisbury 1971, 57). This echoed Bauer's argument that services were crucial from the beginning, in 'quickening' development and extending the market. Influenced by Rostow's *Stages of Economic Growth* (1960), Salisbury posited a social evolutionary model of the role of services. From Sahlins (1958), he drew the insight that, in undifferentiated subsistence societies, political and religious activities are the first to emerge as specialist occupations. Echoing Bauer's notion of 'imperfect specialization', he suggested that, in circumstances such as those of the Tolai, the true proportion of labour power engaged in services would be considerably higher than suggested by the apparent numbers of full-time specialists. This would be due, for example, to 'part-time involvement in politics and religion' (Salisbury 1971, 57). If trading and gift exchange were also regarded as tertiary activity, the share of subsistence labour employed in services among the colonial-era Siane may have been as much as 20 per cent. For both Siane and Tolai, increased levels and frequency of Maussian gift exchange were a culturally appropriate way to enjoy additional leisure made available by labour-saving innovation.

A state of underdevelopment emerges, however, if subsistence economies are diverted from a 'normal' path of development, causing the labour-intensity of agriculture to increase, and absorbing a larger proportion of labour power in that sector, while centralizing the provision of services – either in capital cities or metropolitan countries – instead of continuing to have them provided organically in rural and/or poorer areas (Salisbury 1971, 58). Absent such centralization, groups such as the Siane and Tolai would follow the 'normal' path of development, on which services provided within villages would act as the leading sector. Political consolidation and the retention of local decision making were crucial elements in this scenario, for without them villagers would likely succumb to what Geertz (1963a) called 'agricultural involution'. This is a situation diametrically opposed to what Salisbury (1971) regarded as development through the expansion and elaboration of service industries.

Salisbury showed that among the Tolai most subsistence cultivators also engaged part-time in a range of service activities. Often voluntarily and without remuneration, they provided a range of socially beneficial services to their fellow villagers in the absence of formal, specialized agencies for such purposes. In places where 'internal self-sufficiency' in food production exists, a process of development through the elaboration of the service sector enables improvements in living standards and social welfare, without the necessity for large external investment funding. Development achieved through the service industries, in 'education, marketing, artistic endeavour, housebuilding, athletics, or leisure', inter alia, can provide a framework for 'grassroots' development (Salisbury 1971, 65).

By calculating Tolai time-budgets, Salisbury found that official data exaggerated their engagement in self-employed agriculture while failing to suggest the importance of their work in services (ibid., 59). This mirrored Bauer's observations in West Africa. Salisbury's trust in the Tolai and Siane to throw up energetic community organizers encouraged him to believe many services could be provided by local government and church entities. These would be local *public goods*, provided informally and autonomously as dividends of the political consolidation process. Bauer's critic Lipton would have regarded the Siane and Tolai homelands as 'lucky' places, just as Salisbury assumed the prevalence there of an 'affluent' environment. These ideas will be discussed below, as will the attributes that make a place 'lucky' and their significance for informality in Melanesia.

Following Rostow's social evolutionary model of economic growth, Salisbury posited four successive stages of labour-saving agricultural change experienced by Tolai over the period 1875–1960. These released successively larger proportions of labour time for service activities, leading to a kind of prosperity less evidenced by greater material consumption than by more time for leisure and an active social life (Salisbury 1970, 60). 'Leisure' appears to have included engagement in group activities such as ceremonial exchange, local government, and church and community affairs. Such a shift to leisure could occur only if existing demands for material consumption – food and other components of subsistence – were already satisfied; that is, in a relatively 'affluent' society (ibid., 11). The supply of labour was not unlimited. In fact it was scarce, relative to the resource endowment and productive potential of the Tolai lands. Salisbury's data for land-use and labour inputs in Vunamami supported his contention that the Tolai were affluent in subsistence terms. Thus, for 1961 he reported that, because of women's labour, Vunamami still remained 'virtually self-sufficient' in food production while using little more than fifteen acres of land and no more than 11 per cent of its available labour power (ibid., 146). This encouraged investment in, and movement of labour to, other activities for which demand was more elastic. Among both the Siane and Tolai, labour moved from subsistence agriculture to services (Salisbury 1962, 152; 1971, 61).

After reading Geertz (1963a) on agricultural involution, Salisbury (1971, 61–62) contrasted the Tolai situation with that in cash-cropping peasant societies in Java. The latter were typified by mono-crop export production systems and reliance on imported food staples. This was a situation of excessive specialization, characterized by falling wages, deficient services, vulnerability to external economic shocks, and failure to innovate or to diversify the local economy. These circumstances led to agricultural involution, such as described by Geertz. Salisbury believed such situations might be avoided if local service activity were maintained, and with it the flexibility of action necessary for economic diversification.

Drawing a questionable parallel with the very different circumstances of Javanese agriculture, Salisbury (1971, 64) saw a kind of agricultural involution as threatening the Tolai on the Gazelle Peninsula. He warned of simultaneous dangers: Geertz's involution in rural areas and overdevelopment of services in the cities. Urban centralization of services was inimical to progressive rural communities, leading to what he understood as agricultural involution. But declining rural living standards would also cause *service* provision to become progressively less productive and 'technologically involuted'. For the idea of an involution of services, Salisbury acknowledged discussions with the economist Benjamin Higgins (formerly a colleague of Geertz). Paraphrasing Higgins, Salisbury noted that low-productivity service provision may absorb excess manpower, but that this amounts to disguising underemployment without eradicating it. The result is involution of services – taking in one another's washing – which leads to the use of technologies of increasing labour intensity (ibid., 65, n2). This suggests Salisbury had conceptualized *two* informal service sectors. One was rural and prosperous, the other urban and marked by poverty and disguised unemployment. The former could flourish in an 'affluent' society unconstrained by shortage of land. The latter would emerge from an increasingly land-short subsistence economy in which people are forced to migrate to urban areas.

Insofar as Salisbury discerned an informal Tolai economy, in Hart's sense, it was a *rural* informal economy, operating in what Lipton would call a 'lucky place'. Salisbury also deserves credit for recognizing the possibility of a future involution of services. This would involve increasing intensity in the application of labour to services, and would lead to the immiserization of service workers. This informal economy would occur in urban areas and be driven by the threat of rural poverty. Salisbury's premonition of urban informality, such as described by Hart in Ghana, is clear. His comparison of the 'affluent' Tolai lands with the intensive rice cultivation of Java was spurious, and his social evolutionary approach rather laboured, but his analysis yielded insights of genuine originality. These have continuing resonance for twenty-first century Melanesia.

To continue the discussion of precursors of informality, the next chapter deals with J.C. van Leur, a historian of the ancient trade of the Malay Archipelago. Van Leur studied small travelling peddlers, a group that can be seen as historical forerunners of Asian informal micro-entrepreneurs. They operated in a pre-colonial environment in West New Guinea, where Asian trucking and bartering came into contact with Melanesian ceremonial (i.e. Maussian) exchange. This situation is presented here as a historical analogue of the much later encounter in colonial PNG between the Smithian worldview of European colonialism and the Maussian logic of *The Gift*.

Notes

1. While Basil Yamey was joint author of some studies cited here, he has acknowledged the primacy of Bauer's original fieldwork and observations. See Yamey 2005.
2. Ennobled by Mrs Thatcher in 1983, Bauer was styled (in a nice touch) Lord Bauer *of Market Ward* Cambridge.
3. Not listed in his comprehensive bibliography published in a posthumous tribute volume (Silverman 2004).

Chapter 3

Melanesia in the Trade of the Malay Archipelago

J.C. van Leur's study, *Indonesian Trade and Society: Essays in Asian Social and Economic History* (1955), documented a complex trading system extending across the full, east–west span of the territory that is now modern Indonesia. It reached as far as the western fringe of historical Melanesia (present-day Indonesian Papua [Map 3.1]). As I read van Leur's account, historical Papua appears as a transitional zone between the traditional exchange of Melanesia and a system of trade and tribute imposed on Papuans by Asians. The latter were the Muslim sultans of Tidore and Ternate in the *Maluku* group (English, the Moluccas), and 'Malay' traders (mainly from Maluku and Seram), as well as traders from China. The taking of slaves as booty, and their gift as tribute, was integral to the system, while commercial slave raiding was a well-organized trade.

This archipelagic trade extended to Papua a pre-colonial system of what (in van Leur's account) sounds very like an early Asian form of mercantile capitalism. That system had its own conventions of bureaucratic regulation and market exchange, so much so that when Portuguese mariners arrived in the archipelago in the early sixteenth century, they came into seas where they found a system of 'shipping, trade and authority as highly developed as the European', and varieties of 'political capitalism' no less developed than those of southern Europe. There were ships capable of carrying more than those of the European merchant marine, involving 'every conceivable valuable high-quality product', and conducted by a 'great multitude' of peddlers, together with 'merchant gentlemen and harbour princes' with

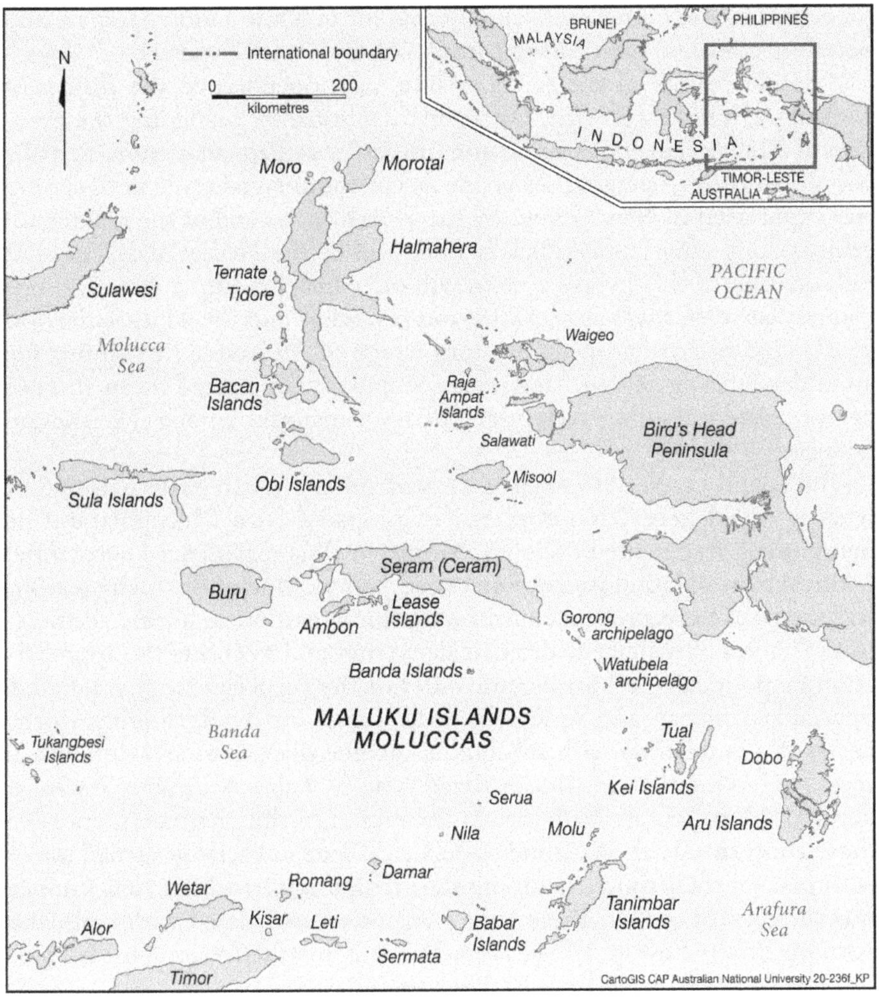

Map 3.1. Maluku and the Bird's Head of New Guinea. Permission granted for reproduction of this map by CartoGIS Services, Digital Scholarship, Scholarly Information Services, The Australian National University.

financial resources no less than those possessed by European 'merchants and princes' (van Leur 1955, 117).

While this Asian system would be superseded by Dutch mercantile capitalism from the seventeenth century, that outcome was more a matter of naval force than superior economic organization. The institutional framework of the older Asian system continued to shape much of the archipelagic trade, even after the ascendancy of the Dutch. This was perhaps especially true in regions contiguous with western New Guinea, where for centuries the Dutch were largely content to allow Tidore, Ternate and Seram to continue their earlier patterns of trade with Papuans.

Another feature of the Asian system, as it operated on the fringes of Melanesia, was its *hybridity*. 'Tributary' relationships, including the exaction of Melanesian slaves and commodities from Papuan communities by Moluccan rulers, operated alongside Asian commercial trade until slavery was suppressed in New Guinea by the Dutch at the end of the nineteenth century, long after it was officially outlawed by the Netherlands. A closer examination of this hybrid system will offer insights into a historical encounter between trade as 'trucking and bartering' and the Maussian world of *The Gift*, occurring on the western fringe of Melanesia. It will provide an understanding of that Melanesian 'singularity' indicated by an absence of specialized trading and intermediary functions among Melanesian peoples.

The island of New Guinea is located on the south-eastern fringe of what is called here 'Monsoon Asia'. Compared with Melanesia and its many small, fragmented societies, Monsoon Asia experienced substantial political consolidation in the premodern period. One of the many reasons was the need to secure and control water for irrigation, requiring administrative cadres to manage hydrological systems, and to ensure the appropriation by political and bureaucratic elites of the surpluses these generated. Specialized artisan and service-provider castes emerged, catering to the needs of a population with substantial income disparities and differential access to land, and an institutionalized system of slavery. Among the most developed bureaucratic activities in the region in the premodern era were those concerned with maritime trade. Local bureaucracies governed major entrepôts on trade routes spanning the archipelago, of which New Guinea was the eastern outlier. These routes were also articulated with mainland ports in South East and East Asia, and it is instructive to consider how western New Guinea related to that system.

The limited specialization and exchange of premodern Melanesia was in marked contrast to the economic organization of Monsoon Asia, where traditions of household crafts and manufacturing, the use of 'general purpose' monies as media of exchange, and a complex division of labour facilitated domestic and international commerce. Most Asian households remained anchored in agriculture, but many developed post-harvest and off-farm sources of income to supplement farming livelihoods. With declining land availability and urbanization, many households became increasingly dependent on trade, services, petty manufactures and wage labour for livelihoods. Such influences contributed to the relative complexity of social structure and occupational differentiation in much of Monsoon Asia, by comparison with a fairly general lack of ascribed social status in

Melanesia and the undifferentiated character of livelihoods in its small-scale subsistence economies. Melanesian societies did not throw up anything approaching the degree of economic or occupational differentiation (or landlessness) sufficient to create 'Asian' patterns of productive activity and income distribution. This may suggest some historical antecedents of modern Melanesian 'singularity'. It certainly helps to explain why, in the modern era, a dynamic informal economy was observable in Monsoon Asia, whereas in Melanesia such livelihoods were very limited in scale and scope. A brief account of trade in historical Monsoon Asia, and the trading relationships between it and traditional Melanesia, may assist in considering that proposition.

As previously suggested, the western half of New Guinea (later Dutch New Guinea, now Indonesian Papua) was for many hundreds of years a transitional zone between Monsoon Asia and Melanesia. This has been described from the Melanesian perspective by Charles Rowley (1965), Pamela Swadling (1996) and Clive Moore (2003). Also, as mentioned above, van Leur seems to have regarded premodern Asian trade as exhibiting a degree of mercantile capitalism comparable with that of contemporary Europe. Whereas modern industrial capitalism requires the efficient organization of free labour, mercantile capitalism in the Malay Archipelago – whether of the earlier Asian variety or the later Dutch version – relied heavily on slaves, including those from Papua. Commercial slave raiding was a highly organized trade. It was conducted alongside, although only ambiguously separated from, the enslavement of Papuans in a continuing premodern system of tribute and plunder imposed by the rulers of Tidore and Ternate. The parallel yet intermingled operation of these two modes of extraction bestowed a degree of hybridity on the system.

Slavery was ancient, and Papuan slaves may have been held on the island of Java as early as the tenth century CE (van Leur 1955, 355, n64). For at least five hundred years Malay traders established bases on offshore islands and on the 'Birds Head' of West New Guinea, where by intermarriage and Islamic conversion, they created small 'mixed intermediary' populations (Andaya 1991). These served as local agents of the archipelagic traders, and their Muslim descendants remain identifiable today. Commercial trade across the archipelago was facilitated by various local and/or regional media of exchange, although the degree to which trade destinations were incorporated into monetary exchange tended to diminish across the region from west to east. The vigorous monetized commerce seen further to the west assumed a more liminal character on the fringes of Melanesia, so that trade at the end of the line, in Papua, was conducted by barter. Introduced commodities (metal implements and weapons, cloth, other manufactures) were exchanged for slaves and marine and forest products. These Papuan commodities were monetized (or bartered for other 'monetizable' commodities) by the Asian visitors at entrepôt markets on their return voyages to the west. The natural scientist Alfred Russel Wallace (1869) observed trading in several such markets within close range of the Bird's Head as late as the mid-nineteenth century.

Among commodities introduced to Papuans in such trade was *kain timur* (Malay, 'eastern cloth', traditional woven cloth from Eastern Indonesia). This was exchanged for 'kidnapped people and birds of paradise' (Miedema 1998, 194, n3). Over centuries, this trade effected considerable social change among Papuans of the interior of the Bird's Head, as *kain timur* acquired prestige value, with the varieties most coveted by Papuans regarded as *kain pusaka* (Malay, 'heritage cloth'). Christopher Healey (1998, 346) claimed that for Papuans of the Bird's Head *kain pusaka* came to acquire the status of 'inalienable things'. Inalienability is the hallmark of the Maussian *Gift*, the exchange that represents 'relations between non-aliens by means of inalienable things' (Gregory 1997, 52). For Gregory (in *Gifts and Commodities*, 1982) such inalienable things are gifts, not commodities (the latter connoting 'relations between aliens by means of alienable things'). Both occur in Gregory's analysis of Melanesian indigenous economy because it is an 'ambiguous' economy where, depending on context, things may now be gifts, or commodities (Gregory 1982, 117; Hann and Hart 2011, 87). This may explain how Indonesian *kain timur* became a valuable (a *Gift*) in Papuan bride price exchanges. In the interior of the Bird's Head, bride price exchange evolved over time from 'women for women' exchanges, to '*kain* for women'. On the coasts, such exchanges morphed further, to the commodification of women as slaves ('women for *kain*') (Miedema 1998, 227, n58). Some interior populations became slave reserves for the conduct of these exchanges.

While this commodification was said to have involved an emergent class of Papuan 'warrior-capitalists' (Miedema 1998), their activities did not fit any modern understanding of capitalism. Papuans saw trade in Maussian rather than Smithian terms, and were often persuaded to surrender commercially valuable commodities on terms that a modern observer might see as unequal exchange. Commodities (and slaves, as commodities) passed from the interior to the coasts between parties with radically different understandings of the transactions in which they engaged. Malay merchants, whom Goodman (1998, 438) described as 'trade-savvy', bartered with Papuans on the frontier for commodities that they could subsequently monetize. To understand this situation it is necessary to consider how trade was conducted among Melanesians, and how their traditional exchange practices conditioned their approach to trade with aliens.

Here a conceptual divide exists between orthodox economic and Maussian views. While making some allowance for cultural practices, neoclassical economists such as E.K. Fisk (to be discussed in the next chapter) modelled the operations of Melanesian subsistence 'units', assumed as self-sufficient. His conception of how such a society makes 'the transition from subsistence' was predicated on a propensity to 'truck and barter', assumed as operating in what Adam Smith had called 'natural' economies. By contrast, Marcel Mauss rejected any innate propensity to truck and barter in such situations, asking instead, '*What power resides in the object given* that causes its recipient to pay it back' (Mauss 1925, 4, emphasis added). Keith Hart saw the answer everywhere, in the circumstance that human beings 'find the personal character of the gift compelling' and are drawn to 'its evocation of the most diffuse social and spiritual ties' (Hann and Hart 2011, 50). This understanding of human behaviour is antithetic to the individualism and impersonality associated with neoclassical economic analysis; in Hart's account, 'spiritual ties' are set against 'trucking and bartering'.

Such situations proved richly productive of misunderstanding – as seen on the Bird's Head where commercial exchange was conducted with Papuans by Asian traders. The Maussian expectations of Papuans were confronted by the shrewd and knowing commerciality of Moluccan and Seramese merchants. From a contemporary Western perspective it appears that traditional Melanesian trade and exchange provided inadequate preparation for Papuans exposed to Asian commercial exchange – likewise for their later engagement in the monetized, commercial exchange introduced by European colonial powers. Some evidence of this incapacity, from the most recent episode of West New Guinea's colonial history, will be presented below, in the conclusion to this chapter.

J.C. van Leur made a crucial distinction that illuminates this Melanesian trait, this 'incapacity' as it is described here. He distinguished between the practice of trade as a 'secondary occupation', in which it complemented agriculture or artisanship, and trade as a 'self-sufficient profession' (van Leur 1955, 53). Writing of the archipelagic trade, van Leur asserted this distinction as applicable to both local and long-distance trade and to its occurrence in disparate agrarian civilizations in both 'pre-capitalistic' and 'early capitalistic' periods (ibid.). Recalling his characterization of the pre-colonial archipelagic trade as an incipient form of mercantile capitalism it seems appropriate to re-examine the economic behaviour of Asians and Papuans on the Bird's Head in terms of van Leur's secondary/self-sufficient distinction.

Malays, Chinese and Arabs on the western fringe of Melanesia pursued trade 'as a self-sufficient profession', bartering for commodities with Papuans and monetizing their gains elsewhere as opportunity allowed. But Papuans approached these transactions from the standpoint of traditional Melanesian exchange, and cannot be categorized in terms of van Leur's secondary/self-sufficient duality. Only later, in the modern colonial era, would the spread of monetized trade in Dutch New Guinea enable some Papuans to become 'secondary' traders (as, for example, in the sale of copra, vegetables or forest products).

The Dutch colonial 'touch', when it came to the island of New Guinea, was both late and light. In 1892 they established an onshore administrative presence in *Nederlands-Nieuw-Guinea*, and by the early 1960s its capital, Hollandia, resembled no place in the world more than Port Moresby; it was a relatively high-waged, white-administered, import-dependent 'whitebread' tropical town, ordered along European lines. Apart from some formal wage employment, Melanesians participated in the urban economy to only a very limited degree. Other than selling produce in the town market (as what Scarlett Epstein [1982] called 'producer–sellers'), they essentially had no urban informal economy.

In 1962, the international community acquiesced in Indonesia's claim to *Irian Barat* (west New Guinea) on the basis of historical connections. Within ten years of the takeover, Jayapura (as Hollandia was renamed) had become an 'Asian' town (Garnaut and Manning 1974, esp. Ch. 4). It developed a flourishing informal economy in which Indonesian immigrants played the part of van Leur's travelling peddlers to increase the range of local goods and services, reducing import dependence for basic consumer goods and pushing down cost levels closer to Asian levels. Papuans played little part in this transformation, and seemed destined to remain essentially a rural people. While the possibility that indigenous Papuans were unable to make their way in the new urban informal economy due to bureaucratic or other forms of exclusion cannot be excluded, it appears more likely they were simply unprepared to engage with this new economic environment.

The brevity of this account has precluded discussion of a distinction van Leur made between commercially motivated 'petty traders' (described above as comprising the 'great multitude' of traders in the archipelagic system) and 'wealthy money-holders'. The latter term was an analogy from the classical European world, applied to the Malay Archipelago. 'Money-holders' were members of a pre-capitalist class whose primary concerns were political, as 'the classical *polis*' of the Mediterranean was not dominated by "'bourgeois" economic life, but [by] war, booty, and political tribute' (van Leur 1955, 60). For Papuans, until the Dutch established an onshore presence, the sultanates of Tidore and Ternate in the Moluccas were the principal centres of such activities – a regime of "trading and raiding" – directed against them.

It is not difficult to identify the counterparts of van Leur's *peddlers* in modern-day West New Guinea. But what of his dominant group, the *money-holders*, concerned not so much with trade as with 'war, booty and political tribute'? Could van Leur possibly have foreseen the circumstances of modern Indonesia's Papuan possession: rich in land, timber, fisheries and mineral resources, and governed since 1963 by a new colonial administration that is top heavy with senior military figures who commit the public resources of the Indonesian state to the cause of private enrichment?

Chapter 4

Melanesian Singularity

Insights from Neoclassical Economics

When the Faber mission visited PNG at the end of the colonial era, Hart and his colleagues were intrigued to find economic *informality* largely absent from Port Moresby and other PNG towns. The Faber Report concluded that 'urban artisan and service activities are as yet virtually non-existent' (ODG 1973, 4.11). This unexpected finding, the absence of a phenomenon almost universal in towns and cities of Asia and Africa, might appear to challenge the generality of, or the capacity to generalize from, Hart's observations in Nima. It was a conundrum, derived from a particular singularity in traditional Melanesian economic behaviour – the absence of specialized trading and intermediary functions. That absence derived from a deeper incapacity stemming from the character of trade and exchange in traditional Melanesia, dramatized in this study by the account of exchange between Monsoon Asia and Melanesia (Ch. 3).

Here 'incapacity' refers simply to inability or unwillingness to conform with the expectations or requirements of market economy norms. 'Singularity' implies something distinctive or unusual rather than unique and deterministic. Hart has explained informality as flowing from the merely *partial* institutionalization of people to economic orthodoxy (Ch. 1). In late colonial PNG this situation caused the Faber team to recommend measures to encourage informal economic activities – an urban 'informal sector' – expecting this to increase the degree of acculturation (or institutionalization) of people to the market economy, and hence their participation in it.

Keith Hart later acknowledged the 'decisive' influence on his thinking of the Faber experience, for the case of PNG represented perhaps the most dramatic example of a modern state formed by the unification of a multitude of primitive groups. Although he was speaking of West Africa when he wrote of 'local material and social conditions' posing daunting barriers to growth (Hart 1982, 2), it is argued here that such endogenous factors were also crucial in PNG. These led to an incapacity that Melanesians could only overcome slowly. Among the objectives of this study is to explain why economic informality was very largely absent from towns in late colonial PNG, and to examine the significance of this absence for broader processes of economic development there. In what follows, efforts by economists from the neoclassical tradition to explain what E.K. Fisk (1971, 378) called the 'unfamiliar economic setting' of PNG are considered for the light they might shed on this issue.

The Idea of Subsistence Affluence

Before the independence of PNG in 1975, neoclassical economists, most notably Fred Fisk, were responsible for formal analyses of PNG's traditional agrarian economy. Acknowledging the influence of Richard Salisbury (1962) he originated the notion of 'subsistence affluence' in the country's rural sector (Fisk 1962, 1964, 1966, 1971). Subsistence affluence became an influential idea, and it retains some contemporary relevance because it may still contribute to an explanation of the Melanesian informality 'conundrum'. While Fisk's formal analysis of the subsistence sector employed the marginalist techniques of neoclassical economics, his underlying assumptions were those of the classical economists. This placed him in the same ideological camp as Peter Bauer. Both employed the metaphor of transition from subsistence economy to market exchange, and accepted the validity of that propensity to 'truck, barter and exchange' which Adam Smith thought innate to humanity. Both adhered to what Lipton (1984) called the 'classical' prescription, that 'enterprise, trade, enlargement of markets' would act as the 'engines of development' (Ch. 2).

For these reasons Fisk might also be thought vulnerable to Lipton's critique of Bauer: that his analysis applied only to the special case of certain 'lucky places'. Fisk described the particular and unfamiliar problems of economic planning in PNG, where a majority of the population conducts its economic activities in the setting of an isolated subsistence society. This is a 'primitive' economy where 'exchange and the use of money is either unknown, or only marginally significant'. His simple, stylized model of the 'pure' subsistence unit shows it as completely independent of the external world, and responsible for life's necessities and all the customary consumption of its inhabitants: 'food, clothing, shelter, tools and recreational requirements' (Fisk 1962, 462–63). This was his *oikos*, his chosen unit of analysis. The term derives from Aristotle, who envisioned a community, or extended household, seeking communal well-being within the *oikos* (Hann and Hart 2011, 57). In Fisk's model we see simplifications and 'stylized facts', but should not imagine he confused such constructs with reality. Fisk intended them as abstractions involving a 'recognizable caricature' of reality, in which 'complicating details' may be left out so long as they do not materially affect 'the principles governing the interaction of the main factors retained in the model' (Fisk 1962, 464).

The Fiskian *oikos* was a 'pure subsistence unit', defined as the population of all groups among which a major instance of Maussian exchange, the 'pig cycle', occurred. This enabled him to internalize all such exchanges within the unit, defined so as to remain self-sufficient. The unit operated at a low-level equilibrium of production, founded primarily on tubers as staple foods. People had access to abundant arable land and employed simple production techniques, with negligible capital accumulation. Production levels were set by maximizing returns per unit of labour, rather than per unit of land, in the context of a limited set of known production possibilities and modest consumption aspirations. The limit of subsistence output was not set by scarcity but rather by a 'demand ceiling'. This situation was akin to the 'zen affluence' later articulated by Marshall Sahlins – the state of enjoying plenty by reason of wanting little (Sahlins 1972). It also brings to mind Salisbury's description of the Tolai as 'affluent' (Ch. 2). Within the production unit there existed a stock of untapped resources which could become available for use once its isolation was disturbed. This resource surplus might be measured as a quantum, either of labour or of the additional subsistence output that labour could produce.

Fisk's model of the self-contained Melanesian *oikos* had undeniable elements of caricature. Nonetheless, it conveyed a sense of the contrast between small-scale agricultural societies with low levels of technology and the capacity for self-sufficiency prevalent in Melanesia, and the developed systems of specialization and exchange found in Monsoon Asia. In Fisk's terms, 'subsistence affluence' is a situation in which land is abundant relative to labour, and the productivity of labour (with 'applied' labour as the denominator, rather than 'available' labour) is high. Under such conditions, most subsistence farmers will have the capacity to produce all they can consume, 'with satisfaction', of their customarily essential requirements. They will be able to maintain living standards at a customarily adequate level and can manage this with a labour input of 'as little as fifteen or twenty hours a week' (Fisk 1971, 368). This is a recognizable 'lucky place' scenario, based on the existence of surplus resources in a favourable environment. It is significant that Fisk was inspired by just such a setting in the region around the highland town of Goroka. This was close to the territory of the Siane, of whom Salisbury had written in *From Stone to Steel.*

Dependent on a favourable balance between population and land resources at a given level of agricultural technology, the 'affluence' of highland peoples such as the Siane was not a permanent condition, since it would be eroded over time by population growth (Fisk 1962, 469ff). Fisk specified the conditions under which this temporary margin of resources, hidden within the subsistence sector, could be tapped to finance development. The analysis was essentially Smithian, echoing Bauer's 'well-known theme' (Ch. 2), the role of trade and transport in extending the monetized economy. Fisk's concept of a macroeconomy consisting of 'subsistence', 'transitional' and 'modern' sectors provided the taxonomy around which late colonial national accounting estimates and economic policy were formulated for PNG. As previously mentioned (Ch. 2), Fisk's account of subsistence economy influenced a number of anthropologists, including Scarlett Epstein and Ben Finney. They appear in later chapters, in discussions of indigenous enterprise in Goroka and Rabaul, both seen here as among Lipton's 'lucky' places.

The idea of subsistence affluence also carried an important implication for the narrative here: so long as some degree of affluence remained in the countryside this would act to reduce the willingness of rural–urban migrants to endure unemployment and to 'hustle' for a living in towns. Moreover, their 'incapacity', that inability to go beyond simple market exchanges to more complex forms of specialization and exchange, limited their urban self-employment options. To the extent this was still the case when the Faber team visited PNG in 1972, Hart's attempt to introduce the idea of urban informality into policy discussion (and, more especially, the recommendation that such activity should be encouraged as a matter of public policy) might be seen as premature. This proposition is discussed later (Ch. 25) in the context of urbanization, unemployment and demographic change.

Hybridity in Melanesian Economic Life

Although Fisk did not question the applicability of conventional neoclassical theory to the transition from subsistence, he made some concessions to Melanesian culture, including his definition of the social/economic *oikos* as incorporating ceremonial exchange of pigs, and allowing for its 'demand ceiling' to include food required for Maussian feasting and exchange (Fisk

1962, 467). An agricultural economist, W.R. (Bill) Stent (1973, 1984), departed further from neoclassical convention with an analysis of subsistence recognizing that 'goods' can become 'bads', if consumed to excess. This incorporated satiation into neoclassical method, in which *insatiability* of demand and constrained equilibria (elements synonymous with the scarcity underpinning orthodox analysis) are normally the default assumptions (Stent 1973). Karl Polanyi had equated the substantive and formal meanings of 'the economic' with (respectively) subsistence and scarcity – two conditions represented as alternative existential states. In doing so, he challenged the assumption on which conventional economic theory is grounded, that scarcity is universal. Stent's intention was, by means of an 'adaptive use' of orthodox economic analysis, to advance the theorization of Fisk's affluence. In particular, he sought to identify 'a number of *hybrid types* of economic activity in the transition from subsistence to a market economy' (Stent and Webb 1975, 522, emphasis added).

Stent incorporated into his model examples of hybrid economic activity – behaviours inconsistent with orthodox utility-maximizing principles. These came from his observation of Abelam shifting cultivators, when employed as an agricultural officer in the Sepik district of PNG in the 1950s. Abelam gardeners often worked on widely separated parcels of land for personal satisfaction, rather than choosing their plots on criteria of accessibility. This was due to a 'feeling of duty to the soil', a duty pursued to the point where the marginal productivity of land could become negative, as it might do 'where a gardener takes delight in cultivating all the land to which he has rights' (Stent and Webb 1975, 526). Another instance of Abelam hybridity was their habit of taking pleasure from garden work (although only up to a point, because even the demand for labour by gardeners was considered 'satiable'). Accordingly, Stent included garden-labour in the household utility function of his model, as a *positive* source of satisfaction. His analysis also incorporated the possibility that cultivators might produce commercial crops simply for prestige, even before marketing opportunities had become available. Again, as the transition proceeded, householders might continue stubbornly to produce food for their own household consumption, even though orthodox economic *rationality* would seem to require a fully specialized, commercial mode of farming. These behaviours were hybrid, in the sense they evidenced continuing Abelam adherence to traditional subsistence values, in an agricultural system experiencing technical change and commercialization during the transition to market exchange.

Even after markets and bureaucracy emerge in a society, some activities and attitudes left over from earlier socio-economic formations will likely continue. The instances discussed above are examples of what Hart called 'residue', seen as 'parallel to' what he called 'the formal order' (Ch. 1). The persistence of Hart's residue – leading to what Stent understood as hybridity – is key to understanding many aspects of Melanesians' economic behaviour in the colonial period, including their resistance to becoming institutionalized to market norms. Lingering beliefs and customs continued to influence the conduct of modern economic affairs by inducing hybrid behaviours. This occurred where what Hart calls 'legal pluralism' existed, where usages of custom are confronted by an imposed bureaucratic system. It might often be better for authorities to show some degree of tolerance for 'plurality of form' (Hart 2008, 15) in the hope that people's energies can 'be harnessed... in partnership with bureaucracy' (ibid., 19). This is an injunction to loosen up the regulatory frameworks governing engagement with formal market economies, to involve the poor more productively – perhaps especially in urban areas. The latter part of this study includes a series of case studies and an account of economic policy in late colonial PNG, told in the hope of amplifying that message. First, however, it is necessary to consider dissenting voices, specifically those of Keith Hart and Chris Gregory, severe critics of the ideas of 'subsistence', 'affluence' and the 'transition' to market exchange.

Hart was introduced to Fiskian ideas in 1972 as a member of the Faber team, while Gregory – a lecturer in Economics at UPNG – was familiar with Fisk's model as part of the late colonial economic orthodoxy. Without controverting Fisk directly, the Faber team had taken a politely sceptical view of his ideas, although Hart was privately dismissive. Some years later, in his *Political Economy of West African Agriculture* (1982), and without identifying Fisk personally, Hart rejected all analyses employing notions of transition to market exchange from a presumed 'subsistence' economy. Chris Gregory had become radicalized at UPNG after completing an ANU Master's degree in orthodox economic theory. During a period of student unrest (see Preface) he became a leading participant in debates urging curriculum reform at UPNG, including the introduction of Marxist economic theory on an equal footing with orthodox economics. Late colonial economic policy, with 'Fiskianism' at its centre, was also subject to attack.

Gregory would later challenge Fiskian neoclassicism explicitly in his Cambridge doctoral thesis, published as *Gifts and Commodities* (1982). His intention was to create a 'theoretical alliance' of political economists and anthropologists against neoclassical economists (Gregory 1997, 42). Designed as a general critique of neoclassical development theory and its application in PNG, it represented subsistence economy as misconceived, and subsistence affluence as a chimera. Neoclassical economists – armed with utility analysis – focused on individuals' subjective view of *goods* as 'objects of desire'. But Gregory (citing Bukharin) adhered to the 'objectivist' method of political economy. Reflecting French Marxist thought from the late 1960s, he concerned himself with *class relations in production* (Ch. 21, below). In 1970s PNG this played out as a contrast between consumers' 'subjective relationship' with the objects of desire (Fisk's 'incentive goods') and personal relationships created by exchanging 'things' in particular social situations. The things exchanged are *gifts* and *commodities*. In Gregory's argument, gifts and commodities fit comfortably within a political economy framework but are jointly incompatible with the orthodox economic theorization of 'goods' (Gregory 1982, 7–8).

Gregory (1982, 107–8) challenged Fisk by attacking the work of Bill Stent, discussed earlier. The latter had sought to adapt orthodox economic analysis to elaborate Fisk's theory of subsistence affluence and to identify forms of economic hybridity occurring during the 'transition' to market exchange. Arguing from within the neoclassical paradigm (in an effort to falsify Stent in his *own* terms), Gregory attempted to show a flaw in Stent's analysis of the hybrid behaviour of Abelam cultivators. Two such hybrid instances were, first, in their working on widely separated parcels of land to the point where the marginal productivity of land became negative; and, second, taking pleasure from garden work – up to a point of 'satiation' – so that such labour could be included in the household utility function as a *positive* source of satisfaction. Unfortunately for his case, Gregory appears to have confused these two behaviours. His attempt to refute Stent's 'adaptive use' of orthodox microeconomic analysis reveals a failure to comprehend the latter's argument. The matter is abstruse, and it seems unlikely that many readers of *Gifts and Commodities* ever went beyond Gregory's assertions to examine the case on its merits.[1] Stent paid the price often imposed on interdisciplinarians, risking incomprehension or misrepresentation from both sides of the divide they seek to bridge.

At the height of his influence, Fisk asserted a wider applicability for his ideas, in (among other places) Africa. There much of the population of certain territories was maintained in the condition Fisk described as 'subsistence affluence' (Fisk 1971, 368). Hart would have rejected Fisk's assertion, for he claimed that while the terms self-sufficiency and subsistence economy had frequently appeared in European accounts of African traditional economy, they were antithetical to 'commodity economy'. The latter was a form of production common in traditional West Africa, occurring in both 'precapitalist' and 'noncapitalist' forms. For this reason he rejected any formulation of a West African transition to commercial agriculture from an original state of subsistence (Hart 1982, 8–9). His account stressed diversity, fragmentation, complexity and the layering of history to counter any romanticized generalization of Africans as living in isolated groups in a peaceful condition of pure subsistence agriculture (ibid., 35).

Hart's *West African Agriculture* (1982) did contain hints of something like affluence, and he gave grudging acceptance to the notion – albeit oversimplified in his view – of labour as the scarce factor of production. Fred Fisk seems to have interpreted this situation as self-sufficiency, enabling affluence. Hart would counter that it was not so much a question of land, because people beset by warfare, isolation or environment were compelled to group together in societies with the capacity to perform all functions necessary for them to survive, even flourish, while holding their territories against such threats (ibid., 10). Ian Hughes had earlier adopted a similar position. Fisk's self-sufficient groups generally had that capacity, 'in principle'. The circumstance that they were constrained in their movement by enmities with neighbours, limiting their capacity to trade, supported this notion (Hughes 1977, 204).

Cultivator communities in West Africa were subject to external pressures towards self-sufficiency and, to the extent they possessed that capacity *in principle*, could be supposed to resemble Fisk's *oikos*. But whereas the Fiskian representation of pre-colonial agriculture was static in the manner of neoclassical models, Hart's argument was framed across some five hundred years of history. Hart was critical of any narrative cast in terms of a colonial 'intrusion' of money or the cash economy into West Africa. Any suggestion that supposed self-sufficient household units, as conceived by Fisk, might have been subject to external 'disruption' in West Africa during that period was ahistorical. The next chapter will return to this argument to consider whether marketplace trade in West Africa had any counterpart in pre-colonial Melanesia.

Note

1. For readers wanting clarification, Gregory's critique of Stent is discussed in my paper 'A Guide to Subsistence Affluence' (Conroy 2012; at 22–23, and in an Appendix at 44–45).

Chapter 5

Traditional Trade and Exchange in Papua New Guinea

Previous chapters have made the case for an economic incapacity, posited as inhibiting Melanesian engagement with the colonial market economy. General purpose monies and market economy had no precedent in Melanesia, while pre-contact production and trade were alien to 'Smithian' principles of specialization and exchange. PNG's introduction to the market will be described in subsequent chapters, in which the informal economy lens is applied to historical case studies of Port Moresby, Rabaul and Goroka, and their respective hinterlands.

The roots of the Melanesian 'incapacity' lie in the manner in which traditional trade and exchange were conducted. This chapter describes three 'pre-contact' trading systems, occurring in the regions in which the three colonial towns were later established. While each region was culturally distinct, the three trade systems had broad equivalents in west New Guinea, despite the disruptive influence of Monsoon Asia on accessible parts of the Bird's Head. Many generalizations concerning Melanesian economic behaviour made in Chapter 3 are also applicable to the lands and peoples further east – discussed in this chapter – and later incorporated into modern PNG. The traditional trade systems of PNG described here are those of the interior Highlands, Tolai people in the Bismarck Archipelago, and the maritime trade of coasts and islands.

Traditional Trade in the Interior Highlands

Ian Hughes' study of *New Guinea Stone Age Trade* (1977) applied, inter alia, to the region of what is now modern Goroka. He described trade linking the populations of those remote interior valleys, scarcely known before the 1930s, with the coasts and his account offers a *via media* between a mechanistic formalism and the romantic appeal of *The Gift*. For example, while accepting the Maussian commodity/gift distinction, he nonetheless saw 'pure' barter and 'pure' exchange as abstractions. For Hughes, some degree of what Stent called 'hybridity' was the norm in exchange; while accepting that Melanesians sought psychic and political benefits from trade, he was persuaded also of their concern for material gain. Despite having the 'in principle' capacity for Fiskian self-sufficiency, population groups strove nonetheless for utilitarian advantage through trade.

The inland trade system was 'a successful, functioning, integrating distributive system with its own market forces' (Hughes 1978, 310). It achieved a degree of economic integration across populations in different ecological niches, and with different tastes and productive capacities. No mere formalist validator of orthodox economics, Hughes showed the trade was embedded in specific social arrangements (the system's '*own* market forces'). What is described here as Stent's *hybridity* marked the processes of traditional production and exchange (Ch. 26), just as it would later influence how Melanesian highlanders responded to introduced market exchange. They had the capacity for self-sufficiency, and staple foods seldom entered into their barter trade. 'Every man took part in ceremonial gift exchange and bartered on his own account when opportunity offered; there were no professional traders, no merchants, no itinerant pedlars' (Hughes 1977, 203). Consequently, engagement in traditional trade not only enriched Melanesian cultural lives, it also increased material welfare and prepared them to engage later in van Leur's *secondary* trade, during the colonial era.

Hughes reconstructed the immediate pre-contact history of that 'great network of trade routes from coast to coast transcending the formidable barriers that continued to exist between thousands of mutually hostile groups' (Hughes 1977, 12). Three factors affected the patterns and scope of trade: access by trafficable routes to the sea, 'vertical zonation' due to altitude, and proximity to 'hard, fine-grained metasediments' for the manufacture of stone tools (ibid., 60–61). Aside from tools, other minerals enabled the manufacture of products such as pottery, pigments, salt and mineral oil. Traded stone objects included 'cooking stones, hammer and anvil stones, drill points, awls, scrapers, knives, bark-cloth beaters, axe blades and the prehistoric mortars, pestles and naturally weathered curiously shaped stones used in magico-religious rituals' (ibid., 132). Marine shells were of great importance, for these were 'the trade goods [that] most frequently performed some of the functions of money ... Shells played their role as valuable ornaments with brightly coloured feathers, especially bird of paradise skins and plumes, and they shared their role as durable valuables with axe blades' (ibid., 184).

Hughes' discussion of the mechanics of trade is relevant to his claim that specialist traders were vanishingly rare in the interior. Exchanges occurred in 'a series of chain-like steps', a string of 'dyadic' encounters in which a series of intermediaries was involved. Hughes pointed to the absence of any 'proto-markets', representing local concentrations of trade. Neither were there obvious 'trunk routes' for flows of goods, most of which 'had a multiplicity of alternative routes' (Hughes 1977, 206). A trade network extending across the whole island 'was created by and built up of the interlocking and overlapping personal trading networks of individual men' (ibid., 210). Not even the ceremonial grounds used periodically for major prestations served as proto-markets. Multiple decentralized barter transactions were quantitatively much more important. The reference above to 'the whole island' emphasizes that external disruption of the patterns and cosmology of traditional trade in the pre-colonial period, such as was described for the western fringe of New Guinea (Ch. 3), was confined substantially to that region – the Bird's Head. Further east, the trade systems and social structures of inland Papuan peoples essentially mirrored those described by Hughes for eastern New Guinea. Another, and related, instance of external disruption occurred in the waters off the Bird's Head. This is mentioned again below, in a discussion of the trade of coasts and islands.

Fiskian models were based on the assumption of small-group self-sufficiency (Ch. 4). But political and social change quickly transformed the trading landscape in Australian New Guinea. Soon after pacification by the colonial power, 'a remarkable expansion of trading, and in particular *travel* for trade' occurred, as fighting was repressed (Hughes 1977, 204, emphasis in original). This dramatic and swift transformation made it difficult for later commentators to judge the merits of the Fiskian case. More than anything, the difference between the accounts of Hughes and Fisk is one of methodology. Hughes required Fiskians to re-examine their approach, and to decide whether the insights it yielded justified the stylization of fact (for the purposes of neoclassical 'comparative static' analysis) on which it was based. On the other hand, Hughes' account of the inland trade (Hughes 1977) should also have obliged Chris Gregory to refine his application of Maussian constructs to the case of PNG in his later, very influential study, *Gifts and Commodities* (1982).

Tolai Trade of the Gazelle Peninsula

The Tolai, whom Salisbury recognized as 'affluent', traded on the Gazelle Peninsula of East New Britain, in the Bismarck Archipelago (Map 7.1). This was later the site of Rabaul, an important centre of colonial economic activity. Tolai conducted maritime trade with the Duke of York islands, a food-deficit area whose people exported canoes to the Gazelle, although Tolai were most interested in obtaining *tambu*, a form of shell money. They supplied staple foods to the Yorks, acquiring in return the shell from which they processed *tambu*, the principal item of Tolai wealth as well as their medium of exchange. Inland trade on the Gazelle was driven by local ecology, and displayed many similarities with barter in the New Guinea Highlands. Concerning traditional trade, Bill Epstein wrote that the Gazelle ecology supported a complex trade system, each locality having its particular environmental advantage. Strings of marketplaces linked coastal, hinterland and interior places in which intermediaries in long-distance trade supported flows of commodities to and from the coast, both 'on their own account and as middlemen' (Epstein 1969, 12).

As in the Highlands, intergroup enmities limited the distance over which exchanges occurred. Women traded in markets on territorial borders, guarded by armed men. The latter were more interested in specialist commodities – ochre and megapod eggs, live cockatoos, headdresses and stone clubs – than foodstuffs. Women exchanged foods at standard valuations influenced by traditional notions of 'fair exchange', denominated in terms of other commodities or *tambu*, while men were more opportunistic and engaged in some bargaining (Salisbury 1970, 175ff). The missionary Benjamin Danks observed this impersonal trade, in which market days appeared scheduled to avoid other local market days. A seller could then attend a market one day and another one close by on the next day (always providing it was safe to do so). Coastal and inland trade were distinguished from one another by the importance of trade in *tambu* shell, fish and garden produce in the former (Danks 1888, 310), and the range of garden produce in the latter (ibid., 315).

Coastal Tolai profited from the value added in processing raw shell, as the most important element in the cost of *tambu* is the input of Tolai labour (Salisbury 1970, 187). Any man who acquired it could process shell, and younger men voyaged to obtain it. *Tambu*'s scarcity derived from the effort necessary to collect and process shell, coupled with the Tolai propensity to hoard it. Danks concluded that the possession and use of *tambu* made the Tolai 'a commercial people' who, by using intermediaries, extended their commerce to 'places they have never visited'. Exchange was individualistic; rather than entrusting their capital to intermediaries, traders required go-betweens to finance their own transactions and to extract their own margins from each transaction. The scale of trade was petty, each trader handling only the volume of produce immediately required, so that '*we see no wholesale business done*' (Danks 1888, 310–15, emphasis added). While Danks referred to 'a commercial people' and 'intermediaries', it is clear from the broader context that he did not suggest any specialized trading. What he saw was akin to van Leur's secondary trade, conducted by subsistence cultivators, rather than any specialized or self-sufficient trading.

Tolai secondary trade involved what Chris Gregory called relations between aliens, by means of alienable things – an impersonal mode of exchange differing greatly from transactions occurring *within* groups. The latter is the form of exchange described by Gregory as occurring between non-aliens and involving inalienable things (Ch. 3). This led individual Tolai to hoard *tambu*, retaining it for ultimate redistribution within their groups. Such an occasion, marking the end of a life, was associated with the procurement and exchange in ceremony of great quantities of foodstuffs. Tolai were exemplars of that 'part of mankind' described by Mauss (1925, 3) as 'wealthy, hard-working and creating large surpluses', exchanging 'vast amounts in ways and for reasons other than those with which we are familiar from our own societies'.

Danks's description of premodern Tolai trade shows the emergence of Gazelle marketplaces and a regular cycle of market days. This contrasts with Hughes's account of highland trade, from which even 'proto-markets' were absent. Together with Tolai use of *tambu* as a medium of exchange, this suggests a system of commodity exchange among the most advanced in pre-contact PNG. However, a reading of Hart's *Political Economy of West African Agriculture* (1982) suggests that these Tolai markets were only comparable with the least advanced rural markets in pre-colonial West Africa. Commodity exchange was widespread in West Africa, whether in what Hart called 'precapitalist' or 'noncapitalist' forms (Ch. 4) or by assuming increasingly capitalist forms, and the evolution of systems of commodity economy had been an organic element in the expansion of markets (Hart 1982, 8). Even in the pre-colonial era, and alongside barter, commodity exchange was facilitated by special purpose currencies, which included metal bars, cowrie shells, cloth, cattle, slaves, and tokens from trading houses (ibid., 115), while in the most advanced rural markets in pre-colonial West Africa, among the Nigerian Hausa, all foodstuffs were traded as marketplace commodities, while cotton was widely grown for textile manufacture (ibid., 9).

The West African markets most comparable with those of the Gazelle were local, rural and remote, enabling cultivators to trade away any surpluses of staple foods, to vary their diets by obtaining foodstuffs from different ecological niches, to buy luxuries – such as salt and cloth in minute quantities imported from other regions – and to obtain simple manufactures such as handicrafts, tools and utensils from people whom Hart characterized as 'part-time specialists' (Hart 1982, 37). But even here the variety of special purpose currencies employed and the degree of specialization and exchange in manufactures suggest qualitative differences between the regions. In terms of the sophistication of premodern trade, any overlap between these rural markets in West Africa and those of the Gazelle appears to have been slight indeed.

Hart would probably not endorse this conclusion; he has been critical of any narrative cast in terms of the *intrusion* of money or the cash economy into West Africa. Such a scenario implies an 'abrupt confrontation', something that never occurred in the modern era. The emergence of market economy in subsistence agricultural society cannot be depicted as the 'disruption' of a self-contained household unit producing and consuming its own food (Hart 1982, 9). Recalling oblique criticism of Fisk in the Faber Report (ODG, 1973), this comment implies Hart's rejection of the Fiskian narrative, of which he was well aware. Hart returned to the subject later to clarify for me what he characterized as an 'insidious' opposition between 'subsistence' and 'market' in my own thinking. In his study of *West African Agriculture*, as he noted:

> I replaced the idea of subsistence with a pressure towards local self-sufficiency, which was never divorced from commerce. Mauss and Polanyi both held that local societies may aspire to self-sufficiency, but they never achieve it, so that markets and money (often taking forms quite unlike ours . . .) are necessary to extend the reach of such societies for purposes of trade with foreigners. (Hart 2012a, emphasis added)

Despite this judgement, my argument in this study proceeds from the proposition that Hart's expression – an 'abrupt confrontation' – *is* a reasonable description of historical events in 'lucky' places in PNG, where 'local self-sufficiency' was only ever modified by such 'commerce' as Ian Hughes described. The discussion below of maritime trade will introduce new perspectives concerning the meanings of subsistence and commerce in certain *less* lucky regions of Melanesia, but without compromising the essential argument here. The 'penetration' of the market mechanism into PNG was indeed a 'disruptive' event.

The Trade of Coasts and Islands

Along the south-eastern margins of the island of New Guinea the most significant traditional system of trade and exchange was conducted by trans-coastal voyagers. For example, the trade conducted by two peoples, the Motu and Mailu, extended hundreds of miles in an arc north and south of the Motuan village of Hanuabada. The village was close to the site of modern Port Moresby, and this narrative will later consider the importance of that circumstance for colonial history. Traditional Motu and Mailu trade were elements in a larger, interlinked set of trade routes strung along much of the coastlines of New Guinea. But there was at least one notable gap in this ring, situated south of the Bird's Head in the south-western quadrant of New Guinea. Ian Hughes noted that 'a trans-coastal canoe trade was absent' from this region (Hughes 1977, 32), and it has been suggested that endemic violence, associated with predation and the exaction of tribute by the Moluccan sultans of Monsoon Asia, acted to suppress indigenous maritime trade along that coast (Goodman 1998, 425). This was another element in the wider disruption of pre-colonial trade on the Bird's Head by external forces (Ch. 3).

In the part of New Guinea that became modern PNG, traditional maritime trade was markedly different from the inland trade described by Hughes. In pre-colonial times, coastal regions exhibited 'an intensification of trading as an economic option which surpasses anything inland'. Less 'lucky' than the Highlands or the Gazelle in terms of natural resource endowment, many coastal places lacked 'not only sufficient space and suitable climate for an agricultural basis for life, but also a variety of other necessary raw materials' (Allen 1982, 197). This certainly applied to Hanuabada, which nonetheless sustained a population much greater than its own dry and infertile land was capable of supporting. Hanuabadans possessed inadequate resources for agricultural subsistence, let alone ceremonial exchange, but like the people of Mailu they specialized in domestic pottery production. Both groups traded pottery and other valuables for food along their respective swathes of coast (Map 5.1).

From studying archaeological evidence of this trade, Jim Allen concluded that Melanesian specialist traders 'use trade as a basic mode of *subsistence procurement*. They are not merchants, they are subsistence traders' (Allen 1985, 50, emphasis added). Moreover, 'Melanesian specialized trading villages are very different from specialized traders as a class' (ibid.). Implicitly rebuking both anthropological formalists and Fiskian economists, Allen asserted that the trade of coastal potters was not 'the disposal of surplus production for profit'. This amounted to rejecting any analogy between such trade and what in classical political economy was called the 'vent for surplus'. A mechanism derived from Adam Smith by Hla Myint, this 'vent' enabled an agricultural community to break free of its subsistence confines, reaping the benefits of specialization and exchange in a wider world (Myint 1958). Dismissing such ideas as 'deterministic', Allen

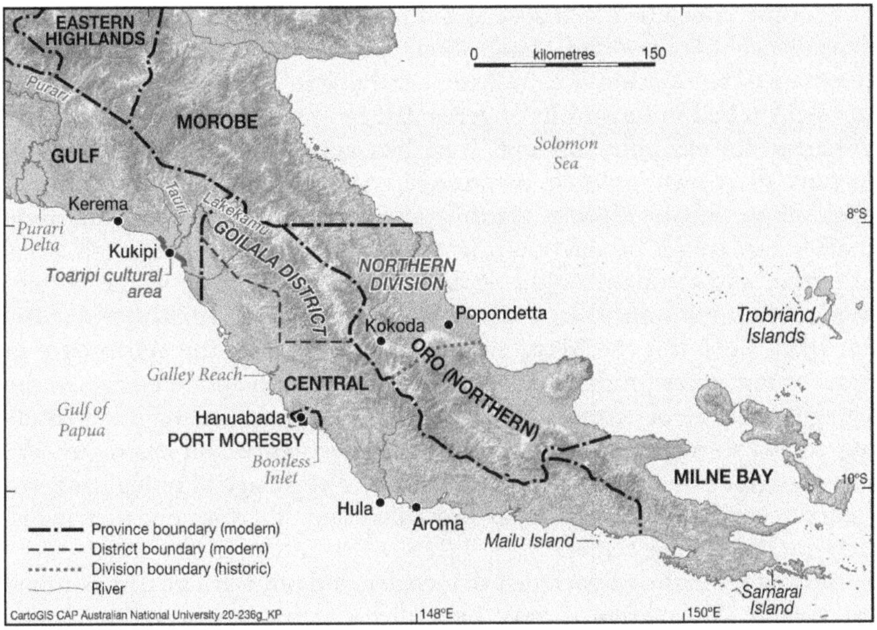

Map 5.1. Territory of Papua (part). Permission granted for reproduction of this map by CartoGIS Services, Digital Scholarship, Scholarly Information Services, The Australian National University.

argued that coastal trade in the south-east could not be explained 'by laws of trade, which are immutable across space and time'. Instead, Motu and Mailu were groups whose trading was 'a basic subsistence mode, as well as a central factor in their social lives' (Allen 1984, 409–11).

Thomas Harding (1994) recognized that every traditional Melanesian society had engaged in trading, and at least some retrading (or intermediation). He identified characteristics distinguishing specialized maritime traders from traders in agricultural societies, including the advantages of water transport in the carriage and distribution of commodities. Jim Allen also identified low transport costs and the advantage bestowed on certain coastal communities by the centrality of their locations. Location was crucial for 'retrading'; that is, for the middleman function – passing on goods received in trade to third parties (Allen 1985, 51). The importance of geographic centrality was supported by Irwin (1978, 406), who described Mailu Island as 'the point of articulation of both local and long-distance trade networks' – a description applying equally to Hanuabada on its own stretch of coast. In time, Hanuabada's centrality would inspire the London Missionary Society to establish its headquarters there.

Harding concluded that specialized maritime traders displayed a 'twin dependence' on imported staple foods for quotidian consumption and ceremonial distribution (i.e. Maussian exchange). Their *political or prestige economies* relied upon surpluses generated by trade (Harding 1994, 118). Whereas, for example, 'affluent' Tolai had agricultural resources enough to fund their own 'political or prestige economy', the Motu and Mailu could do so only by trading. Harding also found that successful maritime traders displayed a 'production orientation to trade', achieving high levels of output and standardization of their commodities, such as the pottery produced on the south-east coast (ibid.; see also Irwin 1978, 409–11; Allen 1984, 423). But the Motu and Mailu did not abandon subsistence in order to maximize production; they continued to fish and to engage in the voyaging culture of ceremonial exchange, while their trading and 'retrading' served to augment their capacity for subsistence and ceremony. We may recognize their system of production and exchange as prefiguring van Leur's 'secondary' trading; for, as Jim Allen said, 'they are not merchants, they are subsistence traders'.

Similarly, Harding concluded that traders did not form an occupational category in Melanesian society. Specialist merchants whose 'livelihoods rested exclusively on middleman transfers in the absence of local production for export' were nowhere found in Melanesia (Harding 1994, 118). Turning to linguistic evidence, in no Melanesian language could Harding find any 'monolexemic term' representing the categories of trader or merchant, despite all such languages having words for 'trade partner or trading friend' (ibid., 123, n14). Regarding people such as the Motu and Mailu, Harding concluded that what he called their 'production orientation' to trade was decisive in their conception of themselves. They were more likely to consider trading in terms of 'their distinctive *productive* roles' as an element in a 'regional division of labor, rather than as traders' (ibid., emphasis added).

Harding's conclusion confirms the case made here for recognizing later, colonial Melanesian trade as 'secondary' in van Leur's terms. As Harding argued for the pre-contact period, trading was 'a household function, *one of several special activities pursued*' (ibid., emphasis added). It is reasonable to conclude that Harding's 'production orientation to trade' carried over into the modern era when what Scarlett Epstein described as the 'producer-seller' became the archetypal trader in informal monetized produce markets (Epstein 1982). Therein lies the Melanesian singularity which, together with Fisk's rural affluence, underlay the situation described here as a conundrum.

Chapter 6

National Capitalism in the Three New Guineas

Economic activity can only be seen as informal by reference to some model or ideal of formality (Ch. 1). Such a model emerged in the nineteenth century with the rise of Weberian bureaucracy, which served to underpin what Hart called 'national capitalism'. This is a synthesis of industrial capitalism and the nation state, a centralizing bureaucratic effort to manage 'money, markets and accumulation' within a national community that is bound, at least notionally, by a common culture (Hann and Hart 2011, 30). German national capitalism developed a coherent ideology to inform its colonial policies, and economic informality was among its artefacts. Informality arose in response to the introduction of market economy, as administered by an alien bureaucracy. It became apparent when subject peoples proved unable (or unwilling) to conform with bureaucratic norms defining 'appropriate' economic behaviour. The Germanic impulse from which modern bureaucracy originated had distant consequences in the Pacific possessions of the Reich where, as previously mentioned (Introduction), New Guinea was divided between three European powers in the last quarter of the nineteenth century. As was shown in Map 0.2, German New Guinea (GNG) occupied the north-east quadrant of the 'big island', together with the Bismarck Archipelago.

Woodruff Smith discerned two colonial ideologies contending for influence in Germany between 1840 and 1906, described as 'emigrationist' and 'economic'. The former called for emigration to colonies as a remedy for contemporary German ills. The latter saw colonies serving German economic interests as sources of raw materials and export markets, but without large-scale emigration (Smith 1974, 641–42). The emigrationist party aimed to ameliorate domestic social disruption and unemployment, the result of industrialization and structural change. The 'economic' tendency originated with Friedrich List (1789–1846), an influential forerunner of the German 'historical school' who advocated pursuing industrial growth in a German core, supported by an agricultural periphery. Initially the periphery was to be in Eastern Europe – where it would have catastrophic echoes in the twentieth century – but later it was seen as better placed in the tropics. When Germany acquired tropical dependencies, including GNG, it sent traders, missionaries and officials carrying, as their conceptual baggage, the institutions of bureaucracy and market exchange. Their preconceptions and institutional innovations explain much about the character of these colonies.

In the face of the 'preclusive imperialism' practised by the British – particularly evident in New Guinea – German imperial expansion served domestic objectives. It offered 'a means of integrating a state torn by class differences, whereby the enthusiasm for colonies and crude anglophobe nationalism could be manipulated as crisis ideologies for electoral and party political purposes' (Wehler 1970, 153). State propaganda aimed at creating a climate of opinion supportive of overseas adventures during the 'second wave' of European colonialism. For example, over six months in 1896 a 'Colonial Exhibition' was staged in Berlin to impress Germans with the exoticism of their colonial empire. 'Native' groups were persuaded to demonstrate traditional activities as if 'in a circus or a zoo' (Firth 1982, 151). The New Guinean delegation consisted of six Tolai men and a boy, and a contemporary German account recorded how they and their African counterparts were expected to learn lessons of 'respect and subservience' to Europeans (ibid.). But when Richard Salisbury met the last survivor of the Tolai party in 1961 he found his memories rather more matter-of-fact. His informant remembered Masai and Cameroonians dancing at the exhibition, and fondly recalled the quality of German beer (Salisbury 1970, 34, n7).

Propaganda might explain the tenor of displays mounted at the Berlin Exhibition, but it did not say much about the underlying rationale for German colonization. Action to expand and develop Germany's overseas possessions was guided by the 'Treitschkean formula', a doctrine that by 1900 had 'become official German policy . . . that Germany's position as a power depended on her overseas empire' (Moses 1969, 53). Emigrationist and economic schemes of colonization were implemented in various German possessions, while in East Africa under Governor Rechenberg (1906–12) both models were tested. The governor was firmly in the 'economic' camp, incurring the enmity of German farmer-colonists by investing in a railway intended to link native smallholders with markets (Smith 1974). Colonial Secretary Dernburg backed Rechenberg, and Woodruff Smith commented that Dernburg had attempted 'to apply economic colonialism in a consistent manner throughout the colonial empire' (ibid.).

The colonial enterprise inspired by national capitalism came to GNG by degrees from the 1870s. In a neat correspondence with the Weberian model of bureaucracy in Bismarck's Berlin, this occurred primarily at the hands of the highly bureaucratized Deutsche Neuguinea-Kompagnie (the German New Guinea Company). It was a private, for-profit entity to which the German government delegated administrative responsibility for its new possession. Under Kompagnie recruitment policies, most European staff were not plantation managers but were either ex-military or government officials on extended leave (Ohff 2008, 257). This entrenched a markedly Teutonic bureaucratic culture in GNG before 1899 (when the Kompagnie yielded control to the imperial administration). This culture was sustained until the ouster of the Germans by Australia in 1914, and nowhere was it more firmly impressed on Germany's Pacific possessions than among the Tolai of the Gazelle Peninsula.

Given that the subsequent Australian administration commenced with this German template, and was itself military in composition, it is reasonable to suppose that elements of a distinctly Germanic bureaucratic culture lingered well into the Australian period. This is supported by Charles Rowley, who noted that Australian policy declarations and legislation give the impression that German administrative practice was retained in the Mandated Territory under the successor Australian regime (Rowley 1965, 90). Such an official culture provided the model in opposition to which informality may be defined in the circumstances of German (after 1914, Australian) New Guinea. This is consistent with Hart's view that national capitalism found its antithesis in informal economy, and with his characterization of the formal/informal duality as representing, respectively, 'bureaucracy' and 'popular self-organization' (Hart 2008, 5).

National capitalism's impact was much weaker in British New Guinea (from 1906, Australian Papua). There the bureaucratic culture was less commercially focused, more concerned with native welfare, and relatively punctilious in regard to matters of traditional land tenure, all to the frustration of its European trading and planting communities. In the case of West New Guinea, due to Dutch preoccupation with their 'Malay' possessions, the engagement of this remote Papuan territory with the world economy more closely resembled the mercantile capitalism of previous centuries than the industrial capitalism of nineteenth-century colonial powers. Until almost the end of that century, the Bird's Head region on the eastern frontier of the Dutch East Indies (now the Indonesian province of West Papua) remained vulnerable to a pre-colonial regime of trading, tribute and plunder imposed upon them by Moluccan sultans and 'trade-savvy' Malay mariners (Ch. 3).

GNG was linked to industrial capital by the demand for vegetable oils, which increased rapidly in Europe and North America from the late nineteenth century, stimulating investment in the production and processing of copra. By contrast, British New Guinea/Australian Papua's embryonic plantation industry largely missed the copra boom of the pre-war period to 1914, while Dutch New Guinea had no plantation sector to speak of. Australian Papua never achieved a surplus on merchandize trade. Gold mining, an enclave activity with quite limited and localized benefits, was its principal link with the international economy until the First World War. Dutch efforts at 'development' in the eastern half of the island were largely confined to an energetic but necessarily limited spurt of activity between 1949 and 1962, when the writing was on the wall for this last fragment of the Netherlands East Indies. This narrative will not concern itself further with the former Dutch colony, now incorporated into Indonesia.

Economic informality, as it emerged in GNG and Australian Papua, was defined by the nature of the prevailing bureaucratic regulation and its commercial culture. It would be surprising if there were not differences between the two colonies, reflecting their different populations and economies, and the divergences between their bureaucracies. The presence of Asian workers and entrepreneurs in German (later Australian) New Guinea, by contrast with Australian Papua's adherence to 'white Australia' principles, provided a rich point of comparison – as did the disparity in levels of investment and market output in the two territories.

The narrative that follows will examine the response of native peoples to the influence of the expatriate-dominated market economy in Rabaul and Port Moresby from the 1870s, and in Goroka from the 1930s. The intention is to sketch the outlines of an emerging indigenous informal economy in the period to the independence of a united PNG in 1975. As previously mentioned, there is an intriguing synchrony here. At the end of that period, a visiting World Bank/UNDP team, the Faber Mission, presented recommendations for the economic policies of the soon-to-be-independent state. Among these were measures to stimulate the growth of an informal 'sector' of economic activity among the indigenous population, a sector the mission noted was grossly underdeveloped. PNG was one of the first ex-colonies anywhere in which the 'informal sector' became an issue of public policy, whether or not it was appropriate in the circumstances of the time.

The next chapter marks the beginning of Part II of this study, devoted to the early colonial period before the Pacific War (1941–45). Chapters 7 and 8 deal with the experience of German (later Australian) New Guinea, followed (in Chapters 9, 10 and 11) by an account of contemporaneous events in British New Guinea (later Australian Papua). Part II concludes with a narrative of the short period of colonial contact in the central Highlands of Australian New Guinea before the war (Ch. 12). The account of these three regions focuses particularly on rural economic activity, seen in terms of formality and informality and encompassing the extension of rural activity into urban areas, and urban reach into rural areas. In the case of German/Australian New Guinea these processes created rural–urban linkages, inducing reciprocal flows of people, information and commodities between the town of Rabaul and its hinterland on the Gazelle Peninsula of East New Britain, in the Bismarck Archipelago. Extending the idea of economic informality to rural activities and identifying a distinct *rural* informal economy is justified by analytical dividends. Central to the narrative is the early colonial experience of the Tolai and Chinese populations. While the Gazelle Peninsula in the colonial period was in many respects atypical, it provides rich material for a case study of the transition from subsistence in an economically advanced (or 'lucky') region, to which the formal/informal lens may be applied usefully.

Part II

From Early Colonization to the Pacific War

Chapter 7

German and Australian New Guinea before the Pacific War

As a place fit to be dubbed 'lucky' by Michael Lipton, the colonial Gazelle Peninsula (Map 7.1) exhibited 'the components of the classical growth pattern – initial foreign capital flows, promising and elastic export crop markets, spare land, and people able to finance savings to transform it' (Lipton 1984, 45). Expatriate plantations and associated services were established, and a comparatively high standard of infrastructure installed. Fertile land was available and German administrators acquiesced in the alienation of significant areas by foreign investors. External markets were generally favourable for staple export crops (copra from the late nineteenth century, cocoa in the twentieth). And the indigenous Tolai demonstrated an impressive propensity to save for investment in introduced economic activities (S. Epstein 1968; Salisbury 1970).

Albert Hahl landed on the Gazelle in 1896. He was impressed by the 'vigour' with which Tolai traders responded to the presence of colonists: they grew food for plantation labourers, door-knocked settlers with produce for sale, and attended traditional marketplaces in their hundreds. Soon after his arrival, Hahl commenced planning a network of roads to encourage such trading (Firth 1983, 62). Their vigorous response to market opportunities seemed to mark Tolai out from other New Guineans. All of Lipton's 'lucky place' circumstances were present to support rising productivity and wealth accumulation. Bill Epstein was impressed by the more entrepreneurial response of the Tolai to such opportunity – as compared with other indigenous groups 'apparently similarly placed'. He took this to

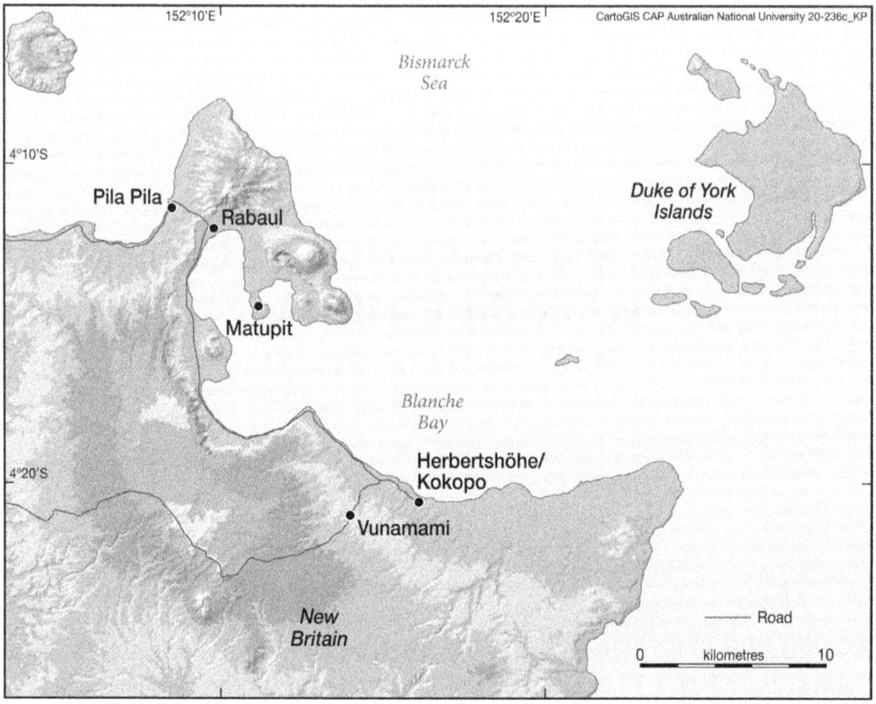

Map 7.1. Rabaul and the Gazelle Peninsula. Permission granted for reproduction of this map by CartoGIS Services, Digital Scholarship, Scholarly Information Services, The Australian National University.

suggest that 'indigenous Tolai *pre-dispositions* have also to be brought into the equation' (A. Epstein 1969, 21, emphasis added).

This view needs tempering. Gazelle traditional trade was characterized by ecologically based specialization, facilitated by *tambu*, a shell-money medium of exchange. It was conducted through a network of customary marketplaces, where trading was essentially a secondary activity, supplementary to subsistence agriculture. I have suggested (Ch. 5) that Tolai 'territorial border' marketplaces were comparable only with their *least* sophisticated equivalents in West Africa, and that any overlap between Melanesian and African modes of commodity exchange was slight. Epstein's assertion of a superior Tolai predisposition to trade should be seen as applying strictly in the PNG context.

Tolai used *tambu* for many transactions, quotidian and ceremonial, facilitating both utilitarian truck and barter, and the Maussian economy of *The Gift*. Debating whether *tambu* might be regarded as general-purpose money is less important than accepting that the Tolai need for it cannot be analysed satisfactorily using orthodox economic concepts such as the

Keynesian 'transaction' and 'asset' demands for money. The latter term is especially problematic. The word 'asset', with its implication of *commodity*, is a pallid representation of the qualities with which the Tolai imagination invested *tambu*. Their use of it did demonstrate the commonly described economic attributes of currency (means of exchange, unit of account, store of value) and, consistent with her view of the Tolai as 'primitive capitalists', Scarlett Epstein (1968) tended to emphasize these utilitarian qualities. Others accepted that the value Tolai perceived in *tambu* was less material than a matter of the potential for power, prestige and influence accruing to its holder (A. Epstein 1969, 230–31). Salisbury explained that while Tolai appreciated the need to earn cash for consumption, it was universally agreed that 'only *tambu* can maintain the fabric of social relationships' (Salisbury 1970, 278).

Salisbury is seen here as a precursor of informality who privileged the role of services in the transition from subsistence, as labour shifts out of agriculture (Ch. 2). Among the Tolai this occurred in 'sequences' – a notion he drew from Rostow's (1960) 'stages of growth'. His historical account is helpful for understanding Tolai accommodation to 'the market'. First, from about 1875, Tolai bartered surplus coconuts with Europeans for trade goods. In a second stage, from the 1890s, they expanded their plantings. Third, from the late 1930s, they added value to their raw product by adopting hot-air copra driers. And finally, in the late 1950s, they adopted cocoa as an export crop, together with its mechanized processing (Salisbury 1970, 13). These sequences required 'a succession of technological changes, each one associated with a political change' to trigger transfers of labour-time from agriculture to services. Many services were communal, involving the creation of social capital and public goods in communities. This was made possible by Tolai 'self-sufficiency in food supplies' (Salisbury 1971, 60). He also described individuals responding to opportunities for private profit, through what van Leur called 'secondary' trade, causing an informal market economy to emerge in the rural hinterland of Rabaul. Salisbury showed prescience by foreseeing the possibility of what (following Geertz and Higgins) he called an *urban involution of services* (Ch. 2).

German National-Economic Purpose and the Indigenous Pushback

Geopolitical influences shaped colonialism in New Guinea, as German national capitalism adopted a more assertive *Weltpolitik* – adopting an imperial foreign policy to achieve global status – from the late nineteenth century. The Wilhelmine state dispensed with the Kompagnie in 1899, a policy shift reflecting the 'Treitschkean formula' (Ch. 6). By 1907, Colonial Secretary Dernburg had enunciated a quite explicitly 'material and mercantilist' economic ideology, defining a 'national-economic purpose' for Germany's colonies. This required 'an exchange of goods and men for culture and civilization', the goal of which was 'the acquisition and development of raw materials' (Moses 1969, 53 and n46). This policy extended to GNG, providing ideological foundations for a Weberian rational-legal bureaucracy in Rabaul. Pushback against this system would produce the particular modes of informality observable among indigenous Tolai and Chinese immigrants.

In GNG, the raw material of greatest interest to Berlin was copra, for vegetable oil. Governor Hahl thought economic development would only be possible if GNG could impose a 'well-regulated system' of government on the population, and convince them that it was in their own interests to work for the good of the country (Hahl 1980, 10). Dernburg's *scientific colonialism* allowed for production by indigenous 'peasant' producers as well as foreign plantations (Firth 1983, 89), but where the latter mode was preferred (as in GNG), national-economic purpose required wholesale labour recruitment. Plantation workers were to be contracted under formal indenture. Their recruitment involved varying degrees of suasion, but Dernburg rationalized this as 'impart[ing] pleasure in work and gainful activity' to the colonized (cited in Moses 1969, 53).

Signing indentures represented formal compliance by a subdued population with the colonial will. But after a few years, Tolai became increasingly resistant to contracted labour, an early instance of what was to become a pattern – Tolai pushback against unwelcome bureaucratic impositions. Head taxes were imposed in 1907 to make them comply, but when Hahl raised the matter at a meeting with Tolai elders he was told that they had the money and were prepared to pay their dues. Any German expectation that taxation would force young men into servitude was mistaken, because money 'drops down to us from the palms which we own and which we planted at your behest' (Hahl 1980, 112).

The Tolai were in Salisbury's second 'stage', establishing copra smallholdings; it was left to other, less 'lucky' places to supply plantation labour. Collecting fallen coconuts, planting palms and processing copra, done by stay-at-home Tolai smallholders, were informal responses to (the repudiation of) early German attempts to impose a bureaucratic model of formal employment upon them. Although Hahl's initial encouragement of what he called Tolai 'private agriculture' was consistent with Dernburg's 'scientific colonialism', it worked against the primary goal of recruiting labour. The GNG Annual Report for 1910–11 canvassed agricultural extension to increase productivity on native smallholdings, but noted the dilemma this might pose: European enterprise needed to secure Tolai labour, but if young men were induced to cultivate their own land it would become even more difficult to persuade them to accept wage-labour (Rowley 1958b, 242–43).

In this period, Tolai benefited from Lipton's 'promising and elastic export markets' as colonial copra traders competed to buy their unprocessed coconuts. Early armed conflict suggested to Europeans the wisdom of accepting Tolai as 'peasant proprietors', although some might be induced to perform day-labour. After the Pacific War, prosperous Tolai would themselves become employers, usually of workers from elsewhere. But such arrangements would not be contracted under labour ordinances, for Tolai labour-hire, like their copra production, would be informal. Consequently, from the early twentieth century the goal of bureaucratic activity became to maximize opportunity for European traders and planters in their dealings with independent native producers, who were to be cultivated as consumers.

Tolai were to comply with a regulatory regime designed to achieve certain objectives, as links in a copra supply chain leading to German trading houses. Their earnings were to be recycled to those same houses as Tolai embraced new forms of consumption. This, and numerous similar instances in both the German and Australian periods, demonstrated the colonial state's determination to provide bureaucratic protection to metropolitan capital, to the detriment of indigenous enterprise (Ch. 1). The Tolai response often failed to meet German expectations however, and their pushback threw up many instances of informal economic behaviour. GNG's Chinese community were an important influence because they often cooperated with Tolai in ways calculated to frustrate bureaucratic objectives.

Hart distinguished between 'legitimate' and 'illegitimate' informal activities (Ch. 1), with legitimacy defined by laws and the morality of 'respectable' citizens. In Rabaul, respectability resided in the small population of colonial officials, planters and traders whose bureaucratic culture set standards for economic activity. The town was stratified by race and zoned in ethnic quarters, with 'illegitimate' activity quarantined largely within its Chinatown. In a formulation akin to Antonio Gramsci's approach to 'cultural transformation' (Ch. 20, below) Hempenstall (1978, 160–61) described the German belief that prosperity depended on 'creating an ordered existence'. The 'life and thought' of the colonized must become 'assimilated to that of the German people' to achieve the Dernburgian national-economic purpose.

National capitalism depended on a citizenry institutionalized to national goals and broadly accepting of the associated norms. Modern nation states might fit this description in varying degrees, but scepticism is more appropriate for colonies in which the compliance of alien peoples was assured by real or implicit coercion. Western bureaucratic norms had no precedent, while any suggestion of a 'common culture' (Ch. 7) is fanciful, at least until the appearance of an indigenous bourgeoisie. So long as people are (in Hart's terms) only 'partially institutionalized' to the economic orthodoxy of the state, their economic behaviour will display 'palpable discrepancies' in relation to the 'prevalent intellectual model' (Ch. 1). Informality will occur.

If the earliest evidence of this was seen in a Tolai preference for independent production, a later instance flowed from German efforts to substitute coinage for *tambu*. For a period after 1887, when the Kompagnie first circulated silver coinage on the Gazelle, two rival currencies competed. Authorities had earlier accepted *tambu* for taxes and fines, and in 1899 the new administration found it necessary to pay *tambu* to induce Tolai to work on the roads (S. Epstein 1968, 35–36). It became evident that Tolai preferred shell currency in exchange for coconuts, rather than silver or trade store goods (Salisbury 1970, 284–85). As Tolai tended to hoard *tambu*, this acted as 'a dampener on trade' (A. Epstein 1969, 22). As international demand for vegetable oils grew, the terms of trade shifted so decisively in their favour that Tolai were able to '*insist* on payment in their own shell-money' (ibid., 21, emphasis added). As Stewart Firth explained, with some admiration, Europeans needing to buy copra had to source the necessary *tambu* from Tolai, at what seemed 'absurdly high' rates of exchange. In a sellers' market, many also agreed to demands that they accept 'whole' coconuts from the Tolai instead of 'ready-cut copra'. Rather than acquiring 'valuable habits of industry' from the foreigner, Tolai proved to be 'inconveniently independent' (Firth 1983, 69).

As *tambu* disappeared into Tolai stockpiles, its scarcity hampered copra trading. Tolai pushed back against German attempts to substitute an *ersatz* alternative, and some traders were forced to finance Tolai shell-collecting expeditions or to voyage to the source themselves (S. Epstein 1968, 35). Although more *tambu* was produced, supply was relatively inelastic while demand for copra continued to rise. For a brief period at the end of the nineteenth century, the exchange value of *tambu* appreciated dramatically against the German silver Mark (Salisbury 1970, 284–85). Differential access to *tambu* disadvantaged major trading houses, putting pressure on the authorities, who also hoped Tolai would consume more trade goods if paid in cash. This situation was galling for German authorities because the trade was more profitable for Tolai than for German planters and traders (ibid.). German ordinances forbade the use of *tambu* in trade with Europeans from 1901, but this measure was not wholly successful. *Tambu* continued to change hands in covert (informal) trade, although the Mark recovered as more copra was traded for cash. This prompted Salisbury to claim that, in this first contest between Tolai and the 'German financiers', the latter emerged victorious, but only after being forced to take 'repressive political action' (ibid.). Salisbury's assertion of a 'currency war' may perhaps be discounted as formalist exuberance, but it does capture something of the difficulty the Reich experienced in institutionalizing Tolai to a formal legal tender.

Similarly, the head tax of 1907 was intended to force Tolai into formal contract labour; instead, it propelled them further along the path of independent (informal) smallholder production. Further disappointing the Germans, Tolai were slow to adopt new forms of consumption. They seemed to hoard cash just as they did *tambu*. After initial enthusiasm, Tolai spending stalled towards the end of the nineteenth century, causing GNG to suffer a perennial shortage of specie. This forced authorities to maintain coinage in circulation by annual imports of silver. Nor did increasing cash incomes after 1901 translate immediately into higher demand, suggesting the Tolai were no more malleable in serving the national-economic purpose as consumers than they had been as labourers. However Scarlett Epstein (1968, 41) calculated a threefold increase in their purchases of clothes and textiles between 1905 and 1913, suggesting that by the end of the German period Tolai had come to appreciate a wider range of commodities (which Fisk would categorize as 'incentive goods').

Further discussion of German attempts at bureaucratic control of trade between 1907 and the outbreak of the First World War will be provided in Chapter 8, dealing with the Chinese. This is appropriate because the primary goal of much regulatory effort was to formalize (and thereby contain) burgeoning Chinese economic activity in favour of European interests. Tolai were affected by these restrictions, and many colluded with Chinese to avoid mutually irksome regulation. Later discussion of Chinese activities will reveal the synergy involved in Tolai–Chinese economic relationships, and will emphasize their largely informal character in comparison with the formality of dealings with European enterprise.

By the outbreak of war and the Australian invasion, Tolai engagement with the market economy included production and processing of copra, various forms of service activity, and wage labour. Village production of copra in the Bismarck Archipelago totalled 5,000 tons, some 80 per cent by Tolai, while from 1896 to 1913 the per capita value of their copra almost quadrupled (S. Epstein 1968, 40–41). In Vunamami from around 1910, some wealthy men began to acquire symbols of a European mode of affluence – horses, buggies and metal-roofed houses – while Tolai house building and church construction suggested that some Tolai now owned

European tool kits and engaged in independent contracting (Salisbury 1970, 243). The volume of foodstuffs produced for market continued to increase to meet the needs of a growing plantation labour force, while the informal marketplace in Rabaul had become an important food source for the European, Chinese and non-Tolai populations. In the peri-urban village of Matupit, people engaged with the urban economy through various forms of off-farm formal wage employment (ship building, stevedoring, ships' services and domestic service), as well as vending their garden produce and fish (A. Epstein 1969). By 1914, rural informal economic activity was well established, albeit with varying degrees of engagement, as between emerging Tolai entrepreneurs and their fellow villagers, and between coastal and peri-urban communities and the more remote villages of the interior.

The Australians in New Guinea

The Germans were ousted in 1914, but although the incoming military administration might adopt a new, Australian 'national-economic purpose', the Germanic bureaucratic culture remained. Believing their contracts no longer binding, many labourers 'deserted'. They were soon put right; their new overlords explaining that, while the Germans were no longer in charge, the plantation system would continue as before. It was 'the old colonial order under new management' (Firth 1983, 2). It appears Colonel William Holmes, the Australian commander, had only vague instructions: to overcome the Germans and occupy their territory, and then to maintain this asset in good running order, 'with an eye to international law' (Rowley 1958b, 3). Although Australia's international obligations would be defined in 1921 by a League of Nations mandate, there emerged an essential continuity of policy and practice, underpinned by an Australian nationalist economic agenda. If prior to the Australian occupation the emphasis was very much on economic expediency, the evidence suggests that German practices were maintained under the new military administration. And, for most of the mandate period, Australian practice was at least as partial to the 'interests of profit-seekers' as before, while native protection was probably less effective (Rowley 1965, 90–91).

Continuity of objectives is less important than the degree to which bureaucratic culture was maintained. Holmes noted the need to discharge his mission with minimal change to 'existing customs' and to 'trade and commerce'. He concentrated on restoring supply chains for copra and the materials and trade goods necessary to maintain economic life (Rowley 1965, 5). German civil officials were to act in an advisory capacity, while

German planters continued working their holdings. Many increased their plantings, whether because of confidence in an ultimate German victory, or perhaps the belief (mistaken, as it turned out) that any peace settlement would protect their interests. As a result, the Australian military regime 'swung into action under the tutelage of those German officials who chose to remain', and the new administration gave priority to the economic value of its new territory (Reed 1943, 157–58).

When the military administration yielded to civil control in 1921, the Australian government's primary concern was to seize German assets rather than to pursue administrative change. In fact, there was little discontinuity between the occupation administration and its mandated successor. Reed commented that between 1914 and 1921 there were 'few new European innovations or adjustments' in native administration. Instead, the Australians sought to preserve 'the social order built up by the Germans' (Reed 1943, 160). Although a recognizably Germanic bureaucratic culture was maintained, Dernburg's 'national-economic purpose' was succeeded by an Australian design for expropriation. Australia's own *national purpose* became explicit when German mercantile assets fell cheaply into Australian corporate hands. Settlement of Australian ex-servicemen on some German plantations achieved a politically popular distribution of spoils, while assuring the Australian character of New Guinea as a buffer against future military threats to the Australian mainland. Meanwhile a Germanic bureaucratic culture, in reaction to which informality had emerged, continued to hold sway.

The Experience of Stagnation

At the time of the Australian invasion, Tolai were experiencing Salisbury's second 'stage', with the emergence of service and off-farm economic activities. These are interpreted here as rural informality, conducted as secondary trade. Much later, in the early 1960s, Salisbury described Tolai as undergoing a fourth stage of their 'service-driven' economy. To achieve continuing progress in the face of a burgeoning population they would need further technological innovation and political consolidation (Salisbury 1971). A less benign set of possibilities also existed. These could lead to economic stagnation due to some combination of population growth, natural disaster, political regression, or failure to identify and exploit new technologies. Such reverses might lead to rural distress, impelling rural–urban migration and the emergence of an 'involution of services' in Rabaul. Conditions precedent to so dismal a scenario could be found in a period of stagnation experienced by the Tolai between 1921 and 1935 (Salisbury 1970).

Before the Australian takeover, Rabaul had been central to German operations in the Pacific. Close to major shipping routes, it was a strategic base for the imperial navy's East Asia Squadron. Norddeutscher Lloyd was subsidized by the Reich to maintain inter-island and international services around Rabaul as a hub, and most of the trade of the region passed through its harbour. But after the takeover, Rabaul, formerly a sea-transport focal point, became a terminal port with a few inter-island connections, a situation imposing additional costs on traders and producers.

Although the war period saw generally rising copra volumes and prices it was unfortunate for Tolai producers that these events occurred in a regulatory environment tilting towards the interests of European copra traders. Cost pressures increased again after 1920, when protectionist provisions of the Australian Navigation Act were applied to New Guinea. This coincided with a copra price slump, and it disrupted production on German plantations undergoing expropriation. The navigation legislative changes were repealed in 1925, but in the interim Australian carriers had become entrenched, while regulation of copra buying and trade store operations to favour European interests had intensified. By 1922, the coastal village of Vunamami – with prices for its copra and consumer goods regulated, and independent (i.e. Chinese) copra buyers excluded – had become a 'captive labour force' for local plantations (Salisbury 1970, 124). Whether or not employed by planters, Tolai were increasingly bound to them. These circumstances, general throughout the Gazelle, ushered in a period of stasis during which 'increasingly direct administration from Australia and a lack of technological innovation brought Tolai society into an incipient phase of involution. Both technological and political change was needed to reverse the process' (Salisbury 1971, 65, n3).

Stasis was prolonged by the Great Depression, and Tolai were not the only parties affected. Many independent European planters were bankrupted and their plantations fell into corporate hands, while much Chinese commercial activity stalled due to the combination of discriminatory regulation and conglomerate market power. During this period, formal copra production increased as wartime and early post-war plantings came to maturity, causing demand for labour to rise. Smallholder production diminished in relative terms, making Tolai interests of even less political consequence. Signs of positive change appeared from 1937, with a recovery in prices and the formation by government of a few 'non-statutory village councils' near Rabaul (Fenbury 1978). The Pacific War put an end to this political experiment, and formal local government had to wait until the 1950s. Tolai political energies had begun to revive at an unofficial level, however, with the emergence of *kivung* (young men's organizations) from the mid-1930s. These would contribute to Tolai political ferment in the post-war period.

More positively, the interwar period was marked by greater Tolai engagement in non-agricultural formal employment. Described by Bill Epstein as a 'pattern of relations' between Tolai and colonial society that they had managed since German times, this was managed even as the Tolai maintained a secure subsistence base. Tolai were prepared to accept semi-skilled jobs, and some travelled outside the district for employment. In Rabaul, men from Matupit were averse to indentured labour, preferring 'free' engagement in roles such as boat-crew or domestic service. Epstein reported a somewhat rueful discussion of Tolai workers in the *Rabaul Times* in 1936, a time of rising copra prices and labour shortage. Tolai had no fear of dismissal from paid employment because 'everyone was a landed proprietor'. Epstein thought that Tolai, living in 'their own hamlets and settlements' near Rabaul and resorting occasionally to the town to earn cash, remained aloof from urbanism. They retained their independence – both economic and social – while benefiting from 'the produce of the soil' (A. Epstein 1969, 29–30).

If not actually 'integrated into an urban system', the Tolai were certainly developing an active set of rural–urban economic relationships, in which the Rabaul town market and nearby Chinese shops played an important role. Such relationships would come to define the character of their informal economy after the Pacific War. Meanwhile, change in the late pre-war period was signalled by Tolai shaking off the unofficial but pervasive culture of discouragement engendered by Australian rule – the feeling that independent New Guinean business activity was somehow 'forbidden' (Salisbury 1970, 243). This positive phase of development, corresponding to Salisbury's third 'stage', was abruptly interrupted in January 1942. Japanese invasion converted the Gazelle into a vast military base, the Australian residents and administration having essentially abandoned the Tolai people. Military occupation caused the remaining population, Chinese as well as Tolai, much suffering and loss of life. Allied bombing inflicted enormous damage on the town, its infrastructure and plantations, while Tolai coconut plantings and food gardens were severely affected. As Allied forces struck back, their 'island-hopping' military strategy isolated Rabaul for more than two years until the Japanese surrendered in August 1945.

Chapter 8

Chinese in New Guinea before the Pacific War

German national capitalism institutionalized a bureaucratic framework in GNG and ordained a racial division of labour in which indigenous people and Chinese immigrants were to play specific, subordinate roles. After accepting that Tolai could not be compelled to labour, the Germans tolerated their working as independent (and informal) smallholders supplying copra to European trading houses. Chinese traders had been active on the margins of Melanesia for centuries (Ch. 3), and the Kompagnie recruited labourers and artisans for the Bismarck Archipelago from Hong Kong. At least one independent Chinese, the legendary entrepreneur Ah Tam, had by the turn of the century established a shipyard in the Bismarcks at Matupit on the outskirts of modern-day Rabaul (Cahill 2012, 21). This account of the Chinese will be divided between two chapters, mirroring the narrative of Tolai economic activity in the periods before, and after, the Pacific War. It will emerge that the Chinese presence was an element contributing to the Gazelle as a 'lucky place'.

The roles allotted to Chinese in the colonial design were as formally contracted wage workers, labourers and skilled artisans. But among the Chinese who remained after completing initial contracts, most aspired to free employment and then to independent informal commercial or artisan activity. This was a form of pushback, the voluntary *de-formalization* of Chinese livelihoods in reaction to the limited appeal of formal jobs. Such men were embraced in a Chinese informal economy, operating in parallel with the formal colonial economy, in which after acquiring enough capital they became self-employed. Some hoped to progress, as Ah Tam had done, to larger-scale operations. But this would necessarily incur more regulatory scrutiny and require increasing degrees of formalization.

By 1907 there were no longer any Chinese under indenture (Cahill 2012, 45), and official policy had turned from further recruitment towards acceptance of free immigration. Bowing again to the inevitable, Europeans sought to link 'free' Chinese into copra supply chains, as agents sent among the Tolai to gather coconuts and processed copra in exchange for trade goods. By the end of the German era in 1914, fewer than one in seven Chinese was a labourer (ibid., 24), and a small number of Chinese firms were large enough to attract substantial regulatory attention. However, as these were typically multi-activity enterprises, they almost certainly retained informal elements 'under the radar'.

In the broader Chinese business community, mixed modes of operation, involving varying degrees of conformity with colonial bureaucratic requirements, were normal. Peter Biskup gave an account of the early stages of an individual's career progression. This showed a classic Monsoon Asia mode of 'hustling', with Chinese typically pursuing multiple activities to get ahead. While they worked initially for wages, trade was the 'Chinaman's forte'. Typically, immigrants would start in a menial position, and after saving some money would become 'under-traders' to a European or Chinese master. More savings would equip them for independent copra trading, opening the possibility of independence as a storekeeper in a rural area, or in Rabaul. But few relied on trade alone; whether as under-traders or free agents, they typically had sidelines – 'recruitment of labour, building, a small copra plantation, a vegetable garden, a tea-house or a hostelry' (Biskup 1970, 99–100).

Reminiscent of Bauer's account of West Africa, Biskup described a pattern of Chinese commercial activity escaping the attention of GNG census-takers. Bauer and Yamey (1957, 34) had shown a reality of entrepreneurial livelihoods 'masked by the unreliability of census data'. Enumeration errors occurred because such activities displayed 'imperfect specialization of labour' and 'occupational fluidity', enabling people to work in a manner 'better described as the performance of a number of different tasks than as the pursuit of a definite occupation' (Ch. 2). Chinese immigrants were acculturated to trade in a semi-industrial environment, were thrifty, could turn their hands to a variety of tasks, and were given to 'moonlighting' away from formal employment.

Chinese influence on the Tolai was potent, and, for two reasons, subversive of the Dernburgian ideology. Bureaucrats found it difficult to confine men such as Ah Tam to dependent and subordinate roles, and Chinese often colluded with Tolai to frustrate German (later Australian) efforts to regulate economic activity to their own advantage. The model of economic activity demonstrated by Chinese traders encouraged native people to accommodate themselves to 'the market' in a manner unorthodox in Dernburgian terms. This was both hybrid (in the sense of retaining important elements of traditional behaviour) and informal (in the sense of failing to conform with bureaucratic prescriptions).

The Business of Cultural Frontiers

Reviewing the experience of the Chinese in western (now Indonesian) New Guinea, Rowley (1965, 56) spoke of their special aptitude for operating on cultural frontiers. Later, in GNG, they displayed a great capacity for conducting business without any hint of cultural prejudice – a trait that, when coupled with an easy indifference to legal technicalities, distinguished them from the more bureaucratically observant Europeans (Rowley 1958b, 79). Such attributes were useful in early colonial New Guinea, where the capacity to survive on slim pickings enabled Chinese traders to act as what Sapper (1910, 107) termed 'cultural pioneers'. They prepared the way for formal European enterprise by familiarizing indigenous people with how immigrants lived and traded, and introduced them to new consumer wants (Biskup 1970, 106). Towards the end of his tenure, Governor Hahl encouraged free immigration of Chinese with such considerations in mind, and Biskup commented how well they served Hahl's policy of acculturating native peoples to the commercial economy, 'on European terms' (ibid.).

Chinese entrepreneurs were not usually minded to yield gracefully to Europeans the territories they had pioneered. Commercial contestation of such opportunities, and the different Chinese and European approaches to exploiting them, resulted in much friction. European traders often appealed to bureaucratic authority, and systematic efforts were made to weight the regulatory scales in favour of formal (that is, mostly European) investors. Chinese were convenient scapegoats for abuses against native people, even as they were trusted to provide certain services disapproved by respectable society. Yet, in retrospect, Hahl concluded that Chinese workers had shown their capacities in the better jobs – 'artisans, cooks, overseers, ships' engineers and traders' – and had become indispensable. Pointing to the positive example of Chinese immigrants in Indo-Chinese mining and agriculture, Hahl thought it necessary to secure their permanency as residents so that others would be encouraged to follow (Hahl 1980, 144–45).

Ruefully, Hahl recalled that his immigration proposals had generally been opposed by the European community and rejected by a new secretary for colonies in Berlin (Biskup 1970, 99). In a much-quoted trope, he observed that while no one 'wished to or was able to do without the Chinese . . . no one wanted to have them in the country' (Hahl 1980, 145). In an equally rueful comment, Lieutenant-Governor Murray complained that Australian Papua was disadvantaged by the application there of Australia's more rigorous immigration restrictions. Murray was especially troubled by the shortage and high cost of skilled artisans in Papua, noting that GNG pay rates for Asian artisans were half those of Europeans (Rowley 1958b, 73). Rowley concluded that, without the Chinese, GNG might have appeared to the Germans very much more like Papua (ibid., 76).

Much of the history of Chinese Rabaul may be understood through the character of Ah Tam. Other than at the outset, he was a formal businessman, as the later scale of his operations made regulatory scrutiny unavoidable. Nonetheless, much of his income was gained informally, by means such as using *tambu* for trade with Tolai after the practice had become illegal (Salisbury 1970, 286). His influence is particularly important in the German period, during which Chinese stamped out a template of informal economic activity for Tolai. Ah Tam married a Matupi woman, on whose land he constructed his enterprises, including a trade store and a hotel. Hahl gave Tam permission to import Japanese prostitutes, as a 'public health measure' (Davies 2002, 68). So many boats were built in his shipyard that he found it necessary to import Chinese artisans as well as hiring Europeans (Rowley 1958b, 74). Other Chinese patrons were also sponsoring migrants, and Biskup (1970, 94) suggested that immigration controls and official supervision of employment conditions in Rabaul avoided exploitation – common elsewhere – of migrants by compatriots. This suggests that Rabaul was a place of opportunity where Chinese immigrants could more readily 'buy their independence' (Cahill 2012, 22). Again, in the late colonial period, Christine Inglis was struck by the limited influence there of 'particularist' tendencies common in other Chinese immigrant communities (Inglis 1977). Early-period regulation may have contributed to this failure of clientelism to become entrenched in Chinese Rabaul, encouraging their dynamism.

Whether or not Ah Tam had rivals, Hahl 'appears to have recognized Ah Tam as the business leader and patron of the Chinese community'. In 1907, Hahl granted him a substantial land lease in Rabaul (later known as Chinatown) in consideration of his agreeing to import carpenters, cooks, coolies, and Chinese women to give greater stability to the Chinese community. They were to reside on Ah Tam's lease, and their businesses would be confined to it (Rowley 1958b, 75). Aside from this, Ah Tam gained other franchises. By 1914 he had the sole licence to import opium, and he seems also to have collected levies on gambling in Chinatown (ibid.), while between twenty and thirty Japanese prostitutes were working there (Davies 2002, 68). Hahl's toleration of illegal activities and his decision to quarantine them in Rabaul's small and (to European eyes) squalid Chinatown was simple pragmatism, with notions of legitimacy or legality honoured in the breach. It would give an unbalanced impression, however, to ignore the many legitimate, albeit still informal, business activities conducted there. Just as in Hart's Nima (Ch. 1), Chinatown was a substantial supplier of legitimate goods and services to 'respectable' households. Even so, visitors from the European town viewed it with a mixture of curiosity and prurience, for it was 'vice' that made this 'little East Asiatic village' most alluring (Lyng 1919, 125–27).

Rabaul market (the *Bung*) was adjacent to Chinatown, reproducing a symbiosis found in towns throughout the Pacific. Chinatown and the marketplace were the urban focus of a system of rural–urban relations that Chinese and Tolai had constructed. Chinatown was the locus of *urban* informal economic activity, while the Bung was the primary outlet for produce marketed by a growing Tolai *rural* informal economy. Chinese were patrons of the Bung, while rural Tolai vendors, acting as 'producer-sellers' (S. Epstein 1982), spent much of their earnings in Chinese stores. Chinese and Europeans encouraged Tolai to grow a range of exotic vegetables, and both communities purchased these in the market, while many Tolai and other town-based New Guineans bought traditional staple foods there. The Bung was also a point of intersection and exchange between the two rival currencies, German silver (the Mark) and Tolai shell (*tambu*).

Bureaucracy, Regulation and Discrimination

Tightening the Fetters

An account of the bureaucratic regulation of Chinese enterprise must include many instances of authorities 'weighting the scales' to favour metropolitan capital against informal operators (Ch. 1). In the early part of the twentieth century, the formal/informal categories corresponded closely to European and Chinese, respectively. This simple duality would break down as many Chinese entities grew in scale, and their operations became more formal (although elements of informality continued to characterize even the largest Chinese entities). Nonetheless it was true that, under both German and Australian administrators, the primary goal of much regulatory effort was to contain burgeoning Chinese economic activity. Intended to advantage European commercial interests, such regulation was anticompetitive and the subject of lobbying by vested interests. Tolai were affected by these processes insofar as constraints on Chinese informal business often disadvantaged them; Tolai often colluded with Chinese to avoid such irksome bureaucratic constraints.

Regulatory measures impacting the Chinese were directed to numerous areas of commercial life, including the copra trade, retailing, land tenure, business practices (including bribery), licensing, taxation, and their residential/legal status. Such initiatives sometimes served as a pretext to exclude them from trading with Tolai. Some early cases concerned activities of copra traders, many of them Chinese, who purchased dry coconuts or 'cured' copra from Tolai. The terms of trade so favoured Tolai at the turn of the twentieth century that they were able to insist on payment in *tambu* (Ch. 7), to which Chinese traders often enjoyed preferred access. In response, the administration imposed an ordinance in 1901 forbidding the use of *tambu* in commercial trading. It was not wholly successful; *tambu* continued to change hands in covert – that is, *informal* – trade, conducted mainly with Chinese. A related source of friction soon after 1900 concerned the processing of copra. Cahill (2012, 44) recounted how fierce rivalry led to unethical behaviour, with complaints about the shoddy quality of 'trade' (informal) copra as a result of inadequate processing. Chinese were often willing to buy poorly cured copra and to 're-cure' it for resale. This gave them the edge in trading with Tolai. Such complaints may have been an attempt by trading companies to channel all purchases of copra through their stores, by having quality standards embodied in regulation. If so, this failed, because the Chinese were able to find other buyers.

An ordinance in 1903 imposed a licensing requirement for traders in copra and other natural resource products. This forced unlicensed Chinese traders further out into 'uncontrolled' and dangerous territory. Cahill commented that the government did not or could not enforce the regulation, and was indifferent to the loss of lives among those Chinese who ventured further out (Cahill 2012). Meanwhile, the issue of processing standards continued to simmer. European commercial interests lobbied in 1906 for the Chinese to be required to have contracts with registered European firms (ostensibly for purposes of quality control, but actually to tie Chinese hands in negotiations). These pleadings failed. Cahill commented that the trade was so profitable that by 1907 most Chinese were associated with copra at one level or other (ibid., 44–45).

Other Chinese trading practices incurred disapproval, including the tie between copra-buying and credit. Many Tolai villagers entered into arrangements with Chinese buyers because the latter, unlike European corporate and independent buyers, were prepared to lend money against future production (Cahill 2012). An ordinance of 1909, described by Cahill as directed against the Chinese, attempted to regulate such lending. It was a futile exercise because such arrangements suited both sides and so continued beyond the ken of authorities. Another ordinance in 1910 prohibited supplying alcohol to natives as an inducement to supply copra (a charge often levelled against the Chinese). This also failed because of enforcement difficulties outside town limits. In Rabaul itself, European traders fretted over Chinese competition. They claimed, in effect, that the Chinese worked too hard – keeping longer trading hours than European storekeepers while paying 'too much' for copra (Biskup 1970, 99). Eventually, under the Australian occupation, a regulation (*Closing of Stores Order* 1917) was imposed to limit trading hours. But by then the Chinese had achieved effective dominance of trade store operations in Rabaul and its hinterland (Cahill 2012, 81).

By 1917, the Australian administrator, Pethebridge, had decided to curb Chinese business, with the intention to 'fatten' German firms ahead of their expropriation. This strategy was challenged by the growth of Chinese business, although the danger lay more in trend than magnitude (Rowley 1958b, 82–83). It may be seen as the assertion of an Australian 'national-economic purpose', weighted 'in the interests of profit-seekers'. The 'profit-seekers' were Australian ex-servicemen taking up expropriated plantations and, later, Australian corporates whose grip on the mandate economy tightened as private planters went to the wall. In the meantime, in 1917, Pethebridge issued an *Order on Trading in Coconuts and Copra in the Gazelle Peninsula*, the purpose of which was to protect German firms from the competition of small traders. Rowley concluded that the traders moving into the established territories of older European businesses, or who were offering more 'trade goods' for copra, were very probably Chinese, supported by Chinese firms, which in turn had their own links to larger Chinese entities (ibid.). This order was said to have been ineffective because Chinese informal modes of trading were more congenial to Tolai producers (Cahill 2012, 88). Another measure, the *Control of Chinese Trade Order 1917*, was designed to block more wealthy Chinese, such as Ah Tam, breaking into wholesale trade. This was quickly withdrawn because of protests from other Australian commercial interests (Rowley 1958b, 82–83).

The year 1920 was an active time of fetter-tightening. A *Non-Indigenous Persons (Amendment) Ordinance* prevented new Chinese immigrants establishing themselves in the copra trade; a *Sale and Disposition of Copra Ordinance* allowed sales to take place only in designated places; a *Trading Stations Leases Ordinance* created local monopolies for planters in trade goods and copra-buying. Finally, in an echo of the earlier 'currency war' (Ch. 7), a *Currency and Coinage Ordinance* assured only natives could use German currency (which both Tolai and Chinese had been hoarding). This measure reduced trading options open to the Chinese, and must have induced ingenious and surreptitious (that is, informal) modes of dealing. In any case, it failed to break Chinese dominance of direct copra trade with Tolai.

Authorities turned their attention to increasing the colony's tax yield, and gave priority to raising revenue from the Chinese. In 1905, Hahl increased import taxes and imposed export taxes on copra and other natural resource products handled by them. Such imposts, calculated at the wharf, are efficient in that transactions are simpler to trace. Hahl also attempted to replace the income tax (especially problematic when dealing with enterprises lacking formal accounting systems) with a graduated tax calculated on business turnover and other more observable criteria (Cahill 2012, 49). A business register was established to assist authorities in assessing tax liability, but the difficulty of extracting accurate information from Chinese entrepreneurs continued to vex officials.

Cahill noted that from 1916 the Australians found it necessary to place greater reliance on more easily collected indirect taxes (Cahill 2012, 50) and these were conscientiously applied to growing businesses owned by Chinese (Rowley 1958b, 68). From taxation it is only ever a short step to bribery, and Pethebridge was forced to take measures to avoid bribery of officials, a practice thought to be particularly prevalent among Asians. A 1915 ordinance gave Chinese, Malays and 'other coloured races' (although not including the indigenous people) a higher civil status and a new, separate jurisdiction. Rowley thought this measure was really intended to bring those affected under Central Court jurisdiction, to deal with bribery (ibid., 25). The problem was not easily solved; as late as 1920 the *Government Gazette* warned again of penalties applicable to bribery, singling out the Chinese community for specific mention (ibid.).

On the other hand, improved Chinese legal status may have contributed to a gradual formalization of their business, in that it also gave them the capacity to enforce contracts with Europeans in the Central Court. Notwithstanding this, Chinese business remained essentially insecure as they had no assurance of future citizenship attached to their 'quasi-European' status before the law (Rowley 1958b, 83). Other civil disabilities remained in force. Chinese could not purchase land, for they were effectively blocked by '*Principles of the Transfer of Land*' circulated in 1912 and 1914. Although not discriminatory per se, these were administered in a discriminatory fashion (Cahill 2012, 51). Some Chinese had relatively short-term leasehold rights to plantations on government land, but freehold title or long-term leasehold was more acceptable as collateral for formal bank credit. After the First World War, Lyng (2019, 69) observed that certain Chinese traders, 'since the establishment in Rabaul of a branch of the Commonwealth Bank, [had] commenced to emancipate themselves from the controlling influence of the European firms'. Whatever the reliability of this information, it is possible that more secure access to land would have improved Chinese 'bankability'. Instead, discrimination in access to land served to increase Chinese disadvantage vis-à-vis formal European business. They had been barred from tendering for expropriated German plantations after the war, and in 1933 the *Companies Ordinance* required British subjects to form a majority on boards, though the appointment of 'dummy' directors enabled some larger Chinese entities to continue trading (Cahill 1996, 82).

The Rise of 'Legitimate' Chinese Business and the Persistence of Informality

Despite a history of discriminatory regulation and partisan administration, successive GNG annual reports suggest the growth of Chinese business. Data reported by Biskup (1970, 100) reflect increases in activity but also suggest improved bureaucratic coverage, made necessary by the imposition of a business tax. Considering the simplest indicator – a head count of enterprises – in 1908, of the 48 entities in GNG, only 4 were Chinese. By 1911, when the Chinese population had for the first time outnumbered Europeans (Rowley 1958b, 76), 36 of the 81 concerns enumerated were Chinese. Among 334 entities in GNG that paid business tax in 1912, no fewer than 207 were Chinese and, suggesting the economic importance of the Gazelle, 120 of these were in Rabaul and 15 in Herbertshöhe (modern Kokopo). The raw numbers are misleading to the extent they did not distinguish German conglomerates with trading, planting and shipping interests from the typically smaller Chinese enterprises. The data must have lumped together entities ranging from those highly formal in terms of management, accounting and technology with others that were quite rudimentary and informal in character, enumerated simply because they failed to escape official attention. We might expect many firms at that end of the spectrum to be Chinese, although there were difficulties in assessing them. As an official quoted by Biskup (1970, 101) lamented in 1913, control was difficult because 'the Chinese make palpably untrue statements' in their tax returns. No doubt language difficulties and a paucity of records – characteristic of informal business – also contributed to this situation. Some Chinese paid substantial tax bills while others were doing better than the group suffering most keenly from Chinese competition – the small, independent white planter-traders.

Biskup concluded that larger Chinese enterprises were narrowing the gap with major European firms (Biskup 1970). Cahill was more expansive, declaring that by 1914 Chinese enterprise threatened to assert control over the whole commercial landscape (Cahill 2012, 51). But this was surely an overstatement. On the factual evidence, economic dominance was a distant prospect, notwithstanding the Chinese had an important role in Hahl's plans for German New Guinea, which the abrupt end of German rule in 1914 brought to nought. In the face of fiscal pressure from Berlin he had concluded that Chinese entrepreneurship would make GNG self-supporting. Ohff (2008) claimed that Hahl very nearly managed to persuade Berlin that the Chinese should have equal civil status (as indeed the few Japanese in GNG had enjoyed from the outset). But Hahl did not succeed, and we cannot know whether he would ever have overcome local European opposition and Berlin's reservations.

With each successive annual report there was evidence of population growth and family formation among the Chinese, and by 1914 Chinatown had grown into a busy centre with over a thousand people. In GNG as a whole, from a population of 1,377 fully 583 Chinese were artisans and another 172 were in business (Rowley 1958b, 76–77). But despite this suggestion of progress and the success of some families, most Chinese businesses continued to be small and informal, with copra at the centre of their economy. Chinese were numerically the largest group among those travelling in the copra trade and working in trading outposts; others were labour recruiters, while some combined trade with recruiting. Rowley speculated that the Chinese were better equipped for such roles than Europeans, under conditions in which 'law and order were comparative' (ibid., 79). Outside Rabaul, Chinese patience and grasp of local psychology often proved decisive. Playing a catalytic role in the villages, and with close links to Chinese enterprise in Rabaul, they contributed to the emergence of an integrated and largely informal rural–urban economic system on the Gazelle Peninsula.

Before the First World War, Chinese business had been 'hamstrung' because wholesale trade and trade financing were controlled by Europeans. Chinese entrepreneurs specialized instead in fields such as building and construction or tertiary services – activities relatively neglected in the formal economy (Biskup 1970, 101). They were largely confined to interstitial gaps – by 1910, for example, services for the repair and maintenance of engines were only available from Chinese workshops (Cahill 2012, 24). Inferior legal status limited access to formal finance and, unlike overseas Chinese elsewhere, they were never able to establish their own formal financial institutions (Wu 1974). It is likely that Rabaul Chinese, as Chinese elsewhere, resorted to *hui* arrangements (an informal rotating savings and credit club) to pool financial resources. Also, to finance international transactions during the German period, leading merchants such as Ah Tam were able to enter into trust-based arrangements ('relational contracting') with Chinese counterparts in Hong Kong, Singapore and in other German Pacific possessions. Such informal mechanisms were based on kinship or personal relationships and, although not subject to legal recourse, generally sufficed to cover counterparty risk. This still left them unable to contract formally with offshore European firms, including those based in Australia which were major suppliers to the big European trading houses in Rabaul, as well as importers of copra.

During the Australian occupation from 1914, Ah Tam was able to move into wholesaling, as did a number of other Chinese enterprises. This became possible because certain Australian firms (including the politically well-connected Burns, Philp & Co., which had hastened to establish itself in New Guinea) saw the opportunity to deal directly with leading Chinese businessmen. This secured for Chinese firms direct access and trade financing in overseas markets for copra, and with major suppliers of consumer goods (Rowley 1958b, 82). The ambiguous situation of German firms (which continued to trade during the war), together with Chinese acquisition of quasi-European legal status (albeit they were still 'aliens'), enabled the latter to break into the import–export trade. As mentioned above, higher civil status meant that debts of Chinese firms could now be litigated in the Central Court. And just as the change had strengthened the hand of Chinese in making and enforcing contracts with Europeans, it also increased the comfort of corporate business in dealing with them.

At the end of a war that had been good for Chinese traders they had become entrenched in independent business, while in the post-war period their 'tact' with indigenous customers underpinned their growing share of village copra buying, and in retail trade (Rowley 1965, 193–94). Evidence of rising status came with the 1921 census showing Chinese as now more numerous than the Germans and 'British' combined. It also revealed an upward shift in their occupational status: now there were some Chinese 'professionals', a larger proportion in commerce, in manufacturing and building, and some plantation lessees. Rowley thought this upward mobility reflected the new opportunities of the period, while their inability to take money back to China during the war had encouraged reinvestment locally (Rowley 1958b, 77–78). This committed many decisively to long-term residence.

After 1920, protectionist provisions of the Australian Navigation Act were applied to the Mandated Territory, entrenching Australian carriers in the shipping trade. Regulation of copra buying and trade store operations to favour European interests intensified, penalizing Chinese and Tolai alike (Salisbury 1970, 124). Some Chinese were more fortunate. Cahill related how, although they had been prevented from tendering for expropriated German plantations, Europeans had failed to foresee that Chinese would tender for trade stores located on plantations. These often proved more profitable than the plantations themselves, giving Chinese storekeepers opportunity both to purchase village copra and to sell trade goods to plantation workers and villagers (Cahill 1996, 80). Planters who leased their trade stores to Chinese came to regret it. Caught in a price/cost squeeze during the Great Depression, many were bankrupted, their properties foreclosed by Australian conglomerates holding their debt. Cahill (2012, 120) suggested that Chinese entrepreneurs fared better because they had access to informal 'club' loans (a reference to the *hui*). The depression years had also been a period of economic stasis for the Tolai (Ch. 7), but prospects for all communities improved as copra prices rose after 1935.

Evidence of formalization in Chinese building and construction firms is reported by Cahill (2012). He noted that four Chinese companies won most government tenders for public buildings in the late 1930s, during a rebuilding boom after a volcanic eruption (Cahill 1996, 83). For the period just before the war, the *Pacific Islands Year Book* listed the principal Chinese trading houses and, in addition, more than fifty traders in Chinatown and another score in the town proper, along with a few merchants and copra traders in Kokopo. Activities were quite diverse and, aside from merchants, included a range of service-providers. In addition, many young Chinese educated in Rabaul (and some in Australia) worked for European firms in skilled and semi-skilled occupations. But some less-educated or older Chinese still worked as market gardeners or water- and wood-sellers, operating door to door in the town (Cahill 2012, 137–38). The spectrum of activities included incorporated construction companies, diversified wholesale traders and the vigorous retail and service sector, as well as informal agriculture and petty services. Outside the town, Chinese traders continued to buy copra from Tolai and to supply to them what Fisk would call 'incentive goods'.

Hahl had envisaged the Chinese performing a useful function as a 'middle layer' between Europeans and native people. Rowley believed this vision had been fulfilled, concluding that their economic success was typical of Chinese acting as the 'intermediate layer' in colonial colonies (Rowley 1958b, 76). By contrast, Bill Stanner flatly denied that there was any 'intermediate' race in PNG, such as the Indians in Fiji. The Chinese in the Mandated Territory of New Guinea – only about two thousand in 1939 – were of minor economic importance and without any real social or political significance (Stanner 1953, 14). But the analogy with Fiji (where Indians came to form almost half the population) was surely misplaced. It was not a question of relative numbers, or of degrees of social or political influence, but of catalytic effect in the emergence and spread of a market economy on the Gazelle Peninsula. To underestimate Chinese economic influence is to overlook their function as sinews tying Tolai into the market economy of the Gazelle and the wider world of international markets. This status was cemented during the interwar period. The subsequent history of the Rabaul Chinese, in which the recovery from losses suffered during the Pacific War and the persistence of informality alongside the 'modernization' of their commercial undertakings are important themes, will be recounted in Chapter 19.

Chapter 9

Hubert Murray and the Contending Moralities

In German New Guinea (GNG) a classic plantation economy was created to serve the imperial Reich, while in British New Guinea (BNG, later Australian Papua; see Map 5.1) a notably less well-funded and cohesive imperial experiment was proceeding.[1] The Australian Papua experience before the Pacific War will be described in these next three chapters, which cover successive periods of British and Australian administration. They will consider whether the bureaucracy in Port Moresby was guided by any ideology so compelling or coherent as the 'national-economic purpose' of its German neighbour. Coherence was hard to achieve in a settler community subject to two 'contending moralities'. Among the very small population of Anglo-Papuan colonists (as some called themselves) a fault line had opened up between official and non-official constituencies. Across this divide, attitudes were determined by livelihoods, and the interests of the parties seemed irreconcilable (Lewis 1996, 126).

Private settlers in Papua were not as influential as their counterparts in GNG, where a 'pan-German settler clique' exerted pressure on Hahl (Hempenstall 1978, 160). Greater certainty of purpose prevailed in GNG, where the 'scientific colonialism' of Dernburg (Ch. 7) assured closer alignment between official policy and white commercial interests. The contending moralities in Papua might be seen as, first, an ideology of resource exploitation, conducted by and for alien settlers and corporate interests, and backed by metropolitan capital. This was pitted against another ideology seeking 'the preservation of village life', championed in the main by senior officials and missionaries. Bureaucratic support for either ideology would amount to what Hart called the 'institutional effort to organize society along formal lines', although the outcomes would differ considerably. Back in Australia, opinion was conflicted between maximizing the economic benefits of colonization and the wish to be regarded as having dealt fairly with the Papuan people (Lewis 1996, 7).

In practice, bureaucratic energies in Papua were never so focused as in GNG, and though both 'moralities' were represented to some degree in each colony, they were more evenly matched in Papua. The trajectory for Papua's 'preservation' policy was set originally by the British Colonial Office. It instructed Peter Scratchley, special commissioner from 1884 following the declaration of the British protectorate, to assure Papuans of their personal safety and the protection of their property rights (Oram 1976a, 19). 'Preservation' had antecedents in Arthur Gordon's earlier, liberal stewardship of Fiji, and it was introduced to BNG by his former colonial secretary, William MacGregor, between 1888 and 1898 (Joyce 1971). On the other hand, the 'plantation' morality was an expression of nineteenth-century industrial capitalism and its search for raw materials. The planter faction had its exemplar in GNG, towards which Anglo-Papuan settlers turned envious eyes. Clearing and planting had begun there in 1884, whereas planting on any comparable scale did not occur in BNG until it became the Territory of Papua, under Australian control from 1906.

The Dual Mandate

Conflict between these moralities underlay problems experienced by the Australian resident, Lieutenant-Governor Hubert Murray, whose tenure in Papua in that post extended from 1907 to 1940. Changing policy emphases, when one or other tendency was more dominant, reflected pressures on him and his own evolving sense of what was possible. In 1906, before his appointment as lieutenant-governor, Murray had appeared before a Royal Commission on Australian policies for Papua. At that time he appeared to signal support for the planter faction. In his evidence Murray supported the principles of a 'dual mandate' accepting responsibility for the interests of both Papuans and settlers, although suggesting that the concerns of the latter group had been less well served (Lewis 1996, 64–65).

The plantation 'turn' that followed the commission's findings led to the freer allocation of land and a boom in private investment. Plantation numbers increased from 76 in 1907 to 151 in 1910, and to 228 by 1914, although without yielding much immediate increase in production. Watching the pre-war commodity boom, Papuan planters feared that by failing to enter the rising markets for copra and rubber by 1902, they had 'missed the boat' (Ohff 2008, 411). The pace of new plantings stretched the available supply of Papuan labour, testing the administration's preservationist resolve. Employers demanded longer terms of indenture and stronger labour sanctions, while corporate planters pressed for a 'village' system on estates, as in Java and Ceylon (Lewis 1996, 113–16). This latter bid failed, because Murray believed it would lead to permanent alienation of Papuan workers from their home communities. Some planters called for recruitment of Asian skilled labour, sparking negative reactions from the broader European community in which 'white Australia' attitudes prevailed (ibid., 117–18). In 1919, Murray acknowledged Papua's disadvantage in regard to supply and cost of skilled workers, due to Australian immigration restrictions. Again in 1920, he conceded the economic cost of excluding Asians, but said that Papua would do without such labour, for reasons of 'patriotism and self-protection' (cited in Lewis 1996, 162). Consistent with my account of Chinese immigrants in GNG (Ch. 8), I argue here that the exclusion of Asian workers deprived Papua of much more than cheap labour.

Murray's concept of a dual mandate required government to heed both 'moralities', even though in 1906 he had thought it necessary to redress the balance in favour of commercial interests. As economic realities bit – insufficient private investment, inadequate public financial support, difficult export markets – Murray's views changed. After 1913 he recognized irreconcilable elements in the dual policy, due to inescapable conflicts of interest between settlers and Papuans, and by 1920 he had accepted that government had obligations to the Papuan people 'which the white settlers did not share' (West 1968, 175). While Murray continued to accept the need for an economic base to assure self-reliance, the preservation morality had become more important for him.

This was evident from his minority (dissenting) report to a 1919 Royal Commission on the post-war future of GNG. Murray's view was that, while the Germans had regarded colonies as commercial undertakings, British practice had adhered (at least, in theory) to obligations of 'trust' required by the League of Nations Covenant. If an amalgamated territory were to be administered by the Papuan government, the British principle, rather than the German, should be applied to the whole (West 1968, 199). Murray had hoped to become the administrator of such a new, amalgamated territory, but by 1920 Papua was bulking less large in Australian calculations. GNG's plantation economy had fallen into Australian hands without any expenditure commensurate with Germany's original investment (Ch. 7). The government decided to continue it as a separate jurisdiction, and Murray was left to soldier on in Papua (West 1968, 198).

His rejection reflected an official view that Papua had limited economic prospects and might as well continue as it had begun (West 1968, 199; Lewis 1996, 158–59). Successive Australian cabinets viewed Papua largely through a geostrategic lens, and they took the high moral ground, declaring protection of the native people as policy (Lewis 1996, 292).

On the other hand, New Guinea was an economic asset whose value was to be maximized by Dernburgian exploitation under a virtually unchanged bureaucratic system, albeit one with an Australian accent (Ch. 7). The case for this was compelling, as its plantations were three times as large as Papua's and had benefited from much greater expenditure by a far less scrupulous imperial government. GNG gave Australia an opportunity to secure economic returns without having made the initial investment (Lewis 1996, 158–59). For the rest of its brief separate history until the outbreak of the Pacific War, Papua would suffer in popular white opinion by comparison. It was generally thought an 'ungenerous' territory, lacking comparative advantage both in terms of natural resources and in the wage costs or productivity of its labour (ibid., 291). Even more damning, perhaps, was the belief that its bureaucracy was insufficiently dedicated to commercial development and was excessively scrupulous in its native policies. If the Rabaul hinterland was a 'lucky place', Papua was not.

Between the wars, Murray's authority was enhanced by his growing international reputation as an enlightened administrator. After a phase of rabid settler opposition during the 1920s, he was less challenged in imposing his views, whether by an increasingly dispirited local planter constituency or the succession of Australian ministers whom he inducted into their responsibilities. This situation would have long-term consequences for the degree and character of indigenous Papuan engagement with 'the market' and for the character of Port Moresby itself. Under Murray's increasingly personalized regime, normal processes of urbanism would be inhibited in the capital. Autonomous Papuan enterprise, if not suppressed, could scarcely flower and, aside from formal indentured employment, rural Papuan economic activity would receive only fitful encouragement.

The 'Informality' Construct in Colonial Papua

Market exchange and bureaucracy are necessary preconditions for informal economic activity. Weberian bureaucratic processes emerged in parallel during the nineteenth century in Germany and other industrializing states – in Britain and Australia, and then by extension in GNG and BNG. Although Murray had a reputation for impatience with routine, Lewis commented that he was supported by an efficient staff, while Papua's bureaucracy was 'impressive'. Of Murray personally, he said that his records showed a mind both organized and systematic (Lewis 1996, 123). Murray and his predecessors laid sturdy bureaucratic foundations, but not for the prosecution of any orthodoxy as utilitarian as the German 'national-economic purpose'.

The account by Lewis shows how remote the lieutenant-governor was, personally and intellectually, from the middle-class settlers who came to Papua with the pre-war boom; his ethical code and personal conduct were in profound contrast to their 'petit-bourgeois' style. Despite having endorsed white settler suffrage in 1906, he grew to distrust the commercial and planting classes, and for the rest of his career he successfully resisted their enfranchisement. Bleakly, he came to believe that European communities exercising total power over 'natives' would descend to practising slavery within three generations. This he knew, for he could feel the tendency within himself (Lewis 1996, 120–23).

If Murray disdained petty capital he also distrusted large corporations. He opposed oil drilling because of the potential influence of powerful corporations with financial resources greater than those of the colonial government itself and seeking to capture it. Economic activity on such a scale would threaten a principle on which *preservation* depended, that the rate of development must not outrun the labour available (Lewis 1996, 140–41). Later, as it seemed European plantations could not provide an adequate economic base, he would seek a different model of agricultural development. This was necessary because he doubted Papua's capacity to adapt to an industrialized economy. However, Papuans were more than simple 'hewers of wood and drawers of water', and they could be expected to advance in an agricultural economy (West 1968, 185). Many administrators of the period accepted a 'popular pseudo-Darwinism', a set of beliefs supporting social-evolutionary processes (Rowley 1965, 92). At a more intellectual level, Murray was familiar with Maine's *Ancient Law* (1861), and broadly accepted contemporary notions of evolutionary social progress (West 1968, 39; see also 214). Such ideas, incorporated into an Anglo-Papuan bureaucratic orthodoxy, were tempered by Murray's conception of duty towards the indigenous people, and his views – moderating over time – of their ordering on an evolutionary ladder.

As to the other precondition of informality – market exchange – coastal Papuans were introduced to the international economy by early visits of European mariners. These bartered industrial commodities for coconuts, pearl shell and other 'gathered' products. As late as 1900, most copra in international trade still came from 'beach' traders dealing with indigenous producers of fresh coconut or dried kernel (Lewis 1996, 73). Such transactions in Papua, as among the Tolai, became gradually monetized. But, by vivid contrast with the Tolai, Papuan village cash crop production owed more to official suasion than market incentives because, in the final reckoning, Murray lacked confidence in any native policy eschewing compulsion (West 1968, 186).

Policy for native agriculture under both MacGregor and Murray rested on dirigisme. Although bureaucratic regulation was apparently more stringent in German (and later Australian) New Guinea, that was largely because there was more economic activity to regulate. To promote white settler interests, officials in New Guinea strove to contain emerging Tolai and Chinese informal activity within a thicket of regulations. In a telling contrast, their counterparts in Papua felt the need to regulate indigenous economic activity *into existence*.

If the initial Papuan impulse to market exchange resulted from contact with alien traders, many more Papuans were brought into the market economy by labour recruiters. From the earliest engagement of labour mandated by MacGregor's *Native Labour Ordinance* in 1892, until the end of Murray's tenure in 1940, the principal mode of indigenous involvement with 'the market' was by formal contract of indenture for work in plantations and mines. This was profoundly different from any informal, autonomous participation in market activity. Official efforts to encourage independent Papuan market participation were sporadic; bureaucratic energies were less directed towards that end than to maintaining native welfare under the rubric of 'preservation'. In practice, most effort was given to the 'pacification' of new populations, to the governance of the pacified, and to the regulation and inspection of indentured labour. Regulation was intended to minimize the negative consequences of the absence of able-bodied men from their villages. Murray had no intention of converting Papuans from their status as 'peasant proprietors' to that of a 'landless proletariat' – which he believed would occur if they accepted long-term indenture involving lengthy absences from the village (West 1968, 132). The term 'peasant proprietor' (used also by early German administrators in regard to the Tolai; Ch. 7) seems to suggest an unspoken Smithian assumption, implying a Papuan inclination to truck and barter if only inertia could be overcome.

On the other hand, as in GNG, Papuan administrators were aware of the implications of any growth of indigenous commercial agriculture for the supply of indentured labour, and they accepted that village welfare was competitive with maintaining the formal plantation workforce. Statements of both 'Anglo' and German administrators suggested a need to avoid over-recruitment, though in practice they differed in the emphasis given to welfare (generally more in Papua) and to 'veterinarian' concerns, in which principles applicable to the management of game parks were applied to village populations (Rowley 1965, 94). The contradiction inherent in drawing on villages to man plantations, while attempting to maintain their demographic and social viability, laid the indenture system – reliant on recruitment of unaccompanied male labour – open to the charge it was designed to subsidize plantation wage costs.

Cyril Belshaw was perhaps the first observer to point out that 'by far the greater part of the indentured labour sector … is subsidised … by the domestic village production of the labourers' dependents, and male kinsfolk who remain at home' (Belshaw 1957, 244). Charles Rowley would later build on this observation to illustrate the 'obsolescence' of the plantation economy and its negative implications for urban employment, and to argue the case for wage reform (Ch. 11). Again, in the 1970s, followers of contemporary French Marxism would interpret Belshaw's 'subsidy' in 'structuralist' terms. For them, the system was designed to preserve a 'traditional mode of production', thereby sustaining the exploitation of rural labour (Ch. 25).

Regulating Economic Activity into Existence: The 'Murray Policy'

Dirigisme in Papuan policy was intensified by fears of native depopulation. MacGregor's biographer noted his inclination, following Gordon in Fiji, to encourage indigenous commercial agriculture. It would be necessary to teach the Papuans boat building, fishing and how to 'trade on their own account'. He began a demonstration plantation, followed in 1894 by a regulation requiring certain groups to plant coconuts, for unless they were to become independent producers, they 'cannot exist long as a race' (cited in Joyce 1971, 197). The regulation did not specify whether plantings were to be done by individuals or groups, but in the event villages and clans were responsible for most production, with little voluntary planting (Crocombe 1964). Near the end of his term, faced with failure to build an economic base, MacGregor felt compelled to facilitate commercial planting by opening up land for white settlers. As he became more aware of the failure to persuade Papuans to independent production, he wrote despondently that they were not likely, on their own account, ever to 'add much to the exports of the colony' (Joyce 1971, 205).

Soon after the First World War, worldwide expansion of output in territories with lower cost structures than Papua's brought the commodities boom to an end. Murray no longer felt able to juggle the competing demands of his dual mandate, and began instead to renew attention to welfare – an objective central to what came to be known as the 'Murray policy' (West 1968, 143). This would involve establishing law and order in

Papua with a 'minimum of bloodshed' and assuring the 'paramountcy' of Papuan interests over those of Europeans in matters of 'land, labour and development' (West 2006, 113). Perhaps Murray thought it possible to dispel Papuan inertia by education and regulation, speeding the social-evolutionary process. In an attempted new start, he instituted measures in 1919 to stimulate village cash cropping. He was disappointed with the results of an agricultural system based on planters, and with their hostility, and was increasingly aware of how little Papuans themselves gained from participating in that system (Lewis 1996, 149). In any case, after the war European settlement was discouraged by labour shortages, low commodity prices and high shipping costs, so that 'indigenous agriculture was seen as the only hope' (Crocombe 1964, 4).

Murray's new measures proved even more dirigiste than those that had failed under MacGregor. A *Native Taxes Ordinance* in 1919 imposed a head tax on males. This was to be paid in cash, or remitted by delivering cash crops to government, or by working on 'native plantations'. The tax was not intended to force men onto European plantations, because it was also levied on indentured workers. Native plantations were to be established on land alienated by government from the villagers concerned. This initiative had no equivalent across the border; in GNG the indigenous population – not European enterprise or the Australian taxpayer – was targeted by colonial tax policy (Rowley 1958b, 180). A 'Native Education Fund' was created in Papua to receive the taxation proceeds, together with half the earnings of the new collective plantations (the other half to be paid to villagers fulfilling work obligations). Most plantings were of coconuts although some coffee and rice were trialled.

In Murray's ordinance (as also in MacGregor's regulation) there was no requirement for either individual or group production, but it appears again that most plantings were collective. Ron Crocombe suggested that many officials believed group operations to be more congenial for Papuans, and officials certainly found it easier to inspect group plantations than individual, dispersed blocks. Again, taking a position inconsistent with his description of Papuan subsistence agriculturalists as 'peasant proprietors', Murray decided that communal labour applied to communal land – something he regarded as part of Papuan customary life – was a method of production that could be harnessed for economic development. It could also provide a basis for levying taxes, as an element of that 'compulsion' he believed to be essential for native administration (West 1968, 232).

This new direction of agricultural policy led to collective production under a system in which incentives were small and only indirectly linked to effort. Compulsion was always needed to ensure planting, and even more so to secure harvesting, and there was no guarantee that copra would be marketed through approved channels – or even marketed at all. As a result, the record of production and payments to villagers was disappointing (Lewis 1996, 150). Attitudes engendered by memories of village plantations had long-lasting effects on Papuans' willingness to engage as independent producers. In the Northern Division (later part of the modern Northern or Oro Province; see Map 5.1) cash-crop plantings became so strongly identified with group enterprise that, after the Pacific War, agricultural officers found it difficult to encourage people to plant individually. Only then did some Orokaiva realize that 'cash crops could be grown by individuals' (Crocombe 1964, 30).

The Role of Traders

Despite the prevalence of a dependent psychology among many Papuans, some autonomous production of cash crops did occur during the interwar period. More spontaneous mechanisms – consistent with 'peasant proprietorship' – seem to have been at work in dealings between some village producers and small European planter-traders who supplemented their incomes by buying native copra. Although MacGregor's attempt to stimulate indigenous production met with little success, traders had been bartering for coconuts along the Papuan coast since before the protectorate. However, village producers with a secure base in subsistence agriculture demonstrated an elastic supply response to price fluctuations, often preferring to leave nuts ungathered when they deemed returns too low. Furthermore, as coastal village populations were small and dispersed, Europeans had little incentive to set up specialized trading, processing and distribution enterprises. Samarai, a small island off south-east Papua, was an exception as it enjoyed sufficient locational advantage to become a hub for traders and planters. But, unlike the Gazelle, Papua was difficult territory for traders.

After 1906, Murray had felt it necessary to show greater concern for European planters, even if it entailed de-emphasizing indigenous production. In a revealing comment in the Annual Report for 1905–6, Murray confessed that did he not have the staff to enforce the regulation of 1894 adequately, and that when it was enforced it had an unfortunate consequence. Increased incomes of growers '*attracted traders* whom he felt to be *a bad influence* on the Papuan people' (paraphrased by Crocombe [1964], 3, emphases added). This suggests Murray's failure to appreciate the potential of traders to stimulate economic activity (and, perhaps, his awareness that such activity was competitive with indentured employment). The traders he disapproved of were Europeans striving to become planters despite lacking sufficient capital. This was an identifiable category of small trader/

planters who supported themselves by trade while developing copra holdings (Lewis 1996, 25). They operated in a manner similar to the Chinese traders of New Guinea, buying copra from Papuans as a sideline, and supplying them with cheap consumer goods.

Such 'small men' traders became less representative of the industry after 1907 with the arrival of plantation companies, and relatively few ever managed to become fully independent of trading. Planting may have conferred prestige, but over the history of colonial Papua it was trade that offered enterprisers – whether large or small – a more secure living (Lewis 1996, 97). Among such men, struggling to survive after the war, many turned again to trading in 'native' copra to supplement meagre returns from their own plantings. Even during the 1930s, when many small company plantations were acquired by conglomerates, most of these independent operators survived, continuing to provide distributional services to village producers (ibid., 213). They proved more durable than the 'small men' of New Guinea, driven to the wall by debt and Chinese competition (Ch. 7).

This contrast points to the absence from Papua of any intermediate class of 'Asiatic' traders, and raises the question of how effective white traders proved as an alternative. Papua is represented here as an 'unlucky place', but natural resource endowment is not destiny. As Bauer asserted, active traders and transport improvements often act to alter 'the facts of geography' (Bauer and Yamey 1957, 44). Among Bauer's favourite themes were the indispensability of traders and the role of minority groups in trade, as evident from the late nineteenth century in West Africa and Malaya where they 'made' markets and extended their reach, opening new opportunities for indigenous peoples to produce and consume. No agricultural surplus was possible without trade, and through it people learnt how the market economy works, and then acquired the 'attitudes appropriate to it'. Traders 'promoted the *uncoerced* erosion of attitudes and customs incompatible with material progress' (Bauer 1984, 37, emphasis added). Trading proved to be 'a seedbed of entrepreneurial activities extending beyond trading itself'. This had certainly been the experience with Chinese enterprise around Rabaul.

In Papua, European specialist traders had found the pattern of small, dispersed coastal settlements unprofitable. But, as Rowley remarked, Chinese traders were prepared not only to live more simply but also to follow up on what, by European standards, were unpromising trading opportunities (Rowley 1958b, 79). That the absence from Papua of Chinese competitors may have assisted some European 'small men' to survive is of less import than the withholding from Papuans of the superior Chinese distributive services available to Melanesians in other places. Around Rabaul,

Chinese contributed to engaging native people in cash crop production and a diversified set of service activities (Ch. 8). Rowley's judgement was succinct: GNG without the Chinese would have been much more like Papua. But even accepting that Port Moresby and its hinterland was not a 'lucky place', one might invert his logic to say that, *with* the Chinese, Port Moresby might have looked rather more like Rabaul.

The volume and value of 'native' copra entering into private trade in Papua cannot be estimated with certainty, although Lewis (1996, 150, n29) suggested that the cash return to Papuans selling copra to white traders was higher than if selling it through government channels. Some of this copra came, informally, from Murray's village plantations, diverted (in a form of pushback) from official marketing channels (Miles 1956, 322). Other sources were plantings from MacGregor's period, and palms planted with the encouragement of traders. Any such unenumerated trade, conducted in breach of the ordinance (and subversive of its intent) is an instance of rural informal economic activity. It was one of the few kinds of Papuan informality likely to have occurred in Murray's time.

Lewis remarked on the absence of Papuan entrepreneurs, noting that no entrepreneurial class of traders, small businessmen or managers had arisen despite their propensity to engage in exchange with other Papuans (Lewis 1996, 293). This observation is based on a problematic assumption, that traditional modes of exchange should have predisposed Papuans to specialized market exchange. But the findings of Jim Allen (1984, 1985) on Papuan coastal trade as 'a basic mode of subsistence procurement' led him to deny that Hanuabadans, Mailu and other specialized traders engaged in 'the disposal of surplus production for profit' (Ch. 5). My account of the Tolai (Ch. 7) suggested that, while informal trading gave them an entry point to 'the market', they learnt to trade only as a secondary occupation. Like Papuans, Tolai also failed to produce a 'class of traders' – if, by that term, Lewis meant specialized traders divorced from direct participation in agriculture.

Traditional modes of human interaction often impose constraints on participation in the market economy, resulting in *hybrid* economic behaviour. Some degree of hybridity was the norm in much of Tolai economic life, and it was seen also in accounts of early Papuan interaction with the market economy. This, together with the absence of an 'Asiatic' intermediary class, the inhibitory policy and social regime created by MacGregor and Murray, and the handicaps implied by the idea of Papua as an 'unlucky' place, must all be factored into an explanation of the apparent dearth of Papuan entrepreneurialism. With emphasis on Port Moresby, Papua's 'central place', these matters will receive further attention below. But first we should consider Port Moresby itself.

Note

1. The protectorate, established in 1884, and the later crown possession, annexed in 1888, were both named British New Guinea. After Australian federation in 1901, arrangements were made for its transfer to Australian authority, a process completed in 1906 after which it was named the Australian Territory of Papua.

Chapter 10

The Idea of a Town in Anglo-Papua

Nigel Oram, historian of colonial Port Moresby, believed urban administrative decisions often as not derive simply from the way a decision maker conceptualizes *the town*. Such a person has an idea of the town in the 'Platonic sense', distinct from any notion gained by reasoned assessment of the factors at play (Oram 1976a, xii). He was referring to Plato's concept of 'the form of the good', a reality that is perceptible, but not intelligible, and from which are derived all other 'forms'. The 'idea' of a town, which serves to guide urban policy and bureaucratic action, springs from processes internal to the decision maker, 'the soul's activity within itself' (Seyffert 1894, 481). This is potent because, as Keith Hart noted, from the time of Plato idealist philosophers held that 'the general idea of something was more real than the thing itself' (Hart 2008, 12). Hart's 'general idea of something' corresponds with what Simon Blackburn called 'the general concepts making the framework in which we think of things'. In philosophy such general concepts 'are themselves made into the objects of study' (Simon Blackburn, cited in Pyke 1995). In what follows, the 'idea of the town' serves as the object of study.

Here I extend Oram's argument to suggest that in relatively homogeneous societies the 'soul' may be a collective social entity. This is not to say that Port Moresby's colonizing residents were of one mind in all matters. The existence of 'two moralities' (discussed in Chapter 9) certainly contradicted that notion. Still, it is reasonable to think that, in matters of urban environment and domestic arrangements, people of broadly similar background and experience would find comfort in the familiar, and in the exclusion of the unfamiliar and the unsettling. If so, early colonial Port Moresby probably generated such a consensus on the 'idea' of the town among its Anglo-Papuan residents. From such subjective processes emerges a conception of the 'form' of what is good in a town. This consensus defines a particular *urban* formality, requiring behaviour consistent with the maintenance of good urban 'form'. By simple opposition, informality is behaviour inconsistent with correct urban form. While this study is concerned with Hart's *market* informality, it also considers the additional perspective of Plato's *urban* 'form of the good', as both are relevant to a consideration of urban economic activity.

European residents of Port Moresby shared a broad consensus concerning the 'form of the good' in their town. In turn, this form was an important element in norms guiding actions of the town bureaucracy, and Papuans in the town had to become institutionalized to these norms. Here I will examine the elements of social consensus on the idea of the town in 'Port' (as its settler-residents called it). This will require an account of the bureaucratic activity – urban administration – conducted to achieve and maintain the prescribed urban form and to secure Papuan con*form*ity. It will be argued that bureaucratic action to achieve any *idea of the town* has implications for the possibility and character of urban informal economic activity, and that, in the case of 'Port', economic informality was very largely stifled by the particular 'colonial' idea of the town.

Port Moresby became the capital of a British protectorate proclaimed in 1884 and annexed as BNG in 1888 (see Map 5.1). Even earlier, Pacific Islander teachers of the London Missionary Society (LMS) had been posted in the 'great village', Hanuabada, very close to the site of the modern town.[1] The Reverend W.G. Lawes arrived later to establish an LMS station, influenced by Hanuabada's centrality to traditional trade routes, the value of Hanuabadan Motu as a lingua franca, and the belief it was a healthy place. Together with proximity to the nearest Australian telegraph station, these factors would later confirm Port Moresby as capital. None of the reasons for selecting Port Moresby related to its economic potential. MacGregor defended his frequent absences on patrol, saying that Port Moresby, either in terms of its indigenous people or its future development prospects, was 'comparatively unimportant' (cited in Joyce 1971, 128). The eastern town of Samarai would become larger and commercially more important.

A storekeeper set up in Hanuabada in 1880, and with Special Commissioner Scratchley's arrival in 1884 the three elements of colonization – cross, commerce and flag – were in place. A visitor in the following year recorded the few small houses of galvanized iron, in which the British Empire was represented by just seven people (Oram 1976a, 21). Even in

1904, the European population was only thirty-eight men and eighteen women (West 1968, 35) and the total white population of BNG was less than six hundred. Concentrations existed in the two towns (Samarai and Port Moresby), but otherwise people were scattered along the coasts 'in ones or twos' (Lewis 1996, 39). Even with the benefit of a plantation boom from 1906 and Australia's acceptance of responsibility for BNG (then renamed 'Papua'), the white population scarcely exceeded a thousand before the Great War. The indigenous population in the littoral was fewer than two hundred thousand, with the European population never more than fifteen hundred until just before the Pacific War (ibid., 9).

MacGregor commenced laying bureaucratic foundations, setting up a legal code and judicial system. While there is properly a distinction between the bureaucratic, judicial and legislative functions, 'multi-tasking' was unavoidable in a small government service. Often more than one of these functions was embodied in a single officer; in Murray's case, all three. From 1904, as chief judicial officer, he also served as a member of the executive and sat in the Papuan legislature, remaining to do so after his appointment as lieutenant-governor in 1907. He was able to secure greater coherence – according to his lights – in policy and administration, making a habit of yearly working visits to Australia, and imposing close personal control over the Papuan administration (West 1968, 121). This is not to say that Murray could have ruled by fiat; he was obliged to respond to popular concerns, some of which concerned the *idea* of the town.

A policy of segregating non-indigenous residential areas commenced early, under the protectorate. For appropriate urban 'form', a fence was erected around land reserved for European residential and commercial use. The white storekeeper was moved from the native village of Hanuabada to Badili, an area developed initially as a residential zone for South Sea Islanders and other non-European immigrants. In 1910, a native labour regulation allowed only domestic servants, for whom employers were obliged to supply 'sanitary' accommodation, to live in the town. An area at Badili was set aside for labour compounds to house other indigenous town workers (Oram 1976a, 33). An urban form comprising European town, traditional village, and dormitory suburb began to crystallize. A surveyor was appointed to lay out the town grid even before annexation and a framework of urban administration had emerged, based very largely on Australian models. The style was quite 'rational-legal' enough to satisfy any Weberian; Oram remarked that, for its European population, the administration of Port Moresby was as 'impersonal' and 'legalistic' as in any small Australian municipality (ibid., 44). Illustrating Hart's dictum that *form* is the rule – an idea of what ought to be universal in social life – metropolitan precedents were applied reflexively.

Papuans were not subject to the same ordinances, and their administrative regime was quite separate (Oram 1976a, 44). MacGregor had raised an armed constabulary in 1890, and a town guard was established. From 1899, *Native Regulations* affected all facets of Papuan life. Apart from controlling their access to the town, additional controls governed movement in order to protect public health and good order. After 1915 it was an offence for a Papuan to be found after dark on premises other than those of his employer, and further restrictions were designed to prevent gambling. After 9 PM, Papuan employees were bound to their quarters without written consent (ibid., 45–47). By such restrictions, Port Moresby's guardians sought to achieve their idea of the town in the unfamiliar setting of Papua.

The Australian census of 1921 showed 313 Europeans in Moresby town (Inglis 1974, 26). Indeed, in 'Port', 'Europeans *were* the town' and fashioned its institutions 'on the basis of their own whiteness' (ibid., 28, emphasis in original). Demographic change created demands for even more stringent regulation because, by 1933, the proportion of European females had increased from 33 to 45 per cent (ibid., 30). Amirah Inglis documented increasing anxiety in this small community, where agitation flared up periodically during the 1920s due to 'apprehension amounting to panic' over the supposed danger of sexual assault by Papuans on white women (ibid., 56). Anxiety also intensified because of opportunism on the part of Murray's enemies in the business community. In this new round of the contest between moralities, women became 'pawns' in an anti-Murray campaign (ibid., 39). Rather uncharacteristically, Murray 'succumbed' to pressure from residents (ibid., 88), assenting to the *White Women's Protection Ordinance* 1926, under which (despite no white woman ever having been raped) even the attempt was punishable by death.

Further, 'to his discredit Murray administered and extended a long list of discriminatory legislation' (Griffin, Nelson and Firth 1979, 30). Adding to restrictions under the *Native Regulations*, 'a Papuan . . . in a public place could not behave in a threatening, abusive or disrespectful manner towards any European, and he was not to beg or loiter'. No Papuan could wear clothes above the waist without permission; and outside the town, in a measure directed at plantation absconders, uncontracted Papuans were not permitted within five miles of Port Moresby or Samarai unless they could show the means to support themselves (ibid.). They could be 'rounded up' and sent back to work (Rowley 1965, 106). This increasingly onerous restriction occurred during the post-war period of economic depression. Morale was low in the beleaguered European community; to the somewhat down-at-heel residents of 'Port' it may have seemed that maintaining racial prestige was all the more essential in adversity. In 1930, a deputation put to Murray the urgency of teaching Papuans that Moresby was 'a European town', not 'a native playground'. He succeeded in persuading his petitioners that 'emasculation and public flogging' could not occur but yielded to approve 'stricter supervision' of Papuans in the town, while agreeing to a new fence for the European settlement (Inglis 1974, 107–9).

In such details Murray showed himself responsive to community perceptions of the *idea* of the town, while defusing and denying more extreme demands. This had not been the case in his most important test, the *White Women's Protection Ordinance*. Amirah Inglis attempted to explain why this 'thoughtful and benign administrator' had agreed to that measure. He accepted the legislation because he was not completely free of contemporary European assumptions concerning 'black sexuality and inferiority' and 'the importance of white prestige'. Consequently, he had accepted the ordinance under pressure from Port Moresby influentials, despite its adding to the 'burden of inferiority' and the already existing 'injustices' suffered by Papuans (ibid., 147).

In 1937, a Papuan, Louis Vangeke, returned from Madagascar as an ordained priest, giving the Catholic Murray pause for thought. In a passage that says much about Murray's attitude to the restrictive ordinances he had been induced to approve, and his disdain for many residents of 'the white man's town', James Griffin wrote how, '34-year-old Louis was "quite a presentable youth"', although some colonists 'were enraged that a Papuan spoke French, English and Latin'. Murray noted that, 'as drinking by "natives"... was banned', he ought not drink the communion wine; and that 'strictly speaking' he should celebrate Mass 'stripped to the waist'. He should also be 'subject to curfew' (Griffin 2012).

Perhaps irony was Murray's final defence, in a situation for which he shared responsibility while being aware of its inequities. In the town, segregation was social, residential and administrative, and race relations were 'paternalistic'. Discrimination manifested in a thicket of prohibitions – in the cinema, at the swimming baths, in stores and in the workplace (Oram 1976a, 59). These and other restrictions would remain in place until the late 1950s, when their repeal commenced. Perhaps as a harbinger of change, the clothing restriction was removed in 1939. In that same year, however, further change was stifled by new *Native Regulations* limiting visits to the town area for more than four days, without reasonable cause. This measure was additional to an existing *Vagrancy Ordinance* (Oram 1967, 36).

The *White Women's Protection Ordinance* and other discriminatory measures were elements in a collective Anglo-Papuan notion of the 'form of the good'. This (to recall Nigel Oram's invocation of Plato) was a product of 'the soul's activity within itself'. The ordinance was the most dramatic element in a body of regulation – much of it directly relevant to economic activity, and all of it *implicitly* so – designed to realize the 'idea of a town'.

Keith Hart (2013) has remarked on the contrast between pre-colonial cities in West Africa and the settler-created cities of southern Africa. The former retain vivid traditions of urban informality derived from their organic, unregulated origins, while the latter continue to reflect the regulatory cosseting that buttressed the original white settler *idea* of the town.

In the case of Port Moresby, settlers' fear of economic competition – quite explicit in the case made for excluding Chinese – was among the factors supporting such regulation. As for Papuan competition, the convenient notion they could never pose an economic challenge to the Australian workingman required exercising the selective blindness that refused to acknowledge the technical training and industrial achievements of the Kwato mission, in Milne Bay Province, south-eastern Papua (Abel 1969). In so prejudicial an environment, what Hart described as the 'institutional effort to organize society along formal lines' produced neither an intermediary class of entrepreneurial Papuans nor any significant informal economic activity. The preservation morality and an Anglo-Papuan idea of the town combined to produce what Charles Rowley (1965) called *obsolescence*. Explaining this outcome requires considering the working lives of Papuans in the interwar period, and how colonial policies retarded urbanism.

Note

1. 'Hanuabada' is the collective name for a tight cluster of villages of Western Motu and Koita peoples.

Chapter 11

Papuans in Town before the Pacific War

If this chapter and its predecessor give the impression of an extended commentary on the work of Nigel Oram, it is because of the magnitude of his contribution. It is measured in terms of historical and linguistic scholarship, and his grasp of administrative and town planning principles, all informed by a profoundly humane sensibility. That later scholars have so rich a corpus to inform newer speculations, including this attempt to refocus colonial history through the formality/informality duality, is a tribute to Oram's careful documentation. Understanding how Papuans related to the town in Murray's time requires examining two closely related themes. The first – a unifying thread running through Oram's work – was Hanuabada's centrality to traditional maritime trade routes along the southern Papuan coast. The other is the nature and significance of that trade. Any conjecture that traditional trade ought to have 'predisposed' Papuans to commercial exchange is untenable, while my account of the Tolai (Ch. 7) concluded that in the market economy introduced by German colonizers they learnt only to manage secondary modes of trade. That conclusion, supporting the idea of a Melanesian singularity in regard to specialization and exchange, will be shown here as holding with even greater force for the limited market engagement of Papuans in the early colonial period.

If traditional trade did not prepare Papuans for the commerce of Port Moresby, it did equip Papuans from other districts to live there. LMS missionaries regarded Port Moresby as an entrepôt, a strategically located place for trading and, hence, evangelizing (Oram 1976a, 14). Missionaries who learnt the Motu language were able to communicate east and west along the southern coast of Papua, while the government adopted a simplified 'trade' version of it, known as *Police Motu*, for administrative purposes. Hanuabadans had trading partnerships with men from the Gulf of Papua in the west, and from Hula, Aroma and other places in the east. As the town grew and formal employment opportunities opened up, such relationships would become crucial in permitting other Papuans to establish themselves there.

Located in a rain shadow, Hanuabada and other nearby Western Motu villages such as Vabukori were unsuitable for the village plantations encouraged by MacGregor and Murray. Nor did their men show any enthusiasm for indentured labour, instead continuing for a time to mount trading expeditions while gradually taking up formal jobs. Even there they were selective; averse to joining the police or acting as carriers, they were good ships' crew and domestic servants. As their formal educational standards rose they could become 'craftsmen, interpreters and clerks' (Oram 1976a, 55). Some few women worked as laundresses and domestic servants from the 1890s, while mission-educated women trained as nurses (ibid., 56). Until the Pacific War had ended, these were virtually the only occupations open to them.

As traditional landowners in the capital, Hanuabadans enjoyed privileged access to Western education and formal employment, enabling them to acquire a stock of 'human capital' during the interwar period. They would experience more rapid and sustained social change than any other Papuan community before the Pacific War, and in this they resembled people of the peri-urban Tolai village of Matupit. Hanuabada's inferior natural resources meant, however, that its people would become far more reliant on the formal colonial economy than the Matupi. The latter retained a base in subsistence throughout, finding informal, complementary sources of cash income which left them much less dependent on wages from formal employment (Ch. 7). By contrast Hanuabada became increasingly disconnected from subsistence, and its people proletarianized. In what seems a questionable bargain, they gave up fishing, trading and pottery making in order to become dependent on wage employment, which was mostly ill-paid and only semi-skilled.

Lawes prepared scriptural materials in the Motu language, and established an LMS school. In 1884, a hundred children enrolled at another such school, in Hula, could read and write (Griffin, Nelson and Firth 1979, 6), so that by 1941, many people in the Port Moresby area and further afield had reasonably competent English (Oram 1976a, 53). Formal education was left to the missions, and in 1940 some three thousand pupils sat for the examinations on which the government's school subsidies depended (Miles 1960, 9). Perhaps in consequence, Murray's attitude to Papuan capacities changed over time. After the First World War, he 'forsook his earlier views and began to see the Papuan as an independent producer, as a clerk, an artisan and a petty government official'. But influenced by the inescapable barrier of the colour bar, 'he could not see the Papuan as a businessman or a professional man'. Such attitudes may account for the colonial expectation that Papuans would advance themselves on a ladder of formal employment, rather than through self-employment or commercial trade. Western education would equip them for allotted roles in a hierarchical society (ibid., 4) and, indeed, records showed that many retirees in Port Moresby in the 1960s had been in regular employment from as early as the 1920s. Oram suggested that, by 1941, many or even most adult males aged below fifty had some experience of formal employment, while many younger men were in permanent employment. Their advancement, however, was limited; only the lowest ranks of commercial and official employment were open to them (Oram 1976a, 55–56).

Increasing dependence on formal employment brought with it changing consumption habits. The resident magistrate observed in 1919 that, as land under cultivation diminished and men sought urban jobs, family diets were largely restricted to tea and biscuits, and occasionally tinned meat or fish (cited in Oram 1976a, 57). Other needs for money arose, not only for imported consumer goods but also church levies, the native tax and council tax. Traditional labour-intensive activities, such as the collection of 'bush' materials for village housing, became increasingly onerous as time became money. In 1924, Hubert Murray lamented the erection of 'some dreadful structures' in Hanuabada with galvanized iron roofs and sides (ibid., 34). For the same reason, by 1927 the great annual feasts which had galvanized the communal energies of Hanuabadans were abandoned because of the competing demands of formal employment (ibid., 57).

Papuans coming into town from areas of Motu trade were able to communicate, and to call on traditional relationships for assistance. Some married into the villages – for example, men from the Gulf district living on Vabukori land from 1927 (Oram 1976a, 34). Perhaps responding to the decline of Motu voyaging, Gulf people began to sail to town with sago from the late 1920s (ibid., 57). During the First World War, the large traditional Hula trading canoes ceased to ply, but enterprising Hula families in smaller craft continued to visit Moresby for sago, exchanged for fish caught locally, as Motuans neglected their fishing grounds. Much later, after the Pacific War, Hula control of fishing off the town was virtually complete, and Hanuabadan fishing became simply recreational. Men from beyond the traditional trading regions were recruited as indentured labourers for wharves and public works. Others began to practise short-term circular migration to achieve specific goals. Paying head taxes and church dues motivated some, as casual jobs were available in the town for up to three months without indenture (Oram 1968a); however, they were then liable to be sent home because authorities (especially after the *White Women's Protection Ordinance*) policed regulations zealously. It was a source of satisfaction for officials to point to the almost complete absence of 'detribalized' Papuans in 'Port'.

Although the number of migrant workers living in or near Port Moresby was never more than five hundred in the interwar period (Oram 1976a, 38) and few had dependents in the town, they still had to be housed. Short-term visitors from coastal regions could beach canoes at friendly villages, and some permanent settlements originated from such episodes. Others acquired occupancy rights by marrying local women or relying on fictive kin relationships from traditional trade, while many were housed in labour compounds at Badili. That area was so insanitary that we learn from letters to the *Papuan Courier* in 1940 that migrant labourers often built their own quarters, 'unsightly humpies' put together from sheets of tin and corrugated iron, packing cases and timberyard waste (cited by Oram 1976a, 34). Some Hula who succeeded in remaining for extended periods built dwellings as 'permitted' occupants on traditional land, or as squatters on government land (Oram 1968b, 3). These changes suggest the beginnings of Papuan informal investment in urban housing, occurring as pushback against the bureaucratically prescribed urban 'form'. Whether on customary land or in settlements of migration, such informal action challenged the colonial 'idea of the town'. After the Pacific War it would transform the physical fabric of Port Moresby.

Intimations of an Urban Informal Economy

In much of the developing world, incremental investments in non-traditional housing are among the most important elements of an urban informal economy. Such investments, involving the use of industrial materials and introduced tools, were emerging in interwar Port Moresby. There is no evidence of the extent to which these represented monetized (i.e. *informal*) transactions, rather than customary self-help arrangements combining the utilitarian and the traditional. More generally, evidence of economic informality is quite limited in the historical record. For instance, visits by Gulf district voyagers bringing sago to the urban villages, and by Hula families to obtain sago, probably amounted to traditional utilitarian barter (a modernized version of Allen's 'subsistence trading' [Ch. 5] rather than monetized informal transactions). On the other hand, circular migration to earn cash for head tax and other obligations by selling fish in the town (done by those frontrunners of informality, the Hula) *did* represent incipient informal economic activity.

Evidence is abundant of the failure of Motu people to produce any significant food surplus for sale in the town, whether to Europeans or to labourers in the Badili compounds. In any case, white settlers had no interest in Papuan staple foods such as sago or yams; unless they were fortunate enough to 'employ a "shooting boy" who brought in fresh wallaby' (Inglis 1974, 36) they relied largely on tinned food delivered by boat from Australia every five weeks. Nor did demand from Europeans stimulate Hanuabadans to commercial fishing, as they were abandoning subsistence fishing. In the early 1920s the Australian *Navigation Act* (Ch. 7) disrupted shipping to the degree that supplies of 'European' foods were interrupted. Employers unable to feed their indentured workforces threatened to force a resolution by despatching labourers to the capital to be fed by the government (Oram 1976a, 29). From this we can assume that not only were plantation labourers customarily fed imported rice and bully beef but that there was no surplus production of, or trade in, Papuan staples. It is telling that only after 1953, when Koke (now 'Koki') market was established near Badili (Map 15.1), did the town gain a focal point for informal fresh food marketing.

Oram looked for evidence of 'market' economic activity in the interwar period, concluding that it was quite uncommon for Papuans to engage in personal money-making activities. Among the few positive examples was the cultivation-for-sale of exotic vegetables (including tomatoes and pumpkins) by Koita agriculturalists, neighbours of the Hanuabadans. As mentioned above, the latter could not now be induced to provide fish for the town; this was left to people who appear in this narrative as precocious informalists – seaborne visitors from Hula – to hawk catches from door to door. In another, isolated instance, a technically trained and well-paid Motuan named Oala Dagora took the initiative to leave his formal job and buy a lorry, leading Murray to comment in an annual report that perhaps Papuans were overreaching in their haste to advance. In 1929, the people of Hanuabada and Tatana owned cutters in which they shipped sago from the Gulf, and Vagi Rei of Vabukori owned a sailing boat for trading kerosene with Gulf people. Rather exceptionally, he put money in the bank, enabling his son to build up a trade store (ibid., 56).

As suggested above, it is not clear if the efforts to obtain sago from the Gulf using modern vessels showed any intention to then retail sago commercially. More likely, the Motu men concerned were still motivated by a desire to achieve prestige by reviving or sustaining traditional Maussian feasting. At best, these were hybrid transactions rather than 'market' dealings. Murray's negative reaction to Dagora's entrepreneurial gamble hardly suggests official encouragement. Rather, it recalls the mindset leading him to discourage private traders from dealing with village copra growers. Finally, it is telling that it was visitors from Hula rather than Motu residents who hawked fish around town and on the beach near Badili. This is not to deny the truth of other instances of informal activity by local villagers mentioned by Oram, but the record is negligible compared with the situation in contemporary Rabaul.

An 'Obsolescent' Economy and Society

The Second World War came to the island of New Guinea in 1942, with the Japanese occupying Rabaul in January and bombing Port Moresby from February. Preparation for hostilities had commenced earlier in the Papuan capital with some build-up of the white population and in formal indigenous employment, altering the complexion of Hubert Murray's town. His tenure as lieutenant-governor had ended two years before, in its thirty-third year. Maintaining his habits of restless energy, Murray died in harness at Samarai, en route to inspections in the Trobriand Islands. Reflecting on the condition of Papua and its capital at the end of this long career, an expression used by Charles Rowley in *The New Guinea Villager* is revealing. He employed the term 'obsolescence' to describe the unified Territory of Papua and New Guinea after the Pacific War. It signified a dysfunctional state, unsustainable in social and economic terms, and marked for change. But this was true even before the war, and more particularly so in Papua where the condition was acute. In what follows, what Rowley meant by the expression 'social and economic obsolescence', and how this situation manifested in pre-war Papua and its capital, will be discussed.

Historians such as West and Joyce, respectively the biographers of Murray and MacGregor, had remarkably little to say about the town these men created. West, during whose period Port Moresby took a more definitive shape, was perhaps guilty of the same selective vision he ascribed to Murray when he remarked that the latter's concern for the frontiers of government distracted him from the needs of those Papuans with a relatively long experience of European administration, and who were 'ready for innovation'. But Murray preferred 'pioneering' to 'routine' (West 1968, 275). If so, it helps to explain Murray's austerity in regard to furnishing the town as a place for living, rather than simply an administrative centre and port. He was notorious for spending more on the wharves than on urban amenity and 'Port' was the subject of invidious comparisons with the altogether grander town of Rabaul. If West rather neglected Port Moresby in his account of Murray it was because Murray himself thought little of it. He found it 'trying' and its society 'maddening', although the office of lieutenant-governor made it all worthwhile (ibid., 121).

It was left to Nigel Oram to take Port Moresby seriously. For him, in 1942 the formal town was Australian in both appearance and character. Its residents almost exclusively European, they enjoyed comforts comparable to those of a similarly sized Australian town. As to Papuans, other than in daylight hours when their sole purpose was to perform their allotted work, they were excluded from the formal town (Oram 1976a, 41). In Port Moresby and its villages and compounds there were some four hundred Europeans and between three and four thousand Papuans (no more than five hundred from elsewhere in the territory).

There were a small number of Asians and mixed-race people, including just four Chinese men (Oram 1976a, 59), and a few Malays, Filipinos and South Sea Islanders, all mostly resident in Badili. Such non-white immigrants occupied an intermediate social space, better paid than Papuans and filling mid-rank public service jobs – 'clerks, headmen and mechanics' – regarded as subordinate by Europeans. They differed markedly from that other intermediate group, the Rabaul Chinese, in that they were not in general entrepreneurial. There is no evidence of their engagement in informal economic activity, nor of the moonlighting so common among the Rabaul Chinese. Moreover, they were a numerically small cadre with little group consciousness, lacking political voice and with little social influence (ibid., 38).

Papuans in and around the town were still regarded as inferiors, and were often treated by Europeans in 'humiliating' ways. Oram claimed that their acceptance of this was induced by limited aspiration and the Christian missions (influential in inculcating notions of a present 'time of light', which had succeeded a 'time of darkness'). A still undeveloped consciousness of racial discrimination repressed awareness of their objective situation, and they remained subject to 'smothering paternalism', an influence unlikely to encourage entrepreneurial behaviour. Passive and dependent, they were left unprepared for the rapid changes about to overwhelm colonial Papua (Oram 1976a, 61). Such change commenced with the Japanese advance to within thirty miles of Port Moresby, and the Allied response in which Papuans were caught up willy-nilly. Colonial paternalism was suggested by Crocombe's anecdote (Ch. 9) concerning the failure of Northern Division villagers – even after the Pacific War – to grasp that they could grow crops individually. Such a situation diminished Papuan capacity, whether for independent, informal market engagement or even for formal employment. The final chapter of the Murray saga, and the role played in it by Hubert's nephew Leonard Murray, is richly suggestive of this bureaucratic culture. A long-serving member of Hubert's executive, and committed to the 'Murray policy', Leonard was appointed administrator in 1940. He served for a short period marked by disorganization, and friction with the commandant of Australian forces. Leonard Murray was accused of having abandoned Papuans on the eve of the Japanese invasion by withdrawing staff from rural administrative posts (Nelson 2000).

Appearing before a post-war Commission of Inquiry, Leonard defended this decision, claiming – in a revealing passage cited by Oram – that it was central to native policy to defend and maintain the rights of villagers. There were 'no detribalized natives dependent on the white man to live', as found in other colonies. In any crisis Papuans absent from their villages could 'return to them and resume their village life' (cited in Oram 1968a, 69). Oram condemned this statement as an 'epitaph' for Leonard Murray and the Murray regime. Murray was satisfied that the departure of the colonial regime would not have caused much harm to the Papuan people (ibid., 68). Alternatively, we might regard it as his admitting to an official policy of retarding urbanism in favour of the 'preservationist' orthodoxy.

Obsolescence and Retarded Urbanism

Retarded urbanism was a corollary of Rowley's 'obsolescence', achieved by braking normal processes of family formation and economic diversification in towns. In Papua this situation originated in the earliest colonial period, and by the 1930s a fully formed bureaucratic framework existed for discouraging, even repressing, urban development. While elements of such obsolescence were also present in Rabaul, its hinterland economy was more robust and indigenous agricultural innovation was occurring. Such influences lent greater vigour to the town (Ch. 7). Tolai were active in independent cash-crop production and participating in a thriving set of rural–urban economic relationships – activities with little counterpart in the Port Moresby hinterland.

Rowley saw urban and rural problems as two sides of the coin. Post-war PNG was obsolescent in comparison with other decolonizing states because so small a proportion of its population was committed to formal employment. In rural areas, most men who accepted employment persevered for only a single term of engagement. Their experience of plantation management and the rewards received were not encouraging – typical of an immature industry and suggesting that, in the early post-war period, PNG plantations were 'among the most obsolescent in the world' (Rowley 1965, 114). The system was inefficient, and plantations were sustained by the implicit subsidy they extracted from the villages supplying their labour (a subsidy also acting to depress urban wages). In remarks describing the plantation sector of the 1950s, but equally applicable to pre-war Papua, Rowley asserted that the high degree of dependence on indentured migrant labour, permitted by Australian authorities, had social and economic consequences. The recruitment of 'unsophisticated primitives' from remote locations became necessary because local villagers rejected such employment. Employers were forced to accept, as the norm, low levels of labour efficiency while themselves demonstrating low standards of management. Damage also resulted from the circumstance that the rewards of such work – wages and other compensation, and services provided by employers – were set at levels appropriate to the *single* rural worker. This was based on the convenient fiction that the village was the worker's real source of support (Rowley 1958a, 541).

Societal, as distinct from economic, obsolescence was evident from the fact that, in a very high proportion of cases, labourers recruited from villages gained only the most 'transient' knowledge of towns, and acquired such worldly knowledge as they had from 'the brotherhood of the plantation labour lines' (Rowley 1960, 1). This situation, exacerbated by policies to repatriate the unemployed from town and repel independent migration to it, was also unsustainable. People could not be denied indefinitely the exposure to ideas, monetization, movement, communications, formal education and literacy, the things that challenge traditional beliefs and focus attention on a wider world, which Rowley (1965, 196) saw as intrinsic to urbanism.

Even more fundamentally, developing the basic elements of a modern community depends on achieving efficiency and maintaining stability in wage employment (Rowley 1965, 111). But efficiency also demands a greater degree of wage equity, and this was not secured in towns where wages, as in rural areas, were based on the needs of the single man. To achieve stability of urban employment requires a family wage, placing employers in a difficult position. On the one hand, it is insupportable not to pay a 'living wage' in a town where essentials cost the same for white and black. On the other hand, wages must reflect the productivity of labour, and increasing productivity requires attitudes very much opposed to those of traditional life. It also requires higher standards of education and skill, better health, and reform of the 'authoritarian management' still found in both urban and rural workplaces (ibid., 199–200). These deficiencies, underlying both the obsolescence of industrial organization and the retarded urbanism of Port Moresby, were already well in place by the end of the Murray era.

Social obsolescence was evident in a wage structure operating to inhibit 'normal family life' in towns, with negative impacts on quality of life for all residents. Along with discouraging urban family formation, it led to circular migration, threatening the stability of both urban and rural populations. Hanuabadans, their lands progressively enclosed within the town, were in a different category. They experienced the 'full impact' of urbanization by committing to wage employment while losing the subsistence production that subsidized indigenous employment in 'obsolescent' Port Moresby. The convention that geared wages to the needs of single men had 'especially deleterious effects' in villages such as Hanuabada (ibid., 197). Hanuabadans were acquiring some characteristics of the *detribalized native*, whose presence in Port Moresby Leonard Murray had been so anxious to deny. The Matupi in Rabaul were better off because they maintained subsistence agriculture well into the post-war period. They supplemented it with informal economic activities, whereas van Leur's 'secondary' trading was notably lacking in Moresby.

The failure of Tolai and Chinese in Rabaul to conform with social arrangements flowing from Dernburgian orthodoxy, and to accept the economic roles it assigned them, resulted in informal economic behaviour. By contrast, Papuans in and around Port Moresby in the interwar period very largely did accept the orthodoxy implicit in the 'Anglo-Papuan' idea of the town, and they conformed with the economic and social behaviours it required. Normal processes of urbanism were inhibited, and autonomous Papuan enterprise, if not actively suppressed, could scarcely flower in the highly regulated town environment. As mentioned, there was some informal marketing of agricultural produce and fish among Port Moresby villagers, while others took tentative steps towards service activities. But if there was little scope in the town for informal activity, neither was there the open unemployment that might have driven some Papuans to resort to it. This was because urban residence was controlled to exclude 'incomers' without formal means of livelihood.

As we have seen, many men from urban villages had significant experience of formal wage employment from the interwar period, while some others continued to engage in traditional subsistence. The balance between these options altered over time. As wage employment became more important, so subsistence declined. However, traditional sharing within and between families still required wage earners to support unaccustomed numbers of people amid growing deprivation. In rural areas, Papuan market economic activity received only fitful encouragement, under circumstances in which official policy favoured communal activity over individual initiative. Further, for 'unlucky place' reasons – having to do with the unpromising character of the capital's immediate hinterland and the inadequacy of investment to link it with more distant regions – interwar Papua failed to develop any vigorous system of rural–urban economic linkages such as characterized the Gazelle region. The mercantilist ideology prevailing in New Guinea was both more compelling and more coherent than the preservationist orthodoxy guiding policy in Murray's Papua. It is tempting to suggest that this explains the spirited pushback against bureaucratic regulation observable on the Gazelle, as Tolai reached for the economic opportunities available. By contrast, in Papua the native people appear to have been relatively passive in the face of the 'smothering paternalism' of colonial bureaucracy.

This is not to suggest that pushback against bureaucratic regulation was completely absent from Papua in the interwar period. A major exception was the willingness of newcomers to the capital to invest in informal housing, in face of official efforts at control. Among 'pacified' rural populations, resistance took a number of forms, including reluctance by some to 'sign on' for formal indenture and the unwillingness of many to re-engage. Among those accepting contracts, pushback took the form of friction between labourer and overseer, and of desertions. These are scarcely dramatic instances but, although conscious opposition to the plantation regime was uncommon, petty thefts and erratic conduct signalled an underlying malaise, and occurred when Papuans felt sufficiently provoked to assert 'their dignity as men' (Lewis 1996, 268).

Again, some rural villagers sold copra to private traders, rather than through prescribed channels. Few seem to have been as enterprising as those from Hula who, lacking their own coconut palms, obtained nuts through traditional barter, made copra and then resold it to traders for cash. Non-conformity was seen also in the failure of some individuals to return home after indenture. This led to their long-term disassociation from village society, an outcome authorities were anxious to avoid. Some few drifted to urban areas and managed to escape repatriation, while others found their way to mining camps. Independent 'artisanal' gold mining, conducted by groups of former indentured mine-labourers, was another rare instance of rural informal economic activity in the interwar period.

The obsolescence of Papuan plantation economy was due to poor management and a labour system typified by what Rowley (1958a, 541) had called the 'norm' of low standards of labour efficiency. Plantations relied on what Cyril Belshaw (1957) recognized as an implicit subsidy, paid to them by the rural village sector (Ch. 9). This situation had its counterpart in the obsolescence of Port Moresby society, where the regulatory framework and the consequences of racial discrimination, together with a wage structure influenced by rural levels of remuneration and based on the needs of the single male, prevented the small urban migrant community from developing a normal population structure. In terms of their use of Papuan labour, both urban and rural economies were caught in a low-wage, low-productivity trap.

Papuan urban workers were disadvantaged by the regulatory environment; the consequence, intended or not, was a repression of the informal provision of marketed goods and services. Such 'wage-goods' were commodities of potentially great significance for low-paid urban workers. Although Rowley's assertion of obsolescence related to the 1950s, I have chosen to 'back-project' this situation to the 1930s, making the case that not only was the condition already present before the Pacific War but that Port Moresby was in a worse state than Rabaul. Rural–urban linkages on the Gazelle enabled urban workers to enjoy the relatively low-cost wage-goods found in the Bung, the Rabaul town market, which had no counterpart in interwar Port Moresby. Furthermore, innovation was occurring in indigenous cash cropping in the Gazelle hinterland, raising the cash incomes of rural dwellers and permitting the more efficient provision of produce for urban consumers. However, in both territories at that time, the absence of efficiency and stability in formal wage employment prevented the emergence of what Rowley called 'the basic requirements of a modern community'. A substantially higher incidence of economic informality around Rabaul was evidence of its greater progress towards participation in the market economy than had proved possible in Murray's Papua, while Rabaul demonstrated a more vigorous urbanism than its 'Anglo-Papuan' rival.

Chapter 12

Hidden Valleys

A New White Highlands?

Informality challenges bureaucracy by failing to con*form*. The metaphor of pushback is employed in this study as shorthand for such non-conformity – *kicking against the pricks* – as the King James Version has it. Unfortunately for the bureaucratic state and its administrators, Damascene conversions were relatively uncommon among colonized populations; their propensity for informal action was not only persistent but had an almost microbial capacity for mutation when challenged. That propensity was illustrated by a highland population in and around the Goroka Valley, located in the Mandated Territory of New Guinea (and now in the Eastern Highlands Province of PNG; Map 12.1). These 'Gorokans' were a distinct element of the greater highland population, whose traditional trade patterns were described by Ian Hughes (Ch. 5). To complete the narrative in Part II of this study requires an account of their incorporation into the Mandated Territory. This chapter describes the earliest stages in the introduction of Gorokans to a market economy, commencing their transition from subsistence.

When first contacted during the late 1920s by European gold-seekers and missionaries, highlanders had very little knowledge of the outside world and no system of monetized exchange, but by independence in 1975 Gorokans had become active participants in the international coffee trade. This experience involved great change in their modes of livelihood and social organization. The ensuing disruption of their traditional lives and the necessity to adjust led many to cope by engaging in economic informality, while also displaying hybridity in their economic activities. As

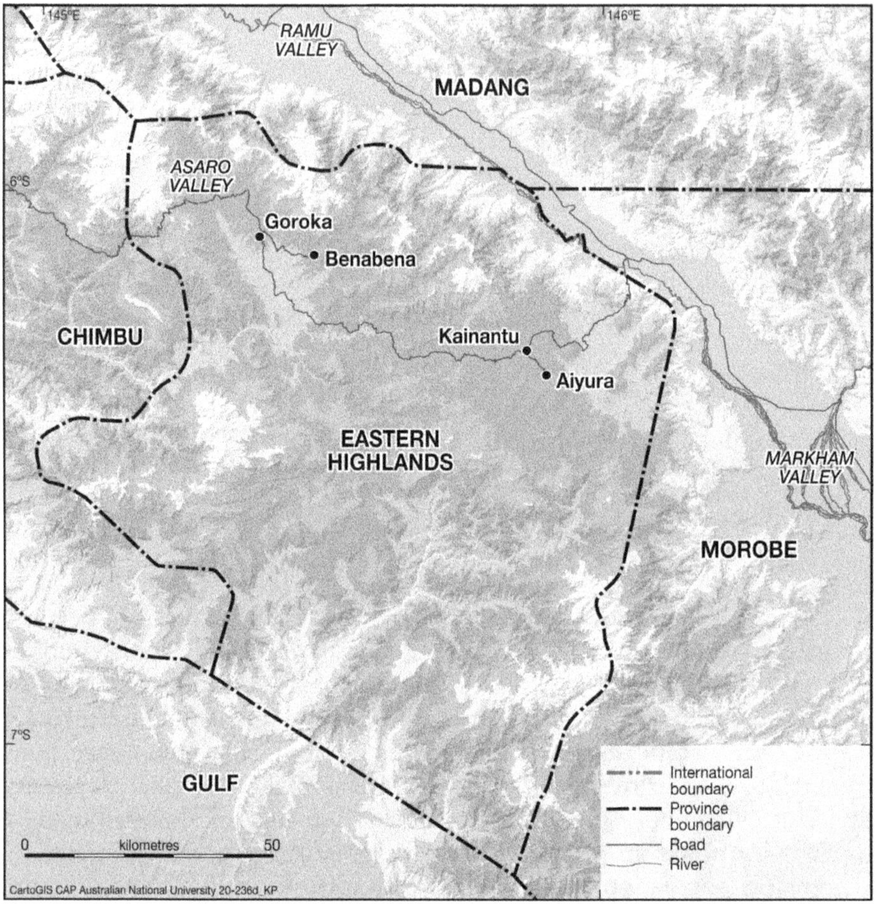

Map 12.1. Goroka and the Eastern Highlands. Permission granted for reproduction of this map by CartoGIS Services, Digital Scholarship, Scholarly Information Services, The Australian National University.

previously explained (Ch. 1), the informality construct cannot be applied to traditional forms of exchange such as occurred in pre-contact Goroka. Informality became salient only with the commencement of market exchange, with the introduction of bureaucratic regulation, and with efforts by traditional subsistence agriculturalists to accommodate themselves to the modalities of markets. Such accommodation normally throws up economic informality, as indigenous people grapple with unfamiliar 'market' norms. It also induces hybrid behaviour, in situations where introduced market economic dealings sit uncomfortably alongside traditional norms, with one apt to compromise the other.

The Colonial Intrusion, 1930–1945

This introduction to early colonial Goroka deals briefly with the 'discovery' by Europeans of the previously unknown central Highlands populations of the island of New Guinea. For most of the interwar period the outside world regarded the region as a void because overstretched colonial budgets and administrators' continuing preoccupation with coastal populations had combined to delay exploration of the interior. As late as 1927, when commercial aviation became established on the goldfields of Wau and Bulolo at the eastern end of the central cordillera (Map 0.1), its capacity for overflight still fell short of the altitude and range necessary to probe the Highlands. Although aircraft would later come to play an essential role in opening up the region, it was left to men patrolling on foot to make the initial, stunning discoveries. An account by Francis West conveys these first impressions, inspiring comparisons with British settlement in the highlands of Kenya. Administrators on the New Guinea coasts and islands had believed the interior to be 'wholly mountainous and uninhabited'. But in the early 1930s, having previously been 'shut off from the coast by high mountain ranges, great grass valleys were discovered . . . green, temperate and fertile'. In these valleys was found a 'concentration of native people' greater than anywhere else in the Mandated Territory or in Papua. The effect of this discovery was electrifying; this 'wonderland', so 'suitable for European settlement', evoked enthusiasm for '*a new white highlands*' which would become the premier region of New Guinea (West 1956, 305, emphasis added).

Highlanders themselves were not totally unaware of a larger world, for among the valuables that changed hands in their elaborate ceremonial exchanges were shell ornaments sourced from the coasts. These were obtained through chains of transactions in the system described by Hughes as 'interlocking and overlapping', and consisting of a myriad of personal trading networks. In the closely settled Highland regions, however, such traders were seldom able to travel more than 'eight to ten miles' from home – and then only in heavily armed parties. Cordillera dwellers were dependent upon poorer folk in Highland fringe communities who acted as intermediaries for utilitarian goods and ceremonial valuables found in the lowland forests and coastal regions and seas. Highlanders received these from adjacent trade partners without any knowledge of the environments from which they originated, or the people who produced them (Hughes 1977).

If during the 1920s some few missionaries had been aware of, while officials suspected, the existence of a previously unknown 'Tibet' in the mountains, both groups had their own reasons for not publicising the fact.

In the event European missionaries and gold-seekers preceded officials into the fringes of the region before the end of the 1920s. Then, in 1933, a seven-month patrol, the first east–west traverse through the central Highlands, was made by an official party led by District Officer Taylor, and including the brothers Mick and Dan Leahy, civilian gold prospectors. They proceeded from 'Upper Ramu' (later Kainantu) at the head of the Ramu Valley, passing through what is now known as the Goroka Valley, and as far west as present-day Mount Hagen before retracing their steps. In the process, the party encountered population groups thought likely to exceed half a million people (Downs 1980, 175–76). Downs commented wryly that the numbers of people for whom the Mandated Government was responsible had doubled almost overnight.

Violence occurring during the subsequent rush into the interior by miners and missionaries caused the government to declare the area 'uncontrolled' in 1936. After this, only Taylor and other government officers, Leahy family members (including a third brother, Jim) and some missionaries were permitted to remain, while 'pacification' of the local people proceeded.

During the Pacific War from 1941, administration activity was confined largely to levying labour for infrastructure works and patrolling around the established government posts, Kainantu and Benabena. The latter was near modern Goroka town, where the construction of a wartime airstrip would establish the settlement's regional primacy. Despite episodes of Japanese bombing, the posting of some US and Australian troops to the district, outbreaks of introduced disease requiring attention from medical patrols, and some agricultural innovation, the area remained comparatively undisturbed. One should not think of pre-contact Highland societies as static, however. The evidence suggests social and psychic changes of a particularly significant, non-marginal character occurring from the early 1930s (Hughes 1978; Strathern 1979). These changes were the result of new, external forces affecting indigenous social structures and exchange patterns. Such change continued throughout the war and into the post-war period, diffusing areally with the spread of colonial influence. The forces impelling change included two almost simultaneous and interacting social disruptions, which stemmed from European contact. These were the introduction of steel tools and the importation of unprecedentedly large quantities of the marine shells that had served as media of exchange in traditional Highlands trade, and as valuables in ceremonial exchange.

Salisbury (1962) showed how the eclipse of stone axes by steel drastically reduced the time required for Highland men to make their normal contribution to subsistence production. Their initial response was to spend much of this extra 'leisure' engaged in warfare. As pacification proceeded, their energies were diverted to an 'efflorescence' of traditional (i.e. Maussian) exchange – contesting for prestige and political influence through feasting and the ceremonial distribution of wealth in pigs, shell and other valuables. Women, by contrast, did not benefit greatly from the introduction of steel. Instead, they suffered escalating demands for labour to make gardens and raise pigs, in order to meet the requirements of burgeoning ceremony conducted by men. Hughes and Strathern documented the widespread occurrence of these changes throughout the Highlands, amplified by a second disruption – an increased availability of shell valuables. This occurred as soon as the European intruders understood how much highlanders prized the comparatively few shells they had been able to acquire through traditional exchange.

Grasping the opportunity, government officers, missionaries, miners and traders alike began to import shell to trade for the labour and food supplies necessary to establish themselves in the region. At least in the beginning, small quantities of shell of trivial cost on the coast could buy goods and services of much greater value to Europeans. In the Eastern Highlands, men could be found to work for a month building airstrips if paid a single egg-white cowrie shell (brought from the coast at the cost of 'a shilling plus airfreight'). A Catholic mission was constructed with 'thousands' of labourers for a few small cowrie shells a day, and the first specimens of large 'green-snail' shells could be traded for pigs at the rate of 'one for one' (Hughes 1978, 311–12). In quite a short time, the shell currency (which Hughes called 'the coin of the traditional realm') was debauched as the quantity in circulation increased, courtesy of airlifts from the coasts bearing quasi-industrial volumes of shell.

Government dealings in shell continued through the war years to finance the labour requirements for maintaining administrative control and building infrastructure, especially airstrips. Substantial imports resumed after the cessation of hostilities, as the demand for shell, especially among more recently pacified groups, continued into the 1960s. Because of the areal diffusion process, 'sophisticates' closer to the centres of European activity were able to benefit from arbitrage, in exchanges with country cousins unaware of changing relative values caused by shell 'inflation'. Smart operators grew rich from this 'shell bubble', and local balances of political and economic power shifted. In the judgement of Ian Hughes, social inequality had always existed in the region because traditional resources were 'discontinuous' in their geographic distribution, and because of other 'economic and political factors'. But what had been 'a rough balance of mutual dependence' among neighbouring groups now gave way to dependence on a 'new elite' (Hughes 1978, 318).

Efflorescence of exchange revealed the capacity of many Highland productive systems to generate substantial surpluses of vegetable foods and pig meat, though it also revealed the limits to such 'affluence' – in particular, the constraint on production posed by demands on the labour of women. Traditional trade flows were interrupted and re-patterned, with (as suggested by Hughes) complex economic and political consequences. The emergence of Hughes's 'new elites' was associated with what Salisbury (Ch. 2) called 'political consolidation' – the forging of larger political groupings and the ascension of leaders with greater power and influence. Among the causes of such consolidation were flows of women and pigs to groups advantaged by access to the new supplies of shell, causing the political and economic decline of less advantaged groups. In turn, the prominence of new leaders often commended them to colonial authorities as interlocuters and village office-holders, further entrenching their elite status. Thus, even in this pre-capitalist period before the introduction of market exchange, inequalities in status and traditional wealth seem to have increased.

The account of Goroka's induction into market economy will continue in Part III of this study. This includes a series of chapters concerned with the period following the Pacific War, and dealing in turn with Port Moresby (ch. 15–16), Rabaul (ch. 17–18) and Goroka (ch. 20–23). But first it will be useful to consider the ideological change represented by the early post-war adoption of the idea of 'economic development' in the Western capitalist world, and its application in what came to be known as 'underdeveloped' or 'developing' countries, PNG among them. As in other territories affected by the conflict, an incoming Australian administration was obliged to face severe problems of reconstruction and rehabilitation in preparation for the task of development, while the economy and society of the territory to be 'developed' were, in important respects, in the condition described by Charles Rowley (Ch. 11) as 'obsolescent'.

Part III

Informality in the Era of Economic Development

Chapter 13

Economic Development

Ideology and Apologetics

A changed world order made restoring the old colonial regimes impossible after the Pacific War. In the south-west Pacific, Japanese invasions of New Guinea and Papua had terminated their civil governments and precipitated a unified Australian military administration. This paved the way for a combined political entity to emerge. As the former German part remained subject to international scrutiny under a League of Nations mandate, this would entail greater external attention focused on the whole. These events occurred in the context of broader change after the Second World War, during what Keith Hart called the age of 'social democracy, Stalinism and developmental states'. It was the period when 'European empires were dismantled ... a new world order was inaugurated ... implementing the accords of Bretton Woods; the United Nations was formed and "development" – a post-colonial compact between rich and poor nations' – achieved ideological status among Western nations and decolonizing states (Hart 2015). Guided by this ideology of 'economic development', a term 'rarely used before the 1940s' (Meier 1984), a new orthodoxy in the conduct of international economic policy was asserted.

The emerging discipline of development economics was 'at once among the oldest and newest branches of economics' (Meier 1984). Originating in the eighteenth century with Adam Smith's *Wealth of Nations*, this agenda had suffered a long eclipse from the second half of the nineteenth century, during which the neoclassical 'marginalist revolution' caused economists' attention to turn primarily to issues of allocation. In the post-war period, however, 'development' acquired a new cogency for capitalist societies. This was certainly the case in Australia, where a social democratic government influenced by wartime events in PNG and the heady experience of participating in the creation of the UN system, 'signed on' very early to the development ideology.

The implications of this new dispensation and its discontinuity with earlier experience were suggested by Bill Stanner. In its previous colonial history, PNG had been merely 'commercialized', not 'developed'. Government investment on any significant scale to create social or economic capital was essentially a post-war phenomenon. Past practice had been for private capital to exploit the best resources selectively, while beyond the centres of investment the economy was still almost 'wholly primitive' (Stanner 1953, 386). When commercialization was replaced by aspirations for development, this had implications for a broader indigenous participation in the monetized economy, as well as signalling a greater role for government in economic affairs.

The Japanese advance on Port Moresby had drawn Australian eyes to the region. The anthropologist and scholar of colonial administration, Lucy Mair, remarked that 'the attention which was attracted . . . prompted more constructive thinking on native development than had ever been given to it in Australia before' (Mair 1948, 17). A Directorate of Research and Civil Affairs (DORCA) operating within the Australian military contributed to this ferment. Reporting directly to Blamey, the Australian commander-in-chief, and through him to E.J. (Eddie) Ward, the minister for external territories, DORCA studied issues including the impact of the war on native communities, native education and agricultural potential. It produced a body of thought with implications for a peacetime development agenda. Most immediately influential was a 'Report on Native Labour' by Ian Hogbin (Pybus 1999, 277, n5), who had been appalled by the wartime military administration's inhumane treatment of indentured (effectively, conscript) indigenous labourers (ibid., 48).

DORCA was led by Alf Conlon. Albeit no Marxist, Conlon has been likened by Cassandra Pybus to the Italian Marxist theoretician Antonio Gramsci; both believed that society is shaped by ideas coming from a small elite 'united by shared intellectual premises' (Pybus 1999, 21–23). Blamey saw a use for Conlon's ideas to advance his own belief in 'a historic and politically sensitive role' for Australia in its region. Under Blamey's patronage, Conlon recruited intellectuals including Stanner, Hogbin and the poet James McAuley to prepare the ground for a 'radical and expanded post-war colonial policy' (ibid., 36–39). Pybus described Eddie Ward as captured by 'Conlon's vision of a "New Deal" for New Guinea' (ibid., 46). An 'old-style labour man' for whom colonialism was 'anathema', Ward found his portfolio 'an embarrassment' and was 'uneasy with the system of forced labour' employed in pre-war plantations, and by the wartime administration (ibid., 53–54). Ward appears to have allowed Conlon and Hogbin considerable latitude in framing post-war policy for the newly combined territories, perhaps especially in the field of labour policy.

Australian colonial policy, it has been argued, was intended to make a place for capitalism in PNG, while labour policy had the purpose of creating the workforce 'to fructify foreign capital' and to control it for the benefit of that capital (Hess 1983, 51). Such a position imputes remarkable foresight and unwavering intent to the colonial power, whereas I tend to suspect that 'cock-ups' affect outcomes more frequently than conspiracy. I agree with John Ballard that 'only those who allow of no autonomy of the state see policymaking as a totally dependent variable and outcomes as determined by social structure' (Ballard 1981, 1). Readers must decide whether my *apologia* here places this narrative in the category of colonial historicism criticized by Peter Fitzpatrick as exhibiting sympathy for the colonial state, showing an inclination to accept its policies and viewing any negative outcomes as *unintended* (Fitzpatrick 1980, vii).

I tend to be sceptical of grand narratives and ineluctable forces, whether rooted in Marxian notions of 'the authority of capital' or in that fundamentalism of the market that demands of its followers 'a crude and naïve trust in the goodness of those wielding economic power and in the sacralised workings of the prevailing economic system' (Bergoglio 2013). This narrative proceeds instead on a social democratic premise – the importance of an active and creative public sector in a market economy subject to democratic oversight. It is informed by my continuing adherence (by no means uncritical) to the idea of economic development as it has been elaborated since the Second World War.

Such enthusiasms may set this writer at odds with the Marxist critic who, after condemning 'capitalist development' studies as ahistorical, targets the apologists for economic development. The tone is sardonic; the apologist – necessarily patronizing – supports colonial action to steer 'backward' people towards creating the new nation (Fitzpatrick 1980, vii). One can only respond that we are confronted by irreconcilable systems. In *Gifts and Commodities*, Chris Gregory wrote of a paradigmatic gulf between arguments from orthodox economics and Marxian political economy. We face a choice between alternatives that employ different concepts (*goods* and *commodities*, for example) and apply different modes of analysis, leaving no 'common ground' for comparing or evaluating the two bodies of knowledge (Gregory 1982, 102). I must be content to state my values and confine my argument to issues of logic and veracity, as well as appealing to that common sense expressed by the maxim 'never attribute to malice that which is adequately explained by stupidity'.

Chapter 14

Obsolescence and the Preconditions for Urbanism

In the last year of the Second World War, the Labor government 'acted on the advice of Ward's advisers in DORCA' to make a series of policy announcements. An early initiative was a sweeping reform of labour legislation (Downs 1980, 13–14). Ward imposed a timetable for abolishing indentured labour and the immediate repatriation, at the end of hostilities, of all men employed by the army and plantations. Courtesy of Hiroshima, peace came earlier than expected, magnifying the ensuing disruption. Aside from the minister's abhorrence of colonialism, his motives for abolishing the old system included a tactical consideration – the hope that labour reform would influence favourably the UN attitude to Australia's proposed administrative union between Papua and New Guinea (ibid., 13). Peremptory repatriation of workers proved counterproductive in terms of other objectives, including restoring plantations and rebuilding infrastructure. It was, in fact, competitive with every other post-war task '*except village welfare*' (ibid., 38, emphasis added). The detailed attention to be given below to post-war labour policy and legislation reflects their importance in shaping PNG's modern formal workforce. By simple opposition, such reform would also define *informal* employment, as well as influencing the experience of urbanism during the late colonial period.

Regarding post-war conditions in PNG, Stanner described the destruction of colonial assets and infrastructure. There had occurred a degree of 'ruination' such that by 1949 significant reconstruction had occurred only on plantations and the goldfields (Stanner 1953, 86–87). Village society had also suffered grievously; among the reasons for delay in overall reconstruction was the priority given to emergency feeding, medication and repatriation of villagers who had been displaced and were distressed (ibid., 112). That immediate task was substantially completed by mid-1946, although payment of their claims for outstanding wages and compensation (seen as important to 'pacifying' a 'restive' population and regaining their confidence) took longer (ibid., 119). These early actions were more a matter of welfare and rehabilitation than of economic development, but they were a necessary foundation for it.

After some years during which a provisional administration devoted itself largely to short-term rehabilitation, Australian legislation (the *Papua and New Guinea Act* 1949) transferred both territories to a formal administrative union. Port Moresby was declared its capital over the claims of other centres, for reasons (aside from inertia) including its comparatively intact status and strategic value. Most important was a political consideration: Papua remained a Crown possession whereas New Guinea was still a trusteeship, held under UN mandate (Oram 1976a, 92). While towns in New Guinea might have stronger claims, Australia preferred to invest in the former Papuan capital so long as the future of the Mandated Territory remained an open question.

With its centrality to the administrative apparatus confirmed, and increasing public resources available to pursue development, Port Moresby would come to house the major institutions of the emerging state. It would provide administrative, legal and other services for the whole country, host the head offices of many companies, and house a large proportion of a burgeoning public service. By 1971, reflecting its national status and functions, the town's population would be three times greater than it might otherwise have been if based simply on the size of the regional population it directly served (Jackson 1976, 4). Despite the unpromising character of its hinterland, and by reason of political calculation and bureaucratic fiat, Port Moresby would come into its *own* luck.

Development and the Paramountcy of Native Interests

With the defeat of Japan imminent, the Australian government made clear it had no intention of returning PNG to the situation existing before the war, although policy would continue to be inspired by the notion of 'paramountcy of native interests' (Ch. 9). After establishing a provisional administration, it announced guiding principles. Combining the primacy of indigenous interests with long-standing concerns for the integrity of village life, these were based on a policy of 'dual development' articulated by Eddie Ward. This concept, as with the upheaval in labour policy, appears likely to have had its genesis in Conlon's group. Ward declared that while the immediate priority was to prevent the 'disintegration' of indigenous social and welfare structures, longer-term economic policy would be based on the development of 'non-native and native industry' occurring 'side by side'. However, 'considerations of native welfare and development' would apply when determining the extent and degree of non-native development (Ward, cited in Stanner 1953, 131).

Under the conservative government that succeeded Labor in 1949, Paul Hasluck, the minister for external territories from 1951 to 1963, more commonly framed policy in terms of Australia's duty of 'trusteeship' or 'guardianship'. J.D. Legge described the conservatives as more favourable than the Australian Labor Party to private enterprise and, although equally committed to native welfare, less inclined to see this as the subject of indefinite subsidy. Dual development had been 'a vague aspiration', and 'differences of emphasis in the general policy statements of Labor and Liberal ministers were of little practical significance'. If Ward's pronouncements had been 'evocative', the new government's approach was 'more empirical' (Legge 1956, 197–98). Scott MacWilliam saw a more purposeful side to Hasluck, whom he described as seeing guardianship as necessary to secure the village life of smallholder households as against the emerging claims of a new class of indigenous capitalists (MacWilliam 2013, 6). Hasluck was determined to avoid the ascendancy of this new class, 'a few "smart boys" and "shrewd heads"' from urban centres (Hasluck in 1955, cited in MacWilliam 2013, 95). From Hasluck's period and essentially until independence, the bureaucratic norms and processes of colonial administration would continue to be shaped by the rhetorical orthodoxy of economic development – which also became implanted in the indigenous imagination over time. And although the term 'paramountcy of native interests' dropped out of official usage, the sentiments underlying it remained influential.

By Stanner's account (1953, 122), dual development seemed to involve nurturing 'a widespread system of peasant production in parallel with or as an alternative to plantation production'. MacWilliam (2013, 78) has described the progression of this idea towards support for peasant production under a rubric of *uniform development*, intended to secure increased levels of production and consumption by indigenous smallholder families. 'Dual' development meant that technical divisions of the Agriculture Department supported expatriate plantations, while its extension division handled indigenous smallholders – though in practice an 'extension bias' towards more wealthy smallholders often operated to reinforce rural inequalities (McKillop 1981a, 240).

In retrospect, Stanner thought Labor had lost an opportunity during reconstruction by failing to resume a policy conversation of the late 1930s concerning the longer-term viability of the plantation sector. This related to what Rowley called economic obsolescence, and Stanner's view supports the assertion made above (Ch. 11) that obsolescence was already recognizable by the time of Hubert Murray's death. Stanner commented that a thorough industry review (including debt levels, ownership, productivity and costs) should have been done soon after the war. Plantations were a form of tropical commercial agriculture, which experience elsewhere suggested would have an early use-by date (Stanner 1953, 120).

This failure may have been due to what Ian Downs described as an 'attitude of resignation' to the limited capacity of indigenous people to operate in any new form of 'tropical economy', and to the shortage of private investment and skills for the task so soon after the war. This defeatism was coupled with a lack of vision, and the inability to see that problems would only worsen if they were not addressed quickly. In the event, while government was preoccupied with more immediate problems, white planters were permitted to return to their pre-war holdings. This wholesale return of planters and pre-war residents resulted in a resumption of the interwar system and the continuation of expatriate economic dominance (Downs 1980, 42). After this, indigenous agriculture would require considerable government support if either 'dual' or 'uniform' development were to be achieved.

The Gordian Knot of Labour Market Reform

Colonial labour policies determined the character of formal employment and thus the environment for informal employment. For this reason, it is necessary to consider how a post-war formal workforce framework was set in place. Eddie Ward had declared Labor's intention to increase the resources available for colonial administration; no longer would outlays be constrained by local capacity to raise revenue. Future policy would secure 'better health, better education, more participation in the wealth of their country, and eventually a say in its government' for the indigenous population (Ward [1945] cited in Griffin, Nelson and Firth 1979, 102). However, Ted Wolfers commented that within this rhetorical framework, directions taken by the Labor Party were primarily applications of their Australian domestic policies to its colonial territories, concentrated in the areas of labour and employment reform, and 'relatively easy to implement' (Wolfers 1975, 119–20). This insight may help to explain Ward's acceptance of the Conlon/Hogbin 'line' (Ch. 13), though as a politician schooled in the Labor industrial wing he understood instinctively that obsolescence was an ill rooted in the archaic and inefficient management of labour. DORCA's early attention to labour issues had implicitly recognized the reality of obsolescence, as later articulated by Charles Rowley at the Australian School of Pacific Administration (ASOPA). The school, to which a number of DORCA staff had been appointed, was another part of Conlon's post-war legacy.

Aside from repatriating labour and abolishing indenture (the latter completed only in 1950, under a newly elected conservative government), Ward announced changed conditions of employment. Professional recruiters were no longer to operate, time limits were to be imposed on absences from home areas, the minimum wage would be increased and working hours reduced. Dual development was reflected in Ward's statement that indigenous people were to be assisted to become independently employed in agriculture where possible (Downs 1980, 14). However, some inconsistency was evident from the 1950 annual reports for Papua and New Guinea where, as Downs (ibid., 31) noted, formal employment was still reported as the principal source of 'native economic development'. In any case, a Department of Native Labour was created and a lengthy process of regulatory and societal adjustment commenced, with the ultimate objective of fostering what Charles Rowley (1958a, 540) called a 'wage-earning class'. This would be typified by its stability and effectiveness, and with workers and their families settled close to workplaces.

This vision would not be realized quickly. While Rowley was still lamenting employers' dependence on migrant labour, including rural plantation labour, his comment bore also on the interrelationships between labour productivity, wage determination and retarded urbanism. Rural and urban labour supply were linked, insofar as the plantation wage was the benchmark for the urban unskilled wage. Plantations' dependence on labour recruited and paid on a 'single man' basis, with negative implications for labour turnover and productivity in the rural sector, had its counterpart in the embryonic urban labour market. Both urban and rural employers were sustained by lower wage rates made possible by what Cyril Belshaw described as a 'subsidy' from the rural dependents of absent labourers (Ch. 9). Achieving a committed urban 'wage-earning class' would require authorities to unravel a Gordian knot, woven (in Rowley's brutal formulation) from the strands of poor management, reliance on those he dubbed 'unsophisticated primitives', and the consequent low standards of worker efficiency (Rowley 1958a, 540–41). The challenge was to break out of a debilitating cycle of low-wage, low-productivity industrial organization, and to manage this while minimizing the costs of what was coming to be known as 'urban drift', leading to open unemployment in the towns. This would be difficult in a volatile post-war environment, where any controls over urban residence were increasingly subject to domestic and international political challenge (as well as being inconsistent with efforts to reform labour markets).

The period 1945–47 was one of acute labour shortage, as significant changes occurred in modes of formal employment available to indigenous people. Opportunities for indenture still existed for a time, but repatriated workers, many of them flush with compensation money, were reluctant to re-engage. Even by 1949, the number of indentured workers was only a third of the 1941 total (Stanner 1953, 137ff). The *Native Labour Ordinance* 1946 made provision for employment of non-indentured labour, and the administration signalled the significance it attached to this by labelling such workers as 'employees'. This was done to distinguish them from 'labourers', the official term for indentured workers (Smith 1975, 51). Non-indentured labour was a form of casual employment, albeit still highly regulated, and contracts could be terminated by either party at will. The ordinance was said by Hess (1983, 57) to have been the first initiative to legislate for a class of free workers. Suggesting the culture shock involved in accepting 'free' employment, Stanner (1953, 136) reported that initially many labourers were suspicious of the innovation and risk-averse. Nonetheless take-up grew rapidly, and by mid-1950, when employment had almost regained its pre-war peak, about half of all private sector workers were 'employees'. This gave authorities confidence for the abolition of indenture at the end of that year.

The 1946 ordinance has been attributed to a post-war 'revolution in thought' (D. Smith 1975, 46). In terms of the new 'development' ideology, it was a step towards acculturating workers to competitive labour markets. While many feared free engagement, others embraced the novel experience of exercising some market power. Stanner reported that labour shortage drove up private sector casual wages around Rabaul, where Chinese plantation owners competed for workers with Europeans (who might otherwise have maintained employer solidarity). This was another instance of the historical Chinese role in acculturating indigenous people to market forces. Presenting authorities with unprecedented problems, agitation for racial wage equality also emerged. In Lae, the administration was discomforted when some indigenous workers demanded conditions similar to those enjoyed by 'Europeans and Asiatics'.

In response some scaling-up occurred, with rates for clerical workers and artisans set closer to those of non-indigenous employees. However, rather than building up wage levels by adding skill increments to the unskilled base-rate, a process of ad hoc adjustments by various departments caused margins to vary widely, without any clear rationale (Stanner 1953, 136).

By mid-1950, the administration, employing 28 per cent of the formal workforce, was competing with the private sector for labour and paying generally higher wages. Government employment had increased substantially, with much unskilled labour engaged in stevedoring, road construction, maintenance and minor reconstruction tasks, although some 20 per cent of indigenous employment was now classed as skilled or semi-skilled. The administration employed proportionally more such workers than the private sector, particularly in Papua where government spending increased rapidly in Port Moresby (ibid.). Together with the declining importance of indenture, this appeared a promising start towards a more modern and diversified workforce, with a wage structure more conducive to labour productivity. Momentum was not sustained, however; even by the end of the 1950s, official attention continued to focus on the needs of rural industry while the case for a committed urban workforce was neglected.

Some high-level ambivalence about the changing nature of employment contracts may have contributed to this. In 1952, Hasluck expressed concern about the alienation from village life of a growing cohort of absentee workers due to casualization of the workforce (MacWilliam 2013, 96). Writing to Hasluck, H.C. Coombs was inclined to agree. He had seen the beginnings of a 'proletariat' in Port Moresby, among whom disaffection could thrive, although he also advised Hasluck that urban development and the emergence of capitalist enterprise would require larger indigenous populations in urban centres (Coombs to Hasluck, cited in MacWilliam 2013, 96–97). Hasluck understood the need for labour force evolution to meet the needs of development. He wrote in 1953 that legislation must be suited to a changing economy – more diverse, with growing demand for urban labour (as distinct from plantation workers), and with increasing numbers of 'natives' gaining skills and becoming self-employed (Hasluck 1976, 159).

It would take time for official reservations about urban growth to be overcome, and for the need for Rowley's objective, 'an effective, stable, labour force', to be accepted. Much later, Hasluck expressed some regret. He thought Australian authorities had been too slow in anticipating a 'wage-earning class' and in shaping the circumstances in which an 'urban proletariat would emerge' (Hasluck 1976, 335). A new system of 'native employees' agreements' had replaced contracts of indenture in 1951. These offered improved service conditions, though some employer control was maintained by part-retention of wages and impediments to group action. This latter circumstance encouraged observers such as Hess (1983) to question the 'real' motive of policy, but it may simply be that authorities, managing a gradual transformation of labour relations in a difficult and unpredictable environment, preferred to adopt an incremental approach.

A vocal white industry lobby was apprehensive of the costs of change, and progress in labour reform was correspondingly slow and fitful.

This situation was most evident in urban areas where, although casual contracts of employment had become the norm by the late 1950s, official attention remained focused on plantation labour issues. After a labour code update in 1958, officials in the Port Moresby Labour Office found themselves responsible for administering new regulations for plantation workers, while the reality surrounding them in the town was one of urban casual workers ('the firstlings of a proletariat'). Insofar as the new (1958) ordinance was relevant to such workers, it 'tended to be a hindrance to full-time employment in the towns' (Hess 1983, 60).

Whatever momentum for change had been created by the 1946 reforms, it had not been sustained. Urban remuneration was still set by reference to the low-wage plantation economy, and (as on plantations) men were assumed to have no family responsibilities. As a result, under circumstances where the relatively novel phenomenon of market forces came into play, the terms and conditions of service specified in regulations were ignored by some employers anxious to get the kind of labour they required. But regulatory uncertainty made other employers hesitant to hire, and the administration was seen by business community spokesmen as 'actively discouraging the sort of labour force they needed' (Hess 1983, 60–61).

Efficiency and stability in wage employment were essential for modern urban life, while wage equity was necessary for efficiency. A 'family' wage must be paid to achieve these ends, posing a grave difficulty for employers whose managerial skills were more suited to manhandling a low-wage workforce with high levels of labour turnover than to achieving productivity growth through encouraging worker commitment and skill acquisition (Rowley 1965, 199).

The Organization of Industrial Labour

During the 1950s, Charles Rowley had argued for a permanent formal sector workforce. This would require legislation to codify rights and duties in the workplace, as agreed by both workers and employers. A corollary of this was the need for workers to organize themselves (Rowley 1958a, 540). His view was that official preoccupation with maintaining village society had resulted in an inability to perceive dysfunctional consequences occurring at workplaces. Sources of urban discontent included labour-related issues (industrial relations and wages), social welfare issues (social and health services, housing and education) public order and delinquency, and increasingly inappropriate welfare legislation (such as that dealing with alcohol). It was becoming evermore difficult for government to manage the problems of social obsolescence in urban areas by using vagrancy laws or other regulations as a 'simple expedient' to expel members of a transient urban population (Rowley 1960, 5).

In 1953, an officially commissioned report on economic policy noted the growing numbers of permanent urban residents, and thought it 'a remarkable fact that there is practically no political activity as yet of a quasi-revolutionary nature among such groups, and there is not even a trade union movement' (Spate, Belshaw and Swan 1953, 19.2). Discussing the possibility of an 'emergent working class', Rowley (in a comment which may have implied government's deliberate intent) suggested that agreement contracts introduced in 1951 might have retarded an emerging 'sense of cohesion' among workers (Rowley 1958a, 541). The correspondence between Coombs and Hasluck (above) suggested the latter might have welcomed such an outcome. Despite this, there had been some instances of 'group action' against employers in the 1950s. Hess believed strikes occurred more frequently than was acknowledged; they were 'disguised' in a contract system of labour where 'strikers were dealt with as individual contract breakers' (Hess 1983, 66).

Bernard Schaffer, a visiting British political scientist, commented on early instances of worker organization, occurring in response to the establishment of a Native Employment Board in 1958. He hinted at emergent class consciousness, though avoiding the term itself: the combination of labour organization and political development might induce some surprisingly rapid '*changes in identifications*' (Schaffer 1963, 8–9, emphasis added). Rowley took strikes as evidence of the beginnings of collective action by workers. He urged authorities against denying, or appearing to deny, workers' rights to 'free association'. A legal framework for worker organization must be created as it was no longer appropriate to manage worker dissatisfaction under an outmoded labour code, treating disputes as master–servant issues (Rowley 1958a, 544).

Then, quite quickly, a policy turnaround occurred. Ross Martin described how 'up to 1960 the Australian Government's official view was that union organization was neither necessary nor desired by Papuans and New Guineans themselves'. But after some indigenous industrial action this position was abandoned 'when it was shown to be false' (Martin 1969, 153). Legislation in 1962 set up machinery for industrial relations and for the regulation of industrial organizations, including trade unions. Wage determinations would be made by periodic boards of inquiry. For the rest of that decade, in Port Moresby and elsewhere, incremental improvements were made to earnings levels and wage structures. By 1963, provision had been made for payment of a full urban cash wage. While still calculated as a 'single man' wage, it represented progress in replacing a resented system of cash deductions for accommodation and supplies.

Even earlier, in 1960, failure to distinguish between rural and urban pay and conditions was corrected when a system of urban employment awards was instituted. This was followed by awards for semi-skilled workers, introduced to reward higher productivity. By 1966, almost half the capital's indigenous workforce was employed at rates above the minimum unskilled wage. Awards in Rabaul in 1967 and 1969 set a pattern for the whole country, with 'a more complex wage structure' recognizing grades of skill and length of service. Reflecting market forces, above-award payments were being earned by many skilled workers, 'higher clerical and supervisory workers, technicians and tradesmen' (Langmore 1970, 32–36). Meanwhile a de facto family wage had been struck for lower-paid administration employees, with a 'family needs allowance' paid to semi-skilled married officers, bringing their earnings closer to skilled levels (in a situation where skill differentials were relatively high). Because of the market-leader status of government, this put pressure on the private sector to respond. The totality of these changes brought PNG closer to an 'industrial relations framework designed to serve an emerging urban wage labour force' (Smith 1975, 49). In the absence of any significant indigenous self-employment, these changes served to define urban livelihoods even more definitively in terms of *formal* regulated employment.

John Langmore was not sanguine, however, because a 'currently insoluble tension' remained. Restating the dilemma described above as a 'Gordian knot', he noted that urban wages were still low 'and should be increased only slowly, and yet many workers should be encouraged to settle in the towns to provide a core of committed workers with high productivity' (Langmore 1970, 18). The difficulty was that while PNG wages (paid in Australian currency) were high in nominal terms in comparison with those of international competitors, their local purchasing power was low. The 'consumption basket' of urban families included a large proportion of imported commodities from high-cost sources (notably Australia) and was comparatively expensive, especially in Port Moresby where local foods were scarce.

In the new era, not all actors would be prepared to accept Langmore's implication of a need for patience, as recognition of unions would imply the right to strike. Fitzpatrick documented legal obstacles to industrial action, short of actual prohibition, after the 1962 legislation. He represented Hasluck as anxious to avoid political organization based narrowly on employment issues – with the potential for confrontation between indigenous labour and indigenous capital in a future self-governing state (Fitzpatrick 1980, 154). But whereas Fitzpatrick saw this as political repression, the minister might instead be understood as managing the transition to a more modern workforce while avoiding the political legacy of an industrial system crippled by institutionalized polarities. Issues such as the structure and modes of political organization were 'for the people themselves to determine in due course' (Hasluck 1976, 235).

In the event, reform did not altogether prevent strikes, as seen in Alan Rew's account (1970, 302ff) of industrial disputes in the town in 1965. Rew concluded that these strikes were not primarily about industrial relations issues; striker grievances were not so much systematic as protests against 'day-to-day indignities' experienced while working as 'boys' in the 'racially divided' capital (ibid., 311). And while, 'superficially', such grievances might seem only 'trivial industrial matters', the intensity with which they were held reflected workers' 'appraisal of the racial structure of the town' (ibid., 314).

The platform of Pangu, the political party founded in 1967 that later took PNG into independence, was not (despite the identification of several Pangu leaders with trade unions) centred on pay issues. Still less was it based on demands for 'freedom', as such rhetoric did not reflect the prosaic reality of late colonial PNG. Pangu was concerned with broader issues of dignity, autonomy and distributive justice, such as underlay the strikes documented by Rew. Fitzpatrick's invocation of popular demands for freedom in a supposedly repressive situation was overwrought. However, Pangu's more immediate concerns did include the search for alternatives to an increasingly inequitable pattern of development in the late colonial period. The narrative will return to this subject when discussing the Faber Report of 1972 (Ch. 24). Suffice to say here that many in Pangu thought that the report (and Keith Hart, its co-author) offered exciting new policy alternatives.

For an explanation of Hasluck's about-face between 1960 and 1962 one might look to external influences, including Harold Macmillan's 'wind of change' speech in 1960, and the 'sooner, not later' epiphany experienced by Australian prime minister Robert Menzies that same year. As the last territory of consequence subject to UN Trusteeship Council oversight, New Guinea caused Australia to come under increasing pressure in international forums, while internally there was a gathering sense of unease. In 1958, Rowley had spoken of a continual state of labour dysfunction. Development should have been occurring based on industries, supported by permanent workforces whose families lived with them. The family unit would be supported by wages and enjoy provision for health, education, pensions and other social services (Rowley 1958a, 543). But there was little sign of progress towards these goals.

Murray Groves recounted a meeting between Hasluck and some younger educated Papuans in Port Moresby, at which he 'for the first time discovered the urban elite which has in fact been there for some years'. Hasluck gained some insight into their discontents (Groves 1960, 8). Perhaps this was among straws in the wind suggesting to him the need for a change of direction, away from the anti-elitism of 'uniform development'. Although he would not be in office to receive it, it was Hasluck who commissioned the World Bank report (IBRD 1965) that articulated a fresh approach. A 'big push' strategy,[1] this policy would come to be known in PNG as *accelerated development*, to distinguish it from the earlier 'dual' and 'uniform' development rhetorics. Peter Fitzpatrick regarded Hasluck's labour reforms of 1962–63 as anticipating this policy turn so that, where necessary for an efficient economy to operate, some good order and industrial discipline could apply (Fitzpatrick 1980, 155).

Whatever the need for a protective legislative framework for those 'unsophisticated primitives' who continued to accept agreement work on plantations, qualitatively different modes of regulation were needed for a permanent *urban* workforce. During the 1960s and early 1970s, in the context of 'accelerated development', successive iterations of the Labour Code groped towards that goal. C.E. Barnes, Hasluck's successor, commissioned the Australian economist J.E. (Joe) Isaac to report on the structure of unskilled wages, including 'the proper balance of the wage structure, especially between rural and non-rural employment', which 'would ensure adequate supply of labour to the rural industries as well as the urban; avoid an undue drift to urban areas in excess of employment opportunities offering there and ... ensure attractive employment opportunities in all fields (including at the managerial level) to the native people' (cited in Isaac 1970).

This language reflected the influence of the economists W. Arthur Lewis and Michael Todaro among policymakers perturbed by burgeoning urban populations and apparently ruinous rates of open unemployment in developing countries. Lewis's article 'Economic Development with Unlimited Supplies of Labour' (1954) considered how the transition from (rural) agriculture to (urban) industry might be managed. Agriculture sheds labour as rural productivity increases, and urban areas absorb rural migrant labour as industrialization proceeds. Todaro's model of rural–urban migration (which took the Lewis model as its starting point) directed attention to the gap between rural and urban wages (Todaro 1969). This was relevant to PNG insofar as Todaro pointed to the earnings gap as influencing rates of internal migration and the willingness of migrants to endure unemployment in towns while searching for formal wage jobs (Conroy 1974a, 1976; Garnaut, Wright and Curtain 1977). Open urban unemployment was not yet serious in PNG, but as the old restrictions on urban residence became increasingly difficult to maintain, awareness of change brought such considerations into policy discussions. An additional factor was rapid growth in numbers of rural school-leavers, increasingly visible among migrants to Port Moresby. Growing numbers of educated youth supported improvements in workforce productivity, but the rate of their increase appeared likely to create near-term problems of 'educated unemployment' (Stent and Conroy 1968; Conroy 1970; Garnaut, Wright and Curtain 1977).

The administration felt the need (expressed in Joe Isaac's brief) to assure adequate labour supplies in both rural and urban sectors while avoiding dysfunctional flows of labour to the towns. Wages policy was assumed to be a necessary instrument for that purpose and for achieving what Rowley called 'the basic requirements of a modern community' (Ch. 11). The discussion will return to these issues below, in the context of rapid urbanization in the years before independence. In the meantime, the narrative turns to the physical and social remaking of Port Moresby in the post-war period. For while 'obsolescence' in post-war PNG had both social and economic aspects, the discussion so far has focused largely on the economic aspects of that malady. In what follows, a distinction is made between formal and informal elements of the built environment of the capital. In the late colonial period a burgeoning informal urban fabric provided tangible evidence of popular resistance – pushback exerted against a regulatory framework designed to realize an alien 'form' of the town. While there was still little evidence of Hart's informal economy in the livelihoods of indigenous urban dwellers, it was abundant in the means by which they housed themselves.

Note

1. The notion of a 'big push' originated in wartime planning for reconstruction in South Eastern and Eastern Europe. It stemmed from a paper by Paul Rosenstein-Rodan (1943) who was at the World Bank in the 1950s. This paper was among the earliest contributions to the literature on 'modern' economic development.

Chapter 15

Remaking Port Moresby

The Formal Town

Japanese bombing of Port Moresby had forced the evacuation of native landholders, damaging both urban villages and the European town. Reflecting its importance to the war effort, Moresby became a command and marshalling centre, and many Papuans, men and boys, were drafted as labourers. While imposing disruption and privation, the upheaval gave Papuans an opportunity to observe the mobilization of the men and materiel required for war between industrial economies, and to interact with Australian and American troops. They seemed so unlike the pre-war colonial masters as to be thought a different race, while the comportment of black Americans and their mastery of technology were revelations.

Aside from this psychological influence there was another lasting consequence. This affected the physical character of Port Moresby as an urban centre, as authorities attempted to minimize the impact of bombing raids. A contemporary traveller whose plane circles above the capital might still relate to the revelation experienced by the geographer Bryant Allen:

> The first time a wartime topographical map of [Port Moresby] came into my possession I was immediately struck by the way the wartime layout of airstrips, hospitals, headquarters and dumps had significantly influenced the post-war layout of the city. The wartime base and the post-war city were almost identical in physical structure. (Allen, pers. com., 2015)

When Nigel Oram, a former British colonial service officer, first came to Port Moresby in 1961, its population was some twenty-nine thousand,

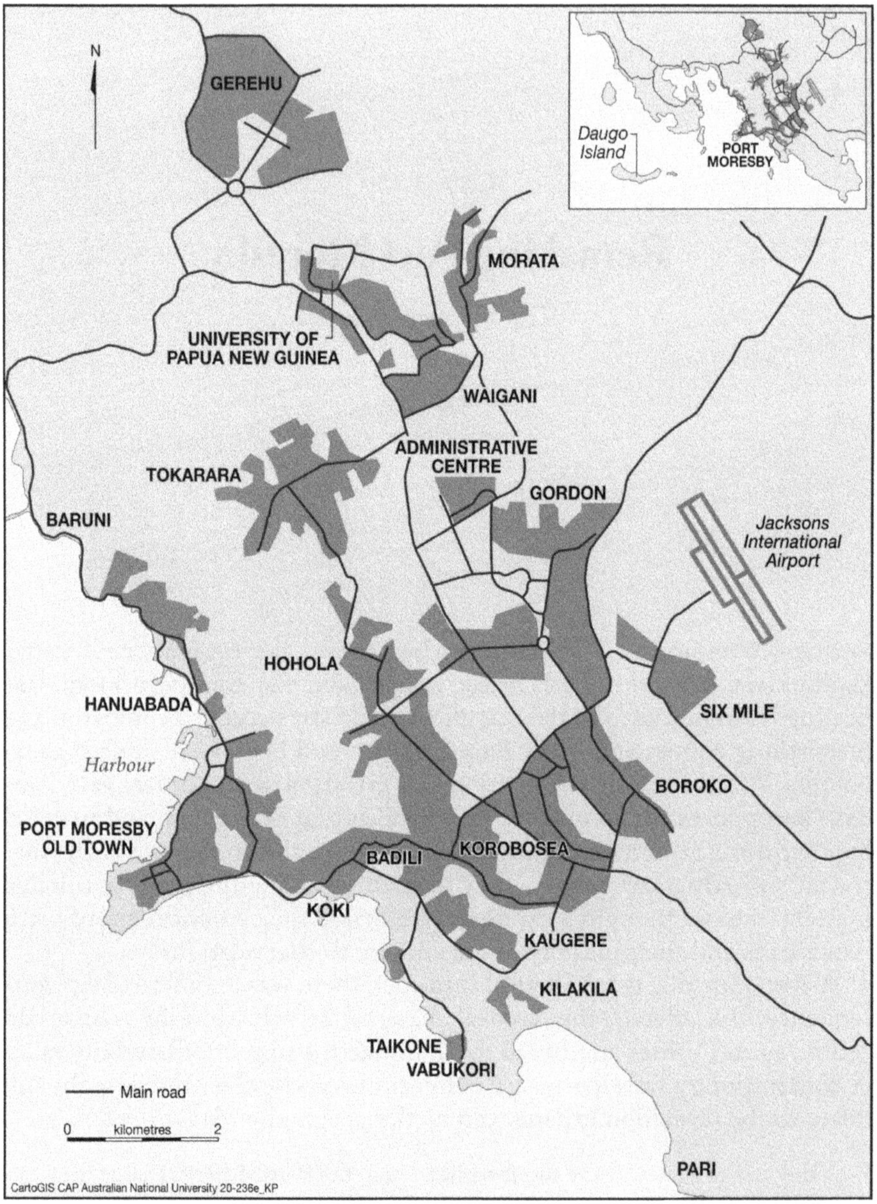

Map 15.1. Port Moresby in 1974. Permission granted for reproduction of this map by CartoGIS Services, Digital Scholarship, Scholarly Information Services, The Australian National University.

having grown from just four thousand in 1946. Later, he reflected on how the 'idea of a town' could influence its character (Ch. 10). He wrote with enthusiasm of Ibadan, a West African city whose colonial character had been determined in pre-colonial times. It exhibited 'magnificently vital and colourful disorder' – mud huts among modern buildings, dusty thoroughfares and dodgy sanitation – all together with 'vigorous economic activity'. In East Africa, by contrast, the ordered British colonial towns had 'sterile and lifeless' indigenous quarters (Oram 1976a, xiv). Port Moresby conformed to the East African pattern. In terms still recognizable today, central business or government districts and more affluent suburbs exhibited planning, building standards and services such as were found in Australian or other first-world cities. In poorer districts there were 'overcrowded tenements', 'uncontrolled and congested' with inferior services (ibid., ix; Map 15.1). Port Moresby was quite unlike Ibadan, where formal and informal manifestations of urbanism jostled side-by-side. The account of undistinguished urban place-making in Papua continues here for the period after the Pacific War, to suggest how Oram's 'sterile and lifeless' East African form was realized in late colonial Port Moresby.

Among the results of Eddie Ward's cancellation of labour contracts (Ch. 14) was slow progress in urban rebuilding (Downs 1980, 39). Building materials were in short supply because reconstruction in PNG was delayed by Australia's own full employment policy. The demands this placed on Australian productive capacity deprived PNG of almost everything it needed 'except money' (Stanner 1953, 112). Nor were shortages of labour and materials the only constraint: delays in preparing town plans restricted urban development in all the main centres, and there was no master plan for reconstruction (Downs 1980, 39). Private rebuilding was 'held up owing to official inability to complete the basic survey requirements of town plans for Port Moresby'. Canberra had been slow to choose the site for a joint capital, holding up decision making for reconstruction. No master plan for the capital would appear for another quarter-century.

Although it compromised reconstruction of the formal town, Ward had promised to rebuild Hanuabada, whose people were living in squalid makeshift huts (Downs 1980, 41). Ward's pledge might be seen as evidencing Canberra's concern to re-establish village life, but equally it may have reflected local authorities' desire to sustain the pre-war idea of the town, with villagers tidily corralled in Hanuabada. In Lae, the absence of a town plan gave authorities license to revert to old habits, when they pegged out separate housing areas for European, Chinese, Papuan, mixed-race and general indigenous labour (Wolfers 1975, 119). In Port Moresby, rebuilding did not proceed in quite so formulaic a manner, though pre-war conventions remained influential. Distinctions (in which land tenure was decisive) were re-established between the European town and urban customary villages, with Badili as a place for 'foreign' natives. Nearby Koki was to become an industrial and commercial area, and to house the town's marketplace.

Old habits of thought resurfaced in regard to the town-ward movement of indigenous people. After 1945, official policies for urban migration were just as they had been before 1942; most officials continued to oppose long-term urban settlement. A degree of policy dissonance occurred in 1947, when Canberra directed that Papuans should be encouraged to find work in the capital, while the district officer continued to warn against the growth of 'shanty towns' and to condemn incomers as parasites. As late as 1955, a senior official was still warning of the dangers of detribalization among rural incomers (Oram 1976a, 168). But given the labour shortages the need for some migration was incontestable, although incomers unable to find work quickly were still liable to be expelled. For some years this mode of managing labour supply allowed annual reports to deny the existence of urban unemployment. Nor was there any significant class of workers employed outside the formal system, as even domestic servants' wages were set by the *Native Employment Ordinance*. Still less was there any group of self-employed, informal workers.

Old-school attitudes would be overcome as circumstances made town-ward migration virtually unstoppable, although their influence would linger on elsewhere. Much later Oram observed that lingering fears of detribalization had given rise to negative, backward-looking policies governing settlement and housing. This was an unfortunate contrast with some other former colonial territories, which had actively sought to stabilize migrants as long-term urbanites (Oram 1976a, 170). Moreover, the continuing official disdain for urban settlements handicapped, even sabotaged, efforts on the part of some officials and community leaders to harness the spontaneous initiatives of migrants to improve their own dwellings and neighbourhoods.

From about 1954, some official efforts were made to house indigenous employees, still mostly quartered in the Badili barracks, by developing new suburbs. Mostly high-standard residential areas for expatriates and institutions, these initiatives spread inland from the historic town. Another planned suburb, Hohola, was created in 1960 to provide formal housing for middle-income indigenous families. Nonetheless, until the 1960s a substantially Western pattern of urban development continued in Port Moresby, designed essentially for Europeans and some few other non-indigenous people (Oram 1976a, 96). The 'vital and colourful disorder' of Ibadan, in which an African informal economy flourished, could not have been replicated in the nation's capital. The very possibility was zoned away by planners.

After 1957, New Guinea Chinese became eligible for Australian citizenship and were allowed to move to Papua. Coming from Rabaul and other towns they inspired a retail revolution. Unlike the Gazelle, where Chinese traders and produce buyers continued to stimulate indigenous smallholder production, few entered rural trade. But in the capital they increased competition to the benefit of all by extending the range of consumer goods appealing to the indigenous market, and establishing shopping locations convenient for local people. These were elements in a general social transformation, altering the town's character and extending to the legal framework for urban residence.

Ted Wolfers (1975, 132) concluded that a visiting UN Mission had impelled the progressive liberalization of discriminatory laws and regulations. It had been critical, inter alia, of the curfew regulations, while in the era of decolonization Australian authorities had become sensitive to the incongruity of 'authoritarian' and paternalistic modes of control, still exercised by patrol officers and other colonial officials. Such administrative methods, historically associated with 'the preservation of a racially divided society', were a source of growing international criticism. A European resident dated the emergence of 'modern Port Moresby' from 1962, when alcohol prohibition was lifted. 'Brown drinkers at once took over the hotel bars for so long the exclusive domain of white men, and in a more subtle way Papuans and New Guineans ... occupied the whole town. For the first time it began to look and feel like a New Guinea town' (Stuart 1970, 163). Quite what a 'New Guinea town' might look like was unclear in the absence of any models, but it was certainly no Ibadan. For while much of the regulation discouraging urban residence had been repealed, authorities could still use the *Vagrancy Ordinance* to send people home.

Authorities also began to deal more systematically with the housing of a broader range of indigenous people. Apart from Hohola, a formal or 'planned' suburb, a first attempt was made to provide 'site and services' blocks. Intended for lower-income people to erect self-help housing, this was not very successful, 'because of red tape which was just too complex' (Surmon 1971, 121–23). More workable approaches would not be devised until soon before self-government. In 1967, a National Housing Commission (NHC) was established to deal with housing problems in rapidly growing towns, though in Port Moresby access to land was a continuing difficulty. While there was no shortage of suitable land, traditional owners were increasingly loth to release it.

Just before independence, Oram could still say of Port Moresby that it comprised two main sectors, planned and unplanned. The first of these – built largely to Western standards – catered to Europeans; but with increasing 'localization' of employment, growing numbers of indigenous public servants occupied relatively high-standard government housing (Oram 1976a, 103). Another dimension of segregation was seen in the tendency for indigenous people of common tribal or regional origins to cluster together, whether in formal suburbs such as Hohola, or in the informal settlements of Oram's second, unplanned sector. The NHC commenced 'intermingling' houses of different sizes and qualities in newer, formal suburbs as a means of producing less segregated housing (Surmon and Ward 1973, 19), but the state could satisfy no more than a small part of the demand. Lower-paid workers were in any case unable to pay economic rents for even drastically scaled-down versions of regulation-compliant housing, and a third of the citizen population lived on customary land, in the second (unplanned) sector of the city (ibid.).

Unlike the promiscuous intermingling that Oram had observed in Ibadan, 'discrete residential and commercial areas' were 'scattered' around the town amidst areas of undeveloped land (Oram 1976a, 100; see also Map 15.1). Such dispersion was Port Moresby's most notable feature, puzzling because it did not fit with 'any theory of spatial development' (ibid.). The explanation may lie in Bryant Allen's observation, reported above, concerning the wartime layout of the town's military facilities. He added that this 'led to the expansiveness of the city, with large gaps of open land between the settled areas'. This was done to minimize bombing damage – which also led to roads up all the valleys where camps had been sheltered from air attack. In the post-war period, these proved 'ideal for the establishment of informal settlements', while 'the wartime roads into these places made it easier for the informal settlers to access them' (Allen, email communication with the author, 2015).

In 1973, an ordinance required employers to provide housing for their workers, though it was little enforced. Other than in the Badili compounds for unaccompanied males, many 'foreign natives' found shelter in the second sector, either in urban villages or by squatting without security of tenure on government or customary land. Such informal settlements were often regarded by the authorities as 'out of sight, out of mind'. As late as 1970, Port Moresby 'was still administered on an *ad hoc* basis through a variety of government departments, and the growing migrant settlements have been nobody's responsibility', although 'the administration at times tried to discourage settlement by cutting off water supplies and by refusing to supply sanitary and garbage services. But the settlers were not discouraged' (Surmon and Ward 1973, 21–22). Wolfers was scathing about the government's attempts to discourage incomers by failing to provide for the influx and insisting on the maintenance of Australian house-building standards: 'The unintended consequence has been a proliferation of substandard fringe settlements just outside the legal boundaries of the towns' (Wolfers 1975, 49).

Although granting some failures, Oram (1976a, 191) was more positive: these were settlements of 'hope', not settlements of 'despair'. The fault lay in adopting Western institutions and policies not related to what the indigenous population either needed or wanted. African experience had shown that attempting to house and provide services at metropolitan standards for whole populations was unrealistic (ibid., xiv). In Port Moresby the most serious policy errors occurred in urban settlements. There the fault lay not in losing control of settlement growth but in failing to provide settlers with secure access to land and minimum acceptable services. Quality of life is not simply a matter of town planning or building and sanitation standards – but only in the 1970s was this insight accepted.

The NHC began to upgrade settlements located on government land to assure secure tenure, basic services and orderly development, and some of these were close to completion on the eve of independence. A related breakthrough occurred in 1973 when building regulations were relaxed to allow authorities discretion to declare 'no-covenant' areas on government land (Jackson 1976, 76). Subject to very low annual land rents and stripped-back building regulations, these areas had minimal provision of water and garbage services, and unsurfaced roads (Wolfers 1975, 156). One of them, Morata, commenced with a thousand building plots and became a largely informal satellite town of Port Moresby, created almost entirely by low-income settlers. Problems of settlement on customary land, over which government had little control, remained, however. In the absence of land markets, and given the reluctance of traditional owners to permit alienation, lack of secure tenure constrained the will of both squatters and government to invest in improving settlements (PNG 1973).

Economic informality derives from the inability or unwillingness of people to conform with bureaucratic norms defining 'appropriate' economic behaviour. Such informality was as yet little evident in the *livelihoods* practised in the capital (Conroy 1973, 1974a; ODG 1973) but it was rampant among people providing their own shelter. The contradictions of a late colonial 'idea of the town' that required a growing and increasingly skilled workforce, while either excluding such people from land and housing or making inadequate provision for them, forced migrants to adopt unorthodox ('informal') means of securing shelter. They were willing to make substantial investments, in money and labour, to create assets that would in time become tradable in informal property and rental markets. Whereas in the interwar period Papuans had largely accepted the 'Anglo-Papuan' idea of the town, radically different circumstances after the war produced irresistible modes of pushback among them. Aberrant, *informal* behaviour, which included unstoppable rural–urban migration, 'squatting' on unoccupied land and the construction of non-compliant housing extended and transformed the town.

In its PNG manifestation, the post-war orthodoxy of economic development reflected assumptions underlying Australia's own version of heavily regulated market capitalism, including the need for centralized wage determination and stringent town planning. Development would be achieved through familiar institutions operating on rational-legal bureaucratic principles. Oram described this as a 'Procrustean' policy, dependent on Australian models for the capital's development (Oram 1976a, 245). Informality would have to emerge if people unable to find formal wage employment or to secure shelter in planned urban areas were to satisfy basic human needs. That Hart found so little evidence of informal *livelihoods* when he visited Port Moresby in 1972 showed how long it was taking to shake off the retarded urbanism entrenched by earlier administrations. How this was manifested in the changing traditional villages and burgeoning informal settlements of Port Moresby will be considered next.

Chapter 16

An Informal Town

Villages and Settlements

Aside from the wartime disposition of military facilities (Ch. 15), traditional land tenure arrangements in and around the capital have also influenced the urban form of Port Moresby – and will continue to do so. Hanuabada and other villages of the Western Motu (notably Vabukori and Pari [Map 15.1]) together with villages of the agricultural Koita people (including Baruni and Kila Kila as well as elements within Hanuabada) constituted the major 'urban villages'. These housed traditional landowners, and were distinct from informal settlements established by incomers. In a broader sense the informal town also included the traditional villages, where housing was also being transformed in ways described in this account as informal.

From before the establishment of the protectorate, some land was acquired directly from traditional owners by private European interests, missionary and commercial, after which the colonial government assumed sole authority for alienating land. While compulsory acquisition occurred for public purposes, alienation of land for economic reasons (essentially for private interests) required landowner consent, which was given with increasing reluctance as independence approached. Much land acquired by government was allocated subsequently for town expansion, particularly after the Pacific War as new suburbs were established. In the meantime, many incomers established informal settlements by 'squatting' – occupying and building on traditional or government land. This survey commences by considering Port Moresby's largest and most emblematic traditional village.

Hanuabada

Located on the fringe of the European town and with access to mission schools, the village cluster known as Hanuabada experienced more sustained social change than any other Papuan community. Returning from wartime exile in 1945, Hanuabadans awaited the reconstruction of their homes, afterwards continuing to improve and extend them. Cyril Belshaw observed life in the village in 1951–52 (Belshaw 1957). This was one of several studies of 'social economics' he conducted in the period (e.g. Belshaw 1954). He reported that Hanuabadan householders were busily adding kitchens, interior walls, wash-places and lavatories, using materials such as scrap iron, timber, and whatever paint came to hand. Permanent building materials were expensive, and traditional materials difficult to obtain because Hanuabadan men had long been fully committed to wage labour. Belshaw did not record how home improvements were done or mention any commercial dealings. By implication, the work was done incrementally by householders, assisted by any friends or affines among tradesmen in the village. Quasi-traditional communal or cooperative activity was responsible for much of the built form of Hanuabada (and by extension, the modern informal town) in the post-war period. This process will be examined later to understand the boundaries between formality, informality and traditional exchange in the provision of shelter.

From a population of some 360 adult males in the named Hanabaduan subgroups of Hohodae and Poreporena, Belshaw found only about 60 not in wage employment, of whom – quite remarkably – fewer than 5 per cent were involuntarily unemployed. In a situation where traditional modes of subsistence had withered and no informal economic activity (in Hart's sense) was evident, wage-employment had become the norm. There were no cash crops, and there was little evidence of supplementary incomes. Practically all adult males were obliged to support their families through wage-labour. Traditional trading voyages (Ch. 5) had not resumed after the war, and agriculture was insignificant by the 1950s. This is not to say that all traditional exchange had been abandoned, as will become apparent.

Hanuabadans were not detribalized (the status urban officials were so anxious to avoid); they were simply enveloped by the town. A genuinely urban community, it differed from the few other such communities in Papua and New Guinea in having no significant migrant population. These pioneer townspeople were also subject to a unique disadvantage, explicable in terms of Belshaw's concept of a 'village subsidy' (Ch. 11). Charles Rowley took up the idea: Hanuabadans bore the full cost of urban development when they became committed to wage employment and lost the subsistence production that subsidized it. They were subject to a system of urban wage determination still focused on the interests of rural employers, so that setting wages according to the needs of single men was especially disadvantageous to Hanuabada (Ch. 11). We should note for comparison that waged workers in the Rabaul peri-urban village of Matupit were much better off because they continued to benefit from subsistence production while earning cash in the town. The effects of Hanuabadan disadvantage were evident from low standards of housing, nutrition, hygiene and health, as well as a scarcity of clean water, high rates of infant mortality and a high incidence of tuberculosis.

It would be a mistake to point to post-war circumstances as the only cause of this sorry state; it seemed to have been longer in the making. Reminiscent of the apathy among many Papuans in the interwar period (Ch. 11), Hanuabadans were locked into a low-level equilibrium of inadequate consumption while lacking the ability, and the political organization and will, to improve their conditions. The men of Hanuabada were losing the labour market edge they had held before the war, as general standards of education were improving and more skilled jobseekers were arriving in Port Moresby. Murray Groves (1957, 46) commented that, '[their] education has lagged behind the industrial and commercial growth of Port Moresby . . . [and] work is a perplexing but necessary drudgery'. Moreover, the tides of rural–urban migration began to wash through Hanuabada itself. Writing only a decade after Belshaw, Rowley observed a striking change. By 1963 a population of some three thousand Hanuabadans was now bearing the burden of some three hundred incomer families – so perhaps fifteen hundred people – imposed by obligations of kinship and custom (Rowley 1965, 197). A token of broader processes of urban growth, this suggests these urban villagers still felt obliged to honour customary obligations to rural affines and traditional trade partners. Increasing pressure on urban land and housing can only have worsened the squalid conditions seen by Belshaw soon after the war.

Informal Migrant Settlements

In pre-European times, Western Motu villages engaged in a far-flung network of trade and exchange relationships with communities along the south Papuan coast (Ch. 5). In the colonial period, coastal people travelling to the capital were able to take advantage of social links forged in such trade. This account draws on the histories of Hula people from south-east of Port Moresby, and Toaripi from the Gulf of Papua in the north-west, to show how such traditional associations assisted migrants to establish themselves. By gaining the consent of right-holders with whom they could claim some link, this early generation of incomers established settlements on traditional Motu or Koita land after the Pacific War. Less commonly, 'squatters' occupied vacant government land, as in the case of Toaripi settlers who occupied a ridge overlooking government offices near Hanuabada.

This suggests how an acute labour shortage, gripping the capital in the immediate post-war years, had eroded official opposition to such incursions. Their dwellings 'were supposed to be temporary, an expedient that would give the administration time to construct proper housing for its employees' (Ryan 1970, 18–19). Men with trade skills, acquired working with Allied forces, were in demand. Some gained government housing but then their supposedly temporary housing was taken over by more recent arrivals (ibid., 19). Settlements continued to grow inexorably, for while both public and private employers were in principle responsible for accommodating staff, provision was never adequate. In the interwar period, swift official action had been taken to defend the 'idea of the town'. In this new era sanctions were initially deferred, then confined to spasmodic bursts during which some evictions occurred and services were cut off, though to no avail (Ryan 1977, 149). Toaripi and other settlers benefited from a lack of official resolve and capacity to deter the inflow of migrants, although there remained an administrative inertia, based on opposition to settlements and what (in Oram's account) reads like calculated neglect. For, while authorities viewed migrant settlements as illegal, in the new post-war order they did little to prevent them. Further, their very illegality disinclined officials from acting to improve settlement living conditions, while many settlers lacked the confidence to invest in self-help initiatives.

Settlers were energetic and resourceful, however, when it came to finding sites for settlement. When incomers wanted to occupy traditional land, diplomacy was necessary. Toaripi incomers would 'invoke some combination of ties' to Motu landholders based on kinship, personal connection or traditional trade partnerships to request permission to build on Motu land. In time this first house would become crowded, and permission would then be sought to build a second, then a third, 'and so on' (Ryan 1970, 19–20). Relations with traditional owners often became strained; as more houses were built, the social distance between hosts and 'guests' increased.

Soon permission was no longer requested, and the original Toaripi occupant became the arbiter of housing arrangements. Within a few years large Toaripi settlements appeared around the capital on traditional Motu land. Relationships with the original landowners were minimal, payment of rents was exceptional rather than the rule, and little acknowledgement of the original status of occupied land was made. Motu might approach authorities for redress but the importance of Toaripi in the formal workforce and the absence of accommodation alternatives usually protected interlopers (Ryan 1970, 19–21). Occasionally landowners prevailed. Tommy Kabu was moved on from several sites before establishing the long-term Purari Delta settlement at Rabia camp in the late 1940s, with assistance from Motu friends (Oram 1967, 93). This was a pattern of pushback: the removal of settlers by officials only for them to set up elsewhere.

A comparatively small group of settlers were Hula people whose home village lay 100 kilometres south-east of Port Moresby (Map 5.1). Mentioned earlier, and described as the 'frontrunners' of informality, the Hula were a fishing and trading community whose traditional activities dovetailed with those of the Western Motu. Before the colonial era Hula families sailed by canoe to the Western Motu villages during the *hiri* season, when Motu men were voyaging to the Gulf region to obtain sago. The Hula fished Hanuabadan waters to supply fish to Motuan villagers during this period, receiving sago from the returning Motu men at the end of the season. The Hula would return to their home villages with substantial sago stocks and with Motuan clay pots exchanged in trade (Oram 1968b, 6).

In the interwar period, Hula had been unusual among Papuans for their copra trading and short-term employment in the capital to earn money for taxes and church dues. They were also, as previously mentioned, early beneficiaries of LMS education. In the late 1930s some lived seasonally on their canoes, beached near the site of the modern Koki market. Others camped on nearby Daugo Island from where they supplied the town with fish (Oram 1976a, 33). After the Pacific War, Hula made use of their local ties and formal education to take advantage of the urban employment boom, bringing families with them. Some Hula began to live on Motu land at Vabukori, facilitated by similarities in their languages and social structures. From 1954 Hula also lived at another beach settlement at nearby Taikone, also on Vabukori land. This Taikone settlement grew in a manner familiar from Ryan's (1977) account of the Toaripi. Other Hula canoes were beached on government land near Koki market. Numbering fifteen vessels in 1959, this 'fleet' was expelled from Koki by government officers. The Hula simply relocated, sailing to Taikone where, according to one Vabukori woman right-holder, 'she gave permission for them to stay initially for two weeks and then allowed them to stay longer. They then began to rest the bows of their canoes on piles'. Against her wishes, the Hula made their occupancy a fait accompli by removing the canoes, while leaving the canoe-houses in place. When Oram first saw the site there were eighteen 'substantial' houses on the shoreline (Oram 1968b, 7–10).

So bald an account might suggest that Hula relationships with traditional right-holders became fraught, as in the case of the Toaripi. However, friendly relations were maintained, as Motu owners came to value exchange relationships with their new neighbours, and benefited from cash they brought into the community. A count of Hula residents in Port Moresby in 1964 totalled 717 individuals, of whom 40 per cent lived within the boundaries of Vabukori. Housing was not a problem because so many Hula people had been able to build their own houses (about 40 per cent) or to find employer housing (43 per cent) while others lived in non-Hula households (Oram 1968b, 11–14). Over 80 per cent of Hula men were in jobs requiring some level of skill. Males comprised less than 55 per cent of the settler community, a degree of demographic 'normalization' very different from other more recent communities. It is striking that during the late colonial period the apparent aptitude of Hula people for informal entrepreneurship was only partially realized, due to their success in the *formal* labour market.

Newer communities included groups with no history of relations with traditional landholders and little educational advantage compared with Papuan coastal groups such as the Hula. These included Goilala from the uplands of Papua, people from the central cordillera (highlanders), and from the New Guinea coast and islands. As each successive group grew, their absorption into the town followed a fairly regular pattern: high masculinity among early cohorts, urban residence punctuated by circular movement between town and home-place, increasing proportions of women and family formation in the group, and increasing stability of urban residence representing commitment to the town. Consistent with this pattern, whereas in 1957 New Guinean men made up only 11 per cent of the urban male workforce, by the census of 1966 this had increased to 25 per cent, while male and female New Guineans were 14 per cent of the total urban population (Surmon and Ward 1973, 15). Port Moresby was becoming a *national* capital in more than just name. However, all newer groups maintained contact with their home communities and frequently hosted visitors, while most still professed the social ideology of an ultimate 'return to the village'.

Among arrivals from the New Guinea Islands region were students, well-educated recruits to private sector jobs or in government (the latter employing 34 per cent of the capital's indigenous workforce in 1966). No doubt some of these people came from the villages of Pila Pila and Matupit on the Gazelle, where investments in 'human capital' were transforming the economic prospects of land-short communities (Ch. 18, below). Such migrants usually found work-related or institutional housing. Other less-credentialed New Guineans, together with Goilalas and the variety of other newcomers without such housing, had to find their own accommodation. A few married into urban villages and others were able to establish themselves in settlements. Many more took the *pasendia* option,[1] moving from house to house to stay with relatives and kin in employer-provided housing. Fully 13 per cent of the urban population lived in servants' quarters attached to high-covenant housing in 1971 (Oram 1976b, 149). Others cast around for land to occupy, contributing to a change in the character of informal settlements. 'Squatter' settlements were increasingly set on government land, away from the coast, their numbers rising from fourteen settlements with some 1,850 people in 1956, eighteen with 4,500 in 1964, and then forty in 1970 with more than 12,000 inhabitants (Oram 1976a, 99). At that time, of eighteen 'major' settlements thirteen were on government land (Norwood 1979, 79).

Settlements were often located in places deemed unsuitable for formal housing, on steep hillsides or in swamps and gullies, reducing the risk of eviction. Some groups with limited formal employment prospects located near land suitable for commercial gardening, along roads outside the capital. Sometimes it suited local landowners, in dispute with rival claimants, to invite migrants to settle and pay rents, to strengthen their hand in future arbitrations (Norwood 1984, 103). Possibly the most disadvantaged settlement was at Ragamuka, established by Chimbu (*Simbu*) highlanders on traditional land whose ownership was disputed. Accessed via a rubbish dump, it was, by reason of landowner opposition, still without running water on Independence Day in 1975, despite more than forty other settlements having been connected. This account may convey something of the complexity of processes by which incomers of diverse cultures, many languages and widely varying capacities for formal employment established themselves.

At the 1966 census, about 16 per cent of the urban population were found in each of the village and settlement areas (Oram 1976a, 101), so that about a third of the urban population resided in Oram's second, or 'unplanned' sector. This was still the case in 1972, when he estimated that villages now held only 10 per cent of the town's people, while settlements had grown to house 23 per cent (ibid., 194). This was a substantial change in weighting, occurring rapidly in a period of fast overall growth. Between the 1966 and 1971 censuses, the enumerated population grew from 41,000 to almost 77,000, while the formal, planned town maintained its two-thirds share.

Escaping Old Habits of Thought

The post-war orthodoxy of 'development' was tempered in its bureaucratic application by notions of 'guardianship', and by a residual commitment to the preservation of village life. Early post-war PNG bore a burden of social and economic obsolescence, originating in a nexus between retarded urbanism, archaic processes of wage determination and low labour productivity (Ch. 14). Official habits surviving from the interwar period delayed the emergence of a committed and stable urban population, and hampered investment in its housing and urban amenity. By pushing back against bureaucratic inertia, indigenous people transgressed the norms of formal market economy. Activities such as migrating to town for opportunity, accessing land via informal channels, and building on it without permission were cases where the people found it necessary to contravene bureaucratic requirements. Meanwhile, customary landowners enveloped by the new urbanism struggled to find livelihoods in an environment where their subsistence resources were increasingly irrelevant.

This and the previous chapter have described how the capital evolved towards a more stable and committed urban workforce, supporting a normalized population structure. It was a system excessively dependent – until late in the colonial day – on unaccompanied male workers, short-term 'circular' migrants. Rural and urban labour supply were linked: the plantation wage served as a benchmark for the urban unskilled wage; urban employers relied on labour recruited and paid on a 'single man' basis; labour turnover was wasteful, and worker productivity hobbled – the policy analogue of a Gordian knot (Ch. 14). Nonetheless, slow and laboured improvements to this dysfunctional policy framework occurred during the 1960s. As a permanent, formal urban workforce emerged, it provided a template against which informal modes of livelihood could be defined.

Such activities (as Hart discovered in 1972) were still relatively unimportant in the capital, even as it came in other respects to exhibit a 'Third World' character. If retarded urbanism was evident in bureaucratic fetters on the self-help housing efforts of migrants, the failure of independent, self-employed, *informal* modes of livelihood to flourish was another telling indicator. Later chapters will consider the implications of these lingering phenomena for the town (or 'city', as Port Moresby became in 1972) at the time of independence. Meanwhile, the narrative now turns to the experience of Rabaul in the aftermath of the Pacific War.

Note

1. *Pasendia* (*Tok Pisin*, 'passenger'): one who is accommodated in a household while job-searching or visiting. *Pasendia* generally wear out their welcome after some period, and are obliged to move on.

Chapter 17

Reconstruction in Rabaul and the Seeds of Post-war Growth

With the Japanese expelled, Rabaul was again under Australian military government. The old German town had largely vanished, and as late as 1950 Rabaul was 'a depressing dusty sprawl of salvage yards, Japanese-built air-raid shelters, black-iron sheds and paper-walled houses' (Fenbury 1978, 49). In Rabaul and more broadly, Stanner felt as though the past half-century of development by Australians and Germans had never occurred. Among the people, significant changes in their outlook and behaviour were evident and 'simple acceptance of European authority and prestige seemed . . . no longer assured' (Stanner 1953, 86). Bill Epstein (1969, 32) thought the ordeal of military occupation and destruction had given the Tolai 'new force and direction'; they were in no mood to return to the status quo of the interwar period.

Nor was the post-war Labor government intending to force such a return, while under the conservatives who succeeded Labor, Hasluck's *guardianship* inspired policies on the Gazelle very different from the interwar years (Ch. 14). In the Mandated Territory, regulation had often favoured Australian economic interests at the expense of Tolai (Ch. 7). But now, with the important exception of Goroka (discussed in later chapters), enterprises thought likely to be 'potentially destructive of village life' were be denied government support (MacWilliam 2013, 2). Invariably these were either foreign investment or resident expatriate initiatives. Historically subject to substantial land alienation, Tolai would be among the primary beneficiaries of this reversal. 'Development' became institutionalized in policy and rhetoric, and the Tolai internalized it as a collective goal.

Compensation payments were important for recovery, and Tolai received among the largest sums. Echoing contemporary opinion, Stanner (1953, 119) commented that much of this was devoted to current rather than investment expenditures, and may have done more for the expatriate private sector than for villagers. Chinese traders certainly benefited, but he probably underestimated the value of supporting Tolai consumption during years when much of their labour was devoted to rehabilitating coconut plantings. They also gained from investing in cheap army surplus trucks and other materiel. Again, while Tolai had benefited somewhat from formal schooling before the war, the Gazelle now became a favoured area for educational expansion, achieving enrolment rates among the highest in the country. Together with reconstruction of pre-war agricultural training facilities, the new official emphasis on smallholder production proved particularly beneficial.

Innovation and Efforts at Formalization

Immediately after the war, few trade stores remained to buy copra in small parcels. Among Tolai smallholders, certain men with access to larger acreages of land took the initiative to directly approach the PCB (Production Control Board) and opened accounts with it (Salisbury 1970, 133). Enos of Vunamami (Map 7.1) bought a truck, founded a cooperative and organized a copra-growing group to deal with the PCB (ibid., 320). The board was prepared to accept small shipments, delaying full payment until after export proceeds had been realized. Although the PCB option disappeared for Tolai when European and Chinese traders returned and the board required increasingly larger shipments, the episode was significant in showing some Tolai striving towards more formal operations, successfully negotiating registration procedures and observing quality standards. Formalization of some Tolai livelihoods was further advanced by the post-war revival of cocoa when agricultural officers distributed planting materials. Few Tolai had planted cocoa before, but now they showed such interest that growth of smallholder cocoa became an official policy objective. Enos was among the first to receive encouragement; in 1949 he deployed his own land, and that of others secured through political influence, to become a substantial producer. Together with other business interests and his subsequent role as a director of the Tolai Cocoa Project (TCP), Enos would become a model Tolai formal entrepreneur and man of influence – an archetypal Melanesian 'big-man' playing a leadership role in the market economy (Salisbury 1970, 319ff).

It is perhaps understandable, but nonetheless piquant, that extension officials selected elite individuals for assistance, thereby reinforcing their political and economic ascendancy. Such 'big-men' often had access to customary land not yet alienated to tree crops, as well as to the labour of 'clan dependants', so that opportunistic action by elements of what MacWilliam referred to as the 'bourgeois and would-be bourgeois' among the Tolai caused cocoa production to run ahead of government capacity for supervision. Not until the 1950s were officials able to exert effective guidance over the industry (MacWilliam 2013, 74–75). On the Gazelle, agricultural extension services were only later directed to turn their attention to smallholder production of cocoa (ibid., 101), rather than favouring those whom Hasluck had described as 'shrewd heads' (Ch. 14). A parallel situation occurred in Goroka during the emergence of a coffee industry, where Bob McKillop saw evidence of an early 'extension bias' favouring 'more wealthy smallholders' (Ch. 14). These were 'big-men' in the mould of Enos of Vunamami, and coffee production in Goroka would also outrun official supervision (Ch. 22).

The progress of cocoa was rapid; by 1954/55, the Tolai population of some 34,000 owned an average of thirty-five trees each; by 1960 their numbers had grown to 40,000, with seventy-four trees apiece. This expansion, together with their investment in processing, marked the commencement of Salisbury's fourth 'stage' of Tolai accommodation to market economy (Ch 3). Even though formal plantation output was recovering rapidly, Tolai became responsible for more than a third of 'dry bean' production on the Gazelle by 1965 (Epstein 1968, 115–66, tables 18, 19). Regulation of smallholders was attempted under a *Cocoa Ordinance* from 1952, which required smallholders to register and to have no fewer than five hundred trees 'in continuous grove' as a condition of registration. This established a de facto criterion for formality that many growers could not, or would not, satisfy. The ordinance was never enforced effectively and, because many small secret plots existed, unregistered (i.e. *informal*) cocoa flourished.

Other regulatory objectives related to quality (an issue of processing) and returns to growers (a marketing matter). 'The Administration was concerned that native growers should produce a uniformly high-quality cocoa which could be sold on the world market at a satisfactory price' (Epstein 1968, 117); this would require modern fermentaries and quality control to produce 'flavour' cocoa – a significant step towards professionalizing Tolai growers. Maximizing prices suggested the need for joint marketing to exert competitive power against 'independents' (private traders and processors, European and Chinese). Concern about the performance of Tolai copra cooperatives prompted the search for an alternative model of community organization, able to achieve both quality and price objectives.

The TCP was established as the chosen vehicle (Epstein 1968, Ch. 7). A significant bureaucratic initiative intended to formalize smallholder production, it inspired pushback among some Tolai in the form of a stubborn informality. The rise and fall of the project has been analysed as a conflict between tradition and modernity (Scarlett Epstein) and as class struggle (MacWilliam). While both accounts are informative, further insights will be gained by viewing the episode through the lens of informality.

Rise and Fall of the Tolai Cocoa Project

Although the TCP was established formally in 1956, its components had operated for some years, processing and marketing Tolai cocoa. The creation of local government councils from 1950 provided it with an institutional anchor. Elected statutory bodies with prescribed, formal modes of governance, local councils were founded on 'rational-legal' principles. Able to operate economic enterprises, to appropriate funds and incur debt, they exemplified Hart's understanding of bureaucracy as an instrument intended to support a 'prevalent economic model'. Councils were among the earliest instances of Tolai participation in bureaucratic management. Their goals were primarily economic – specifically, to implement 'development' based on smallholder communities. Had string-pulling by colonial officials not limited the TCP's autonomy, the powers vested in it might have represented what Salisbury called 'political consolidation'. From 1958 it was administered by a board with council, grower and official representatives. However, as late as 1965 and despite holding a voting majority, Tolai lacked confidence to take charge.

Scarlett Epstein's reference to an active 'breakaway political movement' (1968, 124) suggests some deficit of legitimacy in governance, and this may explain why some Tolai rejected the TCP altogether while others, despite joining it, failed in varying degrees to conform with its rules. Observing the non-conforming manner in which many Tolai continued to grow and sell cocoa, a stubborn informality is apparent. This manifested in what Epstein called 'the drift away from the project' – which may also be seen as pushback against it.

From its beginnings, the TCP suffered from the competition of private traders and processors, European and Chinese, while other Tolai were also free to build and operate fermentaries. These 'independents' could purchase unprocessed beans directly from growers. Attempts to ban Tolai bean sales, other than to the TCP, were disallowed in the interest of competition, but the project still managed to improve its market share, peaking at 70 per cent in 1958, after which it declined.

In 1962, in an attempt to halt the drift, an ordinance concerned with licensing new fermentaries required these to be restricted to Tolai, excluding European and Chinese independents (Salisbury 1970, 60). This was emblematic of the broader policy U-turn since the pre-war period when bureaucratic intervention had been more often intended to advantage European capital. Even so, TCP garnered only 36 per cent of Tolai beans by 1965, and as it had incurred bank debt to ramp up production this decline posed a threat to its viability. In 1967 the project was vested in a single, newly unified Gazelle Peninsula local government council, after which new management and procedures 'appeared to breathe life' into it for a time. But broader political unrest, increasing costs, new debt obligations, a failed attempt at diversification, and growing competition from independents all combined to reverse this recovery. By 1970 preparations had commenced for the TCP to be privatized, a process completed in 1971 (MacWilliam 2013, 186–87).

Why the Project Failed: Rival Explanations

Scarlett Epstein (1968) and Scott MacWilliam (2013) have offered explanations of the erosion of support for the project, representing, respectively, anthropological and political economy modes of inquiry. Their narratives are examined here through the lens of the formal/informal duality. In her account, Epstein recorded some TCP members supporting the project publicly, while selling beans to private traders 'under shelter of darkness'. An informant, To Tama of Rapitok village, was conflicted because he knew the project would pay better in the longer run and deserved his support. Secret dealings with Chinese traders offended his conscience but the situation posed a dilemma from which no escape was obvious (Epstein 1968, 129).

The dilemma arose from To Tama's obligations under Tolai customary land law, a system under pressure as population densities rose. The combination of land allocation on matrilineal principles and the patrilocal residence of many men increased disparities in land distribution, a situation exacerbated by a growing use of land for cocoa, a perennial crop. A traditionally flexible system of land allocation for shifting agriculture was now subject to increasing rigidity and competition. While To Tama acquired Rapitok land through his matrilineal descent group, his wife had no rights in the village and was unable to transmit land to their son. To Tama planted on land registered under the *Cocoa Ordinance*, selling its crop formally to the TCP fermentary. On another, unregistered, parcel he and his son planted more trees, selling the beans secretly (i.e. informally) to

Chinese traders for the boy's benefit. Epstein explained this as To Tama's strategy to give the son some opportunity, in the wheeling and dealing that would follow his death, to acquire part of his father's matrilineal lands. Such 'drift' from the project was caused by the inability of customary land and inheritance law to accommodate introduced, perennial cash cropping. This can be seen as inducing pushback – behaviour that was informal in terms of TCP norms.

MacWilliam rejected explanations couched in terms of a 'growing clash between "tradition", represented by matrilineal inheritance, and "modernity"', represented by land tenure individualization. Scarlett Epstein did not differentiate between the imperative to accumulate motivating the 'indigenous class of capital' and the more modest and immediate motives of most Tolai growers – namely, to acquire consumption goods. MacWilliam's account involved a clash between indigenous capital and household production, whose casualty was the project. But TCP's decline was only incidental; his primary concern was with a developing divergence of class interests between an emerging indigenous bourgeoisie bent on accumulation (including TCP assets) and small Tolai producers concerned with their own immediate welfare. For these small players, clandestine cocoa dealings provided an opportunity for immediate consumption, as distinct from the deferral of gratification required by project procedures. Further (and not surprisingly) assets 'hidden' by the class of accumulators were seen by smallholders as interference with customary rules for the redistribution of land, done by removing land from descent group control (MacWilliam 2013, 191–92). Smallholders pushed back against official efforts to shape them in the bureaucratic mould by resorting to covert informal trade (including cocoa stolen from formal plantations).

The seeds of this conflict were sown, unwittingly but inevitably, by the early prominence of 'wealthy and influential' individuals – such as Enos of Vunamami – in the post-war initiatives of an Australian government intent on stimulating broad-based smallholder development. MacWilliam emphasized the generally benign and positive character of post-war colonial policy while pointing to its longer-run failure (on the Gazelle and elsewhere) to secure an equitable pattern of agricultural development. Increasing levels of economic and social differentiation among Tolai were inevitable, for change in PNG was subject to an ineluctable force, *the external authority of capital*. The post-war world was divided between Western and Eastern blocs, and in the former (including its decolonizing territories and client states) the 'private accumulation of capital' was reasserted (MacWilliam 2013, 12).

From the mid-1960s, in a process by which individuals succeeded in acquiring and 'hiding' assets, a powerful, entrepreneurial group arose on the

Gazelle. Its members' interests 'often spread over a number of landholdings owned and operated under different arrangements'. By 1974, suggesting how far such people had advanced beyond household production, wage labour was employed on indigenous-owned land in East New Britain to harvest 15 per cent of local cocoa production (MacWilliam 2013, 193). MacWilliam's view of the significance of this new class and the timing of its emergence was portentous: an indigenous bourgeoisie became politically powerful 'just as the state was being reformed to accommodate self-government'. In this political environment, a struggle for land was fuelled by opportunities presented by expatriate disinvestment in plantations and other economic assets (ibid., 243). This situation had direct parallels in other 'lucky' places, including Goroka (discussed in Ch. 21 and beyond).

Privatization of the TCP occurred during this period, but by then Salisbury (1970, 1971) was finished with the Gazelle. He had regarded successive rounds of 'political consolidation' as crucial to Tolai progress, and the establishment of the TCP as a signature achievement. In his terms, its acquisition by private interests represented failure. But setbacks had occurred before to interrupt Tolai progress, as for example during the stasis period of 1921–35 (Ch. 7). That situation improved eventually, while under post-war Australian policy representative Tolai institutions were nurtured and smallholder development encouraged. His vision of a rural-based Tolai economy propelled by the increasing elaboration of service activities (Salisbury 1971) should be understood as inspired by this benign policy environment.

MacWilliam (2013, 194) saw TCP privatization in 1971 as introducing a new, more brutal era in which class divisions would be played out in national and regional politics. His suggestion of increasing accumulation by the emergent indigenous bourgeoisie raised the possibility that Salisbury's immiserizing 'urban involution of services' (Ch. 2) would follow as a consequence. In terms of Salisbury's model this would have represented a fifth 'stage' – one marked by regression. But more positive developments (a technological innovation, perhaps, or the success of educated Tolai workers in an emerging national labour market) might emerge to avert such a result. Post-1975 evidence concerning this last possibility is presented in Ch. 18.

Stubborn Informality in the Rural Economy

In Scarlett Epstein's account, despite To Tama's keen sense of the opposing tugs of tradition and fatherly affection, he accepted particular TCP obligations in return for the opportunity to engage profitably in a formal marketing enterprise. But by concealing some cocoa, and creating ambiguity in his relationship with the matrilineage, he chose also to engage in separate, *informal* market dealings. His situation illustrates the hybridity found during transition to market economy, where Adam Smith's view of trade as due to a natural human tendency to 'truck and barter' is counterposed against the Maussian conception of exchange as the product of socially regulated customs. The formal/informal duality is apparent in MacWilliam's version, where some wealthy Tolai led the way to adopting formal modes. Active in local government, they were among the strongest supporters of the TCP, were represented on its board, and hoped eventually to benefit from its assets. But other wealthy men in an 'anti-council' bloc clung to informal modes. They dealt with private traders or even established their own processing facilities, finding customers among their own followers.

Others pursued To Tama's middle way, combining formality and informality by dealing both with the project and independents. There seems no way to establish in what proportions 'indigenous capital' took these options; no pattern emerges from my attempt to read MacWilliam's account in terms of formality and informality. If the duality were salient to his analysis one might expect wealthy Tolai, able to await final payment until export proceeds were realized by the TCP, to deal formally with it. However, political considerations and issues of inheritance ('hiding assets') seem to have counted more for some. Status as an 'accumulator' was no predictor of how an individual might act. One might think small growers, 'reproducing consumption' and with a preference for immediate cash, would be most likely to desert the project. But many did not. Informality in growing and marketing cocoa appears to have been a personal choice, for which an individual's class status was no guide.

Scarlett Epstein's account turns on what is described here as *hybrid* behaviour. While growers were conscious of TCP's bureaucratic norms they were also subject to expectations derived from their own social milieu. Such expectations made it difficult for many to conform with bureaucratic requirements. Because Epstein's analysis focuses on this discrepancy (a conflict between imposed orthodoxy and practical outcomes), her account appears more appropriate to a formal/informal framework than MacWilliam's class narrative. Analysis in terms of informality is of particular value in circumstances of economic hybridity (although not all informal activity is hybrid; Ch. 26).

What is being discussed here is *rural* informality. In an agricultural system undergoing transition, rural informality occurs in households where continuing evidence of earlier modes of production and distribution (household subsistence, non-market exchange, traditional land tenure) is apparent. These are among phenomena described by Hart as 'residue'

(Ch. 1). Such tenacity of customary social arrangements is conducive to hybridity in market exchange, although apparent continuity may also mask changes in rural domestic economy. In the case of the Gazelle, masked changes included efforts to modify traditional land tenure (emphasized by Epstein) and new forms of material accumulation (stressed by MacWilliam). The 'under the radar' character of much rural informal activity provides some explanation for the limited discussion it has inspired in the international literature – certainly by comparison with the abundance of attention lavished on *urban* informality. Perhaps the demarcation of formal from informal poses greater conceptual difficulty in rural areas because developing country agriculture remains, to a greater degree than for urban economic activity, the joint domain of the traditional and the modern. Although it is often assumed that informality will be eradicated by modernization, in practice it appears informal economic activity is tenacious, pushing back against pressures for change. The stubborn informality of those Tolai who resisted the TCP illustrated that tenacity.

Chapter 18

Informal Economy on the Gazelle at the End of the Colonial Era

Insofar as Salisbury described an informal economy, it was primarily rural, although he also foresaw an urban informal economy (the urban 'involution of services'). For reasons of geography and infrastructure, his rural informal economy was well articulated with its urban centre, in Rabaul. He, and both Epsteins, conveyed a sense of thriving rural–urban relationships, expressed particularly in the Rabaul marketplace. Salisbury (1970) estimated some seven thousand people attended on Saturdays in 1961, spending around £2,000, while Scarlett Epstein counted about two thousand vendors and calculated cash takings of £2,750 (Epstein 1968). Women, acting as what she called *producer-sellers* (Epstein 1982), were dominant in this and other Gazelle markets. Sales by individuals were typically small, and (demonstrating hybridity) market days were valued as much for the opportunity to socialize as for profits earned in trade. While using specialized middlemen would have saved them time and yielded higher net returns, women producer-sellers valued the social benefits of market attendance at least as much as their economic gains (Epstein 1968, 145).

Market transactions with non-Tolai were conducted in cash, while in dealings between Tolai both *tambu* and cash were used. Shell money could be exchanged in intra-Tolai trade for a wide range of traditional commodities, and Salisbury (1971, 59) claimed that implied rates of exchange between *tambu* and cash were calculable. Market-women priced their produce in both 'currencies', so that rough equivalents for the cash value of *tambu* transactions could be calculated. While some women used the market to accumulate *tambu*, in most cases their earnings, whether *tambu* or cash, were exchanged immediately for other foods for consumption, or to cover transport costs. All such transactions were in principle 'value-adding' in a national-accounting sense and, as unenumerated trade, should be seen as informal. Although occurring in the town, they were not so much an instance of *urban* informality as the urban activity of *rural* visitors. Nor (as Epstein's designation of vendors as 'producer-sellers' showed) was there any suggestion of specialized trading. It was van Leur's secondary trading, complementary to subsistence production.

Just as the missionary Danks had found men more opportunistic and open to bargaining (Ch. 7), Salisbury thought Tolai men more profit-oriented than women in food production. In the 1960s some men from western villages with relatively abundant land initiated plantings of subsistence and introduced crops for Rabaul market. He called them commercial farmers, because in each village some men 'specialized in producing. . . bulk crops' for market while purchasing their own subsistence foodstuffs from other growers (Salisbury 1970, 214). This occurred amid changing patterns of Gazelle trade in which an older, ecological interdependence was giving way to a new interdependence. This was between food-surplus areas such as Vunamami and food-deficit villages with larger wage incomes near Rabaul, such as Matupit and Pila Pila (discussed below).

Salisbury's narrative might appear to suggest the emergence of specialized intermediaries until we read that these 'commercial' farmers still conducted most of their trade by means of 'delayed barter exchanges' using *tambu*, in terms of 'standard fixed equivalences'. In this trade, profits (while being realized in an accounting sense) were 'supposedly' not the 'driving force' for exchanges (ibid.). Although Salisbury's account is sparse, a strong element of hybridity is apparent. Despite his suggestion of specialized production, such dealings appeared to still retain considerable commonalities with the trading observed by Danks in the nineteenth century. Again, Scarlett Epstein observed entrepreneurs contracting for the bulk supply of foodstuffs to commercial plantations and institutions (schools, missions, hospitals). They bulked up consignments from individuals and trucked produce on commission, thus appearing to perform intermediary functions still absent from Rabaul marketplace (Epstein 1968, 80). The discussion below will return to consider the significance of these two cases.

The Tolai group most engaged in the urban economy was the Matupi, from the peri-urban village of Matupit studied by Bill Epstein (1969). For Matupi women, market attendance was among their most important and regular activities and, unlike other vendors, they sometimes purchased and resold produce. Fish, vegetables, lime and eggs were sourced in Matupit, and other produce in the marketplace itself. They also sold produce around the town, either on the streets or by visiting offices, Chinese shops and other workplaces. Such peddling behaviour, with less emphasis on social interaction and more on resale and profit, set them apart from the bulk of 'producer-sellers'. Whether this constituted middleman trade will also be discussed below. It certainly reflected the changing patterns of Gazelle area trade described by Salisbury (above). He also observed street trading in Rabaul; in addition, vendors were active at sporting events and on other public occasions, although he did not identify where these people came from (Salisbury 1970, 189).

Bill Epstein's remarks concerning the relationship between Matupit and Rabaul in earlier periods were reported above (Ch. 7). For the 1960s, he emphasized the multiple economic activities of villagers; many participated simultaneously in subsistence, cash cropping and wage labour in order to benefit from the economic opportunities offered by Rabaul and its hinterland (Epstein 1969, 305). In this they displayed Bauer's imperfect specialization and occupational fluidity (Ch. 2). Starting from subsistence production, they might earn cash by gardening and selling traditional staples or cash crops. Some had become entrepreneurial and entered contracting, while others were in wage-employment. What Epstein thought most significant was their capacity to pursue multiple and simultaneous roles (ibid., 189). In the context of Africa, such capacity to juggle activities has been described by a modern commentator as 'the reality of a thriving informal sector, the diversity of smallholder livelihoods combining formal and informal, farm and off-farm, urban and rural activities' (Vorley, Del Pozo-Vergnes and Barnett, 2012, 11).

Some small businessmen operated in Matupit, running trade stores and other enterprises. Others had replanted coconuts after the war and rebuilt copra dryers. Eight stores operated in 1960, with capital generally subscribed by members of a descent-group. These stores suffered many difficulties, including interference from kin and pressure to extend credit, and their viability in a commercial sense was problematic. They were hybrid enterprises, for most storekeepers were not entrepreneurs in any commercial sense (Epstein 1969, 65). Beyond the village, there was no simple dichotomy between those with and those without wage employment. Wives worked in gardens but so also did wage-workers at weekends, during holidays, or between stints of formal employment. In this period few absent workers stayed away for very long, though long-term absentees would become more common as independence approached.

Beyond Matupit, Salisbury (1970, 1971) recorded that many individuals and groups in Vunamami tried trucking produce and carrying passengers; ownership of vehicles displayed hybridity in that it both conferred prestige and promised profits. Typically, however, inadequate provision was made for capital replacement, and profits were elusive. Small carpentry contracting was widespread, relatively lucrative though sporadic, and was combined with agriculture and other activities. Pig husbandry had become commercial, while many households raised chickens for sale. Some entrepreneurs obtained beer illegally and resold it; others distilled banana liquor. Commercial *pati* (parties) with music and drinking were frequent and could be quite profitable. Small trade stores were common, though (as in Matupit) often short-lived or spasmodic in operation. Scarlett Epstein was disappointed by the absence of simple manufacturing industries and, like Salisbury and Bill Epstein, she cast doubt on the commerciality of many service ventures. She described these in terms revealing hybridity. Commercial enterprise had become part of Tolai society and economy, and owning trucks, shops and copra-dryers was as much a source of pride for a matrilineage as owning *tambu* had been before the war. This had led, however, to some 'uneconomic investment' (Epstein 1968, 52).

Hybridity was also apparent in rural services, where much activity exhibited continuing adherence to traditional values and goals. Services by traditional specialists (composers of songs and dances, canoe builders, makers of musical instruments and ritual specialists performing ceremonies beneficial to communities) required payment in shell money (Salisbury 1971). Mortuary rites and ceremonies associated with male cults had become more elaborate as part of a Gazelle 'efflorescence of exchange', while specialists in magic and ritual (including workers of spells) may have continued to operate, though Christianized informants were reticent on such matters.

The Late Colonial Period, 1960–75

Assessment of growth and change in Tolai informal economy in the later period is bedevilled by a dearth of studies comparable with those of the Epsteins and Salisbury. In the run-up to independence, local political instability inhibited field research but, among later work, Scarlett Epstein extended her market research, collecting additional data in 1968–69 (Epstein 1982), Bill Epstein returned to Matupit in 1986 (Epstein 1988a, 1988b), and Christine Bradley worked in Pila Pila near Rabaul in 1978–79. A more recent historical account (MacWilliam 2013) complements these field-based studies. Together these sources permit some cautious 'back-projection' to suggest the trajectory of change to 1975, although the conclusions presented here are necessarily tentative.

MacWilliam was confident the tendency towards 'private accumulation of capital' had continued apace, with growing differentiation between 'accumulators' and consumers 'producing for immediate consumption' (Ch. 17). The first formal development plan prepared by colonial authorities acknowledged progress in smallholder agriculture but also pointed to increasing rural inequality. Nationally, it predicted the indigenous share of commercial agriculture (already responsible for half the planted area and some 40 per cent of output) would increase substantially, although 'the trend towards larger holdings in indigenous hands is expected to continue' (TPNG 1968). Nor was it simply a question of land, for the ambitious indigenous bourgeoisie had broader goals. On the Gazelle, around Goroka and elsewhere, members of the class of 'accumulators' entered a range of downstream, service and urban activities (MacWilliam 2013, 233). Growing inequality, suggested by the entry of politically connected indigenous entrepreneurs to higher reaches of economic activity, was much remarked upon at the time. As also occurred in Goroka, such accumulation often involved the acquisition of enterprises from departing expatriates, with continuing use of foreign management skills. Operations at this level and scale marked indigenous entry to the formal economy (rather than the informal 'sector' central to this study). Further discussion of the significance of these changes will be postponed until parallel events in Goroka are discussed (Ch. 23).

Aside from MacWilliam's bourgeoisie, at the more modest level of his 'consumers', another mode of accumulation was operating. Pila Pila, studied by Bradley in 1978, was taking a path other Tolai villages would follow. Its land resources were stretched by population growth and perennial tree crops, to the point where 40 per cent of villagers had little or no land for subsistence and were obliged to buy their food. Nonetheless, it was among the most prosperous of Gazelle villages although with a clear and growing degree of 'economic differentiation'. This was due primarily to villagers' historically good access to formal education, so that formal wage and salary earnings totalled three times the cash crop income. With 62 per cent of households having a resident wage earner (and 15 per cent having two), and with 30 per cent of adult males working away from the Gazelle, Pila Pila was compensated for land shortage by income from the wages and remittances of educated villagers (Bradley 1982, 44–46). This was the return on Pila Pila's accumulated *human* capital.[1] Similarly, in Matupit Bill Epstein found that 'in a completely novel departure' many of its people not only worked in Rabaul town but now also lived there, while educated Matupi had managed to parlay their schooling into well-paid formal employment in other urban centres (Epstein 1988a, 1988b). In 1971 Salisbury had suggested the possibility of an 'urban involution of services' due to rural population growth and economic stagnation. But at independence, in Pila Pila, Matupit and other land-short Tolai villages, a combination of education and migration had postponed any such urban involution. Differential investments in human capital were proving a potent source of economic inequality, however, both between and within Tolai villages (Epstein 1988b, 26).

The growing importance of formal wage-employment accompanied innovation in the rural informal economy. In part this flowed from changes in the status and ownership of *tambu*, whose possession in earlier times had been crucial to the power, prestige and influence of male leaders (Ch. 7). Even in the early years of independence, *tambu* remained an indicator of 'personal worth' for both men and women, as well as continuing to be 'intrinsic to Tolai identity' (Bradley 1982, 84). This continued despite Pila Pila's men having largely abandoned active *tambu* accumulation in favour of seeking success in the cash economy. It was left to women to gather shell-money, and they now possessed more of it than men. *Tambu* also continued in use as a commercial medium of exchange, and it was through informal commercial trade that women exerted themselves to accumulate it. While *tambu* could not yet be purchased for money, household cash earned in cropping and formal employment could be marshalled by women to finance purchases of commodities, for resale in exchange for *tambu*. These transactions were known as *pipiai*.

Pipiai differed from women's food trading because it was occurring outside the usual marketplaces, and the things being sold were not traditional. Often they were imported goods, offered for profit. In land-short Pila Pila, many women now spent more time on *pipiai*, selling commodities bought for cash, than they spent marketing their own garden produce. Bradley described such scenes: wherever people gathered together in numbers, women would be there to offer 'cigarettes, chewing gum, scones, biscuits, rice or potato chips, frankfurters, doughnuts, hardboiled eggs, peanuts, betel nut and lime, frozen drinks, and so on'. Often there was no need to travel; weekly meetings of the Pila Pila Women's Club were also attended by women vendors 'selling snacks', while others were regularly outside the village school to deal with the children. Others worked from home, offering cigarettes and 'pre-packaged snacks' (Bradley 1982, 110).

Leaving aside prepared foods and craft goods, *pipiai* was largely a middleman trade in purchased commodities, conducted for profit (albeit 'profit' devoted to spending cash earned in the accumulation of *tambu*). While it had some precedent in the earlier middleman trade of Matupi women described by Bill Epstein (1969), it differed greatly from Scarlett Epstein's description of marketplace trade. That had been conducted by 'producer-sellers' whose proceeds – whether in cash or *tambu* – were spent largely on foodstuffs for their *own* consumption or on transport costs. Earlier women's market trade was essentially hybrid, but so also was *pipiai* trade, despite its more 'businesslike' appearance. Motives for accumulating *tambu* still derived from traditional values, and reflected a desire to usurp men's dominance of it (Bradley 1982, 109). Whereas Bill Epstein had suggested in 1969 that increasing monetization of Tolai life would eventually spell the disappearance of *tambu*, Bradley concluded that *pipiai* was falsifying that prediction (ibid., 112). Its outstanding characteristic lay in allowing the conversion of cash to *tambu*, providing the link not only between the two currencies but also between tradition and modernity (ibid., 111).

This situation had multiple precedents. Discussing 'state' and 'local' currencies in Melanesia, Robbins and Akin (1999) referred to the experience of many groups with indigenous currencies. These had all seen 'a procession of state currencies come and go' (as Tolai had seen German Marks succeeded by Australian pounds, then dollars, and finally PNG *kina*). Such episodes gave observers an opportunity to study 'the state of play' between rival currencies, and to consider their roles in social transformation (ibid., 2). Reminiscent of Salisbury's 'currency war' between *tambu* and the Mark in German times (Ch. 7), they claimed *tambu* 'has continually "duelled" with money . . . and today remains a vital symbol of identity and autonomy' (ibid., 33). Women's autonomy in Pila Pila involved freedom to resist the complete institutionalization of formal 'legal tender' currency, in favour of conducting some market activity using the indigenous *numeraire*. German 'victory' in the early currency war was merely a setback for the Tolai; the persistence of *tambu* after a century of colonial monetization was another example of their stubborn informality. It was used for a whole category of value-adding transactions, unenumerated and informal. *Pipiai* trading, linking formal and informal currencies and serving both utilitarian and traditional ends, was a prime instance of continuing economic hybridity in the 'modernizing' Gazelle economy. *Tambu* accumulation, an instance of Hart's 'residue', continued to spur Tolai economic activity.

To describe *pipiai* in 1978 as 'businesslike' seems apt when compared with the comportment of Tolai market-women observed by Scarlett Epstein in the 1960s. She saw continuity between Rabaul market behaviour and that observed in inland markets by the colonist Parkinson in the nineteenth century. As in that earlier trade, Epstein's vendors still affected indifference to the prospect of a sale, while husbands still disapproved any sign of 'eagerness' on their part. Competition was not apparent and nor was there any 'sales drive' or undercutting of prices. Presenting a quasi-'monopolistic' front in the marketplace, sellers gave little impression of any individualistic action (Epstein 1968, 142–44).

Yet only a decade later, Bradley commented on what she saw as changing attitudes to marketing by women, allowing them to elaborate and diversify their trading and to display greater 'assertiveness'. *Pipiai* was emblematic of this new attitude. Even in regular marketplace trade, although the exchange of garden produce 'in standard units at fixed equivalences' was still normal, women were now actively drawing their produce to the attention of market-goers – some even reducing prices if necessary (Bradley 1982, 114–15). This might seem trivial to anyone accustomed to Asian produce markets or the barrow boys of Camden Town (Epstein 1968, 142), but in the small world of Melanesian markets such changes verged on the seismic, suggesting progress towards a more recognizably 'Asian' mode of dealing.

The Elusive Merchant Class

This study examines the implications of failure by traditional Melanesian societies to produce an occupational class of merchants practising van Leur's 'trade as a specialized occupation'. It asks whether this was unfavourable to their ready entry to the introduced market economy. But to say that the Tolai experience of traditional 'secondary' trading and retrading allowed them to operate in that economy is not to endorse Scarlett Epstein's (1968) view of them as 'primitive capitalists'.

Reports of innovations in food production and distribution by Scarlett and Bill Epstein, Salisbury and Bradley have been mentioned above. Scarlett Epstein's account (1968, 80) of intermediary functions described the bulking of produce and commission-selling. It is difficult to judge how far this constituted 'trade as a specialized occupation', or the extent to which those concerned had abandoned subsistence. Under Gazelle social conditions it is possible such wholesalers were traditional big-men whose marshalling of food for market was analogous to traditional leadership in the preparation of feasts. Rather than being specialist intermediaries, such men seem likely to have maintained multiple activities, from subsistence and cash-crop production to engaging in individual and group enterprises. From among such people formal wholesalers might be expected to emerge, but there is little evidence to suggest how far this occurred before independence, as detailed accounts of men's trading are lacking for the late period. As to Salisbury's account of men he called 'commercial' farmers (1970, 214), I have noted the continuing influence of traditional trade – delayed barter exchange, use of *tambu*, and fixed equivalences – in the operations of the large-scale producers (or aggregators) he described. This degree of hybridity suggests calling them 'commercial' was premature.

Matupi market-women studied by Bill Epstein were not specialist traders. At best secondary traders, they had portfolios of other livelihood activities commencing with subsistence agriculture, which they combined to contribute to household welfare. By contrast, events observed later in Pila Pila by Bradley were quite different in character – notwithstanding the evidence of hybridity in her account. Bradley's research suggested a late colonial intensification and individualization of petty trading activities, fuelled by growing cash incomes. Having neither access to land nor produce to sell, some Pila Pila women practised *pipiai*, the reselling of purchased commodities as a form of petty specialized trade. This activity was of a different order than secondary trade; *pipiai* traders should be regarded as embryonic peddler/merchants, appearing in land-short villages at around the time of independence.

Leaving aside the activities of MacWilliam's 'accumulators' – who are not the primary focus of this study and whose progress towards 'formal' status is seen as owing more to political entrepreneurship than commercial acumen – the Tolai he described as producing for consumption were responsible for a modest profusion of 'micro' and small enterprises. Such informal activities were typically small in scale, elementary in terms of management and capital inputs, sometimes tinged by illegality, and with pervasive elements of hybridity. Most households enjoyed multiple sources of income and a still relatively secure base in subsistence, although population growth was rapid and pressure on land resources growing. Salisbury commented that a 'lack of avenues for productive investment' deterred further business growth (a theme also taken up by Scarlett Epstein). In Vunamami, many small entrepreneurs progressed from producer-selling to copra drying, and then acquired trucks – too many, in fact, because there was an oversupply of transport vehicles. But market forces did not impel people to branch out; bank savings accumulated, or were used wastefully to duplicate assets intended for local community use (Salisbury 1970, 275). Nonetheless, a new sequence of Tolai economic growth – a possible fifth 'stage' – may have commenced, as suggested by the discussion (above) of human capital, migration and skilled employment among Pila Pila villagers.

In the 1960s, Salisbury had looked forward to a breakthrough to larger-scale and more sophisticated business operations, coming with the emergence of formal investment vehicles. A further wave of political consolidation, these would operate over extended markets and mobilize capital from wider groupings. Such a process would require government to devise new models of business entity suited to indigenous group ownership (Salisbury 1970, 276). A formal legal vehicle for such purposes was created by legislation in 1974 (the *Business Groups Incorporation Act*). Fitzpatrick (1980) claimed that 'big peasants' (MacWilliam's 'accumulators') soon became dominant in these groups, using them as 'springboards' to political and commercial power, though the dynamic was more political than entrepreneurial. By such means, MacWilliam claimed, the principle of *paramountcy of native interests* was appropriated to serve the interests of an emerging class of 'insider' entrepreneurs (MacWilliam 2013, 238).

Leaving aside Chinese activities (until Ch. 19), the *urban* informal economy remained very small at independence (apart from the marketplace activities of rural day-trippers). Despite a growing inequality in access to land, rural distress had not occurred at a sufficient level for an urban 'involution of services' to emerge. Instead, superior Tolai education, deployed in a national labour market, suggested how that danger might be averted or postponed. Scarlett Epstein (1982, 9) was surely too pessimistic when she wrote that Gazelle markets, composed of female producer-sellers, 'do not seem to be transitional types'. In light of the emergence of *pipiai* trade, it seems possible that further and more widespread elaboration of the rural service economy occurred prior to independence, together with incipient specialized trading functions. However, trading as a *self-sufficient profession* still appeared to be confined to some instances of petty specialized trade, albeit amidst signs of a more general change occurring in trading culture.

Note

1. For 'investment in human capital' in late colonial PNG, see Conroy 1976. For a case study of absentee educated workers in a 'human capital' framework, see Carrier and Conroy 1982.

Chapter 19

Chinese Enterprise in Rabaul

Apotheosis and Decline

The Japanese invasion in 1942 converted the Gazelle into a vast military base, the Australian population and administration having essentially abandoned the Tolai, and most of the Chinese, to their fate. Military occupation caused much suffering and loss of life, and Allied bombing inflicted enormous damage on the town, infrastructure and plantations. The suffering of civilians was multiplied when the Japanese garrison was trapped until the surrender in August 1945. Immediately after the war, as in 1914, some Chinese became peddlers to the Australian forces, offering souvenirs, scrap-metal trinkets and Japanese memorabilia. Chinese construction companies regrouped and commenced rebuilding Chinatown, as traders and artisans struggled to recommence operations and contracts were awarded for reconstruction in the town proper. Recapitalization was assisted by compensation for war damage, although (given the opaque character of many of their activities) some Chinese had difficulty documenting losses (Cahill 2012). Tolai also received substantial payments, and their spending in trade stores assisted Chinese economic recovery. Well suited to the new ideology of economic development, Chinese would be freer to exercise their entrepreneurial talents.

Yet there were constraints on that freedom. Charles Rowley observed of the New Guinea Chinese that their community maintains its cultural mores, while producing wealthy individuals who were not given reason to regard themselves as citizens of any realm beyond Chinatown. Even in 1958 when Chinese Rabaul was close to the apogee of its success, he asserted that Chinatown's frontiers were still as clearly marked as ever they had been (Rowley 1958b, 79–80). Originally, racial discrimination and the attempt to impose a particular economic role upon them explained their centralized location. No doubt inertia played some part in keeping them there, but economies of agglomeration were probably more important. There were good reasons for Chinatown to maintain its centrality, so long as Rabaul retained its position as the economic capital of Chinese New Guinea.

Cahill described the 1950s as boom years for Chinese traders, with Tolai keen to 'cut copra' or gather nuts for sale. In 1953, *Pacific Island Monthly* reported the rebound of Chinese enterprise and, rather than crediting hard work and thrift, saw in this a threat. Echoing insecurity felt by European storekeepers and copra traders before the First World War, the magazine claimed that 'perturbation' was evident in the white community because highly capitalized Chinese, able to pay with 'prompt cash', were actively seeking to acquire European enterprises wherever these were available (cited in Wu 1974, 567). Scuttlebutt indicated 'Red China' as the source of this capital, but Wu pointed to compensation payments and the informal *hui* mechanism (Ch. 8) as funding Chinese investment.

Wu asserted that even as late as the early 1970s only some Chinese merchants were dealing with banks, and then simply for transactions (the first bank loan to a Chinese having only been granted in the 1950s – Wu 1974, 571). On the other hand, Christine Inglis suggested that by 1973 *all* her Chinese respondents were using banks, and had been obtaining bank credit where possible 'at least for the past twenty-five years' (Inglis 1977, 249–50). Remembering that the New Guinea Chinese were admitted to Australian citizenship from 1957, the denial of formal credit to them by banks would have been increasingly anomalous after that date. Also, Chinese were encouraged to contract professional accounting services by the introduction of an income tax in 1959, and no doubt this gave greater comfort to bank managers.

Continuing informality in Chinese business is suggested by Wu's anecdote about the owner-manager of one of the largest wholesalers, trading since the 1920s. Even in 1952, this man seemed to know little of Western bookkeeping, or of procedures for debt collection, shipping or insurance, despite supplying Chinese shopkeepers in Solomon Islands, New Ireland and New Britain. Trouble collecting arrears from these distant customers forced him to hire a European to resolve the issues. This man was surprised to find that his Chinese employer had an annual turnover of some £80,000 in 1952 – this, despite his knowing nothing of bank services, including revolving credit arrangements, as he had only ever operated on a cash basis (Wu 1974, 571).

As evidence of growing formalization in much Chinese business, Inglis reported their increasing reliance on formal agreements and other legal documentation in matters such as acquisition of businesses and leasing or purchase of property (including, from the 1950s, in Australia). Larger enterprises consulted European accounting firms for advisory services, and a number incorporated as 'exempt proprietary companies'. These had statutory limits on membership, and relaxed reporting obligations; only two such companies had non-Chinese shareholders in 1973 (Inglis 1977, 206). Nonetheless, Chinese business remained quite heterogeneous on the eve of self-government. For example, in the retail sector, 'stores range from those operated by elderly ladies, carrying a restricted inventory of basic goods obtained entirely from local Chinese suppliers, to large specialist retailers and wholesalers who import direct from Australia and other countries' (ibid., 317). Numerically, the largest class of Chinese business consisted of small trade stores and craft businesses with indigenous staff. Such stores 'lack any form of stock control or check on cash takings, which are often simply put into an old tin behind the counter' (ibid., 138). Such anecdotes suggest a strong continuing strand of informality. Even some larger retail stores continued to exhibit Bauer's imperfect specialization, as a revolving cast of family members and part-time employees took time off from other occupations to work 'after hours' (ibid., 142ff). In some smaller businesses with two owners, Bauer's occupational fluidity also occurred. Owners were obliged to engage in various sidelines if they were unable to achieve the scale necessary to support both proprietors (ibid., 162).

A telling indicator of continuing informality was the widespread participation of business owners in *hui*. A parallel, unregulated credit system, *hui* had members including people with access to formal credit, whose enterprises otherwise exhibited the hallmarks of formality. In Rabaul at the end of 1971 there were fourteen *hui*, each with between thirty and thirty-six members, operating in a town with only about 180 Chinese businesses, so that 'the whole community serves as a general pool for recruitment' (Inglis 1977, 263). Because Rabaul wholesalers often suffered cashflow problems due to a mismatch between payables and receivables they were prominent among *hui* organizers, often participating in several simultaneously. Declaration of *hui*-related income or expenses in some personal tax returns (ibid., 238, n6) marked a degree of enumeration, hence formalization, of the *hui*, and some organizers made explicit attempts at private regulation by circulating printed rule books and issuing receipts for periodic contributions (ibid.). Inglis remarked, however, that 'neither these nor the verbal contracts entered into have ever had their legal status tested in a court, so most participants regard the *hui* as without legal status (alegal)'. Some non-participants described the *hui* as 'risky' and as having 'no legal basis and only informal security' (ibid., 259). That members, whose own enterprises were increasingly formalized, had attempted to establish governance for the *hui* did not amount to its formalization, and it continued to function beyond formal regulatory frameworks. Inglis rejected any suggestion that *hui* membership was based on particularist associations, and she doubted that the integrity of *hui* finances depended on trust derived from such associations. Rather, the existence of 'a network of gossip' in a small community acted to ensure participants were well informed about other *hui* members. It gave 'visibility' to their behaviour. This last was 'probably the most important factor in social control in the *hui*' (ibid., 266).

After Chinese became eligible for Australian citizenship in 1957 they were permitted to move freely to the New Guinea mainland and to Papua. Wu described a substantial movement of population to Lae, Madang and Wewak. But, 'most conspicuously', Chinese moved to Port Moresby, which was growing rapidly due to bureaucratic centralization and Australian development aid. Back home, although other Chinese were ready to step up to replace departing entrepreneurs (Wu 1974, 568–69), Chinese Rabaul had probably achieved its commercial apotheosis by the end of the 1950s. It declined quickly thereafter.

In 1972, on the eve of self-government, Wu counted some 470 Chinese businesses, of which 150 remained in Rabaul, but with almost 140 in mainland New Guinea and some 120 in Papua (Wu 1974, 569, table 3). The latter included those in Port Moresby, which had only had a handful of Chinese residents before the Pacific War. Numbers of businesses probably do not tell the full story; those leaving Rabaul may have been among the more dynamic and formal enterprises, although Christine Inglis (pers. comm., 6 June 2022) was inclined to think they were families with relatively limited resources or opportunities who saw their best chance of advancement in the larger markets of the New Guinea mainland, including the capital.

National census data for 1971 put the Chinese population at some three thousand, with a further five to six hundred of mixed descent. An outflow to Australia was underway by this time, caused by apprehension at the approach of independence. Rabaul remained the largest centre of Chinese population although the total had declined to fewer than 900, while in Port Moresby there were some 620 Chinese and more than 400 in Lae (Wu 1982, Ch. 1). Chinese fear and uncertainty had dramatic consequences in 1972 when one Rabaul *hui* collapsed and a 'run' on others threatened. Only community cohesion enabled losses to be contained and face to be saved (Wu 1974, 581–82). After that, no more *hui* were organized (Inglis 1977, 273). By 1980 Rabaul had fewer than three hundred Chinese residents, the others having 'taken the course of exodus' (Wu 1982, 156).

A relatively new business, cocoa buying and processing occupied many Chinese in the late colonial period. Much of this was conducted on an informal basis, and Chinese traders were implicated in the failure of the TCP, intended to formalize Tolai cocoa. The TCP was undermined by (inter alia) surreptitious informal trading with politically dissident Tolai growers (Ch. 18), and after it closed in 1971 the only cocoa fermentaries operating independently on the Gazelle were Chinese. Their owners had close family connections, and the potential for price-fixing might seem the opportunity for a case study of particularism at work. The freewheeling character of Chinese Rabaul asserted itself, however. Relations between major players were not good, and price competition in cocoa buying remained strong (Inglis 1977, 385).

Yet old habits and familiar tensions continued after the war, as two episodes suggest. In the first case, in 1956, the registrar of cooperatives in Port Moresby alleged that indigenous economic development was being threatened by unfair Chinese business practices. The registrar claimed that Chinese extended credit to natives, and that in New Ireland they had a 'virtual lien' over their crops. In Rabaul, Tolai were either in debt to Chinese or trapped by 'liquor or other vices'. Another senior official, perhaps concerned by the competitive threat to Tolai cooperatives, remarked on the ambivalence of Tolai. While 'jealous' of the Chinese, they were nonetheless led astray by liquor, cigarettes and 'high prices' for their produce (Cahill 2012, 266). A second episode related to an ordinance of 1962 for the licensing of new cocoa fermentaries. These were to be restricted to Tolai operators, to the exclusion of Chinese and Europeans, in the belief that purchasing and processing by non-indigenous traders threatened the viability of the TCP.

These cases differed from pre-war episodes in which Chinese and Tolai aims were often aligned, and opposed to European interests. In this new era, an Australian concern for Tolai welfare (as well as some degree of anti-Chinese sentiment) underpinned the regulatory impulse. Tolai were seen as the proper beneficiaries of economic development, while Chinese had come to be regarded as operating against the interests not so much of Europeans as of indigenous people. The contemporary account of Chinese behaviour is immediately recognizable. It mirrors the conduct of previous generations, and suggests a continuing strain of informality (even illegitimacy) in some business practices, just as the account of official attitudes reflected old prejudices. Two 'legitimate' enterprises, formal in their methods, structures and legal constitutions, were said to be threatened by Chinese business conducted in the old, informal manner. Now, however, these formal businesses were owned by Tolai – the cooperative system and the cocoa project – and Chinese traders were accused of undermining them.

The changing policy environment, together with the rise of Tolai economic nationalism in the 1950s and 1960s, were signals heeded by the Chinese community. Opportunities offered by post-war prosperity, followed by emigration to other towns and/or to Australia, must have seemed a welcome resolution of their ambiguous status.

Chapter 20

Bureaucracy and Market Economy on the Frontier

If bureaucracy and market exchange are necessary for informal economic activity we should examine how each manifested in early post-war Goroka (Map 12.1).[1] The necessary bureaucratic capacity was present, although applied in an unorthodox, occasionally aberrant style owing much to the recent military experience of officials and the circumstances of Goroka as a frontier district. What Francis West described as the establishment of law and order by 'peaceful penetration' was a work in progress there well into the 1950s (West 2006, 113).

Following Antonio Gramsci (Ch. 13), Charles Hawksley (2005) described the post-war Eastern Highlands as a zone of 'administrative colonialism' on which 'cultural hegemony' was imposed to establish and legitimize the capitalist state. In his *Prison Notebooks*, Gramsci (1999) had described hegemonic relationships as producing educational outcomes, and considered how a hypothetical 'Papuan' might be schooled in such a relationship. Should not a nation on a higher civilizational plane accept responsibility to advance the progress of more primitive peoples? This might justify 'a degree of force', though Hawksley emphasized that this would give way to 'increasingly sophisticated techniques of social management' (Hawksley 2001, 14). Regulation and bureaucratic control in Goroka had been central to these techniques; what Hawksley called 'forced cultural transformation' prepared the way for Gorokans to accept the legitimacy of the colonial state and the processes of capitalist accumulation (ibid., 2–3). On this logic one might see the *kalabus*, a prison compound, as an academy in which miscreants learned *Tok Pisin*, the colonial lingua franca, and became schooled to Australian bureaucratic expectations.

Gramsci's notion of colonial hegemony as an educational relationship has some appeal. In a dozen years Australia achieved a great deal in the Goroka region, employing limited force and acting 'primarily through regulation and persuasion' (Hawksley 2001, 301). This was intended to create an environment 'safe for capital' (ibid., 16) by transforming a warlike society into an agriculturally prosperous one. 'Colonial aims and the political economy of capitalism' were to be secured through a population's compliance with regulations (Hawksley 2005, 1). Marxian rhetoric aside, Hawksley's 'administrative colonialism' appears broadly consistent with the *trusteeship* philosophy espoused by Paul Hasluck, the most influential Australian minister of the period, while Alf Conlon, who inspired many postwar changes, has been described by Cassandra Pybus as having Gramscian tendencies (Ch. 13).

Hawksley assumed a consistency between Australian colonial aims and the political economy of capitalism, but Gorokan-style 'capitalism' would prove compromised by the hybrid and informal nature of most indigenous market economic activities. Later chapters will show that the colonized often proved unable or unwilling to conform fully with capitalist market norms and the bureaucratic regulation instilling them. The commitment of successive Australian governments to 'native welfare' (and their relative success in institutionalizing this objective) is difficult to reconcile with wholehearted adherence to 'capitalist political economy'. One might distinguish a realm of good intentions, presided over by Hasluck, while maintaining the inevitability of historical processes. But this would deny the real substance in 'guardianship' and the 'paramountcy of indigenous interests', notions applied to temper the negative effects of development. The account here of Hasluck's ministerial tenure will support these contentions.

To prepare the bureaucracy for its task, the Labor government established an Australian School of Pacific Administration (ASOPA) in Sydney in 1945, to create what Hawksley (2001) called a 'finishing school' for colonial administrators. Although less grand than Conlon (its instigator) had hoped, it would perform a Gramscian role. ASOPA schooled Australian field staff in the new ideology of economic development, encouraging them to consider how it might be reconciled with Eddie Ward's 'dual development' (Ch. 14). Among its graduates was Ian Downs, later the district commissioner (DC) in Goroka (1952–56). His answer to that question would occasionally place him at odds with colonial orthodoxy, as determined in Canberra and then administered from Port Moresby. He was later commissioned to write the official history of the Australian Trusteeship (Downs 1980), so his perspective is well documented in this and other sources (e.g. Downs 1986). His significant role in events discussed here requires the most careful examination of these narratives.

Immediately after the war, the Highlands were not central to Port Moresby's concerns. Conflict had touched the region lightly, and when Minister Ward announced the decision to appropriate resources for development and pay compensation for war damage, the focus was primarily on coastal regions. Colonel J.K. Murray, first administrator of the newly combined territories, was beset by labour and materials shortages, and much criticized by coastal business interests, fretting at delays in reconstruction and outraged by the cancellation of native labour contracts. In the official history, Downs (1980, 176) recorded that because of the relatively benign experience of the region during the Pacific War, development in the Highlands had been set aside. Privately, he charged that the Highlands 'had been deliberately starved of finance, kept in isolation and held back' (Downs 1986, 222). A sense of neglect may have encouraged some non-conformist thinking among Highlands administrators; it certainly appears to have rankled with Downs, who despised the 'centralists' in Port Moresby (Downs 1986, 236; also 233).

While it was Port Moresby's responsibility to ensure Canberra's writ ran in regional outposts, Hasluck was a 'hands-on' minister. When departures from orthodoxy became evident in Goroka in 1953, he found it necessary to rein in DC Downs personally, for decisions he thought likely to infringe the interests of the native people. Administrators in the Eastern Highlands did not always conform with the post-war norm that enterprises thought likely to be 'potentially destructive of village life' were to be denied government support (Ch. 17). Development tempered by guardianship may have been post-war ideology, but in Eastern Highlands practice it was coloured by a local developmentalism. An early instance related to alienation of land for European settlement. In the Highlands, land policy '*as locally applied*' equated development with European settlement (Rowley 1965, 120, emphasis added). It was this attitude that Hasluck found necessary to curb. A second instance concerned transport – specifically roads and their uses. Here Hasluck found himself unable to control the developmentalist impulses of his Goroka administrators. These episodes (described below) exemplified tensions in the 1950s between centrally ordained policies of 'uniform development' and an incipient tendency (personalized here in the character of Downs) towards what came to be known in the 1960s as 'accelerated development'.

Hasluck's early policies were predicated on a long time-horizon, and on gradualism. To some extent tensions in Goroka were also playing out in other 'progressive' districts, exerting pressure on the minister to reconsider the pace of development and the allocation of resources. This was the context for his decision, shortly before his term ended, to seek the World Bank policy advice which crystallized accelerated development (IBRD 1965, 31–35; see Ch. 14). This involved picking winners for preferential treatment among PNG's regions, whereas uniform development, the attempt to achieve racial and regional equity, had been a corollary of Ward's *dual* development. The new approach would have distributional implications, with political consequences that came to a head immediately before independence (Ch. 25).

Private business activity was prominent in Goroka from the beginnings of white settlement, with the boundaries between public and private interests often fluid. J.K. Murray was disconcerted in 1948 to find that District Officer Taylor and a number of other serving field staff had taken French leave to join a short-lived gold rush at Porgera, in the far west of the region (Downs 1980, 174), and by 1949 Taylor had resigned to take up land in the Asaro Valley. By that time, some 'privileged Europeans' including former government officials had secured 'permitted occupancy' of Highland land, some even squatting on land close to Goroka airstrip (ibid.). In due course other senior officers set up post-retirement careers in and around the settlement. These included Taylor's successor George Greathead, who retired with the rank of DC in 1952 and was succeeded by Downs, who would himself resign later to become a planter. On retirement, Downs became chairman of the Highland Farmers' and Settlers' Association (HFSA) in which all three played leadership roles.

Before the war, and for a decade after it, the number of Europeans in the district was small, with only fifteen resident in the hamlet of Goroka in 1950 (Howlett 1976, 247). It is remarkable how few government officers (together with a handful of white settlers and missionaries) managed to implant not so much Gramscian 'cultural hegemony' as a particular local version of Australian colonial aims. Goroka patrol post (later, 'town') was not recognized initially as an urban place, though the Eastern Highlands District was recorded as having 363 non-indigenous residents by mid-1954; by mid-1956 it had 487, with 314 of them in Goroka subdistrict (ibid.). This growth occurred during a period of 'land rush' and the initiation of commercial coffee planting.

Despite his dismissal of 'centralist' bureaucrats, Downs and his colleagues were also bureaucrats. Because, in Weberian terms, it would be a contradiction to speak of an informal bureaucracy, it is better to think of the frontier administration as operating in an unorthodox manner, distinguished by a 'can-do' attitude. A product of improvisation under immediate post-war circumstances, and perhaps because the officials concerned displayed little of the 'hostility to capitalism' displayed by their British colonial counterparts (Stewart 1992, 4), bureaucratic action took on a distinctive character. A propensity to cut corners in Goroka contrasted markedly with pioneering coastal administrations, both the highly formalized German bureaucracy in New Guinea, and the impecunious, centralized and 'correct' administrations of MacGregor and Murray in Papua. Goroka bureaucracy in the 1950s anticipated the phase of accelerated development, while at the centre Paul Hasluck was still prescribing uniform development.

Introducing a Market Economy

Beyond Melanesia, it was uncommon for colonial bureaucracy to precede market economic dealings. In many colonies, as in West Africa, 'the market' had pre-colonial antecedents. Hart pointed out that, at one extreme in traditional society – Hausaland in Northern Nigeria – 'all foods entered the market as commodities, and cotton was grown extensively for textiles' (Hart 1982, 9; Ch. 5). 'Even in remote areas, where the division of labour was less developed, mechanisms usually existed for the circulation of foodstuffs, including local marketplaces' (ibid.), whereas in pre-colonial Melanesia specialized traders were unknown (Hughes 1977, 1978). So also were transactions facilitated by general purpose monies. Late-coming colonial powers in the island Pacific often found it necessary to institute market processes, as devices of compulsion became less available as the twentieth century advanced, as well as being of doubtful efficacy. This was certainly true in the central Highlands where colonialism dated from only the 1930s, by which time New Guinea was an Australian Mandated Territory subject to international scrutiny. It is necessary to examine how the Goroka District Office set out to stimulate a market economy among Gramsci's 'Papuans'. Commencing with efforts to monetize economic transactions, we should then consider how the local mode of bureaucracy dealt with three important and interlinked problems: finding and establishing a staple commercial crop, securing the land on which it would be grown, and managing transport to export markets from a mountainous and land-locked region. The solutions to these tasks reveal something of the unorthodox approach of Goroka-based administrators. Their methods included (at least in the early post-war period) a pronounced degree of dirigisme. In Goroka, 'the colonial state created for itself a key role in the production, distribution and exchange of commodities' (Hawksley 2005, 3).

As early as 1945, District Officer Taylor prepared an advisory note, 'Mercantile Stores and the Circulation of Coinage'. A measure intended to promote 'embryonic capitalism', it laid out a strategy to link local agricultural production with external markets (Hawksley 2005, 18). Commercial vegetable growing came first, with the District Office making a market by acting as buyer and price-setter. The intervention was not insignificant; in the first six months of 1950, officials purchased more than 500,000 pounds [weight] of foods from Goroka alone (Hawksley 2001, 324). This had a precedent from the late 1930s, when administrators stimulated production of food for officials, labourers and troops by offering marine shells (Ch. 12). However, the intention to monetize such transactions was novel. Next, passionfruit and peanuts were trialled as potential export crops, with official purchasing policies supporting growers by stabilizing markets (ibid.). Subsistence and introduced crops, along with labour recruitment, provided the initial impulse for Gorokans to engage with the market economy. Neither passionfruit nor peanuts succeeded, though peanuts were incorporated into indigenous diets and became important later in informal food marketing. A third crop, coffee, offered greater potential as it combined a high value-to-weight ratio with a favourable international market.

While cash and shell continued to circulate as parallel currencies, shell diminished in importance as the adoption of new 'valuables' rendered it less central to traditional exchange. When Jim Leahy opened a store in 1948, Taylor felt able to pay station labourers in cash and required the hospital to pay cash for local foodstuffs (Donaldson and Good 1988, 70). Government land acquisitions were also made with cash from 1949, as were early purchases of smallholder coffee. Acceptance of Australian currency increased after 1950 as returnees from the official Highlands Labour Scheme were paid off in Goroka, spending much of their cash locally, and banknotes, coinage and certain introduced commodities came to be incorporated into traditional exchange as valuables (Strathern 1979). Additionally, some two thousand men were employed on highland plantations by 1955, paid partly in cash. Aside from early instances of coffee barter, by the time local smallholders were producing any significant volume the trade was almost completely monetized. Gorokan demand for cash was stimulated by steel tools in trade stores, and they developed a taste for imported consumer goods and foodstuffs. Later, demand for cash was stimulated by council head tax and school fee obligations, although the boom in indigenous coffee plantings commenced years before these were imposed. And, as discussed below, planting was spurred as much by prestige seeking as by material incentives.

An episode from 1953, arising from road construction, illustrates hybridity in economic transactions and official grasp of the Gorokan psyche. Sensitive to any suggestion of forced labour, Downs (1980, 212) claimed that all road workers were paid. This was not formal payment of wages, however. At the completion of a crucial stretch of road, he assembled workers with their appointed leaders (*luluai*) to attend a ceremony replete with symbolism. As in a traditional prestation, Downs called upon the *luluai* to accept payments for their groups. The media of payment were 'boxes of axes, tomahawks, bush knives, gold-lip pearl shell, tobacco, and five white cotton bags of shillings from the Bank of New South Wales in Lae' (Cleland 2010, 68), and he distributed these valuables, traditional and neo-traditional, in accordance with the size of each group and its contribution. As ceremonial sponsor, DC Downs made a speech to which each *luluai* responded after receiving payment. Downs then distributed the flesh of 20 pigs (ibid., 68–69). As a matter of form, he called for payments to be distributed among all, but (as in the 'efflorescence' of exchange characterizing this period) senior men no doubt benefited disproportionately.

Downs had come to Goroka believing the Highlands 'desperately' needed economic development and an exportable crop to satisfy popular expectations (Downs 1986, 217). Coffee, the chosen staple crop, was rapidly adopted by Gorokans, although there is debate as to whether this was due to settler enterprise assisted by bureaucratic dirigisme or to autonomous Gorokan initiative. Ben Finney (1973, 53–54) stated bluntly that settlers largely took the initiative, and their pioneering activities aroused Gorokan interest in coffee. Michael Bourke (1986) offered a revisionist account, challenging the claims for European planters and imputing more agency to Gorokans than was commonly supposed. Finney's account mentioned village plantings near Goroka as early as 1944–45, which he described as non-commercial, although this appears inconsistent with his statement (Finney 1973, 43) that some Gorokans were bartering cherry coffee at the government station by 1947. If so, this was probably inspired by official encouragement of vegetable marketing (and indeed the Eastern Highlands administration paid cash for 3,200 lbs [1,450 kg] of village 'parchment' coffee in 1948–49 [Hawksley 2001, 337]). Bourke and Finney both attributed the earliest plantings to 'coffee patrols' conducted in 1944 by wartime administrators, during which seeds were distributed to villagers. These were sourced from a government agricultural research station at Aiyura, near Kainantu, where experimental coffee had been planted in 1937, was bearing by 1939, and had already attracted the interest of local people by 1940 (Bourke 1986, 101). Bourke concluded that village coffee in the Eastern Highlands commenced in 1944, not 1952, predating the first European plantations and laying foundations for the modern industry (ibid., 102–3).

In any case, Gorokan take-up of coffee was rapid. A boom in plantings was reported by 1955, even though formal extension effort had only commenced in 1952 (Finney 1973, 64). Finney praised the energy and tact of early extension work, which targeted ambitious individuals. His account is consistent with Bourke's conclusion that the indigenous planting boom was not simply the product of formal extension but flowed from certain 'antecedent conditions'. These included 'familiarity with the crop', some 'very modest returns' to the *first movers* who planted some coffee during the war, the 'example of pioneering expatriate planters', and experience with coffee gained by some wartime labourers at Aiyura (Bourke 1986, 103). Finney emphasized the importance of prestige-seeking behaviour among early adopters, burnishing the credentials of their descent groups through coffee, and enhancing personal leadership positions – early instances of Gorokan economic hybridity.

Whereas Bourke emphasized indigenous autonomy in expanding coffee and Finney credited settlers, Downs pointed to the role of government. The decision to make coffee an important commodity and to involve native people was taken – in a corner-cutting initiative and without consulting authorities in Port Moresby – by field staff. The Highland people had high expectations, and 'time was too valuable to wait' for the approval of his superiors (Downs 1980, 180). In an exercise later cited as evidence of 'partnership' between Europeans and Gorokans, white planters built up seed stock by obtaining coffee seedlings, both for their own use and for distribution to Gorokan neighbours. This was expected to prepare the way for coffee trading when Gorokan-planted coffee became available (ibid.).

Finney credited the first agricultural officer in the district as contributing to coffee's widespread dissemination. When Robert Cottle arrived from Aiyura in 1952 with a brief to develop passionfruit cultivation, he soon recognized constraints limiting its potential as a smallholder crop. Instead, he took the independent initiative to promote coffee in remote areas away from Goroka town, laying the foundation for its mass adoption. His extension methods departed radically from pre-war practices of compulsory planting and communal responsibility (as seen in Papua's unsuccessful 'village plantations' [Ch. 9]). As also happened with cocoa on the Gazelle (Ch. 17), Cottle convinced leading men to pioneer the crop voluntarily, providing them with individual guidance (Finney 1973, 59–61). Less adventurous men would adopt coffee later as the crop's potential became better understood, but the first-mover advantage gained by leaders was in many cases sustained. As also with Gazelle cocoa, this had longer-term implications for economic inequality, flowing directly, whether or not advertently, from agricultural extension.

Land for Planters and Roads for Their Coffee

Although controls imposed on residence in 1936 remained formally in place, Downs commented that, by 1952, the numbers of Europeans in the highlands had rendered the 'facade' of restrictions on settlement 'threadbare of either moral virtue or administrative effect' (Downs 1980, 178). Pressure was building for settlement to be allowed. Downs's use of the term 'facade' is revealing because it directed attention to the arbitrary bureaucratic processes – personalistic rather than Weberian – that enabled a group of 'administration officers, prospectors, aviators and other "old New Guinea hands"' (Finney 1970, 119) to live in the district 'essentially squatting' (Hawksley 2005, 10) on land to which they had no formal entitlement. Downs blamed J.K. Murray in Port Moresby for lacking the will to stop this, though Murray's difficulty may have stemmed from the personal interest of some of his field officers in seeing settlement flourish. The Latin maxim *quis custodiet ipsos custodes* – 'who guards the guards?' – suggested the moral ambiguity of this situation (Hawksley 2001, 407).

Hawksley saw this uncontrolled situation as arising from the actions of European early movers, often *kiaps*[2] with local knowledge and connections to traditional landholders, who had identified agriculturally promising land. Pointing to the absence of bureaucratic process, Finney (1970, 121) alleged that they were using their 'local influence as *kiaps*' to acquire land directly, 'before regulation'. This refers to the 'direct application' system, by which customary landowners could be approached by land-seekers without initial resort to authorities (Finney 1973, 46). Efforts to regularize this after 1949 involved the administration's purchasing land and granting 99-year leases. Consent by landowners and an examination of their present and future land needs were supposed to occur before such transfers, though the latter test was not applied systematically. Available areas were often in 'no man's land' between the territories of enemy groups so that many plantations were placed in 'buffer zones', and European settlement was dispersed. Peace emboldened villagers to move from high ground to valley-bottom positions, which, aside from reigniting old land disputes, revealed that 'vacant' land was scarcer than early European settlers had supposed. As Downs remarked (1980, 175), the imposition of colonial rule and the cessation of warfare permitted people to 'recolonize' their own lands.

What Finney (1970, 119) called 'this trial period' ended in 1952 when the prohibition on European residence was lifted. By then some half dozen plantations totalling about 350 acres [140 ha] had been started in and around Goroka, but when the area was opened for public application and Jim Leahy secured a high price for his first crop, a 'scramble' for land began. A 'land rush' between 1952 and 1954 led to 'dozens' of farm properties being established in Goroka, alienating some 3,550 acres – more than ten times the area pegged out over the previous three years (ibid., 120). Downs listed twenty-six Europeans for whom landholdings were registered between 1952 and 1954, although 'hundreds' of applications were denied;

such firm action was necessary to satisfy the immediate and future needs of highlanders (Downs 1980, 179).

But even at the time there was disquiet. Finney commented that although the area was small, allowing rapid alienation in a region of such high population densities – some hundreds of people per square mile in certain places – was incongruous at a time of rapid decolonization elsewhere (Finney 1970, 120). The matter became politicized in Australia, and Hasluck admitted to having suspicions, prompted by a degree of 'glibness' in the Goroka discourse about *development*. He formed the view that Downs was becoming a 'promoter' of European settlement. The minister had created a land settlement board in Port Moresby in 1952 to assure a centralized approach to land administration, but this was being 'sidestepped', and questionable administrative practices – 'have a yarn with the district commissioner' – were occurring (Hasluck 1976, 120–21).

Hasluck's account reflected his commitment to dual development. He was concerned to find Europeans claiming all the land most suitable for coffee, while it was far from clear that the nutritional, health and social welfare needs of the relatively dense indigenous population were sufficiently considered (Hasluck 1976, 122). In 1953 he imposed a slowdown on acquisitions, directing that more attention should be given to agricultural extension. By October 1954, despite public criticism and bureaucratic inertia, Hasluck had reaffirmed the principles of land policy asserted in the New Guinea ordinance of 1922 (West 1956, 307 and n2). This would involve allocation by public tender, and procedures for assessing future landowner needs. Downs's personal developmentalism had proved increasingly at odds with the 'careful paternalism' of Hasluck, who eventually prevailed (Hawksley 2001, 352). Alienation in the district was effectively frozen, with only slight increases occurring after 1954. Canberra had succeeded in bringing 'the locally held hegemonic view' of development to an end (Hawksley 2005, 12). Central authority was reasserted, orthodox bureaucratic practice was re-established and the Goroka land rush was over.

Avoiding the Embarrassment of One's Superiors

An anecdote from 1939 gives precedent for the character of the post-war Highlands administration. In what was then called the Chimbu district, 24-year-old Downs had used police power and guile to dispense rough justice in suppressing tribal warfare – an action Gramsci would have seen as a necessary evil. For Downs the end justified the means, saying 'I did not embarrass my superiors by seeking official support'. In any case, they were 'a long way' from the scene of the action in Chimbu (cited in Hawksley

2001, 293). This freewheeling approach was seen again, after the war, in the episode of Cottle's launch into indigenous coffee promotion – when 'time was too valuable to wait for official approval'. A more dramatic case was the construction of what later became the Highlands trunk road. Another instance of unorthodox, even aberrant administration, it amounted to a localized 'big push'.

Although not such a contretemps as the land issue, the road was a source of irritation to Hasluck. Early in his tenure he felt burdened by infrastructure deficiencies and the inability to fund capital works. He saw the region's dependence on planes for transporting coffee – described as the 'entrenchment' of aviation – as an additional concern. He came up with a labour-intensive strategy, requiring that each DC should 'encourage and direct' road construction by gaining the cooperation of local populations, which were to provide the necessary labour (Hasluck 1976, 147–48). His intention was to build 'light roads' for jeeps and motorcycles, serving administrative and social welfare needs. Although Downs would later make contrary claims, Hasluck claimed credit for this initiative – despite an important difference between his original concept and the final outcome. In 1954 he had been incensed by a piece of boosterism from Goroka that referred to increasingly heavy traffic on highlands roads due to the 'rapid expansion and development' of this 'progressive district'. This flew in the face of a warning that Hasluck had issued concerning the negative effect on indigenous morale if heavy vehicles owned by Europeans were seen to be damaging roads that villagers had been persuaded to build. In response he issued a directive for public (i.e. non-indigenous) use of the road to be contained (ibid., 149–50). This proved a counsel of perfection, beyond the minister's capacity to enforce.

Downs's version of these events in the official history stated his own claims. The Highlands needed access to the port of Lae in time for an expected surge in coffee production. He was concerned to counter the monopoly of air transport operators, upon whom land-locked Goroka depended. Downs claimed to have persuaded Cleland, J.K. Murray's successor as administrator, to approve efforts 'to explore the possibility' of constructing a road to access the Markham Valley from Goroka (Downs 1980, 181; see Map 12.1). In the event, the *exploration of possibilities* took a rather practical turn. Thousands of labourers were deployed to complete a motorable road of 272 kilometres, east from Goroka into the Markham Valley, within six months. Only Administrator Cleland in Port Moresby was fully briefed on these events (ibid., 181–83). The achievement was celebrated by a motorized re-enactment of the central Highlands east–west traverse of 1933, in which a group of the original explorers – Taylor, Leahy and others, all now in coffee – were hosted by Downs. But the event spoke just as eloquently of the permeability of boundaries between public and private interests in Goroka.

What is incontrovertible is that the road from Mount Hagen, east to Goroka and on to the head of the Markham Valley, knitted together an emerging system of local access roads crucial to the region's economic development. The Highlands Highway would later be constructed on the carriageway of this 'exploratory' exercise. Meanwhile road haulage commenced within the Highlands, centring on Goroka, and airfreight operators were put on notice (Downs 1980, 181–85). Perhaps official suasion was effective, for airfreight costs remained essentially constant between 1953 and 1961 (P. West 2012, 86). Downs's developmentalist goal was secured and Hasluck's gradualism frustrated. Economic infrastructure was in place to support the entry of Gorokan coffee to the international market.

Downs resigned in 1956 to become manager of six Goroka coffee plantations totalling 400 acres, of which he was a joint owner. He also became chairman of the HFSA, and his departure may be seen as bringing the freewheeling period to an end.[3] What followed was not any deceleration of development. Rather, the new policy of accelerated development caused the pace to pick up elsewhere in the 1960s, following the Goroka precedent. Downs later justified his resignation by citing the district's flourishing condition and his conviction that he had achieved as much as was possible within the powers of his official office. He would be better placed in the private sector, where it would be possible to address marketing problems facing the industry, including 'the highlands people' engaged in it (Downs 1986, 259–60). This formulation ('the highlands people') should be understood in terms of a particular rhetoric for which Downs was responsible – an economic 'partnership' between Gorokans and Europeans.

The Rhetoric of Partnership

In the official history, Downs constructed his road narrative in terms of a 'racial partnership' with highlanders, a mutually beneficial enterprise in which building the road had been a community project (Downs 1980, 182). He emphasized that payment was made to the tribal groups conducting roadwork and to landowners for alienation of the carriageway, but that distribution of coffee seedlings and the promise of future marketing opportunities also secured compliance (ibid.). Not all compliance was voluntary; Downs used some *kalabus* labour, transferring prisoners to a temporary road-camp for the purpose (Cleland 2010, 25). Further, commentators who have described traditional Highlands leadership as despotic (e.g. Salisbury 1964) or have emphasized the power of 'big-men' (e.g. Donaldson and Good 1988) would see traditional leaders as pressing their followers into service, while themselves benefiting disproportionately. Such considerations suggest the value of examining the notion of *partnership*, as promulgated in Goroka in the 1950s, and its implications for indigenous welfare.

Administrative style during Downs's tenure was marked by this local rhetoric of partnership, which may have been promoted as a riposte to Hasluck's rollback of personalistic land administration in Goroka. A variation on the theme of 'dual development', it was at once a tacit admission that pretension to a 'white highlands' was anachronistic and an accommodation to the precarious position of settlers amidst a dense and warlike population. More positively, Howlett (1973) believed partnership could be seen as acknowledging the economic interdependence of black and white, while promising a shared prosperity. The expression appeared late in 1954, in commentary by the Eastern Highlands District Advisory Council on Hasluck's new land measures. This consultative group (of which Downs was an ex officio member) noted that these measures threatened the 'partnership' between settlers and Gorokans that had been emerging in the district (Finney 1970, 121–22). Again, in his annual report for 1954/55, Downs stressed the positive contribution of European settlers. In the Highlands they were 'a force for good', very different in outlook from the managers of coastal plantations, and conducive to 'a genuine and sincere Partnership [*sic*]' between planters and highlanders (ibid.).

Capitalization suggests reification, and *Partnership* became central to the rhetorical armoury of white Highlands planters for more than a decade. This claim was advanced again, a quarter-century later, in the official history, where Downs asserted that development in the region had brought settlers and highlanders together. This was evident in the creation in 1955 of the HFSA as a 'non-racial organization' with prominent indigenous members, which honoured commitments 'beyond our own self-interest' (Downs 1980, 185).

Partnership had merit enough to persuade otherwise critical commentators that it was an 'impressive ideology', assisting Gorokans to engage with new economic opportunities (Donaldson and Good 1988, 72). Howlett (1973, 258) thought the idea 'probably appropriate', at least in the early years, because it recognized the generally positive relations of settlers with landowners and the demonstration effects and technology transfer flowing from their dispersion among villages. Finney (1970, 17) puzzled over whether to label partnership 'a cynical rationale for old-fashioned land-grabbing'. In the end, he accepted the sincerity of some of the idea's proponents, the eagerness of many highlanders to make land available and to cooperate with European neighbours, and the rapidity with which

Gorokans embraced coffee cultivation. Hawksley's conclusion (2001, 348) was pungent. Partnership was 'an example of mass delusion, as Australian administrators and settlers went to some lengths to deny that what they were engaged in was in any way colonial'.

As early as 1956, Francis West had reported that 'an energetic administration in the Eastern Highlands District . . . has tried to draw natives into partnership with Europeans in economic development'. West warned of the danger of disappointed expectations, 'caus[ing] despondency and indifference among natives who have been encouraged to enter this partnership' (West 1956, 310). Disappointments did soon occur, due to an emerging sense among Gorokans that 'the personal relationships with settlers that [they had] thought they were entering into when they sold their lands seldom turned out as they had hoped'. Gorokan economic achievements would become considerable in the aggregate, but individual Gorokans became increasingly aware of a gulf between them and the Europeans, alongside whom they grew coffee (Finney 1970, 129–31).

Finney described numerous cases of Gorokan dissatisfaction in commonplace dealings with Europeans, such as labour hire and vegetable sales, together with lingering expectations associated with their having surrendered land to settlers. Reminiscent of pre-colonial dealings between Seramese traders and Papuans on the western fringe of old Melanesia (Ch. 3), these might be seen as instances where the Maussian expectations of Gorokans shattered on the rock of Smithian contractual understandings held by Europeans. 'Sales' of land by Gorokans were hybrid transactions bearing a weight of expectation. They anticipated continuing relationships in which they might manipulate new European neighbours, much as successful Gorokan trade partners had always sought advantage from traditional exchange relationships.

In practice, however, rules of engagement were determined by Europeans, acting on market principles of individualistic action, of which they were the masters. 'Partnership', as defined, was seen to be unrealistic, and so conflict was inevitable. Finney reported that by 1957 relations with Gorokans had worsened to the point where local authorities became concerned, while over the following decade the two sides became largely estranged. This occurred as plantations changed hands and new owners felt little obligation to the original landholders, and as European coffee operations became increasingly corporatized and impersonal. Larger corporate entities, appearing from the 1960s, dispelled any illusion that plantations in Goroka could somehow operate differently from those on the coasts (Finney 1970, 130–32).

Donaldson and Good (1988) pointed to a later phase of partnership rhetoric, commencing soon after 1957 when it was clear that relations were turning sour. This involved a few well-performing Gorokan entrepreneurs on whom HFSA 'deftly focused', enlisting them as a local bourgeoisie to act 'as bulwarks of the plantation system'. This was not so much an attempt to influence broad Gorokan opinion as to co-opt an emerging elite, who would be an influence for political stability in the coffee industry (ibid., 73). Finney discerned a mixture of motives among white planters, some genuinely concerned for the welfare of Gorokans, but others regarding efforts to promote leading highlanders as 'insurance' (Finney 1970, 132–33). Stewart (1992, 74) described the HFSA as hoping to facilitate takeovers of mid-sized formal plantations by Gorokans in order to prevent corporate interests increasing their dominance. But despite such hopes, the HFSA remained dominated by its European members and continued to be 'identified with the interests of European plantation agriculture' (Hawksley 2001, 417).

Ultimately Downs acknowledged the failure of partnership. Relationships had soured because the 'fantasy' of real racial harmony was unmasked by the 'commercial greed' shown by 'both races' (Downs 1980, 186). This conclusion may indicate the difficulty Downs experienced in accounting for the episode in the official history. Despite the mixture of idealism and calculated self-interest involved, he exercised authorial privilege to attribute blame to both sides. The partnership episode suggests a need to examine the growth of Gorokan informal engagement in coffee growing and ancillary activities, and how this related to the larger, formal economy of Goroka dominated by settlers and corporate interests.

Notes

1. A note on place names: Eastern Highlands Province (EHP) is the administrative area of contemporary PNG where these events took place. It is the eastern portion of the geographic 'central Highlands' region. 'Goroka' is used both for the principal urban centre of EHP and its immediate district, corresponding broadly to the Goroka and Asaro valleys. For the early colonial period (without considering later boundary changes), EHP may also be referred to here as 'Eastern Highlands District', or simply 'Eastern Highlands'. The title 'Gorokan' is reserved for indigenous inhabitants, while 'European' and 'expatriate' are used for white residents (mostly Australian).
2. *Kiap* (*Tok Pisin*): a government patrol officer.
3. See Hawksley (2001, 415, n74) for an interesting account of this career transition.

Chapter 21

Gorokans and Coffee in the 'Lucky Place'

From 1945, Australian bureaucrats in Goroka chafed under a programme of post-war reconstruction in which the Highlands were accorded low priority. As reconstruction gave way to the new imperative of economic development, they showed themselves unwilling to accept the implications for their district of Hasluck's 'uniform' application of development effort. As a consequence, Goroka became the site of initiatives that anticipated later policies of 'accelerated' development. The achievements were considerable; from 1947 to 1957 the Goroka district office, although 'understaffed and underfunded', achieved 'a social transformation unlike any other area of PNG'. It did this with 'a minimum of force', and its goal of economic progress was at least 'partly realized' because it succeeded in 'ushering eastern highlanders into the international economy' (Hawksley 2001, 423).

While my narrative may have personalized this process in the character of Ian Downs, he is better seen as holding particular values and priorities in common with his predecessors and subordinates. These coloured the bureaucratic culture of a district that Europeans viewed as exceptionally promising. Entering the Goroka Valley in the 1930s, early patrol officers and prospectors quickly recognized the physical elements of what Michael Lipton called a 'lucky place' (Ch. 2), including an apparent abundance of arable land. It is understandable that local administrators, smarting from perceptions of 'centralist' neglect, should have seen Goroka as ripe for economic development.

Fred Fisk saw early colonial Gorokans as living in circumstances of 'subsistence affluence', a condition opportune for development (Ch. 4). His policies amounted, as Diana Howlett (1973) said, to 'modernisation via the addition of commercial crops to the traditional base of subsistence foodstuffs'. This would secure the Smithian 'vent for surplus', overcoming narrowness of internal markets by exporting product surplus to domestic requirements. Such a strategy would succeed only so long as surpluses of labour and land were available to fuel expansion. These resources amounted to what Hla Myint (1958, 330) called 'discrete blocks of surplus productive capacity being drawn into a widening circle of money economy and international trade'. In Goroka this process was seen in the areal expansion of coffee production, extending from Kainantu and Goroka through the Eastern Highlands and further west to Mount Hagen and beyond. The circle of market economic activity was widened, in accordance with principles emphasized by Peter Bauer (Ch. 2), by improving transport (feeder roads and the highway) and economic organization. The latter goal required creating processing and marketing facilities, and making imported 'incentive' goods available. Thereafter, if what Howlett (1973) called 'terminal development' were to be avoided, it would be necessary to secure improvements in productivity based on 'continuous improvements in skills, more productive recombinations of factors, and increasing returns' (Myint 1958, 321).

Gorokan Leadership as Seen by Finney and His Successors

Almost all subsequent studies of coffee in Goroka are heavily dependent on the original accounts of Gorokan entrepreneurship by Ben Finney (1968, 1969, 1970, 1973 and 1987). He acknowledged a debt to Fred Fisk, whose approach to the task of linking subsistence cultivators into the cash economy he found 'most stimulating'. Accordingly, Finney determined to study how this had been achieved in Goroka (Finney 1973, xvii). Later commentators have generally taken a less benign view of the linkage process, but Finney had an implicit notion of Goroka as a 'lucky place' with a broadly advantageous experience of colonialism. This included its relatively benign experience of early colonial contact, investments in infrastructure, and – under the rubric of 'partnership' – know-how and encouragement (ibid., 124–25).

While Lipton (1984) emphasized both foreign capital inflows and the propensity of local people to save for productive investment as marking 'lucky' places, Finney gave more weight to the latter. Employing a trope analogous to Scarlett Epstein's evocation of the Tolai people as 'primitive capitalists' (Epstein 1968), Finney thought Gorokans 'pre-adapted' to *bisnis* (introduced market economic activities) by reason of their savings and investment behaviour. They showed a propensity to save cash, to aggregate it, and to apply it to a range of enterprises. They proved to be 'conspicuous investors' (Finney 1968, 395–96) who desired wealth and enjoyed the prestige that flows from gaining and deploying it (ibid., 398). In arriving at this conclusion, he had been influenced by research on the 'need for achievement' by David McClelland (1961), which posited a causal relationship between this 'need' and the promotion of entrepreneurship and economic development (Finney 1973, xiii).[1]

Finney's assertions reflected something approaching a late colonial consensus on Melanesian social structures. These were seen as typically fluid, while traditional leadership was regarded as most commonly open and competitive (Conroy 1976, 13–18). Such views carried strong implications for prestige and leadership status, which could be seen as matters of *achievement* rather than *ascription*. Greatly influenced by the 'thoroughly bourgeois' Melanesian 'big-man' depicted by Marshall Sahlins (1963), this consensus was evident in anthropological entries in the *Encyclopedia of Papua and New Guinea* by Langness, de Lepervanche and others, published soon before self-government (Ryan 1972; Hogbin 1973).[2] Assuming a lack of centralized authority, Langness (1973, 153) thought 'such authority that does exist is most often based on personal authority', while de Lepervanche (1973, 22) asserted that '[a]lthough leadership is everywhere achieved in competition with rivals, the nature of the competition varies. And depending on the enterprises to which male prestige attaches, the role of big-man varies'. Finney adopted a more singular focus, reflecting his judgement of how *economic* enterprise appeared to gain prestige in Gorokan society. Such enterprise involved introduced forms of *bisnis* activity whose success yielded renown, both for leaders themselves and for followers persuaded to contribute labour, money and even land to activities conducted under an ideology of group enterprise (Finney 1973, Ch. 5).

Finney's position, that Gorokan societal norms were favourable to the emergence of entrepreneurs due to a 'high degree of achieved status mobility' (ibid., xix), provides us with the entrée to a 1970s debate inspired by French structural Marxism. Radical scholars who rejected Finney's analysis sought to discern an indigenous class structure within Melanesian 'traditional social formations'. This required them to discredit the late colonial consensus and to show evidence of an emergent capitalist class whose status (and opportunity for economic success) rested on principles of ascription (see, for example, Donaldson and Good 1981, 1988). This would have implications for new forms of social stratification and wealth distribution. They thought this emergent class already evident by the late colonial period, so further economic growth in the new era of independence could only magnify its wealth and political influence.

Finney's view of capitalist accumulation was complacent. Together with an implicitly meritocratic view of entrepreneurial success, it reflected his tolerance of economic inequalities generated by development. Although Donaldson and Good (1988), like Finney, saw traditional leadership as the precursor of modern entrepreneurship, in other respects their analysis was very different. Whereas Finney declared Gorokans 'pre-adapted' to accumulation, Donaldson and Good seem to have regarded them as pre-adapted to class warfare. Their argument was unpersuasive, insofar as they failed to show that mechanisms for the intergenerational transmission of status and wealth, a necessary condition for the emergence of a continuing rural capitalist class, were present in pre-contact societies.

Donaldson and Good scoured the anthropological literature, settling on a congenial case from the Western Highlands to illustrate their thesis. In Mount Hagen, class formation was 'more than embryonic', and from 1930 the efforts of emerging leaders were directed towards power and accumulation. They acted '*in favour of the formation of what was in the process of becoming a nascent class, certainly of big-men but perhaps of hereditary chieftains*' (ibid., 25, emphasis added). This generalization, as tentative as it is questionable, provided only pallid support for their proposition that the foundations of an indigenous rural capitalism were to be found in the social structures of traditional society. By comparison, Rolf Gerritsen (1979, 48), while similarly selective in his choice of anthropological evidence, was more robust in asserting that the evolution of rural capitalism 'had a strong element of inherited advantage, a mechanism that predated the international capitalist economy penetration of the supposedly egalitarian Melanesian societies'. He felt confident to assert that 'this factor of inherited advantage . . . is becoming permanent'.

Fitzpatrick (1980) enlisted the HFSA to the cause, observing that as independence approached colonists identified willing elements of the rising bourgeois class, employing a strategy based on the existence of 'hierarchies and inequalities in highland societies' (ibid., 15). However, like Donaldson and Good, Fitzpatrick left the essential question unanswered – whether mechanisms existed for the intergenerational transfer of private entrepreneurial status. But he did suggest that Western education would enable the children of entrepreneurs to enter state employment. By contrast, MacWilliam eschewed analysis of capitalist accumulation in terms of sociological abstractions (see MacWilliam 2013, 230, n66) in favour of a determinism in which motive force was provided by the 'external authority of capital'. In a similar vein, Hawksley (2001, 2005) employed an analytical framework of administrative colonialism, the purpose of which was to create conditions 'safe for capital'.

Marxian commentators had in common a distaste for Finney's individualistic values. But his analysis was not exclusively individualistic for, as mentioned above, Finney also took account of prestige attaching to *groups*, whose standing could be enhanced by the achievements of individual members. Late colonial Gorokan investment behaviour demonstrated hybridity, in that, for example, no great prestige attached to the accumulation of working capital. Gorokans sought instead to possess the visible, prestigious markers of success – coffee groves, trade stores, trucks and processing equipment – and the group took pride in their accumulation by individual members. Finney emphasized the capacity of big-men to mobilize finance and labour from their followers, invoking customary ties in support of projects seen as bolstering the solidarity and prestige of the group. Nonetheless, as the experience of 'business groups' incorporated under the legislation of 1974 suggests, big-man entrepreneurs in the hinterlands of Goroka and Rabaul were not above parlaying their influence into projects for personal enrichment (Ch. 18).

A number of writers stimulated by the challenge of Marxian narratives re-examined the achievement/ascription debate towards the end of the 1970s (including Standish 1978, Brown 1979, Chowning 1979 and Douglas 1979). With the exception of Paula Brown – who took a position consistent with the Finney 'line' – these reappraisals were not so much a rejection of the late colonial consensus as an effort to rebalance the argument. Despite its appearance in a modest, mimeographed format, the paper by Bill Standish was particularly influential. Like Brown, Standish was principally concerned with the Chimbu district (later, Simbu Province) located immediately west of the Eastern Highlands, although his characterization of Chimbu leadership differed substantially from hers. She appeared to be defending her own turf: a return visit in 1976 had 'substantiated [her] view that competition is the active binding force of Chimbu society' (Brown 1979, 100), in which 'there was no true stratification or much inherited advantage' (ibid., 103).

Controversy was only implicit in Brown's account whereas Standish was direct. He noted that while political economists were concerned with capitalist 'penetration' it was necessary also to consider 'political culture'. Indeed, 'the two modes of analysis complement each other, showing the way the continuity of past modes of behaviour can allow a receptive environment for alien modes of production' (Standish 1978, 31). Here, 'political culture' is shorthand for whatever ideology is held to explain leadership, and Standish's reference to 'modes of production' suggests a willingness to continue the debate on neo-Marxian premises. Bronwen Douglas rejected this position. In New Guinea and its islands, rather than classifying leadership according to 'distinct structural categories' – a reference to the preoccupations of 1970s French Marxist theory – it is better to think in terms of 'relative emphasis on ascribed status and/or ranking of descent groups or their segments' (Douglas 1979, 5). She also stressed the importance of distinguishing, so far as possible, between historical situations and the 'ethnographic present'. Similarly, Ann Chowning (1979, 66) cautioned that 'professional anthropologists usually arrived only after indigenous patterns of leadership had been drastically altered', and were dependent on *ex post facto* accounts.

Many contributors to the discussion have made this point, referring to the impact, sometimes traumatic, of colonialism on traditional societies, and the emergence of new forms of political power and economic opportunity. These new forms had implications for the exercise of leadership and entrepreneurship in the colonial and post-colonial contexts. Both Brown and Finney were interested primarily in those contexts (and had studied culture regions – Chimbu and Goroka, respectively – in which the case for a conjunction of achieved leadership and entrepreneurship might plausibly be made). Such situations can be generalized: '*When* leadership is based on achievement the pattern tends to be similar throughout Melanesia [and] . . . the realm in which achievement is most stressed is economic' (Chowning 1979, 71, emphasis added).

Douglas (1979, 2) wrote from a comparative, Melanesian/Polynesian, perspective, starting with Marshall Sahlins (1963) and his heuristic pairing of 'sociological types' of political leadership. She warned against stereotyping by region, pointing in particular to the generalization-defying diversity of Melanesia. Thus, societies oriented to achievement could nonetheless also demonstrate 'the operation of ascriptive principles in some social contexts and at some levels of segmentation'. Again, in coastal regions there were 'many societies with a bias towards ascription'. In the face of this diversity, anthropologists have too often come up with 'essentially static' models, neglecting the reality that ideology and practice are interrelated in particular social settings. Sometimes this produced normative constructions of reality (Douglas 1979, 4–5). Readers might see this tendency in positions taken by both formalists and Marxians in the ascription/achievement debate. The same charge might be levied against me, although my position is reasonably robust in the 'particular social setting' of Goroka. Nonetheless, reappraisals of what I have called the 'late colonial consensus' – by Chowning, Brown and Standish as well as Douglas – have demonstrated the perils of generalization in this rather fraught area.

Advance of the Gorokan Smallholders

Soon after the Pacific War and into the 1950s, coffee faced just such 'promising and elastic' markets as Lipton (1984) had described, and Gorokans adopted the crop eagerly (Bourke 1986). Their success would not have been possible without Hasluck's adherence to the principles of 'dual development' and his determination to prevent the destruction of Gorokan village life by any privileging of capitalist production (MacWilliam 2013, 5–6). Compared with the practice of an earlier German administration in the hinterland of Rabaul, land alienation in Goroka was conducted with greater regard to the future needs of village populations. As Gorokans became engrossed in coffee they soon ceased offering for contract employment. Before long, local demand for wage labour (both on European plantations and larger smallholdings established by some enterprising Gorokans) was filled largely by migrant workers from other, less 'lucky' places.

Ian Downs pointed out that some female Gorokan seasonal workers also took casual plantation work to supplement their domestic cash-crop production. During the coffee 'flush' period, they benefited from piecework made available by plantations (Downs 1980, 165). Further, in the communal savings movement known as *Wok Meri* (*Tok Pisin*, 'women's work'), which flourished during the late colonial period, women met to pool the proceeds of marketplace or coffee sales and earnings from casual labour. Finney (1987, 53) commented that this reflected resentment of 'the near monopoly by men of coffee-money and business', while Lorraine Sexton (1982, 196) described it as intended to address 'women's grievances' collectively. She saw their activities as 'building on traditional structures, selecting elements of Western economic institutions, and creatively transforming both'.

In a hybrid ritual, relationships between savings groups were cemented by 'exchanges mimicking traditional marriage payments' (Sexton 1982, 167). In a group's early phase, loans between members established mutual confidence, after which they invested jointly. Again, suggesting hybridity, success in *bisnis* was thought to require not only hard work but also adherence to prescribed ritual, while ceremony and the accumulation of money were sources of group prestige (including vis-à-vis husbands and their lineages). By the end of the 1970s, groups had invested in plantations and coffee buying, retail and wholesale stores, and a leased truck (Sexton 1982). In many instances, however, women had handed these operations to their sons who, unfortunately, 'tend[ed] to be poor managers' (Sexton 1983, 138). At independence, few individual women had significant business interests, although thousands – as producer-sellers – earned modest incomes from sales of staple foods and 'European' vegetables.

Expansion of indigenous coffee in Goroka was among the earliest manifestations of its later, widespread adoption in the Highlands. Finney reported Gorokan production at 100 tons in 1958–59, worth almost $41,000.[3] As young trees fruited, output rose rapidly to 2,500 tons by 1967–68, worth more than a million dollars (Finney 1973, 68). Gorokans had planted almost 2 million trees by 1962, rising to some 3.5 million only three years later, and to 4.5 million by 1967. This occurred in a period of active official discouragement of indigenous plantings (discussed below), during which government effectively lost control of the growth of smallholder coffee production. In 1967–68, as a growing proportion of these trees came into bearing, Gorokans produced an estimated 2,500 tons of parchment coffee, amounting to more than 12 per cent of all PNG production. Indigenous smallholder output quickly challenged the formal, European plantation sector.

At the national level, the acreage of coffee on plantations was exceeded by that of smallholders by the late 1950s, while actual smallholder production overtook the plantations a few years later (MacWilliam 2013, 180–81; see also his table 5.1). Again, smallholder production grew from under 11,000 tons to almost 30,000 tons in the nine years to 1975–76, an annual rate of growth of about 12 per cent. Average plantings were 450 trees per smallholder in 1977, and more than 200,000 indigenous growers were responsible for over 70 per cent of the national crop (Stewart 1992, 28).

The structure of the industry in the Eastern Highlands on the eve of independence may be seen in data for 1972–73. Some 45,000 indigenous coffee growers were reported as cultivating over 5,000 ha (a mean of 0.11 ha per holding) and producing more than 6,000 tons of 'green bean equivalent'. Averaging about 140 kg, this was a very small output on a 'per household' basis and the mean household return was only about $45 (Stewart 1992, 54). Nonetheless these returns provided some cash to households still embedded within subsistence agriculture. Dispersion of incomes was substantial as larger indigenous operators emerged, and income inequality was reflected in their demand for wage labour. In the 1970s, of some 11,000 paid labourers on coffee holdings perhaps 30 per cent were outside the formal plantation sector (ibid., 50). Workers were employed informally by Gorokan big-man entrepreneurs, some of whom the HFSA had recruited as members from the late 1950s.

Hasluck's dogged support for dual development moderated the growth of a capitalist plantation sector while offering opportunities for synergy between planters and smallholders. Aside from any altruistic considerations of 'partnership', active encouragement by planters of their Gorokan neighbours' plantings during the early boom reflected their own interest in coffee trading. Early planters provided essential (and profitable) marketing and processing services until sufficient scale was realized to justify the creation of specialized, corporate intermediaries. These began to emerge from 1959. Growth and elaboration of 'downstream' activities – not seen as an immediate threat to the integrity of village life, and in any case essential for the viability of smallholder coffee – was a phase of capitalist development that proceeded without hindrance from official policy during the 'uniform' development period.

Advance of the Gorokan Entrepreneurs

Goroka, the first town in the Highlands, became a transport and marketing hub. An indigenous population gathered, and at the census of 1961 these urbanites numbered almost 1,100, growing to 3,900 in 1966, then increasing with astonishing rapidity to 10,500 by 1971. Despite their both being 'lucky places', Goroka and Rabaul differed in one important respect; Chinese traders played no role in acculturating highlanders to market dealings comparable with their impact on the Gazelle. The confrontation, implicit in Downs's reference to the 'greed' of 'both races' (Ch. 20), was played out purely between Gorokans and Europeans.

Meanwhile, growing economic differentiation among Gorokans provided further potential for conflict, as some entrepreneurs adopted increasingly large and more formalized modes of *bisnis*. The town developed a diversified economic base, founded on administration and private sector activity serving the agricultural and consumer needs of a thriving hinterland. Rural–urban economic links stimulated heavy vehicular traffic flows, including to and from the town's thriving urban produce market, where female 'producer-sellers' were responsible for most trading. By 1968 Goroka had a European population of more than a thousand, and Ben Finney commented on the continuing dominance of expatriate commercial interests. Financial services, airlines, long-haul trucking, urban retail and wholesale trade, motor vehicle distributorships, timberyards, hotels, and other major urban businesses were all in expatriate hands. As Finney recalled, the degree of European commercial dominance extended to the ownership and control of all major firms. And while Gorokans had made their greatest progress in coffee, that sector was still dominated overall by Europeans (Finney 1973, 159).

Rowley described late colonial PNG as 'obsolescent', a term he also applied to the Highlands region in the wake of Hasluck's crackdown on land alienation. White settlement in the Highlands should properly be regarded as 'anachronistic' – a mode of investment more appropriate in the early twentieth century than in the 'unfavourable political climate' of mid-century Goroka, and likely to be the last such experiment (Rowley 1965, 121). Despite this, he believed European enterprise had a continuing role. The end of land alienation should not spell the loss of further private Australian capital. Logic suggested that the New Guinean should be the grower of export crops on his own land and that expatriate capital should fund investment in processing and finance (ibid.). This was a common European view. Finney observed that, in the late 1960s, many Europeans still thought it would be possible to maintain their stake in plantations, processing and exporting. They did not anticipate how quickly political events would move, or how resolutely a new, independent government would move to localize foreign ownership of the coffee industry (Finney 1987, 23).

Rowley's 'logic' had taken too little account of an emerging, more urgent reality; in parallel with the growth of expatriate-controlled downstream activities, another form of capitalist development was occurring. Increasing economic differentiation among Gorokans was producing new entrepreneurs with the wind of political change at their backs. While some 80 per cent of all indigenous adults were engaged in coffee, mostly for very small returns, younger men were finding it increasingly difficult to find land for coffee. Meanwhile, substantial inequality in plantings was also reflected in access to other productive assets. Emergent, quasi-traditional big-men, whom Finney called *bikfela man bilong bisnis* ('big-men' or 'business leaders'), were not content simply to grow coffee. They were preparing to challenge European commercial dominance.

In 1967 Finney selected ten prominent Gorokan entrepreneurs for study. His analysis of these big-men has been subject to several reconsiderations, in which they were dubbed 'rural capitalists' (Gerritsen 1979), 'rich peasants' (Donaldson and Good 1988) and the 'bourgeoisie and would-be bourgeoisie' (MacWilliam 2013). As against the district's average of about 450 trees, they had mean plantings of some 9,000 trees in 1968. They had also diversified into trade stores, trucking, cattle and restaurants, earning annual incomes of between $4,000 and $10,000, when Gorokan per capita cash income was perhaps $25 (Finney 1973, 85). Gerritsen's 'rural capitalists' (Gerritsen 1979) were distinguished from coffee-growing 'big peasants' by earning a significant proportion of their cash income from non-agricultural activities. MacWilliam's indigenous 'bourgeoisie' wanted to acquire plantations offered for sale by expatriate growers and foreign corporations. 'Rich peasants' were becoming an identifiable rural class and (in class analysis logic) this required an underlay of 'middle and poor peasants' (Donaldson and Good 1988, 105). In each of these three 'post-Finney' studies, an opposition is posited between a rural class consolidating and 'formalizing' itself as recognizably capitalist, and other, lesser growers called here 'informal' smallholders. The latter group in Rabaul was described by MacWilliam as producing for 'immediate consumption', but they also entered into producer-seller trade (Ch. 17), and had their counterparts in contemporary Goroka. Almost all of Finney's 'business leaders' were active in the new political institutions. Together with newer men, they would take advantage of access and information acquired in politics to benefit from economic opportunities arising in a rapidly changing environment. The election of Pangu Pati to government in 1972 and the redistributionist rhetoric of the Faber Report (discussed in Ch. 25) increased uncertainty among foreign plantation owners. This led many to divest, while the emergence of new formal modes of indigenous investment facilitated the takeover of expatriate-owned assets. Even before 1974, when the *Business Groups Incorporation Act* offered Gorokans a simplified model of incorporation, individual business leaders had been trialling formal modes. They took shares in expatriate-owned enterprises or formed limited companies to acquire them (often with guidance from expatriates seeking to divest). Whereas these were formal modes of investment, the new business groups could be seen as innovative in adapting incorporated company structures to PNG customary modes and conventions (Fitzpatrick 1980, 231; see also Ch. 18). Necessarily hybrid, these new entities served as vehicles for politically astute Gorokans to advance personal interests.

Fitzpatrick was disillusioned to see business groups captured by big-man leaders (as was also occurring on the Gazelle) deploying political influence to create a variety of group capitalism which turned out 'to favour them in particular' (Fitzpatrick 1980, 233). Similarly, MacWilliam remarked that powerful politicians were prime movers in these organizations, mobilizing support from local populations and securing access to the resources of the state (MacWilliam 2013, 233). The indigenous bourgeoisie secured power and influence just as the state was being reshaped for independence (Ch. 17). A Plantation Redistribution Scheme (PRS) operating from 1974 provided opportunity for business leaders, heading formalized business groups styled as 'development corporations', to bid for European coffee assets. The PRS also aroused hope among smallholders and landless men; ensuing debates over land redistribution were often framed in terms of 'equity' versus 'efficiency'.[4] Development corporations asserted the equity of their claims (in terms of having numerous smallholder member-beneficiaries) but also their efficiency – undertaking to maintain plantations and other productive assets as modern profitable entities managed professionally by expatriates. The latter was an important consideration for a new government nervous about loss of export income. With their claims resting simply on equity, 'poor peasants' found it difficult to prevail. Some landowner groups were unable to mount credible bids to regain ancestral lands, due to inadequate organization and a lack of capital. Civil disturbances ('tribal fighting') in the Highlands from 1974 seem to have reflected such frustrations. The PRS was discontinued in 1980, after independence, by which time indigenous ownership of plantations in the Eastern Highlands was substantially complete.

A frost in Brazil in 1975, leading to high international prices, enabled recently acquired plantations to be paid off quickly. This good fortune entrenched the positions of a number of leading entrepreneurs. Acquisition of bankable collateral increased their access to formal finance, enabling further diversification of interests. Such ventures included 'crop processing and export, transportation, trade, urban real estate and other areas of commerce'. Some adopted holding company structures with expatriate participation, hiring foreign management and professional services. These gains were enabled by the accession to political power of the indigenous bourgeoisie and its allies in small business. Power gave access to information, and to state allocatory mechanisms. The establishment of provincial governments after independence and a devolution of authority to them delivered decision making in Goroka into the hands of this rising class (MacWilliam 2013, 233; 2016).

It does not require acceptance of Marxian analyses or the prescriptions flowing from them to acknowledge the force of such arguments, or to see how rent-seeking among the new class would motivate their take-up of opportunities created by political change. Events reflected the political economy of the period, and established a trajectory for future accumulation by individuals in the independent state. In his retrospective account of Gorokan business achievements and prospects (based on a return visit in 1986), Ben Finney was untroubled by the evidence of inequality in access to income and productive assets resulting from these events. Instead, although disquieted by Gorokans' continuing reliance on expatriate management expertise, he emphasized the still-modest consumption habits of a number of the early business leaders, and their continuing genuine concern for the distribution of gains to followers. But where Marxian commentary focused on the coalescence of family-based business fortunes, Finney was more inclined to see evidence of intergenerational failure in transmitting wealth (Finney 1987, 33–37). This important question will be discussed further in Chapter 23.

By the end of the colonial period, Gorokan modes of engagement with the market economy had become diverse, with varying degrees of formality and informality, as between smallholders and those called here 'big-man entrepreneurs'. In most cases it was still possible to observe evidence of continuing hybridity – that uneasy coexistence of market dealings and traditional norms – in the management of such affairs. The next chapter will consider how formality, informality and hybridity manifested in Gorokan coffee during the run-up to independence in 1975.

Notes

1. Finney's partner, Ruth Finney, pursued this theme further with a study in the genre of 1960s 'modernization' theory based on surveys of PNG schoolchildren (R. Finney 1971).
2. Readers may find the *Encyclopedia* anthropological entries more accessible in the volume edited by Ian Hogbin (1973).
3. The Australian Pound (£A) circulated in Australian Papua from 1910, and in the former German New Guinea after 1914. With the decimalization of Australian currency in 1966, the Australian dollar (converted at the rate of £A1 = $2) circulated in PNG until 1975, when the kina (PNGK) replaced it.
4. See, for example, the contributions by McKillop (1981b) and Lawrance (1981) in Walter 1981.

Chapter 22

Formality and Informality in the Coffee Economy

This study is an 'informal' economic history, presenting in this chapter a case study of the emergence and character of economic informality in Gorokan smallholder coffee. Except for the need to explain certain implications for Gorokans of international trade negotiations and coffee processing and marketing arrangements from the late 1950s, it is not an account of *formal* industrial organization. Against the background of men's and women's forays into *bisnis*, it considers what the terms 'formality' and 'informality' meant in Goroka at the time of independence.

From the introduction of market exchange in the 1940s, and under pressures of colonial bureaucracy, Gorokans accommodated themselves to cultural norms of 'the market'. Coffee changed modes of livelihood and social organization; the need to adjust led many to cope by engaging in informal economic activities. The uneasy conjunction in their lives of market dealings and traditional norms also led people to engage in behaviours exhibiting hybridity. In the Gorokan context, informality should be seen as encompassing not only distinct rural and urban categories but also rural–urban relationships. These were not central to Hart's account of informality in Nima (1971, 1973, and as discussed in Ch. 1), but the Faber Mission adopted a more inclusive definition. In mapping the PNG informal 'sector', Faber & Co. bundled indigenous urban and rural subsistence and cash activities together under the heading of informal activity (Ch. 25). This was appropriate in 1970s Goroka, where livelihoods of smallholders remained grounded in rural subsistence while the town served as the fulcrum around which their informal cash-earning activities revolved.

Gorokan coffee has been characterized as 'household commodity production' by Stewart (1992) and others, a concept arising from the preoccupation of 1970s neo-Marxian theory with relations of production within particular social formations. Earlier anthropological theorizing was condemned as deficient due to its 'concentration upon exchange rather than production relations' (Donaldson and Good 1988, 12). Household production is also central to the analysis here, although a formality/informality framework governs my argument. Exchange is of continuing significance insofar as distinctions between Maussian and market exchange are essential to understanding the phenomenon of economic hybridity. Gorokan smallholders were engaged in *rural* informal economic activity, in a manner shaped by what Hart (2007a, see also Ch. 1) called their 'partial institutionalization' to the 'prevalent economic model' – one of economic development in a capitalist economy. Behaviour consistent with that model constituted formality, whereas the 'palpable discrepancies' seen in real life (reflecting the messy reality of their adjustment to 'the market') revealed informality.

'Discrepancies' occurred when Gorokans attempted to cope with a host of economic innovations, all governed by an imposed, regulatory framework and an unfamiliar commercial culture. In Goroka, where market economy was incompletely institutionalized, indigenous pushback against colonial economic orthodoxy produced such discrepancies – departures from *form* – as Hart had anticipated. Disruptive innovations to which Gorokans were exposed included the introduction and elaboration of monetary exchange, wage labour, technical change in agriculture (most notably, the introduction of a perennial tree crop into a system of shifting cultivation, disrupting traditional land tenure arrangements) and the emergence of related 'off-farm' activities in marketing and services. Following a process that had proceeded much further in the Rabaul hinterland, most Gorokan households were building on a relatively secure subsistence base to earn cash informally by gardening and the sale of traditional crops, introduced vegetables and livestock; by the production and post-harvest processing of coffee; and by ancillary activities including trade stores, trucking and seasonal paid labour. Many households acquired 'portfolios' of economic activity, giving multiple sources of livelihood.

Women took casual work on plantations, working also at household vegetable growing, pig husbandry and coffee gardens. Just as the earlier 'efflorescence' of exchange had revealed limits to subsistence affluence in terms of demands on female labour (Ch. 12), commercialized economic activity also imposed strains on women. In this environment a monetized regional economic system was emerging on a pattern familiar from the Gazelle. There Salisbury and the Epsteins had found a rural informal economy, well articulated with its urban centre. An observation made of the Tolai would become increasingly true of Gorokans: understanding how Tolai adapted to changing circumstances requires acknowledging their capacity to combine a number of economic roles simultaneously (Epstein 1969, 189). Smallholders juggled time against obligations, displaying agency by 'working and trading outside or at the edges of formal economic and political institutions' (Vorley, Del Pozo-Vergnes and Barnett 2012, 3).

It is intriguing to ask why Gorokans adopted informal modes of action when exemplars of formal economic activity, European plantations and businesses were close at hand. The answer is relatively straightforward where smallholder and plantation production operated side by side, as with coffee. Notionally, all were engaged in a single 'industry', though operations varied greatly in terms of variables such as scale and capital-intensity, sources of capital, relationships with downstream entities, use of purchased inputs, conditions of land tenure, and the sources and conditions of employed labour. In neoclassical economics a 'production function' for a single-product industry specifies the maximum output obtainable for each feasible combination of inputs. A mechanistic formulation, this abstracts from technical and managerial issues associated with 'best practice' production. Just such issues arise, however, in explaining the diversity observable within an 'industry' such as coffee in the Highlands in the late colonial period. It comprised production units ranging from households producing coffee as a sideline while still anchored in subsistence, to capital-intensive and highly professionalized plantations within vertically integrated corporations.

Leaving aside quantifiables such as capital- and labour-intensity, diversity within the 'industry' derived primarily from qualitative considerations, or 'quasi-traditional' conditions of production, such as use of family labour and/or informally contracted labour, location on land subject to traditional tenure, and the hybridity associated with household coffee production. The 'industry' comprised an array of producers ranging from Maussian households to Smithian conglomerates, the latter with continuing expatriate participation. It could not be called a producer 'community', as these disparate entities did not share the motivations assumed by the neoclassical behavioural construct of 'profit maximization'. Instead, we observe an 'industry' with varying degrees of formality and informality, located on either side of a basic divide between formal plantations and smallholders.

By 1975, some Gorokan business leaders were engaging in a range of business activities. These included coffee plantations larger and more highly capitalized than the mass of Gorokan smallholdings, whose establishment signalled their intention to bridge the divide between smallholders and planters. Some leaders were entering into formal contractual relationships, involving rights and obligations under tax, land tenure, company and other legislation, while employing professional services. In growing coffee they had moved from relying on the unpaid labour of family and followers to hiring paid workers – though these employment relationships were very different from the formal, contractual labour relations of European planters. Over a longer time span an entrepreneurial transition occurred, from relying on informal sources of finance (including personal savings and the contributions of kinfolk and 'followers' to joint enterprises) to formal credit, although few had access to bank or trade credit as early as 1975. As these trends continued it became possible to distinguish a continuum of formality among Gorokans themselves, ranging from MacWilliam's 'accumulators' at the more formal end, to 'consumer' households at the other. In regard to the latter, Howlett (1973, 262) observed around Goroka that there was 'much spontaneous planting on small scattered plots, usually on the insecure basis of usufruct'. This suggests a relationship between land tenure and formality. The drive to consolidate land holdings at an economic scale was a characteristic of 'formalizing' business leaders, while the mass of growers continued to cultivate sub-economic coffee plots in a subsistence *milieu.*

Regulation and Pushback

Among regulatory issues relevant to informality in coffee were those arising from ineffectual official attempts to control the level of indigenous production. These began about 1959 with a bureaucratic initiative to wind back coffee extension services. An attempt to divert extension resources to other cash crops and livestock, it was inspired by the fear that growth of smallholder coffee output would imperil official efforts to find overseas markets for the total (smallholder plus plantation) crop. As the potential for plantation growth was more constrained than that of smallholders, unchecked expansion by the latter would dilute planters' share in any internationally negotiated export quotas. Stewart described HFSA as taking an 'intensely political' stance on this issue, while Paige West concluded that the association had influenced the official decision in its members' interests (West 2012, 273, n7). For the late colonial period this was an unusual instance of authorities intervening to safeguard the interests of 'metropolitan capital' over those of indigenous growers, although such interference had been common enough in the Mandated Territory during the interwar period (Ch. 1; see also Ch. 8).

By 1961, official policy had hardened to the point of actively discouraging further smallholder plantings. Australia's accession to the International Coffee Agreement (ICA) in 1962 secured a de facto export quota for PNG coffee (Stewart 1992, 94–95), but this was made conditional upon action to slow the overall rate of coffee's expansion and to cease active agricultural extension efforts among New Guinean coffee growers (Finney 1973, 66). There was a difficulty with this commitment, for while government might abandon coffee extension it lacked legal authority to prevent smallholders from continuing to plant coffee. In the international climate of the 1960s, smallholders were in a position to call the bureaucratic bluff. Continued plantings represented their pushback against official suasion, amounting to the 'informal sector' of coffee prevailing – in this matter at least – over the formal, plantation sector.

Aside from such quantitative issues, there were also important qualitative problems in smallholder coffee production troubling authorities. These concerned good practice in planting, husbandry and processing, and were less the subject of formal regulation than of guidance by administration officials, particularly agricultural extension staff, and commercial coffee buyers. During the tenure of Robert Cottle as district agriculture officer, from 1952 to 1954, early smallholder plantings were carefully supervised and correct agronomic practice encouraged, under a regime targeting leading men (Ch. 20). Even after Cottle's departure, some individual growers still benefitted from a continuing 'big-man bias' among extension staff. But as officials lost control of indigenous expansion, informality in the generality of Gorokan coffee production was signalled by smallholders' failure to conform with prescribed agronomic standards.

This failure is suggested by an account of cultivation practices from the 1980s, which (if backward extrapolation is acceptable) may be taken as a guide to conditions during the late colonial period. Among the mass of small householder growers, techniques and equipment employed in production were 'extremely rudimentary'. Simple and inefficient machinery ('pulpers and hoes') were used by unskilled labourers who 'rarely weed and almost never mulch', while 'rarely' pruning their bushes. The result was 'lower yields, difficulties for pickers and a failure to rejuvenate the tree by providing bearing wood' (Stewart 1992, 55).

Such poor husbandry was due to a number of factors. Aside from withdrawal of extension services there was a period of sustained low prices from 1964 to 1974. This discouraged 'subsistence affluent' Gorokans from investing more than minimum labour inputs into maintenance, although aggregate plantings and output continued to expand as smallholders engaged in their own version of the 'scramble for land'. Further output growth caused the quantitative issue to arise again. Confrontation between bureaucracy and informal producers was renewed in 1966–67 when coffee exports threatened to breach limits set under the first ICA agreement. Gorokan pushback continued (described by Stewart as a 'silent class struggle'), while the HFSA renewed efforts to curb smallholder expansion under the guise of 'non-racial' regulations, which it proposed in order to restrict indigenous output. These were to be based on a formula derived from limits already imposed on the plantation sector.

The attempt failed due to a combination of factors. First, the administration still lacked capacity to restrain indigenous expansion, while regulation so prejudicial to smallholder interests ran against continuing official sentiments of 'trusteeship'. Further (as occurred also in the later case of the Faber Report; Ch. 24), other Australian agencies including the departments of Treasury and Trade were prepared to overrule the Department of Territories on issues of economic policy. These included the anti-competitive nature of the proposed settlement, as well as concern to avoid compromising either broader Australian interests in international trade negotiations or the longer-term fiscal sustainability of an independent PNG. Ian Downs, still chair of the HFSA, might thunder from Goroka that the Department of Agriculture should, 'forthwith', be made to halt the runaway planting in the industry (cited in Stewart 1992, 102), but the times were not ripe for coercive measures. With the administration increasingly conscious of the approach of self-government, any action that might destabilize the coffee industry could not be supported (ibid., 101–3). Smallholders continued to expand plantings under an informal production regime typified by substandard husbandry, with suboptimal yields.

Pushback and Coffee Processing

The quality of processed coffee beans was a perennial problem. It emerged with the decline of extension services and was exacerbated by low prices, but most importantly resulted from smallholder pushback against professional coffee buyers. Commercial processors acted through a Coffee Marketing Board (CMB) to determine formal grading standards and price differentials. Prices actually received by smallholders were negotiated at the roadside or the factory door – supposedly on formal criteria, but more often reflecting power and information imbalances between smallholders and buyers. Beans were often sold at the roadside as unprocessed, perishable 'cherry' coffee. Processing from cherry to 'parchment', requiring modest investment in equipment and labour, was also done by many smallholders, though with variable quality outcomes. Well-processed parchment could be stored, advantaging the holder – whether smallholder or processor – who then had discretion in deciding when to sell. That some small growers held parchment in expectation of higher returns suggests their capacity to defer immediate income in favour of future returns, implying smallholder progress towards more formal modes of operation. The final stage of processing, to exportable 'green bean', required capital investment and was normally done by commercial millers. To gain premium prices, smaller European planters and some larger, more formal Gorokan producers would pay to have this done.

In practice, as Stewart explained, buyers sent out to obtain coffee by the roadside were ill-informed about quality issues and tested the beans casually (or not at all). They classified and purchased all beans offered as 'Y grade'. The reference is to lower-priced bean, deemed suitable only for soluble ('instant') coffee. This was the dominant element in Australian consumption at the time, whereas plantation coffee was considered to be of higher ('appearance') quality. Under ICA quotas, the latter could be sold more profitably in premium markets. But so could smallholder coffee that was suitable for processing to the necessary standard, suggesting that 'native' parchment acquired cheaply could be very profitable. Stewart explained the problem: if smallholders were only ever paid at the Y grade rate, 'where is the incentive' to improve quality (Stewart 1992). It is not difficult to see that the absence of price incentives could cause pushback behaviour among smallholders, either in terms of becoming indifferent to quality or by employing deceptive practices. The latter included adulteration with foreign matter or concealing poorly processed ('wet') parchment in coffee bags.

In the 1960s, coffee buying was a regulated occupation conducted largely by Europeans, employed by processors or funded by them under 'tied' relationships. Towards the end of the decade, illegal roadside buying by Gorokans appeared, a form of pushback reflecting a determination to enter the more profitable, downstream activities. Then in 1973, under the influence of the Faber Report, Gorokans were encouraged to apply for buyer licences. By 1974 new legislation had attempted to 'localize' roadside buying of cherry and parchment completely, and to free newly licensed buyers from restrictive ties. This proved unworkable; lacking working capital and without assured access to processors, indigenous buyers were caught in what Stewart called a 'pinch point' at the factory gate. Regulations were watered down to legitimize processor financing again, and some private European and corporate processors assisted highlanders to purchase vehicles previously used by Europeans. The net effect of this pushback was to improve the position of a new category of indigenous buyers vis-à-vis informal smallholders, with the latter remaining subject to bargains as hard as they had suffered before. Coffee processors (still largely associated with foreign interests) retained the upper hand.

Two more, closely related, instances of the pushback phenomenon occurred during 1973. In the first, we see evidence of reaction against activities of 'formalizing' Highlands big-man/planters by their wage labourers and local smallholders. In the second, pushback took the form of successful resistance to legislative measures secured by the political representatives of those planters. The latter instance occurred when 'some groups, particularly big Highlands businessmen, wanted to ban the selling of cherry, because they felt that the price was too low and cherry coffee was too easily stolen and sold to passers-by' (Von Fleckenstein 1975, 116). Industry sources suggested that 'hired pickers and others' were responsible for such thefts (Cartledge 1978).

Beneath the surface it is fair to see coffee-stealing as grassroots pushback against rural inequality and the alienation of land by prominent individuals – just as one might see those same phenomena contributing to agrarian violence ('tribal fighting'). Legislation to deal with coffee-stealing restricted the sale and purchase of cherry in specified areas, including Goroka. The victory was short lived, the regulation being amended because of political opposition from an unlikely coalition of smallholders and the CMB. Many smallholders, especially women, wished to retain freedom to make immediate small cash sales without the trouble of processing, while the board expressed concern about 'the likely effect on the overall quality and price of smallholder coffee being exported, and doubts . . . about the return to the grower being any more favourable by producing only parchment' (Cartledge 1978, 161). It is piquant that both sides – 'formalizing' big-men and formal processors and marketers – affected to take the high ground by expressing concern for the interests of informal smallholders.

Processors (represented by the CMB) may have been correct to assert that smallholders gained little benefit by processing to parchment stage. It was almost certainly true that commercial processing of cherry would improve quality and secure higher returns for the industry as a whole. But given the stranglehold on downstream purchasing and processing held by corporate interests, it is not clear that higher returns would have flowed back to smallholders – a situation that Stewart (1992, 65ff) explained in terms of 'pinch points' in the purchasing/processing/marketing chain. The ban on cherry sales may be interpreted as protecting the interests of a class of formalizing indigenous planters (who, incidentally, owned most of the small pulping machines hired to smallholders, to process cherry coffee in villages). Pushback exerted against this by smallholders displayed stubborn informality, in support of their freedom to sell coffee in its least-processed (i.e. least *formal*) condition, although their action benefited commercial interests represented by the CMB.

In summary, episodes of pushback (efforts to cope with bureaucratic pressure) entrenched informality in the mass of Gorokan peasant producers. Most significant was their refusal to bend to official suasion to curtail the expansion of plantings – a resistance that assured their quantitative (if not commercial) dominance of the industry. In qualitative terms, smallholders reacted against any pricing policies that did not reward them for careful processing. Their consequent indifference to quality and frequent resort to deceptive practices were evidence of stubborn informality, causing a 'low price/minimum effort' mentality to become normalized among them. Other rural behaviours suggested dissatisfaction among particular groups – informal growers, informally hired coffee workers and younger people facing land shortage. Coffee stealing, and even some instances of 'tribal' fighting, are also interpreted here as informal economy pushback against alienation of customary land by Gorokan entrepreneurs.

Just before independence, Donaldson and Good (1981) identified a group of rural capitalists who were capable of 'class action' (opposition to regulated wage increases, office-holding, and agitation in regard to law and order issues). The aborted ban on the direct sale of cherry was an attempt by these entrepreneurs to protect their own interests, while political reaction against it represented the defence of informality in production by small growers. Illegal coffee-buying was evidence of Gorokans pushing to move 'downstream' from production to marketing, and, to the extent this contributed to further decline in processing standards, the result may have been to entrench smallholder informality further. Episodes discussed here give insight into what Downs called the commercial greed displayed by both races (Ch. 20), particularly evident in 'the purchasing and marketing of coffee'. Alternatively, we might see them simply as characterizing the direction of change in Goroka at the end of the colonial era.

Chapter 23

The Triumph of Capitalism?

If a low price/minimum effort malaise marked much smallholder production, a related weakness plagued Gorokan planters striving towards formalized operations. Their problem was a low wage/low productivity trap. The rise of Finney's *bikfela man* produced economic differentiation between Gorokans in coffee, as well as the entry of others into downstream and service activities. Some aspiring rural capitalists, who might be called 'coffee entrepreneurs', appear to have focused on growing coffee at a scale closer to that of European plantations (Ch. 22). They were distinct from the mass of Gorokans ('smallholders') growing some coffee as part of a portfolio of activities grounded in subsistence agriculture. There was also another group of more ambitious 'formalizing' Gorokans. They extended their reach to commercial activities, such as trade stores and trucking, and gained positions of influence in cooperative societies or savings and loan institutions (Stewart 1992, 75). This narrative considers first the Gorokans – entrepreneurs and smallholders – who were active in coffee.

Gorokans in Coffee: Entrepreneurs and Smallholders

Finney (1969, 37ff) characterized the coffee entrepreneurs as unable to access bank or trade credit, and starved of working capital. Cash-flow problems reduced their capacity to pay wages during the coffee 'flush', and as most could not afford commercial processing they also failed to secure quality premiums on their 'green' beans. Less effective than expatriates in managing labour, they employed workers informally rather than under regulated contract. With such labour as they could afford, they were more likely than Europeans to be locked into low wage/low productivity employment relations. All planters experienced some worker antagonism, but small and medium Gorokan planters suffered because of difficulty in managing the complexities of 'piece rate' employment. Involving payment by results, this was common on larger, formal plantations intent on securing the highest productivity from casual workers.

Piecework involved high costs because some workers cheated by 'forging weight receipts'; others lost these documents, and others – perhaps alienated by the employment experience – damaged coffee trees by rough handling (Stewart 1992, 49). As with coffee stealing, such behaviours were often forms of worker pushback, against industrial grievances that a well-managed and well-capitalized plantation might handle, but that most Gorokan employers could not. Soon after independence, the 'localization' of plantations was essentially complete. In a reference to the 'alienation' observed by Stewart, an experienced analyst remarked that 'the current breakdown of the plantation system in PNG can be related to the lack of acceptance of *the status hierarchy necessary to support the system*' (McKillop 1981b, 28, emphasis added). In consequence of this, and of an inability to realize economies of scale, small and medium Gorokan plantations were unable to rise above their intermediate position between informal smallholders and formal plantations. Also, by reason of greater capital investment and overheads, they were more vulnerable than smallholders to coffee price fluctuations. Smallholders displayed a more elastic supply response to changing prices, becoming at times of low prices both less willing to pick coffee and less careful in processing it. Many preferred to apply their energies to other activities in such circumstances.

Two attempts occurred in the 1960s to create larger entities capable of remedying disadvantages suffered by smallholders at the hands of coffee buyers and processors. Both were settler initiatives, aiming to combine Gorokan capital in joint ventures with European capital and management, and to capture for smallholders more of the value added in processing. One of these, the Highlands Commodity Exchange (HCE), was an incorporated entity and the other an unincorporated partnership. Both were buoyed by initial enthusiasm and Gorokan cash, as smallholder groups saw an opportunity to 'own' processing mills comparable with those of Europeans. In the event, despite reasonable dividends in the early years, HCE's new mill proved insufficiently grand to meet indigenous shareholder expectations. Their loyalty wavered, and in a rather piquant situation of pushback, HCE found itself having to compete with rival buyers for its *own* shareholders' coffee, and to deal with adulteration of bagged coffee purchased from them. Similarly, discontent emerged in the second venture because members' money was employed as working capital – a concept difficult for smallholders to comprehend – and had not acquired 'any visible capital asset to which they can point with pride' (Finney 1969, 77–78). Both cases seemed to illustrate a characteristically Gorokan hybrid mix of motives in which rates of return on capital appeared secondary. Even good returns without 'some visible sign' of success 'may not be enough to satisfy investors' (ibid., 78).

In summary, the evidence suggests informal smallholders did not internalize the market rationality required by the 'development' orthodoxy. They experienced a malaise, cushioned by subsistence, limiting earnings from coffee. Two attempts to create group entities to remedy smallholder disadvantage were undermined by a hybrid preference for prestige. These experiences suggest how frequently 'discrepancies' emerged between prescribed economic behaviour and the untidy reality of Goroka. Secondly, 'formalizing' small and medium planters ('coffee entrepreneurs') had difficulty escaping limitations imposed by the low wage/low productivity trap. They were unable to overcome managerial shortcomings (e.g. the informality and inefficiency of their labour-hire practices). These were uncongenial aspects of the colonial economic orthodoxy, although most Gorokans were enthusiastic about its principal plank – 'development'. They saw this in the parochial and concrete forms of village infrastructure and increasing coffee acreages (however erratically they exploited their *own* acres). Their understanding was encapsulated in the pidgin phrase *kirapim ples* ('local development'). Successful Gorokan businessmen also absorbed the rhetoric of development, and promising to deliver its local manifestations to electors became a prerequisite for political office.

Beyond Coffee

Perhaps one should look elsewhere for a convincing demonstration of acculturation to market norms and the abandonment of hybrid attitudes. More ambitious Gorokan entrepreneurs seeking to diversify beyond coffee, dubbed 'rural capitalists' by Gerritsen (1979), earned much of their income outside agriculture by engaging in economic activities in both town and countryside. It may be possible to judge how far this group, seemingly more progressive, was able to advance towards formal and businesslike commercial dealings, untinged by hybridity. Even before the 'business groups' legislation of 1974 they had entered into more formal, contractual relationships with European interests, and adopted corporate structures, usually with European and/or extension assistance. During the early 1970s these formal measures assisted in opening doors for Gorokan ownership of 'shops, taverns, real estate, coffee buying, commercial vegetable growing, livestock raising, taxis, passenger motor vehicles, and trucks' (Donaldson and Good 1981, 166). Such arrangements, together with the acquisition of urban properties suitable for leasing, encouraged some Gorokans to become *rentiers*, living off capital to a greater or less extent and displaying limited entrepreneurial creativity.

Commencing in the late colonial period, this phase of Gorokan *bisnis* accelerated quickly with political change. As independence approached, the economic power and political influence of indigenous capital gave a new meaning to Hasluck's *paramountcy of native interests*. Replacing old connotations – *preserving village life* – this slogan was appropriated by the new elites to justify the indigenization of commercial activities and assets (MacWilliam 2013, 238). MacWilliam remarked on the electoral success of an indigenous bourgeoisie, and their capacity to mobilize capital from supporter groups and to 'facilitate access to state resources' (Ch. 21). As on the Gazelle (Ch. 18), rent-seeking behaviour – the pursuit of commercial advantage from an insider position – enabled members of this group to profit from opportunities arising in the political climate of the 1970s. Other commentators, from Finney to Donaldson and Fitzpatrick, emphasized the essentially political dynamic supporting this process, in which the entrepreneurship involved was political rather than Schumpeterian. The narrative will return to Schumpeter in Chapter 24 to consider his understanding of entrepreneurship, and its relevance to colonial PNG.

Intergenerational Transmission of Wealth

In Melanesia, wealth, however acquired, cannot easily be retained. Retention requires both strength of character to withstand Maussian pressures and a Smithian capacity to manage capital. This tension was evident in Finney's entrepreneurial biographies, and from his later account of a return visit (Finney 1973, 1987). While attempting to contend with Europeans in the domain of Smithian trade, the big-man strove also to avoid dissipating capital under pressure of the Maussian expectations of his followers. His success in *bisnis* required their support, but the too-lavish reciprocal disbursement of benefits would prevent his accumulating enough for reinvestment and further growth. Success in this delicate task required political skills to achieve the correct psychic balance between communal prestige-enhancement and material distribution. Ultimately, it might require personal willpower to disassociate oneself from the support group, pursuing an individualistic path in the Smithian manner as one of those individuals whom Charles Rowley (1965, 101) called 'isolates in charge of their own destiny'. Some Gorokans, in common with other highlanders and especially the entrepreneur politicians, found it advantageous to take up residence in Port Moresby to narrow their circles of obligation. Later still, some would seek insulation by investing in the northern Australian cities of Cairns or Brisbane. But short of achieving some degree of social distance, the *bikfela man* continued to inhabit a hybrid and insecure reality in which traditional *mores* coexisted uneasily with capitalist accumulation. Further, even to the extent that such men succeeded in conforming with the culture and norms of capitalist commercial activity, their *bisnis* operations would likely continue to be characterized by varying degrees of informality. This is not to deny genuine entrepreneurial achievement among some Gorokan businessmen at independence (as also among Tolai on the Gazelle). Rather it is to consider the cultural obstacles impeding more widespread success, and to suggest that such 'capitalism' proved compromised – at least in the colonial period – by the hybridity and informality common to most indigenous market economic activities.

In Melanesia the death of a big-man often precipitates pressures for the dispersal and redistribution of his wealth (hence the 'hiding of assets' observed on the Gazelle; Ch. 17). In such circumstances, 'capitalists' – whether creative and entrepreneurial, passive *rentiers*, or politically connected rent-seekers – face the common problem of establishing mechanisms for the intergenerational transmission of their wealth (Ch. 21). Some Marxian scholars, represented most clearly in the Gorokan literature by Donaldson and Good, assumed the problem away by asserting that traditional Highlands status was determined primarily by ascription, by attributing success in the market economy to inherited status, and by suggesting that accumulation in one generation would benefit children in the next. By such means, the platform for further accumulation was assured. Similarly, Fitzpatrick saw capitalist accumulation as 'building on hierarchies and inequalities within resident social formations' (Ch. 22). On the other hand, Finney viewed prestige in Gorokan society as determined by personal achievement. While he may have viewed Gorokans as being 'pre-adapted' to accumulation in each generation, he anticipated problems of succession – an issue to which he gave attention during a return visit (Finney 1987). This is not to say that all successful entrepreneurs would lack the wit or opportunity to advantage their offspring, although it was not clear in 1975 how far social advantage, in the sense of capitalist accumulation, had, or would, become embedded among families of entrepreneurial Gorokans. Tracking the fortunes of succeeding generations would require longitudinal studies combining genealogy and business history, and of sufficient scale to provide a factual base for generalization.

While material wealth might not have been reliably heritable, a significant qualification applies. Even before independence, successful individuals in and around Goroka and (especially) Rabaul had invested in *human* capital through the formal education of their children. Paula Brown (1979) observed a similar pattern in the Chimbu district. In the early days this involved getting children into English-medium primary schools, while subsequent cohorts attended multiracial 'A' and secondary institutions, with some continuing to one or other of the universities. Much later, international education options appealed. Unlike physical or financial capital, educational capital is embodied in the young and is not susceptible to dispersal on the parents' death. If the importance of achievement-orientation and social mobility are accepted, it is easier to envisage education as the channel for transmitting status – although if educational capital is not augmented by transfers of material capital the next generation may look beyond *bisnis* for success. Young people equipped with human capital but lacking other resources might see bureaucracy, or the law, as more promising fields.

Fitzpatrick seems to have regarded these as reliable pathways; the sons of entrepreneurs were gifted such educational opportunities that they secured control of appointments and promotions '*in the state system*' (Fitzpatrick 1980, 15, emphasis added). This is relevant because, in a departure from colonial orthodoxy, the 'state system' became an entry point for investment opportunities from the late 1960s. Earlier administration officials (Greathead, Taylor and Downs among them) had been obliged by regulation to avoid compromising their positions by engaging in private enterprise (Ch. 20). While not prevented from making discreet preparations, expatriate officials found it ultimately necessary to resign in order to take up commercial opportunities. This changed with the indigenization of senior levels of the public service, when the barriers and conventions constraining the access of state officials to private investment opportunities were withdrawn (MacWilliam 2013, 232).

The principal beneficiaries of the new environment of the 1970s may have been the political class, but an incoming generation of senior indigenous public servants, advantaged by position and access to information, also found themselves presented with abundant commercial opportunity. This they could enjoy without having to resign. With bank credit readily available, urban real estate opportunities numerous, and the divestment of expatriate interests occurring, some officials benefited handsomely (albeit legitimately, in terms of the new dispensation). The extent to which such activities represented creative entrepreneurialism, as opposed to rent-seeking or passive *rentierism*, is a matter of judgement. There was still little evidence of the corrupt alliances between lawyers, bureaucrats and politicians which later became the staple of political commentary. But at that time, formal education, translated into bureaucratic office, seemed more likely to guarantee the intergenerational transmission of privilege than individual success in business. The process would likely be less mechanistic than posited by Marxians relying on supposed traditional 'social formations' for the maintenance of 'hierarchies and inequalities'. And these processes would increasingly be played out on the national stage, rather than in such provincial theatres as Goroka. Part IV of this study is set on that national stage, with particular reference to the capital, Port Moresby.

Part IV

Birth Pangs

All These Are the Beginning of Sorrows

Chapter 24

The Preparatory Idea

Visiting PNG in 1963, Bernard Schaffer warned of the danger of imagining that development must actually involve the 'working out of transferred Western models'. One version of this seductive myth was the 'preparatory idea', a notion of preparing the ground for Western models of administration (Schaffer 1963, 45). Experience elsewhere provided little evidence of any such preparation until late in the colonial day, while talk of it was usually a ploy for delay. The colonial polity was 'essentially bureaucratic', and colonial governments were 'dominated' by a 'secretariat' aiming at 'efficiency' rather than fulfilling any political agenda that might assure the 'roots of independence' (ibid., 52). These observations should be recalled when considering 'preparatory' measures implemented in PNG. The process of disengagement, in which an alien bureaucracy was expected to prepare the way for its own replacement, was rife with internal contradictions.

In 1964 an appointed legislature with three indigenous members was replaced by an elected House of Assembly. It had an indigenous majority lacking in both parliamentary experience and political coherence, allowing it to be dominated by nominated 'official' members. Multiracial political parties began to coalesce outside parliament, notably the nationalist Pangu Pati, which achieved representation at the second, 1968 election. However 'official' members continued to hold sway, with the acquiescence of nominally independent indigenous 'ministerial members'. None of these members were from Pangu, which had stood aloof from the nomination process. Then after the third national election in 1972, Pangu, under the leadership of Michael Somare, formed a majority coalition on the eve of self-government.

During the second House, economic policy had remained in the hands of colonial officials, who continued to pursue accelerated development on Canberra's instructions. On orthodox macroeconomic criteria this produced impressive results, expressed in terms of the Fiskian taxonomy of subsistence, transitional and monetary sectors. Between 1966 and 1970, output in the combined monetary and subsistence sectors increased at an annual average rate of 9.3 per cent, while the monetary sector alone increased at a galloping 15.6 per cent (Shand 1971, 54). In 1966, subsistence activity still contributed about half of domestic output, with some 44 per cent (nearly a million people) wholly engaged in subsistence. Another 37 per cent continued actively in subsistence while also operating in the Fiskian 'transitional' sector, with some cash income. Rapid rates of measured growth by 1970 suggested the probability of a further significant reduction in the numbers wholly dependent on subsistence, as well as an increased proportion of the population in 'transition' (ibid., 56). On the surface, at least, this suggested beneficial structural change.

The last important expression of accelerated development was a Development Programme (TPNG 1968) aimed at reducing fiscal reliance on Australia, for which it was thought growth should be maximized. Produced by the administration's Office of Programming and Coordination (OPC), it was described by John Langmore as being no more than 'indicative planning' – simply 'a framework for public sector expenditure' – with a wish list of private sector initiatives and internal inconsistencies. Most damning, it paid lip service to indigenous participation while continuing policies that exacerbated expatriate domination (Langmore 1972, 12–13).

Shand judged accelerated development as having primarily benefited expatriates, although in absolute terms the indigenous population had received 'substantial monetary benefits' (Shand 1971, 70). Total monetary sector income rose from $80 million to $300 million between 1960/61 and 1969/70, while the expatriate income-share increased from 62.5 per cent to 68.0 per cent. Despite the absolute level of local people's involvement in the monetary economy having grown, they had 'lost ground in terms of their relative economic influence' (ibid., 73). Inequality also had another dimension, for such gains as were made by local people were unevenly distributed across the country.

Racial income inequality may be illustrated in terms of numbers of workers and their relative earnings. In 1967/68 the indigenous made up 90 per cent of the monetary workforce, and the wage ratio was 1:11, so that expatriates – numbering just 10 per cent – earned a staggering 54 per cent of total wages paid (Shand 1971, 81). Furthermore, over the 1960s a shift in aggregate income occurred, away from wages and primary production in favour of non-wage incomes, especially company profits. Interracial inequality increased because the major modern-sector economic activities – in 'manufacturing, building and construction, transport, storage and communication, commerce, finance and property industries' were all mostly or wholly owned by expatriates. Serious efforts at promoting indigenous interests were confined largely to the public sector and rural industries (ibid., 84–85).

In 1972 the incoming Somare government faced a reality in which nearly all 'modern sector' business was owned by expatriates, who were also the source of skilled labour and managerial skills. Three-quarters of monetary sector spending was on imports, while Australian aid – the main source of growth – was more than double the revenues raised locally by government. In the monetary sector, income inequalities between regions were extreme, as were income inequalities between the indigenous population and foreigners – the latter group comprising no more than 2 per cent of the population (Garnaut 1980, 447).

Ric Shand, though a conservative economist and trusted colonial adviser, felt bound to point to the emergence and growth of 'economically based social and economic tensions'. But he also stressed the continuing adequacy of traditional subsistence as 'a basic structural factor, which has had a positive stabilizing influence on the national economy' (Shand 1971, 56–57). This reflected his belief in the existence of a Fiskian 'floor' to urban livelihoods, provided by an affluent subsistence sector. This 'floor' explained Port Moresby's capacity to maintain the essentially *formal* character of its labour market, despite increasing freedom of entry for rural–urban migrants.

On the eve of self-government, Garnaut wrote that domestic market growth, improved capacities of domestic workers and greater knowledge of PNG's natural resources had greatly increased the number and scope of industries that could thrive in a well-managed PNG economy. It seemed reasonable to expect more diversity to develop on these foundations (Garnaut 1973, 162). Diversification was certainly needed. As Anthony Clunies Ross (1971, 473) had observed, as a national economy PNG was 'one of the least internally integrated'. Almost a decade later Garnaut recalled, ruefully, that PNG had possessed 'none of the characteristics of a national economy when the first Somare government was formed in April 1972' (Garnaut 1981, 157).

Nor did the self-governing state get off to a flying start. Langmore recalled progress being constrained by limited planning and budgeting capacity in an administration only recently freed from Canberra's micromanagement, and by continued adherence to accelerated development (Langmore 1972). Among the problems was a culture of economic management derived from Australia's own 'heavily modified' model of economic liberalism, while the departing Australian bureaucracy was still attempting to fashion PNG in its own image. In this situation, an eleventh hour initiative to reframe the 'preparatory' process originated from an unexpected quarter within the Australian bureaucracy. It was decided to commission fresh advice, from an international group that came to be known as the 'Faber Mission', concerning policy directions for an independent PNG.

The Faber Mission: Ideology and Policy

This study employs the dynamic of informality and the metaphor of pushback to describe the economic behaviour of individuals reacting against bureaucratic orthodoxies. PNG's short period of self-government between 1972 and 1975 was characterized by a similar reactive dynamic, albeit one operating at a more explicitly political level. It took the form of pushback by an incipient political class against the 'bureaucratic and assimilationist' preparations (Ballard 1981, 11) of an expiring colonial administration. Accelerated development had intensified social and economic tensions. To employ Polanyi's metaphor, inequalities arising during the 'preparatory' phase caused livelihoods and social relationships to become increasingly *disembedded* from traditional social foundations (Polanyi 1944).

Events seemed to mirror upheavals elsewhere, typified by dispossession occurring in many forms, 'from the material, to the sociocultural and the moral' (Hann and Hart 2011, 136). In PNG there emerged a proliferation of 'spontaneous local movements, differing in their origins and specific objectives but sharing a broad concern with the achievement of economic, social and political development through communal action' (May 2009, 48). Such tensions, communicated to parliamentarians, inspired political pushback against the late colonial orthodoxy embodied in 'accelerated development'. This may be seen as an instance of Polanyi's 'double movement', the impulse to *re-imbed* morality, culture and livelihoods in a traditional, notionally egalitarian society.

Speaking of the second parliament (1968–72), Garnaut recalled that, aside from predictable demands for higher incomes and government services, parliamentarians were particularly concerned about interracial income inequality. Demands for greater indigenous participation in decision making grew clamorous, and urban unemployment was debated frequently, with calls for the repatriation of rural–urban migrants (Garnaut 1973, 165). Members' concerns were not woven into any coherent narrative; a catalyst was needed to give point and direction to collective discontents. Informed by Polanyi's metaphor, this account considers the catalytic opportunity presented during the third parliament by the Faber Report (ODG 1973).

While perhaps unable to articulate a critique, many parliamentarians associated manifestations of inequality and social change with accelerated development. Amid such uncertainty an alternative, even antithetic, philosophy proved unexpectedly appealing. This is not to suggest that enthusiasm excited by the Faber Report was either universal or sustained, but that a particular serendipity marked its timing and reception. Keith Hart recalled meeting the Somare Cabinet in August 1972, after it had received the report. Somare told the Faber team that their report had shown Cabinet that there were more options available than a single, Australian-inspired, model of development (Hart 2002, 26). The account is credible, reported in similar terms by an observer close to the Chief Minister's Office (Fitzpatrick 1985, 22). Written some thirty years later, Hart's narrative – ever so slightly vainglorious and certainly played for laughs – is helpful in explaining the report's commissioning, reception and impact.

He recounted the experience of the team, which had been commissioned by the World Bank and steered by UNDP to prepare a development programme for PNG on the eve of its independence. After three months there and in Australia in mid-1972, they wrote a preliminary draft and returned for discussions with the Cabinet of the newly elected chief minister, Michael Somare,[1] whose Pangu Party had won government in a general election that year. In fact, only two members (Faber and Hart) of the four person team returned for consultations because the experts in mining and agriculture had opted out. Perhaps they feared their careers in consulting would be ended by what one of them saw as the 'lunacy' proposed by Hart and Faber (Hart 2002, 25).

As to the context of the mission, Hart explained how their arrival in Australia occurred just when a quarter-century of rule by the conservative Liberal/Country Party seemed likely to be overturned by Gough Whitlam's Australian Labor Party. In Hart's account, the Ministry of External Territories had been a 'fiefdom' of the Australian Country Party. From Commonwealth Treasury officials he learned that the existing financial arrangements with PNG had acted as a 'redistributive device' for 'siphoning' half a billion Australian dollars annually to three Australian 'interest groups': trading oligopolies active in PNG and the Pacific, governmental bureaucracies at home and in the region, and the Australian farm lobby. The Faber team's subsequent proposals for change encountered opposition. Their advocacy of a 'grassroots' development focusing on the income share of indigenous Papua New Guineans was described by an official of the World Bank as 'a "racist" deviation' from orthodox economic analysis. 'Everyone' was upset by their proposal to renegotiate an agreement with the copper mine in Bougainville (including the colonial officials responsible for what Hart deemed a 'notorious giveaway' – namely, the mine's operators, the World Bank, and the above-mentioned Department of External Territories) (Hart 2002, 25).

By the time Faber and Hart returned to PNG in August 1972 their draft report had been circulated and leaked to the press. Officials of the World Bank and the OPC (Office of Programming and Coordination, the domestic agency responsible for the 1968 Development Programme) now seemed anxious to cooperate (Hart 2002, 26). Perhaps this was because a White Paper, effectively the last gasp of accelerated development, had been rebuffed in parliament. Seen as 'an effort to outflank Faberism', it had been trumped by another, 'Faberite' White Paper, tabled soon after (Fitzpatrick 1985, 24). Schaffer's 'essentially bureaucratic' colonial polity was turned on its head. By year's end, the OPC and its director were gone, a platform of *Eight Aims* based on the Faber Report had been announced, and a new Central Planning Office was gearing up to implement it.

Soon afterwards the House of Assembly endorsed the Eight Aims as the 'basis for economic planning' in future years (Hegarty 1998, 186). The Faber Report and the Eight Aims, together with a Preamble to the Constitution, were crucial to the official recognition of economic informality in PNG. The report had adopted the informal 'sector' construct as its primary vehicle for increasing indigenous economic participation, and the Eight Aims were suffused with it. As a philosophical framework the 'Aims' were seen at the time as a charter for self-sufficiency, reduction of economic inequalities, and nationalist economic control (ibid., 165). Garnaut saw them as 'expressed in gradualist and reformist terms' and not foreshadowing any 'sudden, radical restructuring of society' (Garnaut 1980, 448). As Hart later discovered, the Australian Treasury had been the unexpected source of the initiative to commission the report. Hart found the experience instructive as an instance of bureaucratic jockeying; the dominant government agencies had intended to maintain the status quo but others hoped to displace them after the expected accession of a Labor government. In particular, this was true of bureaucrats from the Commonwealth Treasury who had engineered the Faber team's appointment. As Hart reflected, 'sometimes an opportunity arises to make a difference, however small' (Hart 2002, 26).

When the Faber Report was first circulated, David Hegarty (1998, 165) had no doubt it 'captured the imagination' of many parliamentarians. Before long, however, ambivalence emerged, reflecting disparate elements within the governing coalition. It became apparent that the Eight Aims were contrary to the 'entrepreneurial ambitions' of some ministers, although their 'pseudo-socialistic overtones' remained 'acceptable at the level of public rhetoric' (Voutas 1981, 46). The then cabinet secretary concluded later that 'the evolution of the ... Eight Aims ... was probably the closest the ministry came to expressing a general ideological stance'. Otherwise, the open contest of ideas was muted by 'the unstated knowledge' that Cabinet consensus was 'too fragile to withstand deep ideological debate' (Lynch 1981, 31).

This fragility, and the divergence of opinion at its core, would have implications for many objectives derived from the Aims, not least the goal of stimulating an indigenous informal economy. In practice, the policy focus was directed elsewhere. Given what Garnaut termed 'an extraordinary concentration of income and wealth' in the expatriate community, redistribution from them to Papua New Guineans of '*high-income employment and business ownership*' was 'the one distributional focus of the Eight Point Plan to be pursued vigorously and effectively' (Garnaut 2000, 32, emphasis added).

The 'entrepreneurial ambitions' to which Voutas referred were not limited to members of Somare's Cabinet. Earlier discussion of *bisnis* in late colonial Rabaul referred to a class of business leaders described by Fitzpatrick as 'big peasants' and by MacWilliam as 'accumulators' (Ch. 18). Similarly, in Goroka there were identifiable groups dubbed 'rural capitalists' by Gerritsen, 'rich peasants' by Donaldson and Good, and members of the indigenous 'bourgeoisie and would-be bourgeoisie' by MacWilliam (Ch. 21). These earlier chapters made frequent reference to political activity as a path to accumulation, one followed by many 'business leaders'. Garnaut's remarks (above), concerning priority given by the Somare government to the redistribution of high-level economic opportunity, suggest the importance of such political processes.

The 'entrepreneurship' involved in this mode of accumulation – in which political access and influence played the dynamic role – bore little resemblance to the Schumpeterian ideal. The latter was a positive model defined by a capacity for constructive innovation. At its most effective, such entrepreneurialism imposed 'creative destruction' on capitalism, renewing its vigour by sweeping away outmoded technologies, products and ideas (Schumpeter 1942). In this universe, political entrepreneurs such as described by Fitzpatrick found no place. But William Baumol enlarged the understanding of entrepreneurialism by arguing it could also assume negative forms, taking as his text an assertion by the Marxist historian Eric Hobsbawm (1969) that whereas private enterprise is commonly assumed to be intent on innovation it has, in fact, 'a bias only towards profit' (Baumol 1990, 893).

Emphasizing the need to recognize both positive and negative entrepreneurship, Baumol cautioned that some entrepreneurs are inclined to lead 'a parasitical existence that is actually damaging to the economy'. Entrepreneurial energies may be allocated either to productive innovation, or to unproductive activities such as rent seeking or organized crime (Baumol 1990, 893–94). In Baumol's account, the choices entrepreneurs make depend to a large degree on the prevailing 'reward structure', the 'rules of the game' (ibid., 894). These determine the 'relative payoffs' to entrepreneurial activities, whether productive or unproductive. Where incentives are perverse, profit-seeking entrepreneurs will be drawn in 'unproductive directions', with negative consequences for economic growth (ibid., 918). He illustrated this by drawing on accounts of earlier historical periods to show how 'relative payoffs' have influenced entrepreneurial behaviour. In the modern context, 'rules of the game' may include both a formal structure of policy and regulation within which entrepreneurs are supposed to operate, and also a less formal framework of norms, conventions and customs derived from the culture and history of a people.

The historical cases considered by Baumol played out over centuries and occurred at the centre of the civilizations in which they were set. None occurred in circumstances such as those of late colonial PNG, where formal 'rules of the game' had been imposed by foreign authority and instituted over less than a single century (much less, in the case of Goroka). The attempt was made to impose rules of an alien game on indigenous people, in the unfamiliar context of market economy, far from the colonial metropolitan centres. In such situations, 'a country cannot meaningfully institute general rules and strict limits unless the informal beliefs and institutions of the people in question legitimate those rules and limits' (Boettke 2009, 45). It should not be surprising that the colonized peoples brought their own 'rules' to this situation; *hybridity* (as defined and reported in this study) is an inevitable outcome of such mingling of cultures.

Nobel laureate Douglass North identified a number of 'stumbling blocks' to economic change and development. While neglected in neoclassical economics because of their institutional nature, they are implicit in Adam Smith's *Wealth of Nations*. Of particular interest here, North emphasized the importance of societies overcoming the stumbling block involved in moving from personal to impersonal exchange (North 2005, 84). The former, broadly equivalent to Maussian exchange, is set against impersonal (or market) exchange, which North viewed as a prerequisite for economic growth (ibid., 133). Achieving this transformation realizes the Smithian potential found within enlarged markets.

The difficulty is that the desired institutional changes 'require fundamental rethinking at odds with our genetic heritage' (North 2005, 84). His reference to 'genetic heritage' is not related to race or ethnicity but should be understood in relation to the mind/body problem – the relationship of thought and consciousness in the human mind to the brain's operation within the body. North noted how limited is our understanding of 'the complex interdependence of the evolving social structure the human mind has created'. But without such understanding efforts to improve the economic performance of our societies are 'crippled' (ibid.). Improvement requires better institutions, but creating them will require fundamental change to the structure of economic and political systems. North's somewhat pessimistic conclusion is that such change is frequently 'not in the feasible set' because of the 'historically derived beliefs and institutions' of the actors in those systems (ibid., 118).

Note

1. Later, after independence in 1975, Prime Minister Somare.

Chapter 25

Hart, Faber and the Informal Economy in Port Moresby

Although he did not use the term, Keith Hart introduced the idea of *informality* publicly in 1971, at a conference on Urban Unemployment in Africa. He argued that Africans in Nima were far from being unemployed, they worked 'for irregular and often low returns'. His account of the experience combined 'vivid ethnographic description ... with some impressive-sounding economic jargon' he had picked up from academic economists. As a result, he was recognized as the author of 'a whole new segment of the division of labour in development studies' (Hart 1994).

The immediate and largely positive reception given to Hart's ideas in Washington and Geneva was due to a panicked climate of opinion, then prevailing among some international agencies and academic economists, concerning a supposed epidemic of 'open' urban unemployment in developing countries. Alarmist and ill-conceived projections of unemployment, such as those published by Richard Jolly (Jolly et al. 1973), depended on defining 'employment' exclusively in terms of formal sector jobs. Hart's contribution, pointing to the nature, extent and value of informal economic activity, assisted greatly in reframing the issue. He established a new understanding of urban realities in development, expressed in terms of the lack of sufficiently remunerative *income opportunities*, as distinct from a notion of open unemployment due to the absence of *jobs* (Ch. 1).

The Faber recommendation that an indigenous informal economy should be encouraged found a receptive audience among economic nationalists in PNG, while the idea of the informal 'sector' – as it was originally called – achieved a degree of influence, at least at the level of rhetoric, on early planning priorities. It also found its way into the constitution of the new state (PNG 1975), which included several clauses implying that it was the duty of government to support and encourage informal economic activity. These appeared in a set of 'National Goals and Directive Principles', derived substantially from the Eight Aims (Ch. 24). Tos Barnett, a member of Somare's staff, recalled that all principles relating to the structure and function of government and social and economic goals 'were intended to be influenced by the wording of the Constitution and the spirit behind it' (Barnett 1981, 64).

In the Preamble to the Constitution, among the National Goals, and in relation to 'integral human development', there is a call for 'development to take place primarily through the use of Papua New Guinean forms of social and political organization'.[1] Recalling constitutional debates at the time, I have no doubt that this was intended to promote a model of development in which informal economic activities would play a leading role. The Preamble calls for 'the family unit to be recognized as the fundamental basis of our society', and for 'every step to be taken to promote the . . . economic and social standing of the Melanesian family'. This recognizes the household as being, inter alia, an economic entity at the centre of the informal economy. Finally, support given to informality in the Preamble was confirmed by a further call, made under the heading of 'Papua New Guinean ways'. It was an appeal for 'particular emphasis in our economic development to be placed on *small-scale artisan, service and business activity*' (PNG 1975, emphasis added).

When Hart came to PNG in 1972, the country was among the first in which the newly minted idea of economic informality (Hart 1971, 1973) was introduced into policy discussion although – oddly enough – PNG was among those developing economies to which the concept was *least* applicable at the time. Hart was optimistic that his ideas would have value for orthodox development planning (Hart 1970), and this would become evident from the tenor of his contributions to the Faber Report. On arrival he discovered that informal economic activity appeared conspicuous only by its *absence* in PNG's few small towns – the circumstance described in this study as a 'conundrum'. The report commented that 'although the *rural* informal sector shows signs of becoming well developed in Papua New Guinea, urban artisan and service activities are as yet virtually non-existent' (ODG 1973, 4.11, emphasis added). This reference to 'artisan and service activities' appears to have been picked up by the drafters of the constitutional Preamble, as cited above.

This observation in the Faber Report is doubly interesting, first because it identified a structural gap in the urban economy of PNG – the absence of a category of economic activity significant elsewhere in the developing world. But secondly, it extended the idea of informality to the rural economy, whereas Hart's original (1973) account of Ghana was very largely urban-focused. The formal/informal distinction was central to the Faber Report's approach, shown by its categorization of the PNG economy as comprising a 'formal' (or modern) sector and an 'informal' sector, the latter embracing 'smallholder agriculture (both cash cropping and subsistence production) and many other small-scale activities in town and country' (ODG 1973, 4.2). While Hart was influential in framing the report, it is possible that his colleagues, rather than Hart himself, favoured extending the concept to rural activities – even including subsistence production. I suggest this because Hart's own view of subsistence agriculture, seen later in his *Political Economy of West African Agriculture* (1982), does not permit such an interpretation. In any case, after the Faber experience and his 'conversion' to Marxism, Hart abandoned the idea of the informal economy for some fifteen years until the fall of the Berlin Wall, 'when its miraculous persistence encouraged me to revisit it' (Hart 2008, 6).

The Faber Report's judgement that urban informality in PNG was insignificant reflected a degree of foreign domination of the urban economy extending to very nearly the lowest rungs of commercial activity. Indigenous participation in the urban monetized economy was limited largely to *formal* employment at regulated minimum wages. Short-term circular migrants, predominantly men, made up the bulk of jobseekers. The absence of a third, 'unprotected sector' of informal employment in PNG towns meant that *open* unemployment, such as was normally associated with industrial economies, typified PNG urban labour markets (Conroy 1973). This made the two-sector analysis of urban unemployment by Todaro (1969) more applicable to PNG than to Asian or African cities with substantial informal economies (Conroy 1973, 1976, 1982b). Another study found a significant positive relationship between the mean earnings of unskilled male migrants and three separate measures of unemployment across all PNG towns. It also found a significant positive relationship between statutory minimum wages and rates of open unemployment among low-skilled males across the towns (Garnaut, Wright and Curtain 1977, Ch. 7). These findings supported the hypothesis, derived from Todaro's original model, of an equilibrium rate of urban unemployment appropriate to any observed differential between urban and rural incomes (ibid.; see also Conroy 1982b, 13–14).

In Port Moresby and other towns, the primary objective of unaccompanied male migrants was to secure employment in the regulated, formal economy. Pending this, most lived in open unemployment supported by 'Maussian' transfers in cash and kind from kinfolk, with little or no informal economic activity (Garnaut, Wright and Curtain 1977). Grumbling about unemployment in Parliament owed more to discontent in urban households obliged to support these *pasendia*, and to concern in rural areas about the absence of able-bodied men, than to the suffering experienced by the unemployed themselves. As seen in my account of Port Moresby settlement life (Ch. 16), and illustrating the mechanism underlying Shand's belief in the existence of a floor to urban livelihoods (Ch. 24), many *pasendia* eventually returned home. Migrants with the alternative of returning to a relatively affluent subsistence sector were not willing to resort to the uncongenial option of urban informal work (Conroy 1974b; Fitzpatrick 1980, 27, 57). The time such men took before returning home was influenced by the level of urban wages, and by their probability of gaining employment (as signalled by the rate of open unemployment).

A 'normalized' urban population structure, showing due representation of families with women and children, was emerging. In Port Moresby, sex ratios became more balanced as families formed; the ratio of men to women, 282/100 in 1961, had become more 'normal', at 159/100, by 1971. But such a level of masculinity still indicated a degree of retarded urbanism – a condition prolonged by continuing in-migration of unaccompanied men from newer source areas. The sex ratio varied between ethnic groups; among people from the four Highlands provinces it was as high as 577/100, which reflected the rapid increase of highlander migration, their proportion of the capital's population having risen from 4.4 per cent in 1966 to 9.1 per cent by 1971 (Oram 1976b, 160).

A contemporary review of circular rural–urban migration patterns posited a continuum, ranging from places whose people displayed a high propensity to migrate and a low degree of circularity in migration, through to places showing a low propensity to migrate combined with a high circularity (Conroy and Curtain 1985). This corresponded with the reality of 1970s Port Moresby, as shown by two urban populations – Toaripi and Chimbu – that lay at either end of the continuum. These people were discussed above, in an account of the city's 'squatter' settlements (Ch. 16). Toaripi settlers were at the stable end in terms of their demographic structure, housing and employment. They were long-established, and seldom returned to their villages other than for short visits (Ryan 1977). The Gumine (Chimbu) people of Ragamuka were at the other extreme: highly masculinized, living in the city's most disadvantaged settlement with a short history of urban life, relatively few formal jobs, and frequent comings and goings.

A contemporary urban household survey prompted Garnaut, Wright and Curtain (1977, 185) to comment on the 'disturbing evidence' that Chimbu migrants appeared willing to endure very low wages and high unemployment, 'even when they maintained close links with home villages'.

Another researcher, Hugh Norwood (1979, 1984), found the greatest reliance on informal economic activities in Port Moresby at the Chimbu settlement of Ragamuka. While formal employment was still the main source of livelihoods everywhere else in the city, the insecure existence of Ragamuka settlers pointed to an unpromising future, likely to be shared by a growing proportion of urban residents in the era of independence.

Debating Informality

In an early account of the Faber Mission, Keith Hart owned to the intellectual transformation he was experiencing. In the early 1970s (a period that included his visit to PNG), like many others of his generation he was undergoing a 'conversion' to French Marxism (Hart 1994; see also Hart 2008). As he recalled, the 1970s were years of economic and political difficulty in the West, and 'the other side' were acquiring increased 'intellectual credibility'. French structuralist Marxism and theories of development and underdevelopment 'achieved widespread circulation among Anglophone economic anthropologists at this time' (Hart 2007b; see also Hann and Hart 2011, 73ff). This 'turn for the worse' in the West had been signalled by faltering economies in advanced industrial nations, as the long post-war boom came to an end. America experienced budget and trade deficits together with 'stagflation', while a 'run' to gold threatened. In response, President Nixon ended US dollar convertibility to gold in 1971, spelling the end of the Bretton Woods system of fixed exchange rates. America withdrew from its war in Vietnam and, with the 'oil shock' of 1973, stagflation became entrenched. This situation challenged orthodox Keynesian prescriptions for macroeconomic management, puncturing the optimism of the post-war period.

These events also threatened the comfortable assumptions of 'modernization' theory in the practice of economic development, described by Hart as 'the notion that poor countries could become rich by emulating "us"'. In retrospect Hart sees 'modernization' as underlying his own initial research in Ghana. But such ideas 'gave way to gloomier scenarios around 1970, fed by zero-sum theories of "underdevelopment", "dependency" and "the world system" advanced by the other side in the Cold War' (Hart 2012b). Together with economic uncertainty, the events of 1968 in Paris signalled changing social *mores*, the influence of anti-colonial struggles and the attraction for the young in France and elsewhere of a revived and repackaged Marxism.

Hart's conversion to Marxism was incomplete during his time in PNG; while there he decided that the country needed a 'Nyerere-style' rural socialist administration prioritizing 'self-sufficiency' (Nyerere 1968), an outcome that would accomplish both 'national autonomy and lower rates of Australian subsidy' (Hart 2002, 25). That remark reflected contemporary interest in Tanzanian socialism, an enthusiasm distinguished from Marxism and shared by a number of academics and students at UPNG. Most notable among these was Anthony Clunies Ross, Professor of Economics. Before the Aims were popularized, he had written that 'there should be some positive human objectives among those toward which policy is directed' (this after noting that, in Africa, Tanzania stood out because it had the 'clearest and most uncompromising commitments to certain social objectives' (Clunies Ross 1973, 228). After the Eight Aims, he did not pursue the subject further, accepting them as an authentic expression of PNG aspirations.

There were also Marxists in the university, and on the fringes of government, including in the Office of Chief Minister. Like Hart, Peter Fitzpatrick was in intellectual transition, for Port Moresby, however remote from the Parisian hotbed, was not exempt from its frisson. French Marxist anthropology achieved 'cult status' in this period (Hann and Hart 2011, 73), and possession of a copy of Althusser's *Pour Marx* (1965) or Althusser and Balibar's *Reading Capital* (1968) was as clear a claim to progressive thought at UPNG as it was on the Left Bank. Marxists were inclined to dismiss the informal 'sector' – which they called 'petty commodity production' – on the principle that it was technically backward and a zone of exploitation (Ch. 2). Perhaps this was why Keith Hart, as he fell under the spell of French Marxism, dropped the idea of informality for more than a decade after the Faber experience.

In the beginning, Fitzpatrick had seized eagerly on the Faber Report and on the idea of informality. He admitted that this had been an error, because Faber had merely inspired a 'populist ideology' encapsulated in the 'anodyne' slogan *Papua New Guinea ways* (Fitzpatrick 1980, 202). It was ineffectual because such populism could not secure necessary systemic change (ibid., 204). By 1980 he had come to accept the negative Marxist view of petty commodity production, and to see the Faber approach as burdened by 'insoluble' difficulties (ibid., viii). Faber had been mistaken to suggest that greater indigenous engagement with the modern economy could operate from a continuing base in the 'traditional' mode – that is, the subsistence economy. To do so would amount to supporting the preservation of village life, the principle espoused by McGregor and Murray (Ch. 9). In *structuralist* terms, the preservation principle acted to conserve the traditional mode, continuing to subsidize capitalist enterprise and to suppress any potential for destabilizing class action (ibid., 2).

Cyril Belshaw originated the idea that, under a system of indentured labour for unaccompanied men, villages effectively subsidized the plantation sector. This was later taken up by Charles Rowley (Ch. 11). Fitzpatrick (who must have been aware of the latter scholar, if not both) preferred to attribute the insight to an ideologically more congenial source, the French neo-Marxian anthropologist Claude Meillassoux (1972). To see the significance of the 'traditional mode' in Fitzpatrick's evolving thought it is necessary to understand the influence on his generation of Althusser and Balibar's *Reading Capital.* Hart thought their reading of *Das Kapital* had removed any remaining elements of Hegelianism from the text. The phenomenology of 'the human subject, dialectical reason and indeed history itself were . . . dropped', to be replaced by a '*deep structure of the ideal mode of production*' (Hann and Hart 2011, 74, emphasis added). The three elements of this structure were producers, non-producers and the means of production – as seen, for example, in writings on the political economy of PNG from the 1970s, which prioritized 'production relations' over 'exchange' (Ch. 22). Varying combinations of these three elements produced situation-specific modes of production (ibid., 73–74).

For PNG, the most complete elaboration of this framework is found in Fitzpatrick's *Law and State in Papua New Guinea* (1980), while its influence on such writers as Donaldson and Good has been discussed above (Ch. 22). The most elaborate application of 'underdevelopment' theory to PNG was a book co-authored by three UPNG academics, Amarshi, Good and Mortimer, titled *Development and Dependency: The Political Economy of Papua New Guinea* (1979). For UPNG, the zenith of academic neo-Marxism may have occurred when Andre Gunder Frank accepted an invitation to interview for its chair of economics in 1976. Its decline probably commenced on the day when, having met his prospective colleagues (including the writer) Gunder Frank declined the university's offer of appointment.

If Hart had ever toyed with these modes of thought it was well behind him by 1982, when his *Political Economy of West African Agriculture* appeared. In that study he rejected both neo-Marxian theories of underdevelopment and the elaborate machinery of French structuralist Marxism, in favour of a return to the liberal and Marxist traditions of classical political economy. Concerning 'underdevelopment', Hart criticized Samir Amin's emphasis on the destructive role of metropolitan capital in extracting value, rather than acknowledging the failure of local economic and political mobilization in the areas where underdevelopment occurred (Hart 1982, 15–17). This is consistent with Hart's own emphasis on 'the massive impediments to growth that originate in local material and social conditions' (ibid., 2; see Introduction). I argue here that such local factors were also crucial in PNG. Hart remains an eclectic Marxian, but as for the French Marxism of the 1970s, it disappeared with that post-war political watershed when social democracy gave way to neo-liberalism (Hart 2007b).

Fitzpatrick's abandonment of the idea of informality may also have reflected the failure of his efforts to promote it as a practical programme. During his Port Moresby years he had collaborated with Loraine Blaxter to pursue a vigorous campaign supporting government initiatives to stimulate informal economic activity, and for the removal of a raft of regulatory impediments. Blaxter and Fitzpatrick (1973a, 1973b) prepared papers announcing 'A New Strategy for Development', and dealing with a wide range of activities and restrictions. They listed a catalogue of impediments, including 'penetration of expatriates into areas that are normally confined to the informal sector', 'comprehensive domination by expatriate interests of most areas of retailing and services', and 'a plethora of laws' that 'effectively debarred indigenous participation' (Blaxter and Fitzpatrick 1973b, 5).

In arguing the necessity for state intervention, Blaxter and Fitzpatrick explicitly dismissed the notion of subsistence affluence as a constraint on the willingness of unemployed urban dwellers to engage in arduous and low-paid informal livelihoods (Blaxter and Fitzpatrick 1973a, 9). The garbage-scavengers of Ragamuka were then among the few concentrations of such desperation found in the capital, and were the people whose tenacious grip on city life had so disturbed Garnaut and his colleagues. At the time it seemed to me reasonable to argue that the reluctance of most *other* urban dwellers to 'hustle' like the Ragamuka Chimbu was primarily due to continuing subsistence affluence in *their* places of origin. In short, Fiskian affluence appeared to set a baseline for the levels of real income and physical exertion most migrants were willing to tolerate. So long as rural societies retained some degree of affluence, this constraint would continue to operate (Conroy 1974b). But affluence was a time-bound condition, liable to be eroded by rural population growth (Fisk 1962).

At the time, I criticized Blaxter and Fitzpatrick for a degree of 'romanticism' in their advocacy of informality (Conroy 1974b). They had claimed that because informal economic activity is essentially social, and 'culturally embedded', there is more scope for 'personal relationships' in which 'economic activities are part of the fabric of life, not compartmentalized work' (Blaxter and Fitzpatrick 1973a). In hindsight, I see this as their laudable attempt to view late colonial Port Moresby through Polanyi's eyes. It recalls Hart's more recent concern – influenced by Polanyi – to explore the notion of a 'human economy' (Hart, Laville and Cattani 2010). But Hart's informality can only be 'embedded' in an economic system in which specialized mercantile functions are performed; these were absent from Melanesian societies represented in the capital during the 1970s. Blaxter and Fitzpatrick's error, shared with the historian Lewis (Ch. 9), was to confuse traditional exchange with a supposed innate Melanesian capacity to 'truck and barter'. Traditional exchange was indeed 'embedded', but in a system of social relations quite unlike those of 'the market' (Ch. 5). In the context of 1970s Port Moresby, utilitarian trade was most commonly a hybrid activity, in which market economic dealings sat uncomfortably alongside, and were apt to be compromised by, traditional behaviours. The analysis will turn to that issue in the next chapter, to examine the uneasy trio of formality, informality and hybridity that is still pervasive in Melanesia.

In a comprehensive account of the informality debate in 1970s Port Moresby, Croz Walsh reported that Blaxter and Fitzpatrick had made thirty-eight proposals to support the development of an urban informal economy, none of which had been implemented by 1983. Yet despite this failure, the informal sector had grown, 'as predicted by its detractors'. Walsh concluded that high urban wages and high rural birth rates would most probably induce a 'new generation' of rural–urban migrants 'sufficiently impoverished' to accept life in the informal economy, even 'without any encouragement from Blaxter' (Walsh 1983, 415, citing Conroy 1974b, 312).

The debate had begun in the context of substantial minimum urban wage increases occurring between 1972 and 1975, and the new government's indifference to burgeoning national population growth, due to the reflexive pro-natalism of the indigenous political class. These factors suggested that (on Todaro principles) informality's time would come as rural subsistence standards declined, when urban communities such as Ragamuka became more numerous, and as town populations grew increasingly distanced from their rural roots. Fitzpatrick came later to concede the significance of Fisk's 'affluence', with an oblique admission that the choice of returning 'to the traditional social formation' (i.e. Fisk's 'subsistence sector') continued as a viable option for urban migrants. They would often find it preferable to return to home villages, rather than to 'attempt to engage in urban petty commodity production' (Fitzpatrick 1982, 27). Fitzpatrick and Blaxter had engaged in one of the earliest attempts at 'formalizing the informal' (Conroy 1974b, 313), but this proved fruitless. The lesson was that the informal economy, rather than being nurtured, would arise in the usual manner – as pushback against the forces of bureaucracy, vested interest and prejudice.

Walsh characterized 'the Blaxter School' as having assumed that substantial economic change could be wrought simply 'by decree', and that the necessary '*political will*' was present (Walsh 1983, 416, emphasis in original). But that *will* never existed, as the fragile consensus on the Eight Aims could not overcome the combination of entrenched interests and bureaucratic prejudice – both expatriate and indigenous – arrayed against the informal economy. One expression of this was unease about urban 'drift', shown in periodic motions and resolutions in the legislature – in 1964, 1969, 1971 and 1973 – calling on authorities to take action against migrants. This even extended to advocacy of apartheid-style pass-laws (Oram 1976a, 169). Displaying an absence of what Hart has called 'openness to plurality' (Ch. 4), indigenous parliamentarians were still so influenced by the colonial 'idea of the town' that they were affronted by manifestations of street informality. They had unselfconsciously absorbed the 'modernization' ethos of aid donors – the belief (as Hart puts it) that 'poor countries could become rich by emulating "us"'.

Note

1. This Preamble is available at http://www.paclii.org/pg/legis/consol_act/cotisopng534/; and the 'Eight Aims' are listed in the Report of the Constitutional Planning Committee (Ch. 2) at http://www.paclii.org/pg/CPCReport/main.htm. Both URLs were last accessed on 16 November 2022.

Chapter 26

An Uneasy Trio of Formality, Informality and Hybridity

In conventional economic theory, actors, formal or informal, are supposed to react in a predictable manner to price signals. Drawing on Adam Smith's notion of an inherent propensity to truck and barter in 'natural' economies, this way of looking at economic interactions was applied to Melanesian societies by anthropological formalists such as Richard Salisbury (1970) and by development economists. For example, Garnaut, Wright and Curtain (1977) applied the Todaro model of rural–urban migration (Todaro 1969) to movements of unskilled labour in PNG (Ch 25). But there is a difference between the initiative required for an economic actor to fill a formal job made available by *another* actor, and the initiative required to make one's *own* livelihood. The first case is amenable to formal analysis, but the latter raises issues of the cultural capacity for entrepreneurship (Ch. 24), and for specialization and exchange – matters less amenable to orthodox economic analysis.

Blaxter and Fitzpatrick's effort to 'formalize the informal' in PNG assumed an innate capacity to truck and barter, among the people thronging its urban marketplaces. Specialized mercantile functions were not performed in traditional Melanesia, and they scarcely emerged before independence, aside from some premonitions on the Gazelle (Ch. 18). But what they mistook for trucking and bartering was traditional exchange, which has both ceremonial and utilitarian elements. Cyril Belshaw showed the persistence of such behaviour in the urban village of Hanuabada after the Pacific War (Ch. 16), even though by then the community was essentially dependent on wage labour, having very largely abandoned subsistence production.

Belshaw found the distribution of household nutrition among families in Hanuabada was more even than for income and expenditure. People were subject to 'specific non-continuous demands for high ceremonial spending, met in large part by small contributions from numerous helpers' (Belshaw 1957, 77). Households often postponed their own consumption to make such contributions. Much food was obtained from other villages, and this was a more important source for Hanuabadans than home-produced food, or even purchased food. These exchanges were of subsistence commodities, not the result of any innovation in a 'petty commodity' sector (ibid.). Since 'petty commodity production' is the Marxist term for what is here called the 'informal economy' (Ch. 25), Belshaw's finding was a convincing (if unconscious) rejection of any suggestion that economic informality was present in early post-war Hanuabada. There, the adult male population exhibited very high rates of *formal* employment and low rates of 'open' unemployment.

If we accept 'gift' exchange and 'barter' as pure types, we see in the latter what Chris Gregory (1982) called 'relations between aliens by means of alienable things', analogous to trucking and bartering. He distinguished this from 'relations between non-aliens by means of inalienable things' – the Maussian *Gift* (Ch. 3). Ian Hughes rejected any notion of 'pure' barter and 'pure' ceremonial exchange, describing this as an unwarranted 'idealization', as they are merely 'the poles at the ends of a continuum of occasions when goods change hands' (Hughes 1977, 209). Along this continuum one might distinguish varying degrees of what Bill Stent called *hybridity* (Ch. 4) occurring where motives for gift exchange are mingled with those for barter. Like Gregory, Hughes accepted that objects may be either 'commodity' or 'gift', depending on context (ibid.). But if traditional exchange can be a hybrid activity, the same is true, a fortiori, of contemporary exchange relationships, where utilitarian monetized exchange (the market analogue of traditional barter) is often tinged with customary elements. Economic hybridity occurs where what Hart called 'residue' persists – and anthropology provides many instances of such hybridity (Ch. 4). An orthodox economist might regard these as arising in situations where Smithian trade is compromised by Maussian exchange (with the latter seen as the product of socially regulated customs). A non-formalist anthropologist might judge Maussian exchange (seen as a valid set of human choices) as compromised by 'the market'. Both perspectives are necessary to understand the reality of late colonial PNG, where some degree of hybridity in economic life was the norm.

In 1972 Faber commented that rural informality was (unlike the *urban* informal 'sector') 'showing signs of development'. In such *lucky places* as the hinterlands of Goroka and Rabaul it reflected changes occurring in livelihoods due to the introduction and elaboration of monetary exchange, as well as to technical innovation in agriculture, off-farm activities, marketing and services. Rural informality occurred in households where Hart's 'residue' – evidence of earlier modes of production and distribution such as household subsistence, traditional exchange and customary land tenure – was still apparent. The tenacity of such customary social arrangements is bound to result in hybridity wherever people enmeshed in the social relations of *The Gift* also engage in market economic activity.

Concerning *urban* hybridity, we should recall how informal construction activity transformed much of the physical fabric of Port Moresby (Ch. 16). While presented here as 'investment', such activity does not fit comfortably into the mould of individualistic, utility-maximizing economic behaviour, because it is hybrid in character. This was shown in Morata and Hanuabada, where quasi-traditional processes of cooperation and exchange between villagers (more of Hart's 'residue') enabled households to accumulate physical capital. In orthodox economic theory, settlement people could be seen as receiving income streams ('dividends' on their 'investments') based on the economic value of shelter provided by their self-built housing. Belshaw's study showed the permeability of boundaries between formality, informality and traditional exchange in early post-war Hanuabada – demonstrating that informality is very often accompanied by hybridity in situations of social and economic flux. It showed the interaction between what might be called the 'uneasy trio' of formality, informality and hybridity (though it is necessary to understand that not all informal activity is hybrid).[1]

Intellectual Precursors of Informality in Port Moresby

Hart had precursors in the academic literature of late colonial PNG, when geographers began to speculate how livelihoods might be gained in towns, other than in formal 'jobs'. In 1970 Gerard Ward (1971, 101–2) suggested that 'an increment in the capitalist sector of the town's economy may well support a disproportionately large increase in the "bazaar" sector', an insight he attributed to Armstrong and McGee (1968). Again, Harold Brookfield wrote that, as town populations became dominated by Melanesians, these urban centres would be transformed both economically and socially. Their 'true cores' would be the marketplaces, while shops would become both 'more specialized and less central' to towns. Urban growth would become responsible for the major part of population growth – a forecast not necessarily dependent on either the expansion of urban (that is, *formal*) employment opportunities or 'on general economic expansion, as experience in Africa and Asia has clearly demonstrated' (Brookfield with Hart 1971, 411–12).

Ward noted how Armstrong and McGee (1968) had applied Geertz's concept of 'agricultural involution' to *urban* South East Asia. In an urban involutionary process, 'the non-capitalist sections of the tertiary sector of the urban economy can continue to absorb increasing labour to an extraordinary extent' (Ward 1971, 101). Coincidentally, Richard Salisbury (1971) had suggested the same possibility for the Tolai. Rural poverty and internal migration would induce an immiserizing 'involution of services' in the town of Rabaul. Based on tertiary sector service provision, Salisbury's model of economic organization was broader than Ward's. Paraphrasing Ben Higgins (Ch. 2), he noted the capacity of services to absorb many workers, 'taking in one another's washing' in increasingly labour-intensive processes (Salisbury 1971, 65, n2). Ward echoed this bleak tone. He saw informality as a sponge, absorbing urban unemployed in a situation of 'shared poverty', and he projected that PNG's urban population would probably be closer to a million people, rather than half a million, by 1991 (Ward 1971, 103). Fortunately, urban populations totalled only some 555,000 in 1990, with the urban share at 15.5 per cent, and the urban male ratio at 126/100 (NSO 2004). Suggesting Todaro's equilibrating forces at work, these numbers indicated an increasing 'normalization' of population structures, rather than runaway urbanization.

Hart did not represent his urban informal economy so direly, although initially he felt unable to resolve the questions with which he had commenced: was the 'reserve army' of unemployed and underemployed urban labour really a passive and exploited majority in African cities? Or did it have some autonomous capacity for generating growth by means of informal economic activity, capable of increasing the incomes of both the urban and rural poor (Hart 1973, 61)? He could not endorse either a Marxian scenario of deprivation or the 'liberal', 'optimistic' possibility of a dramatic *bootstrap* operation to lift African economies through indigenous enterprise (ibid., 88–89). But by 1982 he had come to believe that although a modernizing West African agriculture would inevitably experience an excess of workers beyond the requirements of the formal urban economy, a benign 'trickle-down effect' would occur, due to government expenditures and the 'inherent dynamism' of markets concentrated in Africa's cities. This would generate enough commodity exchange to support an 'almost infinite' variety of economic activity (Hart 1982, 162).

Hart was now pinning hope on an Arthur Lewis transition (Ch. 14) in which excess workers would eventually be absorbed into labour-intensive activities. Most recently, in 2013, Hart felt buoyed by a contemporary wave of optimism for development prospects and economic integration in sub-Saharan Africa. He felt encouraged to declare that everywhere in Africa the urban informal economy supplies 'food, housing and transport; education, health and other basic services; mining, manufactures and engineering; and trade at every level, including transnational commerce and foreign exchange'. Among the challenges for Africans was to build on this dynamism by renewing 'the movement for greater continental unity' (Hart 2013).

The Limited Scale and Scope of Port Moresby's Informality

If it is not too mundane a prospect after such heady speculation, we should return to 1970s Port Moresby. Hart's informality attracted enthusiastic political support, but also some scepticism, notably from Peter Williamson (1977). Williamson's vision was neo-Marxian, with the poor seen as excluded, or marginalized, from access to opportunity. Dismissing the Somare government's support for informality as naive, he asserted the need for a class solution – the radical restructuring of social and economic relationships.

But Hugh Norwood, unlike Williamson, was no sceptic. He had assumed Nigel Oram's task of charting Port Moresby's burgeoning informal settlements and, affronted by my assertion that self-employed economic activity in Port Moresby was more distinguished by *invisibility* than informality (Conroy 1974b), he documented the character and content of the informal 'sector' in the capital. Over a series of publications (Norwood 1978, 1979, 1984), he stressed the significance of informal construction as an element in the physical growth of the city, while recording urban informal livelihoods.

Among informal activities, Hart had distinguished between 'legitimate' and 'illegitimate' activities, and documented the extra-legal provision of 'those goods and services usually associated with any major city's "red-light district"' (Ch. 1). Norwood had no time for Hart's non-judgemental empiricism: 'Hart included thieves, vagabonds and prostitutes as part of the informal sector'. Norwood objected to including 'rascals'[2] as part of the informal sector. To do so would suggest, misleadingly, that in PNG 'the informal sector is thriving' (Norwood 1978, 61). He excluded many informal activities on moral grounds, but apart from residential construction his account of informality in the capital did not show it as thriving by international standards.

Norwood's account of informal construction (written some years after independence) suggests a more monetized process than was seen in Belshaw's account of Hanuabadan 'home improvement' in the 1950s. To call it self-help housing was incorrect, for there was 'a network of small-scale subcontractors' who build with cheap local materials, including 'offcuts from the timber mills' (Norwood 1978, 65). This is not entirely consistent with another account in which he reported that urban self-help housing may employ the labour of friends and affines, or it may obtain 'paid specialist help on difficult bits', commenting that 'short-term use of specialist paid labour is an integral part of every self-help housing scheme (including unplanned squatter areas) I have ever seen in Africa and Asia' (Rabuni and Norwood 1979, 338, n14). The implication was that this was also the case in PNG, but it is more reasonable to suggest that, while informal housing construction was becoming more commercialized, pervasive elements of traditional exchange remained. Most urban home-building or home-improvement projects were still hybrid at independence.

Norwood (1978) also discussed Port Moresby's ubiquitous PMVs (Passenger Motor Vehicles), which were essentially 'operated by the informal sector'. These vehicles, many owned by village groups or extended families, were an important instance of informality combined with hybridity. They often had the character of communal utilities rather than commercial enterprises. He remarked that PMVs were seldom profitable in any commercial sense, despite being essential to urban transport. They were used for a multitude of purposes – carrying passengers, taking produce and vendors to market, family outings, and trips to and from the home village. Capital invested in such vehicles earns a *social* as much as an economic return, especially in the absence of a formal transport system (Norwood 1978, 66).

PMVs were essential to maintaining the active rural–urban linkages that supported urban informal activity. Towns such as Port Moresby tended 'to draw the economic life of neighbouring villages towards themselves' due to the importance of cash flows originating in the capital – such as wages from urban employment or the earnings of other urban economic activities. Improvements in roads and the establishment of village trucking businesses had accelerated this trend to the degree that some village-dwellers were leading 'very urban lives'. Ross Garnaut cited the Motu village of Gaire, some 50 km south-east of the capital where levels of engagement with the capital were quite high. About 8 per cent of working-age men regarded as village residents commuted every day to jobs in the town, while many more (37 per cent) overnighted there during the week, returning home to Gaire most weekends. The trucking and retailing enterprises catering to urban commuters employed fully 6 per cent of village males of working age (Garnaut 1977b, 86).

This showed a mix of formal and informal incomes, and evidence of increasing synergy between town and country. The great majority of vendors in the city's marketplaces were just such people as the Gaire village commuters. Their market dealings were not so much a matter of *urban* informality as the urban face of a *rural* informal economy – a phenomenon also typical of Rabaul market. Such activity cannot be advanced as evidence of urban informality. Only if urbanites produced food for sale on town land (as some did) or purchased rural produce for resale in the town (as few did at the time) would this constitute *urban* informal activity.

Norwood's tally of informal economic activity suggests the limited scale and scope of Port Moresby's informal 'sector' in the mid-1970s. There were almost no petty manufactures. Service activity, aside from the important instances of construction and transport (and a rather vague reference to vehicle repairs) was very limited. Quasi-subsistence activities (gardening, fishing, firewood collection) were relatively important – a paradox of the urban informal economy in PNG towns, as in most other countries the urban scarcity of such primary resources forces people into service and trading activities more typically associated with urbanism. Concerning trading, Port Moresby's markets combined could muster only half the two thousand vendors recorded by Scarlett Epstein at the Rabaul *Bung* as early as 1961. An apparently trivial circumstance was symptomatic: in an urban economy where firewood was much used for cooking, transport costs were relatively high and timber was abundant outside the town, charcoal was unknown. This is remarkable, because (as Norwood pointed out) it is the essential fuel for much informal economic activity in Africa, South America and elsewhere (Norwood 1978, 67). Blaxter and Fitzpatrick might condemn regulatory barriers to street food in Port Moresby, but these were inconsequential compared with this gaping technology deficit.

Interest in the informal economy following the Faber Report led to an urban household sample survey, conducted across major towns in 1973–74 (Garnaut, Wright and Curtain 1977). Earlier census data had shown little evidence of urban *self*-employment, with totals for the whole country of 432 in 1966 and 1,100 in 1971 (or less than 2 per cent of the employed urban workforce; ibid., 6). In this later survey, across all Port Moresby households, only 3 per cent were without any wage earner. The highest incidence of wagelessness, at 6 per cent, occurred in the city's traditional villages. In the settlements, Ragamuka (mentioned frequently above) was notable for its high incidence of wageless households, but across the town only 8.5 per cent of men (and 15 per cent of women) reported earning some informal income in the previous week. Echoing Hart's findings in Nima, Ghana (Ch. 1), for these people informal economic activity was as likely to be a supplement to wage income as a specialist activity. Moreover, 'very few men or women earned as much as the urban minimum wage from informal businesses' (ibid., 126–27).

Other than in urban villages, the few wageless households had typically migrated from distant and relatively disadvantaged places (Garnaut, Wright and Curtain 1977, 125–26 and Table 6.3). Wageless households in Port Moresby 'sold things' (22 per cent), borrowed money (4 per cent), received food as transfers (24 per cent), grew their own food (18.5 per cent), and had 'other' (26 per cent) sources of support (ibid., Table 6.4). These numbers suggest the 'urban subsistence'[3] and 'exchange' economies were probably more important than monetized informal activities. Finally, Croz Walsh reported some official data for urban household expenditures in 1975–76 (NSO 1976). The average outlay on purchases from market and street vendors in Port Moresby was only 12 per cent of all 'citizen' expenditures (Walsh 1983, 416). But the largest component in this spending was the traditional stimulant betel nut (*Areca catechu*), suggesting that other elements in the urban informal economy were still quite limited in scale and scope.

Why So Threadbare?

Why was economic informality insignificant in the capital on the eve of independence? First, there is the anthropological evidence (Hughes 1977; Allen 1985; Harding 1994) suggesting that specialized mercantile functions had no analogue in traditional Melanesia. This provides some explanation for the tardy emergence of informal enterprise (though not suggesting it could never emerge). On the Gazelle, vigorous rural informality was evident, although only of a 'secondary' character – notwithstanding some incipient middleman activities. Activities there were characteristically tinged with hybridity, suggesting incomplete progression from one mode of economy to another. Similarly, informality in Port Moresby was seen in, for example, investments in private construction and 'communal utilities' such as PMVs. The city offered abundant evidence of hybrid behaviour, although much less of the individual economic activity that was evident in Rabaul.

Blaxter and Fitzpatrick's argument turned largely on the issue of regulatory impediments. But historically, on the Gazelle Peninsula, German and Australian authorities failed to suppress Chinese and Tolai informal activity, despite weighting the regulatory scales against them (chs. 8–9), and it can be argued that the absence of Chinese from Papua until the late 1950s impeded the rise of informal activity there (Ch. 9). Impediments listed by Blaxter and Fitzpatrick can hardly have encouraged indigenous micro-entrepreneurs, but legal measures have had limited effect in preventing antisocial behaviour in other spheres of PNG life.

Other considerations include technological unpreparedness (leaving aside urban agriculture, to which traditional skills are directly transferable). Scarlett Epstein was disappointed by the absence of informal manufacturing on the Gazelle (Ch. 18), and Norwood remarked on its paucity in Port Moresby. Difficulties of remedying this were suggested by Bill Stanner soon after the Pacific War (Introduction). Although dated, his comments suggest the magnitude of the skills gap: handcrafts and productive techniques were still backward in the extreme, using very simple 'cutting tools and equipment'. Traditional techniques often involved great skill, but this did not transfer readily to modern tools and techniques. Although individuals showed the capacity to learn readily, 'conceptions and skills' continued to be pre-industrial. Traditional methods of production were 'closely linked with a simple division of labour, little specialization, and an undeveloped system of trade' (Stanner 1953, 394). There is no hint of determinism, and Stanner's references to division of labour, specialization and trade anticipated the argument of this study.

Other problems held back informal food preparation. Traditional hygiene standards brought street vendors into conflict with health inspectors. The absence of charcoal was relevant to food preparation, but it also had wider implications. Charcoal-making would have been a valuable micro-industry and could have provided inputs for other activities. Walsh suggested that prepared foods for indigenous consumption had been cornered by the formal sector. He neglected the possibility of indigenous operators, appropriately equipped and with a greater understanding of technical possibilities, preparing foods that were more congenial to local tastes than industrial fast food.

As a contemporary Vietnamese observer commented on the 'street food' issue, such food services 'require adequate knowledge and/or modern sector experience'; their development would be delayed until such skilled indigenous people became available. Street food needs 'complementary services and know-how. Sidewalk street stalls not only need cheap and effective sources of energy', they also need 'culinary inventiveness and innovation'. PNG cooking methods 'cannot be easily modified or adapted', while ingredients (especially those imported) are costly for low-income families (Lam 1978, 15). But street food was merely one example of a broader problem, which was the need for an informal production system capable of supplying a basket of goods and services suited to indigenous tastes and incomes, and priced accordingly, rather than one heavily dependent on imported commodities.

Among the reasons for limited informality advanced by Walsh (1983, 416) were historical ('recent urbanization'), cultural ('inappropriateness' of skills, absence of middlemen), and institutional barriers. The latter included the 'lack of opportunity to develop small-scale activities ... in an urban economy [that] itself displayed limited economic functions'. The urban economy was subject to duopoly at the highest level, where two large foreign firms were entrenched, while at the levels of medium and small enterprise control was also exercised by foreigners. Walsh's argument here is persuasive; his account of the industrial structure in Port Moresby overlaps with that of Blaxter and Fitzpatrick ('comprehensive domination by expatriate interests'), and contrasts with late colonial Rabaul. There, the *commanding heights* were less oligopolistic, and an understory of medium and small Chinese enterprise still existed to offer opportunity and example to independent Tolai enterprise. Numerous indigenous people had the experience of working in Chinese trade stores (Ch. 19).

Then there are factors associated with 'the idea of the town', which Nigel Oram thought so deadening in patterning the livelihoods of people in Port Moresby. He contrasted the colourful and chaotic urbanism of the pre-colonial city of Ibadan with the retarded urbanism he found in Port Moresby (Ch. 10). It reminded him of towns established in Eastern Africa by British colonialists – quite unlike Ibadan, where formal and informal manifestations of urbanism were side by side. Where rigid zoning occurred, it robbed colonial cities of the capacity for informality. Keith Hart has made the same point about urban development in West and Central Africa, where very little settlement of white colonists occurred. Cities there were largely created by Africans, their marketplaces were not subject to colonial regulation, and Bauer's 'alien' class of intermediaries (Ch. 2) prospered. By contrast, in Southern Africa, cities were the creation of white settlers, and the movement of Africans was strictly controlled. Even today the informal economy in South Africa is 'hedged in by rules and interests' in the interest of economic modernization. Elsewhere in the region – in Zimbabwe, Mozambique and Kenya, for example – governments have always exerted more control 'than would be considered normal today in Lagos or Dakar' (Hart 2013).

Finally, there is the relative 'affluence' of the subsistence economy. In conditions still applying in the mid-1970s, rural affluence set a base rate for the levels of real income and physical exertion that most urban incomers were willing to tolerate (Conroy 1974b). However, rural population growth would whittle away Fisk's surplus margin over time, and increasing numbers of urban migrants would be forced to 'hustle'. The construct of subsistence affluence rests on the same foundations as another generalization central to the argument here: that PNG's subsistence societies neither needed, nor did they throw up, any professional traders, merchants or itinerant peddlers. In Fisk's model (1962) the social groups enjoying affluence were self-sufficient, though in practice they engaged in traditional, non-market exchange – both ceremonial and utilitarian. But the essential feature of such societies – what Fisk called a 'recognizable caricature' of reality, and others called a stylized fact – was an *in principle* self-sufficiency. The idea of 'affluence' was founded on this construct, sufficiently close to the truth to justify also the generalization (arrived at independently by Allen, Harding and Hughes; Ch. 5) that PNG lacked mercantile societies. These linked ideas, of subsistence affluence and the absence of a mercantile tradition, provide further explanation of the slow emergence of an informal monetized economy in colonial PNG.

Notes

1. International agencies such as the ILO campaign for the elimination of informality from middle-income states in Latin America and Eastern Europe, where the weight of official corruption, excessive regulation and criminality encourages otherwise 'modern' enterprises to operate informally, 'under the radar' (ILO 2007). The activities of such enterprises are not normally 'hybrid' in the sense the term is used here.
2. 'Rascals' (Tok Pisin, *raskol*): criminals, possessing little of the raffish charm the term suggests in English.
3. On the concept of 'urban subsistence', see Evers 1981.

Chapter 27

Dilemmas and Consequences of Urban Growth

Having dealt with post-war events to the Faber period, and political developments to independence in 1975, this study turns now to other late-period matters significant for the informal economy. To avoid distortions from an arbitrary cut-off date, the narrative will touch selectively on the post-independence era. This will enable some conclusions to be drawn concerning the longer-run significance of events between 1972 and 1975.

At independence, formal wage employment was still of overwhelming importance to Port Moresby livelihoods, while Garnaut and colleagues (1977) demonstrated that urban informal incomes were no more important than either urban subsistence or traditional exchange (Ch. 26). Wage determination processes were examined for their influence on the stability and productivity of a growing urban workforce (Ch. 14). That account left off after describing how, during the 1960s, colonial authorities felt their way towards a tripartite regulatory framework and a wage structure supporting a committed urban workforce. By 1972, with a new government including former and serving trade unionists, the stage was prepared for a structural change in the wages system. That change would deliver a shock, with implications for rates of urban migration and employment.

The Gordian Knot of Wages Policy, Revisited

In 1972, a newly constituted Minimum Wages Board (MWB) raised Port Moresby's unskilled wage from $8.00 to $11.50 weekly (and to $13.80

after 12 months). Ross Garnaut thought the initial increase to $11.50 significantly exceeded the opportunity cost of labour attracted from rural villages. It alone was enough to tip the balance of advantage, between working in village or in town, decisively in favour of the town (Garnaut 1973, 173, n9). Rapid inflation in 1974 impelled another MWB hearing, as public demonstrations and student protests rattled the government (Hegarty 1998, 221). Garnaut was dismayed to learn that the government, on advice from remnants of the colonial administration, had decided against making any submission to the wages hearing. Reading signals that the board would react extravagantly to political pressures, and in the absence of any coherent input from employers, Garnaut made a private submission to the MWB. Arguing that if the board judged real wage increases to be warranted – and he acknowledged that circumstances might eventually justify real wage increases, even large ones – he urged that such increases be phased in over time, and with caveats applied. He thought, on reasonable assumptions, that 'it would be probable that the nation could afford an increase of 50% in real wages over the decade' – even 100 per cent in the event of major improvements in PNG's external economic environment (Cunningham 1974, 8–9).

In the event, the 1974 hearing established the principle of an 'Australian-style' family needs-based wage. It increased the urban minimum to $20.00, to be followed by a further increase to $25.80 in 1975. It also determined that another Australian precedent – automatic indexation of wages against consumer prices – should apply. As Garnaut recalled, the board awarded substantial urban minimum wage increases without any guidance from government and after proceedings that were 'well tuned to the political hysteria of the time'. Subsequently, government came to the realization that this outcome 'had forced much of the burden of adjustment to later, harder times onto poorer, rural communities' (Garnaut 1977a, 16).

Automatic indexation had the effect of 'locking in' these substantial real wage increases; its consequence was to install what one commentator called 'the fatal Australian system of wages indexation' (McGavin 1991). PNG would be burdened by an inappropriate and crippling piece of Australian industrial relations machinery. In an intervention reflecting hard-nosed metropolitan industrial relations tactics rather than developing country circumstances, Australian advocate Bill Kelty appeared at the hearing for PNG trade unions, and called Chris Gregory (then still a UPNG economist) as an expert witness to argue in favour of indexation (Cunningham 1974). Much later, another economist commented that the minimum wage decision had 'feathered the nest' of 'privileged' urban workers who already had a job. The 1972 and 1974 determinations (an 'explosion' of urban rates) served to entrench the 'dichotomy' between urban and rural wage rates. Between 1972 and 1975, 'the real urban wage for unskilled workers increased by 118 per cent while the real rural rate increased by just 2 per cent' (Levantis 1997a, 54).

After these events, Garnaut made an enigmatic observation: in the early years after independence 'the coincidence of the large increase in urban wages and increased difficulties of obtaining employment would have quite complicated effects on perceptions of the attractiveness of urban residence' (Garnaut, Wright and Curtain 1977, 187). This statement is decodable if Todaro (1969) is understood as his starting point. Garnaut anticipated substantial wage increases to precipitate increased rural–urban migration by jobseekers, emboldened to endure more extended periods of urban unemployment. In the longer run, the migratory impulse would be countered to some (unknown) degree by a reduced availability of employment opportunities. This would result from the presumed negative reaction of private employers to increased labour costs. A further complicating factor was Australia's decision to 'taper' its aid programme to PNG after independence, presenting the young nation with a fiscal challenge and imposing financial stringency upon it. Wage increases would reduce labour turnover among the employed, making life more difficult for jobseekers. 'Family-based' wage rises would encourage greater inflows of women and children, contributing to the normalization of urban population structure. Over time, these processes would also increase the numbers of those whom Garnaut called the 'dispossessed'. These were people (perhaps born in the town) who had lost contact with village society and had no option of returning.

The net effect of these disparate forces on 'perceptions of the attractiveness of urban residence' was problematic. Any increase in net inward migration would probably raise the incidence of open unemployment and increase incentives for the unemployed to engage in legal or illegal informal economic activity. In the longer run, the propensity to engage in urban informal activities would also be increased by rural population growth and the continuing erosion of subsistence affluence (Conroy 1974b). As against that, greater *rural* market economic activity, including cash cropping and a thriving rural informal economy, might operate to counteract the forces of urban immiserization to some degree. This latter set of possibilities has been explored in previous chapters concerning post-war Goroka and Rabaul.

The first Somare government did not formulate a coherent wages policy before the end of 1975. By then, however, much of the increased funding due from a five-year commitment of support made by Australia 'had been appropriated by urban workers and public servants' (Garnaut 1981, 187). Once ministers understood this, the government strongly opposed further real wage increases, but found it difficult to face up to 'the large *reduction* in real wages' needed to restore 'balance between rural and urban benefits' (Garnaut, Wright and Curtain 1977, 191, emphasis added).

On this point, at least – the importance of the balance between rural and urban benefits, and the need for sacrifice – Keith Hart might have agreed with Garnaut. In a paper addressed to a PNG audience, Hart (1974) emphasized the importance of the distribution of welfare. This distribution, 'distorted in favour of towns', draws people away from agriculture even when they are not in any immediate danger of 'penury'. Hart is scornful of orthodox economics, as embodied in constructs such as the Todaro model employed by Garnaut and others (including the writer) for the analysis of such situations. 'How perverse, then, to draw attention to the "minimum wage" or to "education" as *causes* of rural–urban migration!' (ibid., 11, emphasis in original). Hart's alternative was spartan. He urged the new PNG elites to recognise *themselves* as the greatest threat to PNG's 'well-being', with their 'borrowed' lifestyle, attitudes and money. Rather than accepting 'imported Western notions' they must accept the necessity of lower, nationally affordable standards of living for the elites, together with policies 'inspired by local needs and availability' (ibid., 14).

Failure by the PNG elites to accept this counsel of perfection must be central to an explanation of subsequent events, whether framed according to orthodox economic theory or Hart's own political economy. Garnaut's analysis started with wage levels, though his account of *causes* was more nuanced than Hart might admit, as it also revolved around the 'distribution of welfare'. Garnaut articulated a contemporary, more complex, version of the 'Gordian knot' (Ch. 14). Wages policy is a crucial element in maintaining rural–urban balance, but PNG governments face dilemmas: urban living standards are supported at much higher levels than in rural areas because of statutorily imposed wage differentials. Yet PNG has relatively large numbers of foreigners in towns whose living standards make those of urban citizens seem very low. Although living standards in the wealthiest villages are superior to those of people on urban minimum wages, those wages are still very high when compared with rural incomes overall. And yet, if urban wages were much lower, urban workforce stability would deteriorate, reducing productivity in some crucial occupations. Further, while wage and salary levels for workers with particular skills and education are very high when compared with village standards, skills development is hampered because occupational differentials within the overall wage and salary structure are unduly small, compared with those in similar countries (Garnaut, Wright and Curtain 1977, 191).

Policy options were limited because real wage levels and wage differentials were now mostly 'locked in' by the indexation mechanism. Garnaut suggested government had some flexibility to improve rural–urban balance by skewing the allocation of its spending to benefit rural people. But this was beset by political difficulties, not least 'pressures for conspicuous expenditures in urban areas'. He thought urban unemployment would likely worsen, though the problem should not be exaggerated: 'Urban unemployment is one symptom and, at this stage, one minor cause of the very large national problem of inequitable income distribution'. And, in another enigmatic observation, he suggested that as this situation grew more serious the realization might '*expand the range of politically feasible policy options*' (Garnaut, Wright and Curtain 1977, 193, emphasis added). His analysis was guided by a political economy not so very different from that governing Hart's spartan policy prescription.

Urban Growth and Change, in the 1970s and Beyond

To consider the demographic consequences of wage increases between 1972 and 1975 we should examine the record of urban population and employment into the early years of independence. At the national level, rates of urbanization experienced in PNG were exceptional. The urban sector population increased more than threefold between 1966 and 1980, and as a percentage of total population it grew from less than 5 per cent to some 12 per cent. Among 'citizens', the annual national population growth rate over the same period was about 2.1 per cent, while in the urban sector it was at least 9 per cent for the whole period, and about 8 per cent between 1971 and 1980 (Walsh 1984, 79).

Urban growth was most rapid in Port Moresby where, by comparison with other urban centres, inward migration was of more significance for population growth than natural increase (Conroy 1982, 18). Also, from the 1960s, the capital experienced secular demographic change. This involved a shift from circular labour migration to more permanent urban residence. An index of this shift was the progressive *normalization* of the city's population, the convergence of urban age, sex and dependency ratios towards national averages. From the national census in 1980, data on duration of urban residence and inter-provincial movement confirmed for Walsh that Port Moresby 'had experienced a high, and possibly an increased rate of migration, and therefore of [population] growth, *since* Independence' (Walsh 1984, 80, emphasis added). Reflecting its political and bureaucratic importance, the capital emerged as unquestionably the national primate city. Typical of its experience since the Pacific War, Port Moresby was making its *own* luck.

Because this account has referred frequently to the 'Todaro model' and made the case for its applicability, we should consider how the trends described above may be interpreted in terms of it. Todaro was concerned with inflows of adult *jobseekers* to the urban labour market, rather than the total inflow of *migrants* to urban populations. It is an oversimplification to relate changes in incomes and job prospects to the rate of growth of *total* urban population in a city undergoing the dramatic normalization processes described above (Conroy 1977, 7–8; Garnaut 1979, 11). The Todaro model makes predictions about changes in unemployment levels, subject to countervailing forces. These forces were income differentials (raised dramatically by the wage increases of 1972–75) and employment opportunities (actually increasing in the capital in a buoyant economic environment immediately after independence). One would expect the Todaro model to predict greater involuntary (open) unemployment in the face of increased in-migration of jobseekers responding to wider rural–urban income differentials, and that is what Garnaut found. Between 1973 and 1977 the proportion of men actively seeking work (i.e. the 'involuntarily' unemployed) increased, while the proportion of short-term visitors to the capital (the 'voluntarily' unemployed) decreased. In sum, open (or involuntary) unemployment increased in Port Moresby between 1973 and 1977 (Garnaut 1979, 10). Further, the 1977 data suggested 'a workforce characterized by much lower rates of employment turnover, which possibly emerged in response to the increased wages through 1974' (ibid., 11). Lower labour turnover made jobs more difficult to find.

These countervailing forces produced a situation in the capital in which a more highly paid workforce was operating in a tighter labour market. But because the rewards for patience in job-search were higher than ever before, the unemployed were prepared to hang on longer in Port Moresby. This situation should have been more favourable to the emergence of informal economic activity, particularly as the numbers of young people, 'dispossessed' by reason of having grown up in the city, were also increasing. In future years the longer-term implications of inordinately high urban wage levels (inordinate in comparison with rural living standards) would work through urban society, often with unpleasant results. Levantis later attributed the spectacular increase in criminality in late twentieth-century Port Moresby to the operation of these forces (Levantis 1997b). Economic crime, recognized as informal by Keith Hart (Ch. 1), became significant in the growth of urban informality.

National Economic Integration

Evidence of the degree to which demographic change in the capital diverged from changes occurring in other urban centres raises the question of how far newly independent PNG constituted a single economic system. A study whose concerns include the prospects for a viable rural informal economy should consider how far geographic barriers and colonial history had 'compartmentalized' economic activity in the young state, denying it the benefits of Smithian specialization and exchange in domestic trade. Before self-government, Clunies Ross had written that as a national economy PNG was 'one of the least internally integrated' (Ch. 24). In the absence of anything resembling a national road system, a number of port towns (Rabaul, Madang, Lae, Port Moresby, and others) had each served its own hinterland. They were oriented to local export-agriculture or mining, and largely cut off from the rest of the country. Aside from the administrative functions of governments and Christian missions, these towns were decentralized focal points for local commerce, transport and communications.

At the end of the 1960s, aggregate commercial production was centred primarily on exports (40 per cent of market sector net national product in 1969/70), while imports of goods and services were 55 per cent of market sector gross national expenditure. The national economy was extremely open, whereas markets for domestic produce were small and localized. In consequence, traditional staples – vegetables, fruit, fish and meat – formed only a very small proportion of urban cash spending. Clunies Ross commented that imported rice, flour, sugar and tinned fish are 'more conveniently procured' and often 'much cheaper per unit of food value' (Clunies Ross 1971, 473).

Suggesting potential for incremental import-replacement of foodstuffs, domestic production and marketing of food in and around Port Moresby had increased 'markedly' in the 1960s (though only to an annual total of $5 million, as against food imports to the town of $37 million, by 1970) and prices were rising in the face of excess demand (Langmore 1972, 26). A decade later, Garnaut was more sanguine about the state of the domestic produce market, citing estimates of annual national marketed produce worth some K100 million, perhaps as much as 12 per cent of private final consumption expenditure. Sales were growing faster than population in urban areas (Garnaut, Baxter and Krueger 1983, 94–95). But such improvements represented no more than incremental progress towards self-sufficiency.

At independence, PNG remained a predominantly agrarian society capable, in principle, of feeding its rapidly growing urban populations but unable to do so because of its extremely low degree of internal market integration. Accordingly, import-dependence for marketed food supplies remained very high. Correcting this imbalance would require non-marginal change, a shock capable of altering the sluggish trajectory of internal market development by stimulating indigenous food production and marketing. While detailed discussion of the post-independence period is beyond the scope of this study, the following, concluding chapter will sketch the events that played out over the last quarter of the twentieth century, and which delivered the necessary 'shock' of structural change in urban wages.

Conclusion

Starting this Conclusion with a discussion of macroeconomic policy may seem rather bloodless, but I hope these chapters have not lacked humanity. Perhaps it lacks that sense of 'the reality of people's lives' found in the best anthropological narrative? But what economists call 'the numbers', as cited here, speak to a wrenching process of adjustment, involving much personal hardship for ordinary people. 'Rules of the game' set in place by MWB wage determinations allowed no happier alternative if PNG were to be placed on a sustainable path to economic growth and higher real incomes.

The independent state had assumed responsibility for managing its own exchange rate in 1975, but the circumstance that wages had become subject to indexation against consumer prices (the 'lock-in') remained. This entailed an unfortunate consequence: the price effects of any currency devaluation (in PNG's open economy, where a large proportion of wage-goods was imported) would flow through directly to the consumer price index. This in turn would, through the statutory wage determination process, result in further increases in nominal urban wages. The destructive events of 1974 – reflecting what Garnaut had called 'the political hysteria of the time' – were driven by inflation. If such circumstances were not to reoccur it would be necessary for authorities to work around the situation, and to find a feasible approach to macroeconomic management.

The main thrust of macroeconomic policy became to maintain the external value of the new national currency (the kina), and devaluation was necessarily eschewed as a policy option. Described by Garnaut as 'a simple, low-maintenance economic policy', it was designed to maintain low inflation, currency convertibility and the stability of the financial system (Garnaut 2000, 32), with the objective of avoiding import-induced wage-price spirals and the consequent loss of international competitiveness. This *hard kina strategy* (Garnaut, Baxter and Kreuger 1983) was largely successful in securing macroeconomic stability. It also achieved modest, positive levels of economic growth during the period of its application (Garnaut 2000, 33). However, the essential problem of excessive urban minimum wage levels locked-in by wage indexation remained (Garnaut, Baxter and Kreuger 1983, 233). Macroeconomic stability was hostage to fiscal indiscipline and external shocks.

During one such episode, between 1980 and 1982, Garnaut and colleagues recommended that a macroeconomic adjustment of major proportions would be necessary. To avoid the threat of 'entrenched stagnation', this would require, among other measures, increasing the price of 'tradable goods' relative to Port Moresby adult labour costs by between 25 and 30 per cent (Garnaut, Baxter and Kreuger 1983, 234). Such a target, implying the need for a corresponding kina devaluation and real wage reductions, was 'simply not possible to achieve' so long as real minimum wage levels remained locked-in by indexation. At this time, a government submission to the 1983 MWB proposed gradual changes to indexation procedures in order to achieve the desired result over an extended period. A more drastic alternative – a 'sudden approach' – was also canvassed. Applying shock treatment, the 'sudden' option would require a substantial *one-off* currency devaluation. It would also be necessary to abandon or suspend indexation. An overnight reduction of living standards would be imposed on urban formal wage earners (ibid., 234–36).

As mentioned above, Keith Hart, in a paper delivered to a Port Moresby audience before independence, had foreshadowed the need for PNG elites to accept lower living standards and implement policies that are 'inspired by local needs and availability' (Hart 1974, 14). He had hoped for an initial policy framework encouraging such expectations, but this proved a counsel of perfection. So it was no surprise that the 1983 MWB decided the 'gradualist' approach should prevail over the 'shock' option. But the underlying problems continued, and as late as 1990 it remained the case that 'minimum wages remain . . . at much the same real level as in 1975; . . . an inflexible wages policy that inhibits economic growth had been set in place' (McGavin 1991, 39).

It would take a crisis for this stalemate to be broken. The *deus ex machina* emerged in 1994 to compel PNG authorities to float the kina, removing the policy settings responsible for the wage/price impasse. These events occurred almost two decades after Garnaut had suggested, with grim foresight, that economic distress might eventually '*expand the range of politically feasible policy options*'. Armed conflict in Bougainville in 1989 had led to closure of the copper mine and the associated disruption of agricultural exports, jointly inflicting a loss of some 15 per cent of GDP and necessitating an immediate 10 per cent kina devaluation (Bank of PNG 2007, 240). An MWB determination in 1992 followed up by establishing a substantially lower urban minimum wage for new job entrants, a measure intended to lower average wages over time. The MWB also dispensed with automatic wage indexation, removing the damaging feedback mechanism behind import-induced wage–price spirals. Then in 1994 the kina was allowed to float, after fiscal indiscipline had made assignment of the exchange rate to manage domestic inflation no longer feasible. As a result, the kina's exchange value declined dramatically to the end of the century, forcing up import prices and imposing substantial effective wage cuts on the urban workforce.

An account of these events (Chand and Yala 2009) gave a rather bleak summation of their impact on the formal economy, suggesting that earlier hesitation had been costly. Wage distortion had contributed significantly to urban joblessness and social instability, raising the costs of doing business. Labour market deregulation only occurred after a lengthy experience of formal sector unemployment, crime, and social problems in urban settlements. Wage distortions lay behind these phenomena, but when the MWB took action to abolish the statutory minimum wage in 1992 it was already 'too late'. On its own, wage deregulation was insufficient to revive private sector investment in the conditions of that period (ibid., 49).

This account will say no more about PNG's macroeconomic travails. On the other hand, the change in economic environment appeared favourable to the emergence of indigenous micro-entrepreneurs, providing a fillip to informality – what Hart called 'people's activities in the places where they live'. Reduced purchasing power of urban workers and higher kina costs of imported wage-goods stimulated demand for domestic production, especially fresh foods in urban markets (Conroy 2000, 216–17). Intermediary processes began to emerge that increasingly reached beyond the hinterlands of the old colonial centres, with the effect of creating national markets for some commodities, notably root-crop staples and betel nut.

For better or worse, the devaluation of the last years of the century offered the prospect that an informal economy serving the consumer needs of low-income urban people might at last become feasible. Meanwhile, continuing erosion of subsistence affluence in many rural areas acted to increase its *social* feasibility. This is not to deny gradual progress towards developing domestic markets for agricultural produce in the earlier period after independence (see, for example, Connell 1997, 71–74). However, the drastic changes in price ratios after 1994 were of a different order, and their effects correspondingly more dramatic.

While producer-sellers remained dominant in Goroka, specialized *kaukau* (sweet potato) traders emerged in Port Moresby towards the end of the century as supply chains from the interior were forged. This was a step towards market integration at the national level, a problem identified earlier by Clunies Ross (Ch. 24). Dealings in some other lines of produce were even more advanced. Benediktsson (2002, 218–19) observed that highlander commercial 'exporters' of [Irish] potatoes now sold directly in bulk to 'specialized market traders' in the Port Moresby marketplaces. He reserved his highest commendation for dealers in *buai* (betel nut), whom he called 'highlander assembly traders'. These had established the 'most complex system' of intermediation in the capital, and had also introduced intermediation into the Highlands *buai* trade. Benediktsson thought the new intermediaries – in *kaukau*, Irish potatoes and *buai* – symptomatic of a broader trend towards 'informalization' in the economy of Port Moresby. Informality, such as found in neighbouring South East Asian states, 'may finally be taking hold' (ibid., 218). This was despite the far from complete integration of a national market for *kaukau* due to (among other impediments) limited access to inter-regional market information (ibid., 219). But later, the widespread adoption of mobile telephony in the twenty-first century would promise to improve that situation.

From a longer time-perspective, revisiting the capital's produce markets in 2009 after an absence of thirty years, I was astounded at the increase in quantity, range and quality of fresh produce – an 'efflorescence' of production for market in which the increased relative costs of imported wage-goods had played a catalytic role. These circumstances encouraged me to hope that the Melanesian 'singularity', inhibiting participation in specialized trade and exchange, was becoming less significant among what Hart called the 'impediments to growth' originating 'in local material and social conditions'. In the warp and weft of the cloth of Port Moresby life, informality's elusive thread was becoming increasingly visible.

References

Abel, Cecil. 1969. 'The Impact of Charles Abel', in Second Waigani Seminar, *The History of Melanesia*. Canberra: ANU and UPNG, 265–81.

Allen, Jim. 1982. 'Precontact Trade in Papua New Guinea', in R.J. May and H. Nelson (eds), *Melanesia: Beyond Diversity*, Vol. I. Canberra: Research School of Pacific Studies, Australian National University, 193–205.

———. 1984. 'Pots and Poor Princes: A Multidimensional Approach to the Role of Pottery Trading in Coastal Papua', in S.E. Van der Leeuw and A.C. Pritchard (eds), *The Many Dimensions of Pottery: Ceramics in Archaeology and Anthropology*. Amsterdam: Instituut voor Prae-en Protohistorie, University of Amsterdam, 407–63.

———. 1985. 'Comments on Complexity and Trade: A View from Melanesia', *Archaeology in Oceania* 20(2), 49–57; https://doi.org/10.1002/j.1834-4453.1985.tb00102.x.

Althusser, Louis. 1965 (trans. 1969). *Pour Marx*, trans. by B Brewster [*For Marx*]. London: Allen Lane, Penguin Press.

Althusser, Louis, and Etienne Balibar. 1968 (trans. 1970). *Reading Capital*. London: New Left Books.

Amarshi, Azeem, Kenneth Good and Rex Mortimer. 1979. *Development and Dependency: The Political Economy of Papua New Guinea*. Melbourne: Oxford University Press.

Andaya, Leonard. 1991. 'Local Trade Networks in Maluku in the 16th, 17th and 18th Centuries', *Cakalele* 2(2): 71–96.

Armstrong, Warwick, and Terence McGee. 1968. 'Revolutionary Change and the Third World City: A Theory of Urban Involution', *Civilizations* 18(3): 353–77.

Ballard, John. 1981. 'Policy-Making in a New State', in J. Ballard (ed.), *Policy-Making in a New State: Papua New Guinea, 1972–77*. St Lucia: University of Queensland Press, 1–18.

Bank of Papua New Guinea. 2007. *Money and Banking in Papua New Guinea*. Carlton, VIC: Melbourne University Press.

Barnett, Thomas. 1981. 'Policy-Making in the Transfer of Powers from Australia', in J. Ballard (ed.), *Policy-Making in a New State: Papua New Guinea, 1972–77*. St Lucia: University of Queensland Press, 48–74.

Bauer, Peter. 1948. *Report on a Visit to the Rubber Growing Smallholdings of Malaya*, Colonial Research Publications No. 1, Great Britain Colonial Office.

———. 1954. *West African Trade: A Study of Competition, Oligopoly, and Monopoly in a Changing Economy*. Cambridge: Cambridge University Press.

———. 1984. 'Remembrance of Studies Past: Retracing First Steps', in G.M. Meier and D. Seers (eds), *Pioneers in Development*. New York: Oxford University Press, published for the World Bank, 27–43.

Bauer, Peter, and Basil Yamey. 1951. 'Economic Progress and Occupational Distribution', *Economic Journal* 61(244): 741–55; https://doi.org/10.2307/2226978.

———. 1957. *The Economics of Under-developed Countries*. Cambridge: Cambridge University Press.
Baumol, William. 1990. 'Entrepreneurship: Productive, Unproductive, and Destructive', *Journal of Political Economy* 98(5), Part 1: 893–921.
Belshaw, Cyril. 1954. *Changing Melanesia: Social Economics of Culture Contact*. Melbourne: Oxford University Press.
Belshaw, Cyril. 1957. *The Great Village: The Economic and Social Welfare of Hanuabada, an Urban Community in Papua*. London: Routledge and Kegan Paul.
Benediktsson, Karl. 2002. *Harvesting Development: The Construction of Fresh Food Markets in Papua New Guinea*. Ann Arbour: University of Michigan Press.
Bergoglio, Jorge Mario [Pope Francis]. 2013. *Evangelii Gaudium: Apostolic Exhortation to the Bishops, Clergy, Consecrated Persons, and the Lay Faithful on the Proclamation of the Gospel in Today's World*. Vatican City: Vatican Press.
Biskup, Peter. 1970. 'Foreign Coloured Labour in German New Guinea: A Study in Economic Development', *Journal of Pacific History* 5(1): 85–107; https://doi.org/10.1080/00223347008572166.
Blaxter, Loraine, and Peter Fitzpatrick. 1973a. 'The Informal Sector: A New Strategy for Development'. Port Moresby: New Guinea Research Unit (mimeo).
———. 1973b. 'Street Trading and Markets', *Informal Discussion Paper No. 3*. Port Moresby: Office of the Chief Minister (mimeo).
Boettke, Peter. 2009. 'Institutional Transition and the Problem of Credible Commitment', in Emily Chamlee-Wright (ed.), *The Annual Proceedings of the Wealth and Well-Being of Nations, 2008–2009*, Vol. 1. Beliot, WI: Beloit College Press, 41–51.
Bourke, R. (Michael). 1986. 'Village Coffee in the Eastern Highlands of Papua New Guinea: Early Beginnings', *Journal of Pacific History* 21(2): 100–103; https://doi.org/10.1080/00223348608572531.
Bradley, Christine. 1982. 'Tolai Women and Development'. PhD thesis, University College London.
Brookfield, Harold, with Doreen Hart. 1971. *Melanesia: A Geographical Interpretation of an Island World*. London: Methuen.
Brown, Paula. 1979. 'Chimbu Leadership before Provincial Government', *Journal of Pacific History* 14(2): 100–117; https://doi.org/10.1080/00223347908572368.
Cahill, Peter. 1996. 'Chinese in Rabaul – 1921 to 1942: Normal Practices or Continuing the Yellow Peril?', *Journal of Pacific History* 31(1): 72–91; https://doi.org/10.1080/00223349608572807.
———. 2012. *Needed – But Not Wanted: Chinese in Colonial Rabaul 1884–1960*. Brisbane: CopyRight Publishing.
Carrier, James, and John David Conroy. 1982. 'Education and Development on Ponam Island', in J.D. Conroy, *Essays on the Development Experience in Papua New Guinea*, IASER Monograph 17. Boroko, PNG: Institute of Applied Social and Economic Research, 67–81.
Cartledge, Ian. 1978. *A History of the Coffee Industry in Papua New Guinea*. Goroka, PNG: Coffee Industry Board.
Chand, Satish, and Charles Yala. 2009. 'Economic Policy Making', in R.J. May (ed.), *Policy Making and Implementation: Studies from PNG*. Canberra: ANU E-Press, 41–56; http://doi.org/10.22459/PMI.09.2009.
Chowning, Ann. 1979. 'Leadership in Melanesia', *Journal of Pacific History* 14(2): 66–84; https://doi.org/10.1080/00223347908572366.
Clark, Colin. 1940 (and successive editions). *The Conditions of Economic Progress*. London: Macmillan & Co.

Cleland, Bob. 2010. *Big Road: A Journey to the Heart of the New Guinea Highlands 1953–56*. Paddington, QLD: Red Hill Publishing.

Clunies Ross, Anthony. 1971. 'Dilemmas and Expedients in Papua New Guinea's Development', *The Economic Record* 47(120): 470–93; https://doi.org/10.1111/j.1475-4932.1971.tb00771.x.

———. 1973. 'Social Planning: The Relevance of Tanzanian Socialism', in A.I. Clunies Ross and J.V. Langmore (eds), *Alternative Strategies for Papua New Guinea*. Melbourne: Oxford University Press, 228–53.

Connell, John. 1997. *Papua New Guinea: The Struggle for Development*. London: Routledge and Kegan Paul.

Conroy, John David. 1970. 'The Private Demand for Education in New Guinea: Consumption or Investment', *The Economic Record* 46(116): 497–516.

———. 1973. 'The Nature of Urban Unemployment in Papua New Guinea', *Manpower and Unemployment Research in Africa: A Newsletter* 6(1): 3–10; http://www.jstor.org/stable/43390920. Last accessed 19 November 2022.

———. 1974a. 'Education, Employment and Migration in Papua New Guinea: The Impact of Educational Expansion on Occupational and Geographic Mobility in a Developing Economy'. PhD thesis, University of Papua New Guinea, Port Moresby.

———. 1974b. 'Indigenous Small Business in Urban Areas: Informal or Invisible?', *Yagl-Ambu: Papua New Guinea Journal of the Social Sciences and Humanities* 1(4), 310–15.

———. 1976. *Education, Employment and Migration in Papua New Guinea*, Development Studies Centre Monograph No. 3. Canberra: Australian National University; http://pacificinstitute.anu.edu.au/sites/default/files/resources-links/DSC_monograph_03.pdf. Last accessed 19 November 2022.

———. 1977. 'Urban Growth and Unemployment in Papua New Guinea', IASER Discussion Paper No. 16. Boroko, PNG: Institute of Applied Social and Economic Research; https://www.pngnri.org/images/Publications_Archive/IASER_DP16.pdf. Last accessed 19 November 2022.

———. 1982. 'Urban Growth and Unemployment', in J.D. Conroy, *Essays on the Development Experience in Papua New Guinea*. Boroko, PNG: Institute of Applied Social and Economic Research, 1–23.

———. 2000. 'Papua New Guinea', in J.D. Conroy and R. Cornford (eds), *The Role of Central Banks in Microfinance*, Vol. 2, Country Studies. Manila: Asian Development Bank, 213–45.

———. 2012. 'A Guide to Subsistence Affluence', Working Paper. Canberra: Crawford School of Public Policy, Australian National University; https://papers.ssrn.com/sol3/papers.cfm?abstract_id=2059357. Last accessed 19 November 2022.

Conroy, John David, and Richard Curtain. 1985. 'Circular Mobility in Papua New Guinea: The Urban Household and Rural Village Surveys of 1973–75', in M Chapman and R Mansell Prothero (eds), *Circulation in Population Movement: Substance and Concepts from the Melanesian Case*. London: Routledge and Kegan Paul.

Crocombe, Ronald. 1964. 'Communal Cash Cropping among the Orokaiva', *New Guinea Research Unit Bulletin No. 4*. Canberra: Australian National University; http://pacificinstitute.anu.edu.au/sites/default/files/resources-links/NGRB/04.pdf. Last accessed 19 November 2022.

Cunningham, Andrew. 1974. 'The 1974 Minimum Wages Case: A View from the Ring'. Public lecture at University of Papua New Guinea, Port Moresby, 10 October (mimeo).

Danks, Benjamin. 1888. 'On the Shell-Money of New Britain', *Journal of the Anthropological Institute of Great Britain and Ireland* 17: 305–17; https://doi.org/10.2307/2842168.

Davies, Margrit. 2002. *Public Health and Colonialism: The Case of German New Guinea, 1884–1914.* Weisbaden: Harrossowitz.
de Lepervanche, Marie. 1973. 'Social Structure', in I. Hogbin (ed.), *Anthropology in Papua New Guinea: Readings from the Encyclopedia of Papua New Guinea.* Carlton, VIC: Melbourne University Press, 1–60.
Donaldson, Mike, and Kenneth Good. 1981. 'The Eastern Highlands, Coffee and Class', in D. Denoon and M. Snowdon (eds), *A Time to Plant and a Time to Uproot: A History of Agriculture in Papua New Guinea.* Port Moresby: Institute of Papua New Guinea Studies, 143–69.
———. 1988. *Articulated Agricultural Development: Traditional and Capitalist Agricultures in Papua New Guinea.* Aldershot: Avebury.
Douglas, Bronwen. 1979. 'Rank, Power, Authority: A Reassessment of Traditional Leadership in South Pacific Societies', *Journal of Pacific History* 14(1): 2–27; https://www.jstor.org/stable/25168356. Last accessed 19 November 2022.
Downs, Ian. 1980. *The Australian Trusteeship: Papua New Guinea, 1945–75.* Canberra: AGPS.
———. 1986. *The Last Mountain: A Life in Papua New Guinea.* St Lucia: University of Queensland Press.
Epstein, A.L. (Bill). 1969. *Matupit: Land, Politics, and Change among the Tolai of New Britain.* Canberra: ANU Press; https://openresearch-repository.anu.edu.au/handle/1885/115151. Last accessed 19 November 2022.
———. 1988a. 'A Generation On: Aspects of Population Growth and Movement on the Island of Matupit', *Journal of the Polynesian Society* 97(4): 371–90; https://www.jstor.org/stable/20706221. Last accessed 19 November 2022.
. 1988b. 'Matupit Revisited: Social Change, Local Organization and the Sense of Place', *Journal de la Societe des Oceanistes* 86: 21–40; https://doi.org/10.3406/jso.1988.2840. Last accessed 19 November 2022.
Epstein, Scarlett. 1968. *Capitalism, Primitive and Modern: Some Aspects of Tolai Economic Growth.* Canberra: ANU Press; https://openresearch-repository.anu.edu.au/handle/1885/114857.
———. 1982. *Urban Food Marketing and Third World Development.* London: Croom Helm.
Evers, Hans-Dieter. 1981. 'The Contribution of Urban Subsistence Production to Urban Incomes in Jakarta', *Bulletin of Indonesian Economic Studies* 17(2): 89–96; https://doi.org/10.1080/00074918112331334009. Last accessed 19 November 2022.
Fenbury, David. 1978. *Practice Without Policy: Genesis of Local Government in Papua New Guinea*, Development Studies Centre Monograph No. 13. Canberra: Australian National University; http://pacificinstitute.anu.edu.au/sites/default/files/resources-links/DSC_monograph_13.pdf. Last accessed 19 November 2022.
Finney, Ben. 1968. 'Bigfellow Man belong Business in New Guinea', *Ethnology* 7(4): 394–410; https://doi.org/10.2307/3773017. Last accessed 19 November 2022.
———. 1969. *New Guinean Entrepreneurs*, New Guinea Research Bulletin No. 27. Port Moresby: New Guinea Research Unit, Australian National University; http://pacificinstitute.anu.edu.au/sites/default/files/resources-links/NGRB/27.pdf. Last accessed 19 November 2022.
———. 1970. '"Partnership" in Developing the New Guinea Highlands, 1948–1968', *Journal of Pacific History* 5(1): 117–34; https://doi.org/10.1080/00223347008572168.
———. 1973. *Big-Men and Business: Entrepreneurship and Economic Growth in the New Guinea Highlands.* Canberra: ANU Press; https://openresearch-repository.anu.edu.au/handle/1885/115049. Last accessed 19 November 2022.
———. 1987. *Business Development in the Highlands of Papua New Guinea.* Honolulu, Hawaii: Pacific Development Program, East–West Center.

Finney, Ruth. 1971. *Would-be Entrepreneurs? A Study of Motivation in New Guinea*, New Guinea Research Bulletin No. 41. Canberra: New Guinea Research Unit, Australian National University; https://openresearch-repository.anu.edu.au/handle/1885/130936. Last accessed 19 November 2022.

Firth, Stewart. 1982. 'The Germans in New Guinea', in R.J. May and H. Nelson (eds), *Melanesia: Beyond Diversity*. Canberra: ANU Press, 151–56.

———. 1983. *New Guinea under the Germans*. Carlton, VIC: Melbourne University Press.

Fisk, E.K. (Fred). 1962. 'Planning in a Primitive Economy: Special Problems of Papua-New Guinea', *Economic Record* 38(84): 462–78; https://doi.org/10.1111/j.1475-4932.1962.tb01443.x.

———. 1964. 'Planning in a Primitive Economy: From Pure Subsistence to the Production of a Market Surplus', *Economic Record* 40(90): 156–74; https://doi.org/10.1111/j.1475-4932.1964.tb02145.x.

———. 1966. 'The Economic Structure', in E.K. Fisk (ed.), *New Guinea on the Threshold: Aspects of Social, Political, and Economic Development*. Canberra: ANU Press, 23–43; https://openresearch-repository.anu.edu.au/handle/1885/115128. Last accessed 19 November 2022.

———. 1971. 'Labour Absorption Capacity of Subsistence Agriculture', *Economic Record* 47(119): 366–78; https://doi.org/10.1111/j.1475-4932.1971.tb02646.x.

Fitzpatrick, Peter. 1980. *Law and State in Papua New Guinea*. London: Academic Press.

———. 1985. 'The Making and Unmaking of the Eight Aims', in P. King, V. Warakai and W. Lee (eds), *From Rhetoric to Reality: Papua New Guinea's Eight-Point Plan and National Goals after a Decade*. Port Moresby: UPNG Press, 22–31.

Garnaut, Ross. 1973. 'National Objectives and the Choice of Industries', in A.I. Clunies Ross and J.V. Langmore (eds), *Alternative Strategies for Papua New Guinea*. Melbourne: Oxford University Press, 162–84.

———. 1977a. 'Macroeconomic Policy in Papua New Guinea', Seminar Paper, 5 April. Canberra: Department of Economics, Research School of Pacific Studies, ANU.

———. 1977b. 'Urban Growth: An Interpretation of Trends and Choices', in R.J. May (ed.), *Change and Movement: Readings on Internal Migration in Papua New Guinea*. Port Moresby and Canberra, IASER and Australian National University, 71–95; https://openresearch-repository.anu.edu.au/bitstream/1885/114887/2/b12297823.pdf. Last accessed 19 November 2022.

———. 1979. 'Port Moresby', in R.J. May (ed.), *The Urban Household Survey: Town Profiles*, IASER Monograph 12. Boroko, PNG: Institute of Applied Social and Economic Research.

———. 1980. 'The Neo-Marxist Paradigm in Papua New Guinea', *Australian Journal of Politics and History* 26(3): 447–52; https://doi.org/10.1111/j.1467-8497.1980.tb00544.x.

———. 1981. 'Framework of Economic Policy-Making', in J. Ballard (ed.), *Policy-Making in a New State: Papua New Guinea, 1972–77*. St Lucia: University of Queensland Press, 157–211.

———. 2000. 'The First 25 years of Searching for Development', *Pacific Economic Bulletin* 15(2) Supplement: 29–36; http://devpolicy.org/PEB/2019/05/29/the-first-25-years-of-searching-for-development/. Last accessed 19 November 2022.

Garnaut, Ross, and Paul Baxter, with Anne Krueger. 1983. *Exchange Rate and Macroeconomic Policy in Independent Papua New Guinea*, Pacific Research Monograph No. 10. Canberra: Development Studies Centre, Australian National University; https://openresearch-repository.anu.edu.au/handle/1885/132698. Last accessed 19 November 2022.

Garnaut, Ross, and Chris Manning. 1974. *Irian Jaya: The Transformation of a Melanesian Economy*. Canberra: ANU Press; https://openresearch-repository.anu.edu.au/handle/1885/115044. Last accessed 19 November 2022.

Garnaut, Ross, Michael Wright and Richard Curtain. 1977. *Employment, Incomes and Migration in Papua New Guinea Towns*, IASER Monograph 6. Boroko, PNG: Institute of Applied Social and Economic Research.

Geertz, Clifford. 1963a. *Agricultural Involution: The Process of Ecological Change in Indonesia*. Berkeley: University of California Press.

———. 1963b. *Peddlers and Princes: Social Change and Economic Modernization in Two Indonesian Towns*. Chicago: University of Chicago Press.

Gerritsen, Rolf. 1979. 'Groups, Classes and Peasant Politics in Ghana and Papua New Guinea'. PhD thesis, Australian National University, Canberra.

Goodman, Thomas. 1998. 'The *Sosolot* Exchange Network in Eastern Indonesia during the Seventeenth and Eighteenth Centuries', in J. Miedema, C. Odé and R.A.C. Dam, *Perspectives on the Bird's Head of Irian Jaya, Indonesia*. Atlanta, GA: Rodopi BV, 421–54.

Gramsci, Antonio. 1999. *Further Selections from the Prison Notebooks* (trans. and ed. by E. Boothman). London: Elec Books.

Gregory, Christopher. 1982. *Gifts and Commodities*. London: Academic Press.

———. 1997. *Savage Money: The Anthropology and Politics of Commodity Exchange*. Amsterdam: Harwood Academic.

Griffin, James. 2012. 'Vangeke, Sir Louis (1904–1982)', *Australian Dictionary of Biography*; http://adb.anu.edu.au/biography/vangeke-sir-louis-15893. Last accessed 19 November 2022.

Griffin, James, Hank Nelson and Stewart Firth. 1979. *Papua New Guinea: A Political History*. Melbourne: Heinemann.

Groves, Murray. 1957. 'Sacred Past and Profane Present', *Quadrant* 1(3): 39–48.

———. 1960. 'Politics in Port Moresby'. Paper presented to the No. 5 course for Senior Officers. Mosman, NSW: Australian School of Pacific Administration (mimeo).

Hahl, Albert. 1980. *Governor in New Guinea* (trans. and ed. by P.G. Sack and D. Clark). Canberra: ANU Press; http://pacificinstitute.anu.edu.au/sites/default/files/resources-links/ANU_Press_Albert_Hahl_Governor_in_New_Guinea.pdf. Last accessed 19 November 2022.

Hann, Chris, and Keith Hart. 2011. *Economic Anthropology*. Cambridge: Polity Press.

Harding, Thomas. 1994. 'Precolonial New Guinea Trade', *Ethnology* 33(2): 101–25. https://doi-org.virtual.anu.edu.au/10.2307/3773892.

Hart, Keith. 1970. 'Small-Scale Entrepreneurs in Ghana and Development Planning', *Journal of Development Studies* 6(4): 104–20. doi:10.1080/00220387008421338

———. 1971. 'Informal Income Opportunities and Urban Employment in Ghana'. Paper delivered to Conference on Urban Unemployment in Africa, Institute of Development Studies, University of Sussex, 12–16 September.

———. 1973. 'Informal Income Opportunities and Urban Unemployment in Ghana', *Journal of Modern African Studies* 11(1): 61–89. doi:10.1017/S0022278X00008089.

———. 1974. 'A Model of Development to Avoid', *Yagl-Ambu: Papua New Guinea Journal of the Social Sciences and Humanities* 1(1): 8–15.

———. 1982. *The Political Economy of West African Agriculture*. Cambridge: Cambridge University Press.

———. 1994. 'African Enterprise and the Informal Economy: An Autobiographical Note'. English prepublication draft of 'Entreprise africaine et l'économie informelle', in S. Ellis and Y. Fauré (eds), *Entreprise et Entrepreneurs Africains*, Karthala. Online at *The Memory*

Bank; http://thememorybank.co.uk/papers/african-enterprise-and-the-informal-economy/. Last accessed 18 November 2022.

———. 2002. 'World Society as an Old Regime', in C. Shore and S. Nugent (eds), *Elite Cultures: Anthropological Perspectives*. London: Routledge, 22–36.

———. 2004. 'Formal Bureaucracy and the Emergent Forms of the Informal Economy', WIDER Working Paper 11/2005, online at https://www.wider.unu.edu/publication/formal-bureaucracy-and-emergent-forms-informal-economy Last accessed 19 November 2022.

———. 2007a. 'The Informal Economy', in J. Eatwell, M. Milgate and P. Newman (eds), *The New Palgrave: A Dictionary of Economic Theory and Doctrine*, Vol. 2 . London: Palgrave Macmillan, 845–46.

———. 2007b. 'A Short History of Economic Anthropology', unpublished draft, online at https://thememorybank.co.uk/a-short-history-of-economic-anthropology/. Last accessed 18 November 2022.

———. 2008. 'Between Bureaucracy and the People: A Political History of Informality'. DIIS Working Paper 2008/27. Copenhagen: Danish Institute for International Studies; http://pure.diis.dk/ws/files/46171/WP2008_27_Between_Bureaucracy_and_the_People_A_Political_History_of_Informality.pdf. Last accessed 18 November 2022.

———. 2010. 'Informal Economy', in K. Hart, J.-L. Laville and A. Cattani (eds), *The Human Economy*. Cambridge: Polity Press, 142–53.

———. 2012a. Contribution to 'Intimations of the "Informal Economy"'. Online seminar of the Open Anthropology Cooperative, dated 25 April; http://openanthcoop.net/archive/openanthcoop.ning.com/forum/topics/new-oac-online-seminar-johnconroy-intimations-of-the-informal-ec0e5a.html?id=3404290%3ATopic%3A159237&page=3#comments. Last accessed 18 November 2022.

———. 2012b. 'How the Informal Economy Took Over the World'. Online at https://www.academia.edu/30541310/How_the_informal_economy_took_over_the_world. Last accessed 18 November 2022.

———. 2013. 'The Case for an African Customs Union'. Keynote address for a World Customs Organization/World Bank conference on *Informality, International Trade and Customs*, Brussels, 3–4 June. Online at https://perspectivesinanthropology.com/2021/11/01/informality-and-international-trade-the-case-for-an-african-customs-union-by-keith-hart/. Last accessed 19 November 2022.

———. 2015. Draft Preface to *Globalization from Below: The World's Other Economy*, published (in Spanish) as: Carlos Alba Vega, Gustavo Lins Ribeiro and Gordon Mathews, *La globalización desde abajo: LA OTRA ECONOMÍA MUNDIAL*, El Colegio de Mexico, Fondo Cultura Economica, 9–26. English translation online at https://perspectivesinanthropology.com/2020/05/01/new-preface-to-globalization-from-below-the-worlds-other-economy-by-keith-hart/. Last accessed 23 November 2022.

Hart, K., J.-L. Laville and A. Cattani (eds). 2010. *The Human Economy*. Cambridge: Polity Press.

Hasluck, Paul. 1976. *A Time for Building: Australian Administration in Papua and New Guinea 1951–1963*. Carlton, VIC: Melbourne University Press.

Hawksley, Charles. 2001. 'Administrative Colonialism: District Administration and Colonial 'Middle Management' in Kelantan 1909–1919 and the Eastern Highlands of Papua New Guinea 1947–1957'. PhD thesis, University of Wollongong, New South Wales; https://ro.uow.edu.au/theses/1732/.

———. 2005. 'Creating Hegemony: Colonialism, the Social Contract and State Legitimacy in Post-war Papua New Guinea'. Workshop on *Hegemony: Explorations into Con-*

sensus, Coercion and Culture, at the University of Wollongong, 14–15 February, Panel 1, Class and Consensus.

Healey, Christopher. 1998. 'Political Economy in the Kepala Burung Region of Old Western New Guinea', in J. Miedema, C. Odé and R.A.C. Dam, *Perspectives on the Bird's Head of Irian Jaya, Indonesia*. Atlanta, GA: Rodopi BV, 337–50.

Hegarty, David. 1998. 'Political Chronicles from *The Australian Journal of Politics and History*, 1971–74', in C. Moore with M. Kooyman (eds), *A Papua New Guinea Political Chronicle, 1968–1991*. Bathurst, NSW: Crawford House, 134–232.

Hempenstall, Peter. 1978. *Pacific Islanders under German Rule*. Canberra: ANU Press; http://pacificinstitute.anu.edu.au/sites/default/files/resources-links/ANU_Press_Pacific_Islanders_under_German_Rule.pdf. Last accessed 19 November 2022.

Hess, Michael. 1983. '"In the long run. . .": Australian Colonial Labour Policy in the Territory of Papua and New Guinea', *Journal of Industrial Relations* 25(1): 51–67; https://doi.org/10.1177/002218568302500104.

Hobsbawm, Eric. 1969. *Industry and Empire from 1750 to the Present Day*. Harmondsworth, UK: Penguin.

Hogbin, Ian (ed.). 1973. *Anthropology in Papua New Guinea: Readings from the Encyclopedia of Papua New Guinea*. Carlton, VIC: Melbourne University Press.

Howlett, Diana. 1973. 'Terminal Development: From Tribalism to Peasantry', in H. Brookfield (ed.), *The Pacific in Transition: Geographical Perspectives on Adaptation and Change*. Canberra: ANU Press, 249–73; https://openresearch-repository.anu.edu.au/handle/1885/114950. Last accessed 19 November 2022.

———. 1976. 'Goroka', in R. Jackson (ed.), *An Introduction to the Urban Geography of Papua New Guinea*, Department of Geography Occasional Paper No. 13. Port Moresby: University of Papua New Guinea, 243–63.

Hughes, Ian. 1977. *New Guinea Stone Age Trade: The Geography and Ecology of Traffic in the Interior*. Canberra: Department of Prehistory, Research School of Pacific Studies, Australian National University; http://pacificinstitute.anu.edu.au/sites/default/files/resources-links/TA_03.pdf. Last accessed 19 November 2022.

———. 1978. 'Good Money and Bad: Inflation and Devaluation in the Colonial Process', *Mankind* 11(3): 308–18; https://doi.org/10.1111/j.1835-9310.1978.tb00661.x.

IBRD (International Bank for Reconstruction and Development). 1965. *Programmes and Policies for the Economic Development of the Territory of Papua and New Guinea*. Baltimore, MD.

ILO (International Labour Organization). 1972. *Employment, Incomes and Equality: A Strategy for Increasing Productive Employment in Kenya*. Geneva.

———. 2007. *The Informal Economy: Enabling Transition to Formalization* (ISIE/2007/1). Geneva.

Inglis, Amirah. 1974. *Not a White Woman Safe: Sexual Anxiety and Politics in Port Moresby 1920–34*. Canberra: ANU Press.

Inglis, Christine. 1977. 'Social Structure and Patterns of Economic Action: The Chinese in Papua New Guinea'. PhD thesis, London School of Economics and Political Science.

Irwin, J.G. (Geoffrey). 1978. 'The Development of Mailu as a Specialized Trading and Manufacturing Centre in Papuan Prehistory: The Causes and the Implications', *Mankind* 11(3): 406–15; https://doi.org/10.1111/j.1835-9310.1978.tb00669.x.

Isaac, Joseph. 1970. 'The Structure of Unskilled Wages and Relativities between Rural and Non-rural Employment in Papua and New Guinea: A Report'. Port Moresby: Government Printer.

Jackson, Richard (ed.). 1976. *An Introduction to the Urban Geography of Papua New Guinea*, Department of Geography Occasional Paper No. 13. Port Moresby: University of Papua New Guinea.

Jolly, Richard, Emmanuel de Kadt, Hans Singer and Fiona Wilson. 1973. 'Introduction', in R. Jolly, E. de Kadt, H. Singer and F. Wilson (eds), *Third World Employment: Problems and Strategy*. Harmondsworth, UK: Penguin Education, 9–23.

Joyce, Roger. 1971. *Sir William MacGregor*. Melbourne: Oxford University Press.

Lam, Ngo Van. 1978. 'Some Economic Implications of Minimum Urban Wages in Papua New Guinea'. Unpublished paper, Institute of Applied Social and Economic Research, Port Moresby (mimeo).

Langmore, John. 1970. 'Economic and Demographic Forecasts', in *Port Moresby Urban Development*, New Guinea Research Bulletin No. 37. Canberra: New Guinea Research Unit and Australian National University; http://pacificinstitute.anu.edu.au/sites/default/files/resources-links/NGRB/37.pdf. Last accessed 19 November 2022.

———. 1972. 'A Critical Assessment of Australian Economic Policy for Papua New Guinea between 1945 and 1970'. Economics Department, Discussion Paper No. 1, University of Papua New Guinea, Port Moresby.

Langness, Lewis. 1973. 'Traditional Political Organization', in I. Hobin (ed.), *Anthropology in Papua New Guinea: Readings from the Encyclopedia of Papua New Guinea*. Carlton, VIC: Melbourne University Press, 142–73.

Lawrance, Gerry. 1981. 'National Plantation Management Agency', in MAHB Walter, *What Do We Do about Plantations?*, Monograph No. 15. Boroko, PNG: Institute of Applied Social and Economic Research, 190–95.

Legge, John. 1956. *Australian Colonial Policy: A Survey of Native Administration and European Development in Papua*. Sydney: Angus and Robertson.

Levantis, Theodore. 1997a. 'The Urban Labour Market in Papua New Guinea, Post-Deregulation', *Pacific Economic Bulletin* 12(2): 54–71; https://openresearch-repository.anu.edu.au/bitstream/1885/157503/1/122_urban-labour.pdf. Last accessed 19 November 2022.

———. 1997b. 'Urban Unemployment in Papua New Guinea, it's Criminal', *Pacific Economic Bulletin* 12(2): 73–84; https://openresearch-repository.anu.edu.au/bitstream/1885/157499/1/122_urban-unemployment.pdf. Last accessed 19 November 2022.

Lewis, David. 1996. *The Plantation Dream: Developing British New Guinea and Papua 1884–1942*. Canberra: Journal of Pacific History; http://pacificinstitute.anu.edu.au/sites/default/files/resources-links/JPH_Plantation_Dream.pdf. Last accessed 19 November 2022.

Lewis, Oscar. 1966. *La Vida: A Puerto Rican Family in the Culture of Poverty, San Juan and New York*. New York: Random House.

Lewis, W.A. (Arthur). 1954. 'Economic Development with Unlimited Supplies of Labour', *The Manchester School* 22(2): 139–91; https://doi.org/10.1111/j.1467-9957.1954.tb00021.x.

Lipton, Michael. 1984. 'Comment', in G.M. Meier and D. Seers (eds), *Pioneers in Development*. New York: Oxford University Press (published for the World Bank), 44–50.

Lynch, Mark. 1981. 'Ropes, Rules and Ring-Keepers: The Cabinet System as Policy-Maker', in J. Ballard (ed.), *Policy-Making in a New State: Papua New Guinea, 1972–77*. St Lucia: University of Queensland Press, 19–32.

Lyng, Jens. 1919. *Our New Possession (Late German New Guinea)*. Melbourne: Melbourne Publishing Company.

MacWilliam, Scott. 2013. *Securing Village Life: Development in Late Colonial Papua New Guinea*. Canberra: ANU E Press; http://doi.org/10.22459/SVL.05.2013.

May, Ronald. 2016. *Indigenous Commercial Ambitions and Decentralisation in Papua New Guinea: The Missing Driver of Reform*, SSGM Discussion Paper 2016/1, 'State, Society and Governance in Melanesia', Australian National University, Canberra; http://bellschool.anu.edu.au/experts-publications/publications/3574/indigenous-commercial-ambitions-and-decentralisation-papua. Last accessed 19 November 2022.

Maine, Henry. 1861. *Ancient Law: Its Connection with the Early History of Society, and Its Relation to Modern Ideas*. London: John Murray.

Mair, Lucy. 1948. *Australia in New Guinea*. London: Christophers.

Martin, Ross. 1969. 'Tribesmen into Trade Unionists: The African Experience and the Papua-New Guinea Prospect', *Journal of Industrial Relations* 11(2): 125–72; https://doi.org/10.1177/002218566901100204.

Mauss, Marcel. (1925) 1974. *The Gift*. London: Routledge and Kegan Paul.

———. 2009. 'Micronationalism in Papua New Guinea', in R.J. May (ed.), *Policy Making and Implementation: Studies from Papua New Guinea*. Canberra: ANU E-Press, 48–106; http://doi.org/10.22459/PMI.09.2009.

Mayhew, Henry. 1861–62. *London Labour and the London Poor*, 3 Vols. London: Griffin, Bohn and Company, University of Virginia, E-text at http://etext.virginia.edu/toc/modeng/public/MayLond.html (Vol. 1); Tufts University Digital Collections at http://hdl.handle.net/10427/14951 (Vol. 2); and http://hdl.handle.net/10427/15186 (Vol. 3). All accessed on 19 November 2022.

McClelland, David. 1961. *The Achieving Society*. New York: Free Press.

McGavin, Paul. 1991. *Wages, Incomes and Productivity in Papua New Guinea*. Port Moresby: Institute of National Affairs.

McKillop, Robert. 1981a. 'Agricultural Policy-Making', in J.A. Ballard (ed.), *Policy-Making in a New State: Papua New Guinea, 1972–77*. St Lucia: University of Queensland Press, 238–56.

———. 1981b. 'Managing Plantations in Papua New Guinea Today: Who Wants To Be the Labourer?', in MAHB Walter, *What Do We Do about Plantations?*, Monograph No. 15. Boroko, PNG: Institute of Applied Social and Economic Research, 25–31.

Meier, Gerald. 1984. 'The Formative Period', in G. Meier and D. Seers (eds), *Pioneers in Development*. New York: Oxford University Press (published for the World Bank), 3–22.

Meillassoux, Claude. 1972. 'From Reproduction to Production: A Marxist Approach', *Economy and Society* 1(1): 93–105; https://doi.org/10.1080/03085147200000005.

Miedema, Jelle. 1998. 'Culture Hero Stories and Tales of Tricksters: The Bird's Head Peninsula of Irian Jaya in a Comparative Perspective', in J. Miedema, C. Odé and R.A.C. Dam, *Perspectives on the Bird's Head of Irian Jaya, Indonesia*. Atlanta, GA: Rodopi BV, 193–234.

Miles, John. 1956. 'Native Agriculture in Papua', *South Pacific* 9(1): 318–27.

———. 1960. 'The Historical Background of the Development of Native Education in Papua and New Guinea'. Paper presented to the No. 3 course for Senior Officers, Mosman, Australian School of Pacific Administration.

Moore, Clive. 2003. *New Guinea: Crossing Boundaries and History*. Honolulu: University of Hawaii Press.

Moses, John. 1969. 'The German Empire in Melanesia 1884–1914: A German Self-Analysis', in Second Waigani Seminar, *The History of Melanesia*, Canberra, ANU and UPNG, 45–76.

Myint, Hla. 1958. 'The "Classical Theory" of International Trade and the Underdeveloped Countries', *Economic Journal* 68(270): 317–37; https://doi.org/10.2307/2227598.

Nelson, Hank. 2000. 'Murray, Hubert Leonard (1886–1963)', *Australian Dictionary of Biography*; http://adb.anu.edu.au/biography/murray-hubert-leonard-11208. Accessed 19 November 2022.

North, Douglass. 2005. *Understanding the Process of Economic Change*. Princeton, NJ: Princeton University Press.

Norwood, Hugh. 1978. 'Port Moresby Needs a Strong Informal Sector', *Yagl-Ambu* 5(4): 59–70.

———. 1979. 'Port Moresby: Pattern of Settlement among Migrants and Urban Villagers (National Capital District)', in C.A. Valentine and BettyLou Valentine (eds), *Going through Changes: Villagers, Settlers and Development in Papua New Guinea*. Port Moresby: UPNG Press.

———. 1984. *Port Moresby: Urban Villages and Squatter Areas*. Port Moresby: UPNG Press.

NSO (National Statistical Office of PNG). 1976. *Household Expenditure Survey 1975/76*. Port Moresby.

———. 2004. *Demographic Indicators*. Port Moresby.

Nyerere, Julius. 1968. *Freedom and Socialism (Uhuru na ujamaa): A Selection from Writings and Speeches, 1965–1967*. New York: Oxford University Press.

ODG (Overseas Development Group). 1973. *A Report on Development Strategies for Papua New Guinea*. Port Moresby: International Bank for Reconstruction and Development as Executive Agency for UNDP.

Ohff, Hans-Jurgen. 2008. 'Empires of Enterprise: German and English Commercial Interests in East New Guinea, 1884 to 1914'. PhD thesis, School of Politics and History, University of Adelaide.

Oram, Nigel. 1967. 'Rabia Camp and the Tommy Kabu Movement', in *Rabia Camp: A Port Moresby Migrant Settlement*, New Guinea Research Bulletin No. 14. Port Moresby and Canberra: New Guinea Research Unit and Australian National University, 1–43; http://pacificinstitute.anu.edu.au/sites/default/files/resources-links/NGRB/14.pdf. Last accessed 19 November 2022.

———. 1968a. 'Culture Change, Economic Development and Migration among the Hula', *Oceania* 38(4): 243–75; https://doi.org/10.1002/j.1834-4461.1968.tb00972.x.

———. 1968b. 'The Hula in Port Moresby', *Oceania* 39(1): 1–35; https://doi.org/10.1002/j.1834-4461.1968.tb00982.x.

———. 1976a. *Colonial Town to Melanesian City: Port Moresby 1884–1974*. Canberra: ANU Press; http://pacificinstitute.anu.edu.au/sites/default/files/resources-links/ANU_Press_Colonial_Town_to_Melanesian_City.pdf. Last accessed 19 November 2022.

———. 1976b. 'Port Moresby', in R. Jackson (ed.), *An Introduction to the Urban Geography of Papua New Guinea*, Department of Geography Occasional Paper No. 13, University of Papua New Guinea, Port Moresby, 140–72.

Pahl, Raymond. 1984. *Divisions of Labour*. Oxford: Basil Blackwell.

PNG (Papua New Guinea). 1973. *Committee of Inquiry into Land Matters: Report*. Port Moresby.

PNG (Papua New Guinea, Independent State of). 1975. *Constitution of the Independent State of Papua New Guinea*; http://www.wipo.int/wipolex/en/text.jsp?file_id=199188. Last accessed 19 November 2022.

Petty, William. 1690. *Political Arithmetick*, in C.H. Hull (ed.) (1899), *Economic Writings of Sir William Petty*. Cambridge: Cambridge University Press.

Polanyi, Karl. 1944. *The Great Transformation: The Political and Economic Origins of Our Time* (2nd Beacon edition, published 2001). Boston: Beacon Press.

Pybus, Cassandra. 1999. *The Devil and James McAuley*. St Lucia: University of Queensland Press.

Pyke, Steve. 1995. *Philosophers* (2nd edn). London: Zelda Cheatle Press.
Rabuni, Tang, and Hugh Norwood. 1979. 'Informal Settlement Planning in PNG', in R. Jackson with J. Odongo and P. Batho (1980), *Urbanisation and Its Problems in Papua New Guinea: Proceedings of the 1979 Waigani Seminar on Urbanisation*. Port Moresby: University of Papua New Guinea, 326–40.
Reed, Stephen. 1943. *The Making of Modern New Guinea, with Special Reference to Culture Contact in the Mandated Territory*. Philadelphia, PA: American Philosophical Society.
Rew, Alan. 1970. 'Passenger Ship or Cargo Vessel? The Adaptation of Indigenous Industrial Workers to the Social Life of Port Moresby, a Town in Papua-New Guinea'. PhD thesis, Australian National University, Canberra.
Robbins, Joel, and David Akin. 1999. 'An Introduction to Melanesian Currencies', in D. Akin and J. Robbins (eds), *Money and Modernity: State and Local Currencies in Melanesia*. Pittsburgh, PA: University of Pittsburgh Press, 1–40.
Rodrik, Dani. 2016. 'Premature Deindustrialization', *Journal of Economic Growth* 21, 1–33; https://doi.org/10.1007/s10887-015-9122-3.
Rosenstein-Rodan, Paul. 1943. 'Problems of Industrialisation of Eastern and South-Eastern Europe', *Economic Journal* 53: 202–11; https://doi.org/10.2307/2226317.
Rostow, Walt. 1960. *The Stages of Economic Growth: A Non-Communist Manifesto*. Cambridge: Cambridge University Press.
Rowley, Charles. 1958a. 'Labour Administration in Papua and New Guinea', *South Pacific* 9(11): 540–49.
———. 1958b. *The Australians in German New Guinea, 1914–1921*. Carlton, VIC: Melbourne University Press.
———. 1960. 'The Political Significance of the Town'. Paper presented to the No. 5 course for Senior Officers, Mosman, Australian School of Pacific Administration (mimeo).
———. 1965. *The New Guinea Villager: The Impact of Colonial Rule on Primitive Society and Culture*. Melbourne: Cheshire.
Ryan, Dawn. 1970. 'Rural and Urban Villagers: A Bi-local Social System in Papua'. PhD thesis, University of Hawaii, Honolulu.
———. 1977. 'Toaripi in Port Moresby and Lae', in R.J. May (ed.), *Change and Movement: Readings on Internal Migration in Papua New Guinea*. Port Moresby and Canberra: IASER and Australian National University, 147–54; http://pacificinstitute.anu.edu.au/sites/default/files/resources-links/ANU_Press_Change_and_Movement.pdf. Last accessed 19 November 2022.
Ryan, Peter (ed.). 1972. *Encyclopedia of Papua and New Guinea*, Carlton, VIC: Melbourne University Press.
Sahlins, Marshall. 1958. *Social Stratification in Polynesia*. Seattle: University of Washington Press.
———. 1963. 'Poor Man, Rich Man, Big-Man, Chief: Political Types in Melanesia and Polynesia', *Comparative Studies in Society and History* 5(3): 285–303.
———. 1972. 'The Original Affluent Society', in M.D. Sahlins, *Stone Age Economics*. Chicago: Aldine-Atherton, 1–39.
Salisbury, Richard. 1962. *From Stone to Steel: Economic Consequences of a Technological Change in New Guinea*. Melbourne: Melbourne University Press.
———. 1964. 'Despotism and Australian Administration in the New Guinea Highlands', *American Anthropologist* 66(4): 225–39; https://www.jstor.org/stable/668439. Last accessed 20 November 2022.
———. 1970. *Vunamami: Economic Transformation in a Traditional Society*. Los Angeles: University of California Press.

———. 1971. 'Development through the Service Industries', *Manpower and Unemployment Research in Africa: A Newsletter* 4(1): 57–66; https://www.jstor.org/stable/43390885. Last accessed 19 November 2022.

Sapper, Karl. 1910. *Wissenschaftliche Ergebnisse einer amtlichen Forschungsreise nach dem Bismarck Archipel im Jahre 1908* [Scientific results of an official expedition to the Bismark Archipelago in the year 1908] (Berlin 1910–13), Vol. I. Hamburg: E.S. Mittler und Sohn.

Schaffer, Bernard. 1963. *Papua and New Guinea as a Small Territory*. London: University of London, Institute of Commonwealth Studies.

Schumpeter, Joseph. 1942. *Capitalism, Socialism and Democracy* (1st Harper edition published 1975). New York: Harper.

Sexton, Lorraine. 1982. '*Wok Meri*: A Women's Savings and Exchange System in Highland Papua New Guinea', *Oceania* 52(3): 167–98; https://doi.org/10.1002/j.1834-4461.1982.tb01493.x.

———. 1983. 'Little Women and Big Men in Business', *Oceania* 54(2): 133–50; https://doi.org/10.1002/j.1834-4461.1983.tb00341.x.

Seyffert, Oscar. 1894. *Dictionary of Classical Antiquities* (3rd edn). New York: Macmillan; https://archive.org/details/dictionaryofclas95seyf. Last accessed 19 September 2022.

Shand, Richard. 1971. 'Emerging Policy Issues in the Development of Papua New Guinea', in R.T. Shand and M.L. Treadgold, *The Economy of Papua New Guinea: Projections and Policy Issues*. Canberra: Research School of Pacific Studies, Australian National University, 54–100.

Silverman, Marilyn (ed.). 2004. *Ethnography and Development: The Work of Richard F Salisbury*, Fontanus Monograph Series No. 15. Montreal: McGill-Queen's University Press.

Smith, Adam. (1776) 1904. *The Wealth of Nations: An Inquiry into the Nature and Causes of the Wealth of Nations*. Chicago: University of Chicago Press.

Smith, Douglas. 1975. *Labour and the Law in Papua New Guinea*, Development Studies Centre Monograph No. 1. Canberra: Australian National University.

Smith, Woodruff. 1974. 'The Ideology of German Colonialism, 1840–1906', *Journal of Modern History* 46: 641–63.

Spate, Oscar, Cyril Belshaw and Trevor Swan. 1953. *Some Problems of Development in New Guinea: Report of a Working Committee of the Australian National University*. Canberra: Australian National University.

Standish, Bill. 1978. 'The "Big-Man" Model Reconsidered: Power and Stratification in Chimbu', *IASER Discussion Paper No. 22*, Institute of Applied Social and Economic Research, Port Moresby. Boroko: Papua New Guinea; https://pngnri.org/images/Publications_Archive/IASER_DP22.pdf. Last accessed 19 September 2022.

Stanner, William. 1953. *The South Seas in Transition: A Study of Post-war Rehabilitation and Reconstruction in Three British Pacific Dependencies*. Sydney: Australasian Publishing Company.

Stent, William. 1973. 'Perverse Supply in Traditional Societies – an Explanation', *Oxford Agrarian Studies* 2(1): 81–86; https://doi.org/10.1080/13600817308423801.

———. 1984. *The Development of a Market Economy in the Abelam*, IASER Monograph No. 20, Institute of Applied Social and Economic Research. Boroko: Papua New Guinea.

Stent, William, and John Conroy. 1968. 'Little Men, What Now? The Territory's School Leavers', *New Guinea and Australia, the Pacific and Southeast Asia* 3(1): 55–59.

Stent, William, and L.R. (Roy) Webb. 1975. 'Subsistence Affluence and Market Economy in Papua New Guinea', *Economic Record* 51(136): 522–38; https://doi.org/10.1111/j.1475-4932.1975.tb00279.x.

Stewart, Randall. 1992. *Coffee: The Political Economy of an Export Industry in Papua New Guinea*. Boulder, CO: Westview Press.

Strathern, Andrew. 1979. 'Gender, Ideology and Money in Mount Hagen', *Man* 14(3): 530–48; https://doi.org/10.2307/2801873.

Stuart, Ian. 1970. *Port Moresby: Yesterday and Today*. Sydney: Pacific Publications.

Surmon, Albert. 1971. 'The Residential Pattern of a Colonial Town'. MA thesis, University of Papua New Guinea, Port Moresby.

Surmon, Albert, and R.G. (Gerard) Ward. 1973. 'Port Moresby 1973'. Port Moresby: Department of Geography, University of Papua New Guinea.

Swadling, Pamela. 1996. *Plumes from Paradise: Trade Cycles in Outer Southeast Asia and their Impact on New Guinea and Nearby Islands until 1920*. Port Moresby: PNG National Museum in association with Robert Brown and Associates (Qld).

Todaro, Michael. 1969. 'A Model for Labor Migration and Urban Unemployment in Less Developed Countries', *American Economic Review* 59(1): 138–48. https://www.jstor.org/stable/1811100. Last accessed 19 November 2022.

TPNG (Territory of Papua and New Guinea). 1968. *Programmes and Policies for the Economic Development of Papua and New Guinea*. Port Moresby: Government Printer.

Van Leur, J.C. (Jacob). 1955. *Indonesian Trade and Society: Essays in Asian Social and Economic History* (1st English edition [original Dutch edition published in 1936]). The Hague: van Hoeve.

Von Fleckenstein, Fritz. 1975. 'Observations on Coffee Marketing in the Eastern Highlands', *Yagl-Ambu* 2(2): 116–32.

Vorley, Bill, Ethel Del Pozo-Vergnes and Anna Barnett. 2012. *Small Producer Agency in the Globalising Market: Making Choices in a Changing World*. London: IIED and The Hague: Hivos; https://www.iied.org/16521iied. Last accessed 19 November 2022.

Voutas, Anthony. 1981. 'Policy Initiative and the Pursuit of Control', in J. Ballard (ed.), *Policy-Making in a New State: Papua New Guinea, 1972–77*. St Lucia: University of Queensland Press, 33–47.

Wallace, A.R. (Alfred). (1869) 1962. *The Malay Archipelago*. New York: Dover.

Walsh, A.C. (Croz). 1983. 'The Papua New Guinea Informal Sector: Illusion, Dream or Nightmare?', *Australian Geographer* 15(6): 414–17; https://doi.org/10.1080/00049188308702847.

———. 1984. 'Much Ado about Nothing: Urbanization, Predictions and Censuses in Papua New Guinea', *Singapore Journal of Tropical Geography* 5(1): 73–87; https://doi.org/10.1111/j.1467-9493.1984.tb00147.x.

Walter, Michael. 1981. *What Do We Do about Plantations?*, IASER Monograph No. 15. Boroko, PNG: Institute of Applied Social and Economic Research.

Ward, R.G. (Gerard). 1971. 'Internal Migration and Urbanisation in Papua New Guinea', in M.W. Ward, *Population Growth and Socio-economic Change*, New Guinea Research Bulletin No. 42. Canberra: New Guinea Research Unit and Australian National University, 81–105; http://pacificinstitute.anu.edu.au/sites/default/files/resources-links/NGRB/42.pdf.

Wehler, Hans-Ulrich. 1970. 'Bismarck's Imperialism 1862–1890', *Past and Present* 48: 119–55; https://www.jstor.org/stable/650484. Last accessed 19 November 2022.

West, Francis. 1956. 'Colonial Development in Central New Guinea', *South Pacific* 9(2): 305–13.

———. 1968. *Hubert Murray: The Australian Pro-Consul*. Melbourne: Oxford University Press.

———. 2006. 'Two Pacific Biographies: Hubert Murray and Father Damien', in D. Munro, and B.V. Lall (eds), *Texts and Contexts: Reflections in Pacific Island Historiography*. Honolulu: University of Hawaii Press, 111–24.

West, Paige. 2012. *From Modern Production to Imagined Primitive: The Social World of Coffee from Papua New Guinea*. Durham, NC: Duke University Press.

Williamson, Peter. 1977. 'Is There an Urban Informal Sector or Just Poverty?', *Yagl-Ambu* 4(1): 5–24.

Wolfers, Edward. 1975. *Race Relations and Colonial Rule in Papua New Guinea*. Sydney: Angus & Robertson.

Wu, Y.H. (David). 1974. 'To Kill Three Birds with One Stone: The Rotating Credit Associations of the Papua New Guinea Chinese', *American Ethnologist* 1(3): 565–84; https://doi.org/10.1525/ae.1974.1.3.02a00110.

———. 1982. *The Chinese in Papua New Guinea*. Hong Kong: The Chinese University Press.

Yamey, Basil. 2005. 'Peter Bauer, an Unusual Applied Economist', *Cato Journal* 25(3): 449–53.

Index

T

www.ingramcontent.com/pod-product-compliance
Ingram Content Group UK Ltd.
Pitfield, Milton Keynes, MK11 3LW, UK
UKHW020726230926
8686IPUK00002BB/5

9 781800 739680